P9-DDV-313

vegetable gardening

vegetable gardening

from planting to picking—
the complete guide to creating
a bountiful garden

Fern Marshall Bradley
Jane Courtier

Reader's Digest
The Reader's Digest Association, Inc.
Pleasantville, New York/Montreal

This edition published by The Reader's Digest Association by arrangement with Toucan Books, Ltd.

Copyright © 2006 Toucan Books Ltd.

All rights reserved. Unauthorized reproduction, in any manner, is prohibited.

Reader's Digest is a registered trademark of The Reader's Digest Association, Inc.

FOR TOUCAN BOOKS
Design: Bradbury and Williams
Editor: Theresa Bebbington
Managing Editor: Ellen Dupont
Editorial Assistant: Maddy Langford
Index: Michael Dent
Picture Research: Christine Vincent, Maria Bembridge
Proofreader: Constance Novis

Front cover and spine photograph:
Mike Krivit/Krivit Photography

FOR READER'S DIGEST
U.S. Project Editor: Kim Casey
Canadian Project Editor: Pamela Johnson
Canadian Consulting Editor: Trevor Cole
Copy Editor: Marilyn Knowlton
Project Designer: George McKeon
Executive Editor, Trade Publishing:
Dolores York
President & Publisher, Trade Publishing:
Harold Clarke

NOTE TO OUR READERS
This publication contains the opinions and ideas of its author and is designed to provide useful information to the reader. It is not intended as a substitute for the advice of an expert on the subject matter covered. Products or active ingredients, treatments, and the names of organizations that appear in this publication are included for informational purposes only; the inclusion of commercial products in the book does not imply endorsement by Reader's Digest, nor does the omission of any product or active ingredient or treatment advice indicate disapproval by Reader's Digest. When using any commercial product, readers should read and follow all label directions carefully.

The author and publisher specifically disclaim any responsibility for any liability, loss, or risk (personal, financial, or otherwise) that may be claimed or incurred as a consequence—directly or indirectly—of the use and/or application of any of the contents of this publication.

Library of Congress Cataloging-in-Publication Data
Courtier, Jane
Vegetable gardening : from planting to picking : the complete guide to creating a bountiful garden / Jane Courtier and Fern Marshall Bradley.
p. cm.
Includes index.
ISBN 10: 0-7621-0629-8
ISBN 13: 978-0-7621-0629-5
1. Vegetable gardening. 2. Vegetables. I. Bradley, Fern Marshall II. Title.

SB321.C823 2005
635--dc22 2005044338

Address any comments about *Vegetable Gardening* to:
The Reader's Digest Association, Inc.
Adult Trade Publishing
Reader's Digest Road
Pleasantville, NY 10570-7000

For more Reader's Digest products and information, visit our website:
www.rd.com (in the United States)
www.readersdigest.ca (in Canada)

Printed in Thailand

5 7 9 10 8 6 4

Part 1: YOUR GARDEN

1

2

3

Sowing and planting 46

5

Harvesting and storing 108

4

Making your vegetables grow 82

Part 2: THE VEGETABLES

6

7

8

9

10

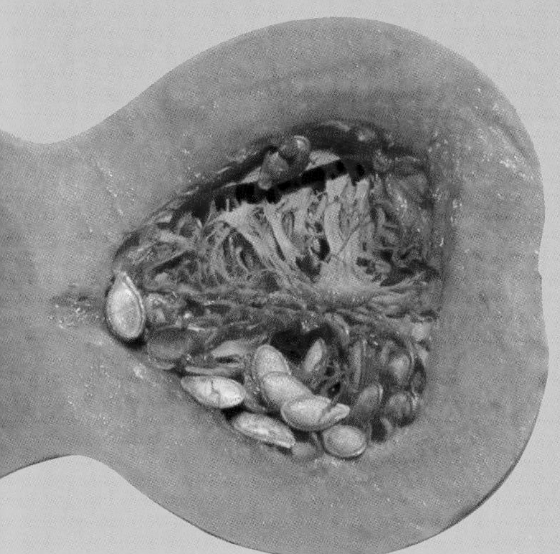

Introduction

There is something satisfying and rewarding about growing your own food. The sense of achievement when you sit before a plate piled high with fresh produce from your own garden is hard to beat. More gardeners are realizing that there is nothing difficult about vegetable growing—and that you don't need an enormous garden to do so.

In Part 1 of *Vegetable Gardening*, Jane Courtier will tell you all about the big picture of growing vegetables. There's information to follow from the beginning of the season to the end: how to design a garden that's just the right size and style for your needs; how to improve your soil and prepare it for planting; how to raise seedlings and plant your garden; how to water and feed your crops; how to protect crops from pest and weed problems; how to extend the season; and how to harvest and store all the bounty of your garden.

In Part 2, Fern Marshall Bradley gives you the low-down on growing specific crops. This section organizes crops according to how they are

FROM A (MOSTLY) ORGANIC GARDENER

Dear Reader,

I prefer to garden without the use of pesticides and manage to do so—most of the time. But sometimes, when caterpillars are on the march against my cabbages or blackflies threaten my beans, I find that a single application of the right pesticide will prevent me from losing the fruit of my labor to pests.

Chemicals aren't all bad. The chemical pesticides that are available to gardeners today bear little relation to those that were common a few decades ago. We no longer use old-style, broad-spectrum, toxic chemicals that persist in the environment for years. They've been replaced by highly regulated, targeted products, often derived from natural sources, that break down quickly and safely after use and leave minimal residues in treated plants.

Ideally, all gardeners would like to grow their food without having to intervene with chemical controls, but it's been my experience that a single, well-timed application of pesticide can prevent a pest or disease problem from ruining a crop. I believe that chemical pesticides should be used only when it's absolutely necessary.

By choosing the right product and following the directions carefully, you can be confident that your garden and your produce will remain safe, healthy, and even environmentally friendly.

JANE COURTIER

grown. Thus, you'll find vines such as squash in the *Vine crops* chapter, and long-term crops such as rhubarb in the *Permanent plantings* chapter. Each entry provides all you need to know to grow a crop successfully, including when to plant, how to care for the crop, and how to harvest.

Best of the Bunch boxes provide recommendations of tried-and-true varieties, including their time to maturity—the average length of time until first harvest from the date of direct seeding in the garden or when transplants are set in the garden.

Problem Solver sidebars summarize the symptoms and signs of the most common pest problems and growing disorders that affect a crop, and they offer quick suggestions on how to solve the problem—or how to avoid it the next time you plant the crop.

Each *Planting Guide* is a quick reference to the essential information you'll need before getting started. Watch for the thermometer icon in some entries. It alerts you to crops that are sensitive to heat exposure or chilling during their development. Where possible, the warning alerts you to temperature thresholds that may cause damage or prevent plants from setting fruit.

In general, keep in mind that when you plant your crop and the precise number of days from seeding or transplanting to harvest will vary depending on the weather conditions in your region and on weather fluctuations from year to year. Crops will mature faster in warmer conditions than in cool conditions, and plants may grow more slowly than usual during a drought, even if you provide supplemental water. The time of year you plant has an effect too, because plants grow more quickly during long days than short days.

FROM A COMMITTED ORGANIC GARDENER

Dear Reader,

Right from the start I decided to garden organically. I had a youthful ideal of saving the environment from chemical pollution. Learning how to garden the organic way was fascinating.

I discovered the intricacies of soil biology and the miracle of earthworms. I enjoyed turning raked-up leaves and kitchen waste into sweet-smelling compost. I planted flowers in my vegetable garden to attract beneficial insects. I learned how simple row covers can protect plants from adverse weather conditions, as well as from animal and insect pests. I enjoyed the adventure of trying out simple, noncommercial, organic methods: Would slugs really come to a beer-baited slug trap to drink and drown? Would spraying a simple baking soda mixture on plants help prevent disease? (Yes, and yes.)

The beauty of tending an organic garden is that each year brings greater success as the natural systems become stronger. For example, I no longer put out slug traps because there is so little slug damage in my garden. I attribute this to healthy populations of slug predators that have grown over the years, especially ground beetles that live under the wood-chip mulch on paths at the border of my garden. I'm now into my third decade as an organic gardener and I am more committed than ever.

Fern Marshall Bradley

FERN MARSHALL BRADLEY

Is organic gardening for you?

In this book, you'll find plenty of advice for gardening organically. Eating delicious, freshly picked produce, enjoying the outdoors, and feeling connected with nature are the top reasons gardeners give for tending a vegetable garden. Many gardeners prefer organic methods, avoiding chemical pesticides—they love the idea that the food they are growing is pesticide-free. But what happens when things go wrong and organic solutions don't seem to work?

The two authors of this book have different answers to this question. Jane Courtier takes the view that organic methods are the first, best choice, but believes there can be a place for carefully chosen chemical pesticides if a serious insect or disease problem arises. Fern Marshall Bradley writes from the viewpoint of a longtime organic gardener who has chosen not to use chemicals in her garden. Together they've created a book that looks at vegetable gardening from both sides.

As experienced gardeners and gardening writers, Jane and Fern know that there are substantive issues on both sides to consider when deciding whether to be purely organic or not—and in the end, it's an individual choice. Let them help you make up your mind!

Part 1

YOUR GARDEN

1 Planning your garden

Planning a vegetable garden can be almost as exciting as growing the vegetables—but, more important, it will ensure that your efforts will bring maximum rewards. Take time to think about the type of garden you already have and the type you want. What vegetables would be the best to grow? How can you make the best use of the space you have? What difficulties are there to overcome? The following pages will guide you through all the choices you have to make and provide some new ideas to inspire you.

Your vegetable garden can be decorative and inspiring or functional and plain—the choice is yours. Among the vegetables in this attractive garden are chard, fennel, lettuce, and cabbage.

The benefits of planning

Once you have decided to grow your own vegetables, endless possibilities open up before you. Just glancing through a seed catalog results in a list of exciting varieties you simply have to try—but hold on, the first step is to come up with a plan.

ADAPTING AN EXISTING PLOT

Although you don't have the option of choosing the ideal site for an existing plot, there are many ways you might be able to change it to make it more convenient for your needs. Adding walkways, making beds, providing shelter with hedges or fences, and adjusting the size of the plot are just some of the possibilities.

Quick Tip

Out of the shade

When planning your vegetables, place tall plantings, such as corn or those grown on trellises, at the north side of the plot so they don't cast shadows on lower-growing plants.

Unless you have a huge garden and almost limitless time and skills, you probably won't grow half the things you would like to. Therefore, good planning is an important part of vegetable gardening. It enables you to think sensibly about how much space and time you can devote to your garden and what type of vegetables will be most useful to you. It also avoids that embarrassment of riches, the glut— you don't want to spend a lot of effort and time growing more beans than your family can eat.

Whether you are about to start a vegetable plot from scratch or plan to adapt an existing one, spend some time with a notepad and pencil before picking up a spade. Draw up a rough plan of your garden to see how the vegetables will fit in and how much space you can afford to give them.

There are many different styles of vegetable gardens, which are discussed in the following pages. You will probably find that some of them are much more suited to your needs than others. Once you have decided on your garden style, you also need to plan which vegetables you intend to grow (see pages 18–19).

Starting a new plot

Creating your own vegetable garden from scratch is a great opportunity—it means you will be able to avoid some of the common pitfalls. Here are some points to bear in mind when planning a new vegetable plot:

Convenience. If the vegetable garden is close to the house, it will be easy to dash out and pick a few herbs or dig some vegetables for dinner. It will also encourage you to visit the vegetable garden more frequently to take care of the plants. The closer it is, the more often you'll weed, water, and check for pests and diseases. Firm walkways around and across the plot will prove a boon for access—and prevent feet from becoming muddy.

Climate. Vegetables will grow best if they are sheltered from strong wind. Fences, walls, and hedges can create a favorable, warm, sheltered microclimate within the garden, but be careful that they don't cast too much shade. Vegetables prefer an open, sunny position. Ideally, run rows north to south within the plot to keep shading to a minimum.

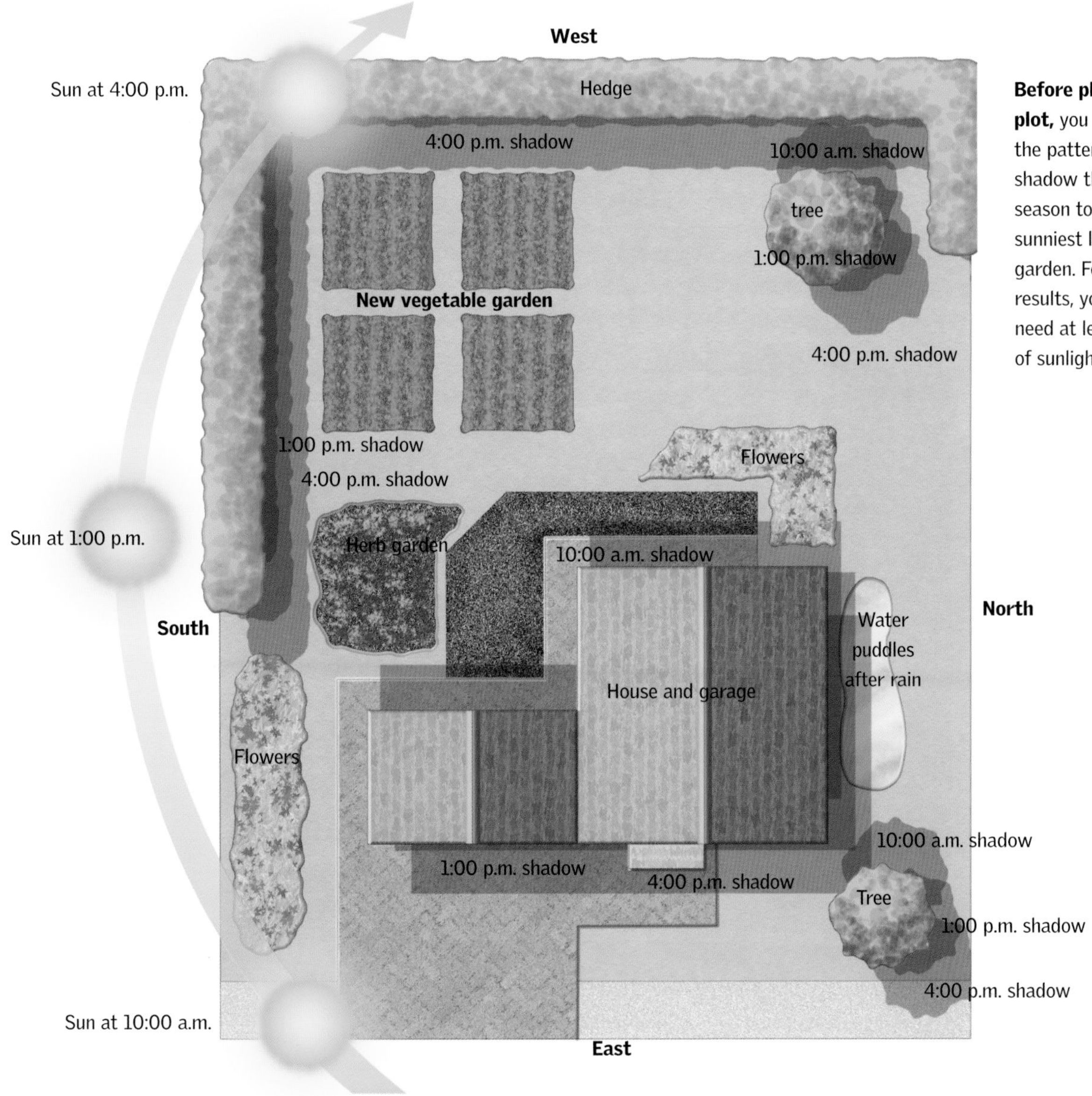

West
Sun at 4:00 p.m.
Hedge
4:00 p.m. shadow
10:00 a.m. shadow
tree
1:00 p.m. shadow
New vegetable garden
4:00 p.m. shadow
1:00 p.m. shadow
4:00 p.m. shadow
Flowers
Sun at 1:00 p.m.
Herb garden
10:00 a.m. shadow
North
South
Water puddles after rain
House and garage
Flowers
10:00 a.m. shadow
1:00 p.m. shadow
4:00 p.m. shadow
Tree
1:00 p.m. shadow
4:00 p.m. shadow
Sun at 10:00 a.m.
East

Before planning your plot, you should observe the patterns of light and shadow throughout the season to determine the sunniest location in your garden. For the best results, your plot will need at least six hours of sunlight a day.

Size. Factors that will affect size include: your enthusiasm, how many mouths you have to feed, how much time you have available, and the overall size of the garden. Don't be too ambitious; a plot that is too big soon becomes a chore instead of a pleasure. As a guide for most standard-size gardens, a vegetable plot of 200–500 square feet (19–49 sq m) is not uncommon. Rectangles and squares are more practical for growing vegetables than flowing shapes.

Ground preparation. What is currently on the site where you want to position your vegetable plot? Bare soil is ideal, but more likely there is a lawn, which means stripping the turf. This is not difficult if you use a sharp spade to undercut it. If it's a large area, hire a sod-cutting machine. Trees and shrubs can be difficult to remove, and a site overrun by deep-rooted perennial weeds can take taming. Consider how much time and effort you are willing to devote to this preparation.

In this typical square plot, lettuce, cabbages, and peas are grown in rows.

Planning your crops

By taking time to think carefully about the crops you're about to grow, you can ensure that you'll get the maximum value from your vegetable garden—no matter its size.

SUCCESSION PLANTING

You can have a constant supply of fresh vegetables for salads, and avoid waste from growing too much of one thing, by sowing seeds in small batches in the spring and summer.

Instead of filling one row with lettuce, another with onions, and a third with radishes, sow only one row—a third of it onions, a third lettuce, and a third radishes. Two weeks later, sow another row in the same way, and two weeks after that, a third row. You'll have a steady supply of the vegetables over a longer season.

Quick Tip

At the root

Never grow plants with long tap roots, such as carrots and parsnips, in freshly manured ground because it causes them to fork and become misshapen.

It's surprising how many times gardeners take a haphazard approach to growing vegetables. Some can't resist the lure of the seed catalogs—and before they know it, they have spent a fortune on at least twice as many packets of seeds as they have room to grow. Others fill half the plot with potatoes and cabbages every year because...well, because vegetable gardens always have potatoes and cabbages. And it's amazing how many gardeners keep on growing Brussels sprouts (or leeks, or spinach, or radishes, or whatever) season after season, despite knowing that nobody in the family actually likes to eat them.

Decide what you like. Write down a list of the vegetables you'll most likely want to grow. Unless you have endless space, concentrate on types that are difficult to buy in the stores (such as scorzonera or black salsify), are expensive (such as asparagus), benefit from being eaten freshly picked (such as corn), or are simply tastier than the commercial varieties (such as many tomatoes). Remember to ask the rest of the family for their preferences, too.

Grow specialty vegetables, such as artichokes, to enhance your choice of vegetables for your meals.

Check the timing. Make a note of the sowing or planting times of all the crops you've listed and when they will vacate the soil after harvesting. A spring-sown crop of bush beans, for example, will probably finish cropping by midsummer, which makes way for a quick-growing "catch crop," such as lettuce, radishes, or French beans, to be sown in the same piece of ground. Make the plot work hard for its keep.

Look ahead to harvesting. Make a note of what should be cropping, month by month. Where several crops are in peak season at the same time, you should consider if some of them can be stored successfully. It's easy to put a surplus of beans in the freezer; however, it's far more difficult to cope with a glut of lettuce (see *Succession Planting*, left).

Grow for health and yield. Different vegetable crops tend to take varying quantities of nutrients from the soil. Members of the cabbage family, for example, are particularly greedy when it comes to nitrogen; conversely, peas and beans need only small amounts of soil nitrogen because of their ability to "fix" nitrogen from the air. Crop rotation—the practice of moving different types of vegetable crops to a different position in the garden each year—helps ensure that the soil does not become depleted of nutrients, which it would do if the same crops were taking the same nutrients from the same place year after year.

Different types of crops may be prone to attack by specific pests and diseases. Clubroot disease, for example, attacks all members of the cabbage family (brassicas), but it has no effect on carrots, lettuces, tomatoes, or other noncabbage-family plants.

Crop rotation can help to prevent the buildup of some of these specific soil-borne pests and diseases; however, it is not 100 percent effective. Some diseases, such as clubroot, can remain dormant in the soil for as long as 20 years, so a three- or four-year rotation plan is unlikely to starve the disease-causing organisms into submission. However, crop rotation is still effective in preventing other disease problems.

By sowing little and often, this gardener would have a steady supply of lettuce instead of a glut.

CROP ROTATION PLAN

The most practical rotation for most gardens is a three-year one. For the rotation to work, each group must occupy the same amount of space. This makes it difficult to follow crop rotations exactly, so don't worry about achieving perfection. Keep the basic principles in mind and do the best you can. Your need to add lime depends on your soil type and pH.

	YEAR 1	YEAR 2	YEAR 3
BED 1	**Roots** Do not add manure or lime; add a balanced fertilizer in spring.	**Others** Add a balanced fertilizer in spring.	**Brassicas** Dig in well-rotted manure or compost in fall; add lime in spring.
BED 2	**Brassicas** Dig in well-rotted manure or compost in fall; add lime in spring.	**Roots** Do not add manure or lime; add a balanced fertilizer in spring.	**Others** Add a balanced fertilizer in spring.
BED 3	**Others** Add a balanced fertilizer in spring.	**Brassicas** Dig in well-rotted manure or compost in fall; add lime in spring.	**Roots** Do not add manure or lime; add a balanced fertilizer in spring.

1 **Roots** Potatoes, carrots, beets, parsnips.

2 **Others** Beans, lettuce, peas, celery- and parsley-family crops, onions.

3 **Cabbage family** Brussels sprouts, cabbage, cauliflower, plus rutabagas and turnips, which are also susceptible to clubroot disease.

The kitchen garden

It's great to have a garden that's big enough to devote a special area to growing vegetables, as well as fruit and herbs—a traditional kitchen garden. However, large plots require careful planning to ensure they will work well without becoming too time-consuming.

IS A KITCHEN GARDEN FOR YOU?

PROS

- Hedges, fences, or walls provide sheltered conditions.
- You can train fruit trees up walls and fences.
- Plenty of room for a variety of vegetables, fruit, and herbs.

CONS

- Hedges, fences, or walls cause problems with shade.
- Hedges will compete for water and nutrients.
- Soil between rows will become compacted; you'll need to dig the plot over at the end of the season.
- Bare soil between rows can be quickly colonized by weeds.
- The size of a large plot can be daunting, especially when it comes to such tasks as weeding.
- If the plot is large, you may sow too much of a crop.

In the past, a large, traditional walled kitchen garden in the grounds of a sizable house was regarded as useful but dull. It was hidden away at the end of the main garden and screened from view by hedges or walls.

A modern kitchen garden

Today, a kitchen garden refers to a garden with a mixture of vegetables, fruit, and herbs. It can be just as decorative and interesting as any flower garden—and there's certainly no need to hide it away from view. In fact, as with any vegetable garden, it is best near the kitchen to make it easier to dig up some leeks or cut a cabbage head in cold weather.

You can provide an old-fashioned traditional touch by including walls, fences, or hedges surrounding the garden, or you can leave the plot open to view. Alternatively, you can train a row of cordoned or espaliered apple and pear trees to make a productive dividing line between the ornamental

Trellises, pergolas, and other types of support frames are ideal in the kitchen garden for growing plants that climb, such as beans and peas. They also break up the space, creating outdoor garden rooms.

and kitchen areas of the garden. This will add interest by creating an extra garden "room" without hiding the vegetables, fruit, and herbs completely from view.

How does your garden grow?

Vegetables are traditionally grown in straight rows in a single, large, square or rectangular plot. There are usually gaps between the rows to allow the gardener to care for the plants.

Instead of growing vegetables in one large plot, try growing them in a bed system, thereby avoiding the drawbacks of a traditional kitchen garden (see *Is a Kitchen Garden for You?* left).

Divide the space into a series of beds divided by walkways. Make sure the beds are narrow enough to be reached from the walkways on each side (see *Creating a Bed System,* below right). This will allow you to work in the garden without compacting the soil by treading on it. (This growing system is also used for no-dig gardens; see pages 42–43.)

Crop rows can be grown more closely together because access is not necessary, so weeds have less of a chance to gain a foothold. The bed system makes it easy to plan rotations and sow in short rows for succession planting (see pages 18–19). Smaller beds also mean work can be divided into small sections at a time.

CREATING A BED SYSTEM

Before marking out the beds, cultivate the whole plot as you would for any vegetable garden, removing all perennial weeds and raking the soil level.

Make the beds 4 feet (1.2 m) wide so you can reach across half the bed from each side. Because you'll have to walk to the end of the bed to reach the other side, a maximum of 10 feet (3 m) is normally a good length. Make the walkways at least 18 inches (45 cm) wide, with a few 2- to 3-foot (60- to 90-cm)-wide walkways, which will be suitable for wheelbarrow access.

Beds can be made level with the surrounding ground, but an edging helps to define them more clearly, and a raised edging allows you to build the beds up by adding organic matter (see pages 22–23).

Surface the walkways in a vegetable garden with bark chips or gravel, preferably on top of a landscape fabric (these are available from garden centers), which will help suppress weed growth.

Raised beds

Raised beds may be low—just a few inches above the surrounding ground level—or about waist height, which is especially useful for gardeners with mobility problems.

Many people who grow their vegetables in raised beds follow the no-dig method of cultivation (see pages 42–43). Because no-dig gardeners add large amounts of compost and other organic matter to their beds, the surface of the beds soon becomes higher than the surrounding soil. Although the soil and organic matter can simply be mounded up with sloping sides, using edging to contain the soil is more practical, especially as the layers build up over a few years.

Low beds

The height of a low bed can vary from 4–12 inches (10–30 cm) high, and it may be made from a range of materials, including wood, bricks, blocks, and edging tiles. Wood is perhaps the most commonly used material, but it should be treated with a safe wood preservative to ensure a reasonably long life.

Old railroad ties were once commonly used to make raised beds, but because they were treated with creosote, these are unsuitable for garden use. (However, safe, untreated ties are sometimes available.) Garden centers and builders' suppliers stock decorative edging materials. These

You can stack a few layers of bricks or use them on end for extra height. Don't slope them on an angle—the corners could scrape your knees as you do your gardening.

DIMENSIONS FOR RAISED BEDS

	Height	Width (one-sided access)	Width (two-sided access)
Wheelchair gardener	24–30 in. (60–75 cm)	24 in. (60 cm)	36–48 in. (90–120 cm)
Standing gardener	30–36 in. (75–90 cm)	24 in. (60 cm)	48 in. (120 cm)

MAKING A LOW BED

A suitable edging can be made from wood planks 1 inch (2.5 cm) thick and 6 inches (15 cm) wide. For rigidity, sink the planks 2 inches (5 cm) deep into the ground and support them with 1-inch (2.5-cm)-square pegs every 4 feet (1.2 m); nail them to similar pegs that will serve as corner posts.

Alternatively, you can set concrete blocks or bricks into a shallow trench, which will provide stability to these edgings. Make sure you pack the soil tightly around them to hold them in place.

can range from inexpensive rolls of plastic to extravagant, beautiful, and sometimes expensive antique-style tiles.

High beds

In situations where growing in the ground is impossible—a yard with a solid surface, for example, or where the soil is polluted—high raised beds are ideal. They are also good for gardeners who find bending difficult or impossible, who are wheelchair users, or who suffer the annoyances of increasing age, such as worsening eyesight, stiffening joints, and tiring easily. Raised beds can also be a design statement, adding three-dimensional interest to the garden scene.

If you want to build a raised bed simply for its decorative appeal, you can make it whatever height you like. However, if it is to make gardening easier, the height and width of the bed will depend on who is going to use it, particularly whether it is a gardener who needs to work from a seated position or a wheelchair (see *Dimensions for Raised Beds,* left), or someone who will work standing up.

Gardeners who use a wheelchair will find it much easier to work at a bed designed like a table, where there will be room to roll the wheelchair underneath; otherwise, access is limited and awkward, involving twisting and stretching. Detailed dimensions and advice are available from many disability groups.

Quick Tip

A super-sized pot

Like pots and containers, raised beds dry out more quickly than the open ground and need frequent watering. Without the proper drainage materials and holes, they can also become waterlogged in wet weather.

CONSTRUCTING A TALL RAISED BED

Tall raised beds are often built from wood, but you can also build them from bricks or stone. If you plan to build the raised bed on soil, start with a concrete footing to provide a firm, level surface.

The walls will need to be only one brick thick; to allow for drainage, leave some weep holes at the base of the walls. Finish the walls with suitable coping stones for weather protection; if you choose wide, flat coping, it can also double as garden seating.

A mixture of peas and lettuces thrives in this raised bed, which also serves as a frame for nasturtiums.

Since plants grow only in the top 12 inches (30 cm) or so, fill the base with rubble, which will also improve drainage. Finish off with 18 inches (45 cm) of good-quality topsoil, so that it is level with or slightly mounded above the walls to allow for settling.

Wood, metal, and other materials are often used for sidings, too.

Ornamental vegetable gardens

Many vegetables are beautiful—a feast for the eyes as well as the palate. Many varieties are worth growing for their decorative value, whether it's in a carefully planned formal plot known as a potager or mingled with flowers in an ornamental border.

GUIDELINES FOR A FORMAL POTAGER

- Keep the design simple so that weeding and general care of the plants are made easier.
- If you want an edging plant, choose one that doesn't need clipping (such as curly-leaved parsley or golden pot marigolds).
- Choose vegetables that you can sample without spoiling their decorative effect. French and pole beans, peppers, and asparagus peas, for example, can all be picked freely, while taking a few carefully chosen leaves from cut-and-come-again lettuce, kale, and Swiss chard won't do any harm.
- Plant late-maturing varieties of vegetables such as leeks, onions, cabbages, carrots, and cauliflower to avoid making a hole in the display.

Originally, the French term "*potager*" referred to a kitchen garden that supplied vegetables for the soup pot. However, today it has come to mean a formal vegetable plot where the plants are grown for their ornamental potential, as well as for their crops.

The potager usually consists of a number of beds that are arranged in a neat, geometric pattern—rectangles, squares, diamonds, triangles, or circles. The beds are often edged with dwarf hedges, traditionally of box, and are filled with vegetables carefully chosen for their shapes, colors, and textures.

While a small-scale potager for the home garden can look splendid, too, don't underestimate the amount of work involved. A formal potager must be kept neat if it is to look attractive, and that means frequent weeding and careful attention to pest and disease control.

Dwarf hedges look lovely, but remember that they will need a lot of clipping (and that "dwarf" usually means crawling along on your hands and knees with the pruners). In addition, unless you're prepared to ruin your carefully planned display, you won't be able to harvest many of the vegetables.

The large cabbage leaves make an impact planted next to flowers in this garden.

Vegetables in flower borders

An easier way to grow vegetables for their decorative qualities is to mix them with flowers and shrubs in an ornamental border. Use plants such as pole beans on a tepee of canes or stately globe artichokes to provide tall focal points at the back of the border, and fill the front of the beds with low-growing edgers, such as frilly-leaved lettuce or parsley, or culinary thyme.

Groups of bold, textured Swiss chard, colorful bush tomatoes, hummocks of French beans, and lacy-leaved carrots can fill in the middle ground alongside flowering perennials or shrubs.

The dark red leaves of chard are the perfect foil for these bright cosmos.

Quick Tip

New favorites

When growing vegetables for their decorative qualities, always check the latest seed catalogs. New, ornamental varieties of old favorites are introduced every year, reflecting their growing popularity.

ORNAMENTAL VEGETABLES

Here are just a few suggestions for vegetables that have decorative qualities. These will look stunning in most flower borders. You can also try experimenting with other vegetable varieties, including bush-type tomatoes.

Artichokes With their tall, stately habit and architectural, jagged-edged silver leaves, globe artichokes make a bold and brilliant statement in any garden.

Asparagus peas An open-growing bush with attractive trifoliate leaves and lovely cinnamon-red, pealike flowers. These are followed by unusual and delicious winged pods.

Bean (runner) These have a normal climbing habit with attractive, scarlet flowers all summer. 'Hestia' is an unusual nonclimbing dwarf with red and white flowers.

Peppers Small-fruited chili peppers are eye-catching; try 'Etna', with brilliant red fruit in upright clusters, or 'Fiesta' with yellow, purple, or red peppers.

Herbs Try varieties in unusual colors, such as purple-leaved or variegated sage, purple basil, golden thyme, and golden marjoram. Fennel has a delicate ferny foliage, and the bronze variety is particularly striking.

Swiss chard 'Bright Lights' is one of the best mixtures, with red, gold, pink, white, orange, and violet stems topped with deeply quilted, rich green leaf blades.

Lettuce Any good seed catalog will feature many handsome lettuces: 'Lollo Rossa' and 'Lollo Bionda' are old favorites with crisply crimped, frilly leaves, and there are some excellent oak-leaved types, such as deep red 'Flamenco' or 'Delicata'.

Green onion Try red-shanked 'Rossa Lunga de Firenze' or 'North Holland Blood Red'.

Summer squash There is no end of varieties here: 'Sunburst' and 'Nova' both have golden, scalloped pattypan fruit; 'Nova' also has contrasting green tips. Slender, bottle-shaped 'Zephyr' has yellow fruit that look as though the tips have been dipped into pale green paint.

The interesting fruit and large architectural leaves of summer squash make an unusual, attractive addition to an ornamental garden.

Vegetables in small spaces

No garden is too small to grow a few vegetables—you can grow reasonably sized crops in the smallest of spaces, even on balconies and patios.

KEEP IT SAFE

If you are growing vegetables on a roof terrace or balcony, make sure it can bear the load—soil-filled containers are heavy, especially just after being watered. Consult a structural engineer if you have any doubts.

Always ensure window boxes and hanging baskets are safely secured, particularly if they are several stories up. Don't be tempted to balance a box on the window ledge without any restraints, and make sure the fixture for a hanging basket is completely secure.

Few gardeners are lucky enough to have a huge garden with limitless space for vegetables. Even in large gardens, vegetables often compete for space with decorative flowers and shrubs. Modern gardens are becoming smaller and smaller, and, in some cases, only a tiny patio garden or compact balcony is available.

With such limitations, it is easy to think that home-grown vegetables are out of the question—however, that's not the case. First of all, vegetables and flowers can coexist happily in an ornamental garden (see pages 24–25), and if soil beds are not available, many vegetables grow well in containers (see pages 44–45), which are ideal for patios and balconies. Even a kitchen windowsill can be pressed into use for growing herbs and perhaps a chili pepper or a compact variety of tomato.

Colorful red and yellow peppers brighten up a small patio vegetable garden.

What to grow

The choice of vegetables is important where space is limited. Consider the following points when choosing them:

High yielding. A container that has been planted with one zucchini will supply you with up to 15 fruit over the summer—enough for several meals. However, the same container planted with spinach might give you enough leaves for only a single serving—if you are lucky. When choosing plants, look for ones that give the maximum return for the space they occupy. Good choices include pole beans, tomatoes, zucchini, and lettuce.

High value. Main-crop potatoes are easy to find and inexpensive when bought from the store, so don't consider growing them if you're short on space. However, early or out-of-season potatoes are a different matter; get the timing right and you could be enjoying homegrown new potatoes at a time when they cost a fortune at the store—or when they are completely unobtainable. Likewise, instead of growing common lettuce, seek out seeds of frilly-leaved or colored varieties that fetch a premium in the stores; grow red salad onions instead of the normal white ones or globe-rooted carrots instead of the usual long varieties.

Easy to grow. The smaller the space for growing, the smaller your margin for error. If one lettuce in a row of 20 bolts to seed, it's not a disaster; however, if it's one lettuce out of only three, it assumes much greater significance. Of course, your success rate will depend on your garden conditions and your experience, and these will affect your choices.

In this hanging basket, French marigolds add a splash of color, while sage and lettuce provide a leafy backdrop.

Vegetables and herbs, such as asparagus, cabbage, sage, thyme, and marjoram, can be confined to a flower border.

CHOOSING THE VEGETABLES

GOOD TO GROW

- **Lettuce** Choose cut-and-come-again varieties to provide a steady supply of leaves; also select varieties that are difficult to find or expensive when bought in a store.
- **Green beans** Look for bush varieties that can be grown in a hanging basket; you can grow pole varieties in containers.
- **Tomatoes** Look for varieties specially bred for trailing over a hanging basket, such as 'Balconi' or 'Gartenperle'.
- **Zucchini** Golden-fruited varieties, such as 'Gold Rush', provide a bright splash of color in a container.

AVOID

- **Cauliflower** Prone to several pests and diseases and will not form good heads unless the soil conditions are perfect.
- **Globe artichokes** Large and spiky leaves are usually hard to avoid in confined spaces.
- **Chicory** Needs forcing and careful blanching.
- **Spinach** Shoots up to seed very quickly in warm, dry weather, so it is not suitable in warm-weather areas.
- **Sweet corn** Needs too much space and doesn't provide a large-enough yield to make it worthwhile growing in a confined space.

Problem gardens

Not every garden is perfect for growing vegetables—however, there are often simple solutions for most common problems. You can enjoy growing your own produce in even the most unpromising situations.

VEGETABLES FOR A PARTIALLY SHADY PLOT

On a partially shady plot, there's little point in growing sun-loving vegetables, such as tomatoes and peppers. However, if your plot receives a minimum of two to three hours of sun a day, you can successfully grow the following moderately shade-tolerant vegetables and herbs:

beet	kohlrabi	rhubarb
broccoli	lettuce	salsify
chives	mint	spinach
garlic	parsley	turnips
kale	radishes	

Quick Tip

Whitewash

Shade cast by buildings can be difficult to handle, but you can maximize the amount of available light by painting all the surrounding surfaces white.

Most vegetables need plenty of direct sunlight to grow and crop well; six hours of summer sun each day is considered ideal. Good light will encourage sturdy growth and good leaf formation, which will enable the plant to carry out efficient food production through photosynthesis. This, in turn, will lead to heavier and better-quality crops.

Shady situations

Excessive shade will result in spindly plants that are more vulnerable to pest and disease attack. They often fail to reach their full cropping potential.

If the shade is cast by tree and shrub branches, this is usually easy to deal with by pruning or removing the plants involved. (However, if the problem plants are on a neighbor's property, preserve good relations by first discussing your pruning plans with your neighbor.) Consider lowering tall hedges to reduce the amount of shadow they cast—you will still retain the benefit of their protection. Walls and fences also offer valuable protection for vegetables, but they can cast a deep shadow if they are too tall. Consider replacing part of the wall or fence with a lower barrier on the side that causes the most shade problems.

Temperature extremes

Vegetables are either warm-season lovers or cool-season types. Warm-season crops are sensitive to any frost and need a long, hot growing season to do well. Temperatures must be above 60°F (15.5°C)—a temperature of 70°F (21°C) is preferable. Cool-season vegetables that are moderately hardy to frost hardy will do best in growing temperatures of 60–80°F (15.5–26.5°C). Sustained periods of higher temperatures will reduce both yields and crop quality.

In most temperate regions, both warm-season and cool-season crops can be grown successfully as long as the timing is right. In cool areas, use cloches and floating row covers to provide extra protection from low temperatures, and start plants indoors to gain an early start to the growing season (see pages 74–81).

Low-lying areas of the garden may become frost pockets. Because cool air sinks, it rolls down to the base of a hill and settles there in a chilly pool.

Terracing will create flat beds for growing vegetables. The walls help support the soil.

A solid barrier, such as a wall or fence, can cause a frost pocket to form by preventing the cold air from flowing down the hill, so bear this in mind when putting up barriers around the vegetable garden.

In hot climates, time the sowing of cool-season vegetables so that they crop in spring or fall, and avoid the hottest months. Provide shade and overhead irrigation to lower temperatures and avoid drought stress.

Slopes

A gently sloping garden is not too much of a problem for vegetable growing, particularly if you are lucky enough for the slope to face the right direction and allow the plants to bask in extra sunshine. However, a steep slope can be a real problem, and it can easily provide you with a demonstration of how soil erosion occurs—it takes little time for rain to wash soil down to the base of the slope. In this situation, terracing is the only answer. Use the "cut and fill" method by cutting partially into the slope and partially building it out to make one or more flat beds for growing vegetables.

Soil problems

The majority of poor soils can be improved (see pages 32–39). However, if your garden soil is completely unsuitable for vegetable growing—it is shallow or stony, or it was polluted by industrial waste—you can grow vegetables in containers or raised beds filled with imported, good-quality topsoil. If the natural soil is polluted, line the base of a raised bed with a landscaping (geotextile) fabric that will prevent the vegetables' roots from penetrating into the polluted area.

Poor drainage is another problem. You can improve heavy clay soil that does not drain freely by applying organic matter, but some sites have a more serious problem where water simply cannot get away because of the underlying ground structure. In this case, it may be necessary to install a drainage system consisting of plastic perforated pipes or tile drains.

Wind

In exposed windy areas, protect vegetable plots by erecting windbreaks. Avoid putting up a solid barrier, such as a wall or close-boarded fence—this deflects the wind over the top only for it to be pulled down and cause turbulence just beyond the barrier. Windbreaks should be around 50 percent permeable to be effective. Hedges, open-style fences, or plastic windbreak netting are all good solutions for reducing the strength of the gusts to less damaging levels as they pass through them.

VEGETABLES FOR THE RIGHT SEASON

Cool-season vegetables: arugula, beets, broccoli, Brussels sprouts, chives, cabbage, carrot, cauliflower, celeriac, celery, chicory, Chinese cabbage, cress, endive, fava beans, fennel, garlic, kale, kohlrabi, leeks, lettuce, onions, parsley, parsnips, peas, potatoes, radicchio, radishes, rutabagas, salsify, scallions, shallots, spinach, Swiss chard, turnips.

Warm-season vegetables: beans, melons, cucumbers, eggplant, okra, peas, pepper, sweet potatoes, squash, sweet corn, tomatoes.

Raised beds and containers are a solution for gardens with poor soil conditions.

2 Preparing the ground

Before you start sowing seeds, buying plants and getting your vegetable garden under way, you need to ensure that the soil—the plants' home—is in good condition. For your vegetables to thrive, they need a well-prepared plot that will provide them with all the necessary food, water, and support from the beginning.

Understanding how soil provides for plants will enable you to decide what you need to do: whether or not you need to dig; what you can add to your soil to improve it; and whether it needs lime or additional fertilizers. Get these right, and you'll have a successful harvest.

A well-prepared vegetable plot will provide ample rewards at harvesttime.

chemin
issue

All about soil

Soil is a wonderful material. It takes thousands of years to form—broken down from rocks by wind, rain, and frost—and it is teeming with life we cannot see. Understanding soil and knowing how to look after it are vital for the production of strong, healthy plants.

Plants miraculously make food out of light and air, but to make that miracle happen, they have a few requirements. They need water and a variety of mineral nutrients; most of them also need somewhere to anchor themselves while they grow. For most plants, this is where soil comes in.

Soil may have started its life as rock, but in the process of its breakdown into tiny particles, it has acquired a few other constituents. Variations in the proportions of these constituents mean there are different types of soil, some of which are better for plant growth than others.

VEGETABLE PH PREFERENCES

Most vegetables prefer soil between pH 6.5 and 7.0, but the following types will tolerate soil with higher levels of acid (below 6.0) or alkaline (above 7.0).

Acid-tolerant plants (below pH 6.0)	Alkaline-tolerant plants (above pH 7.0)	Alkaline and acid-tolerant plants
Carrot 5.5–6.8	Asparagus 6.5–7.5	Celery
Celery 5.5–7.5	Beet 6.5–7.5	Garlic
Eggplant 5.5–6.8	Brussels sprout 6.0–7.5	
Endive 5.5–7.0	Cauliflower 6.0–7.5	
Garlic 5.5–7.5	Celery 5.5–7.5	
Potato 5.8–6.5	Cucumber 6.0–7.5	
Radish 5.5–6.5	Garlic 5.5–7.5	
Rhubarb 5.0–6.8	Leek 6.0–7.5	
Sweet potato 5.5–6.5	Melon 6.0–7.5	
Watermelon 5.5–7.0	Okra 6.8–7.5	
	Onion 6.0–7.5	
	Shallot 6.5–7.5	

Before testing soil, mix it with water and shake it up. The sediment will settle in layers, and you can determine the proportions of silt, clay, and organic matter in the soil.

The main constituents are:

Soil particles. The size of broken-down rock particles in soil varies: The largest are sand; smaller particles are silt; and the smallest are clay. Most soil has a mixture of sand, silt, and clay. An even mixture is a loam, but one type often predominates; the soil is then known as a sandy loam, a clay loam, and so on.

Organic matter. This is any living thing that has died. Plants grow in the soil, die, rot down, and are absorbed back into the soil as humus. Plants are also eaten by grazing animals, who return them to the soil as manure; the animals also die and are broken down and incorporated into the soil, too.

Living organisms. In addition to the larger soil-dwelling creatures that we can easily see, such as earthworms and insects, soil is full of microscopic life forms. These microorganisms are various fungi and bacteria—many of which have an important role in breaking down plant and animal matter into humus. Not all of the soil's living population are helpful; many insects, eelworms, and mites are plant pests, and some types of fungi and bacteria cause devastating diseases.

Air and water. These are essential constituents of soil. The fragile root hairs that grow from a plant's roots seek out the moisture and dissolved minerals that are vital for growth. They also need air to function, as do soil microorganisms. The amounts of water and air within the soil depends upon its structure (see pages 34–35).

Nutrients

While plants make their own food using energy from sunlight, they need mineral nutrients to do so. When dissolved in soil moisture, these nutrients are taken up by the roots.

The major nutrients required are nitrogen, phosphorus, and potassium—often abbreviated to their chemical symbols of N, P, and K. Nitrogen helps leafy growth, phosphorus helps provide root development, and potassium encourages flowers and fruit.

Other mineral nutrients needed in smaller quantities are calcium, sulfur, and magnesium, plus trace elements, which include iron, boron, copper, manganese, molybdenum, and zinc.

SOIL ACIDITY

Soil may be acid, neutral, or alkaline. Most vegetables grow best in soil that is just on the acid side of neutral. However, if the soil becomes too acid, clubroot disease, which affects members of the cabbage family, can become a real problem. Conversely, soil that is too alkaline can "lock up" various nutrients and make them unavailable to plants.

Soil acidity is measured on a pH scale: a pH between 1.0 and 7.0 is acid; pH 7.0 to 14.0 is alkaline, and pH 7.0 is neutral. Simple soil-testing kits, available from garden centers, reveal your soil's acidity, but do several tests in different parts of the garden for the best results. Or send samples to your local Cooperative Extension Service or a commerical laboratory for testing.

Most vegetables grow best at pH 6.5. If the soil is more acid than this, apply ground limestone to reduce the acidity; this is helpful to prevent clubroot in cabbage-family plants. Depending on the soil, the amount of lime to apply varies. As a rule of thumb, add: ½ pound to sandy soil, 1 pound to a mixed loam, and 1½ pounds to clay per square yard (or 270 g, 540 g, or 800 g per sq m). This raises the pH by one unit—for example, from pH 5.5 to pH 6.5.

Lowering the pH of an alkaline soil is not practical, but knowing your soil is alkaline will warn you that you may need to apply a fertilizer containing trace elements.

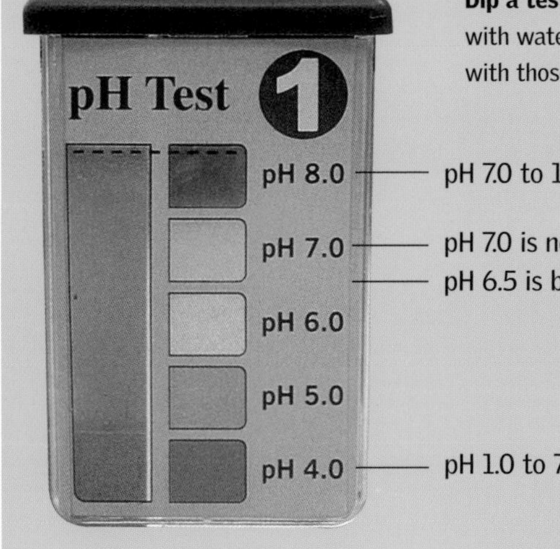

Dip a test strip into soil mixed with water and compare its color with those on the chart.

pH 7.0 to 14.0 is alkaline

pH 7.0 is neutral

pH 6.5 is best for most vegetables

pH 1.0 to 7.0 is acid

Different soils vary in the quantity and quality of these nutrients. If sufficient nutrients are not present in the soil, they can be added in the form of manure, compost, or various manufactured fertilizers. Soil test kits for checking your soil's nutrient status are available from garden centers.

Quick Tip

Telltale blooms

If you have a big-leaf hydrangea *(Hydrangea macrophylla)*, you can use the color of its blooms to determine the soil pH where it is planted: pink, above pH 7.0; blue, pH 6.5 or lower; both pink and blue, neutral at pH 7.0.

Improving your soil

Few gardens are blessed with perfect soil, but fortunately, there's plenty that can be done to improve it. Building up soil fertility will pay dividends in heavier, tastier crops.

Imagine a glass jar filled with golf balls. Because the balls are relatively big, there are large air spaces between them. Now imagine the same jar filled with dried peas—the air spaces between the peas are much smaller. If the jar is filled with sugar crystals, the spaces between the crystals are comparatively minute.

This is a little like soil. Sandy soil has large particles with plenty of air surrounding them. Soil that is mainly silt has smaller air spaces and slow water drainage, while clay particles have tiny air spaces between them and water is often trapped by surface tension around the particles.

Identifying your soil

The best garden soil is loam, made up of a mixture of sand, silt, and clay. Moisten a pinch of soil and rub it between your thumb and index finger. Sandy soil feels gritty, silty soil feels slippery, and clay soil feels sticky. Try molding a handful of moist soil into a ball. If it falls apart, it's sandy; if it molds easily into a ball, it contains a lot of clay. If you can give the ball of soil a polish with your thumb, there's an even higher proportion of clay.

Sandy soil has large particles and drains rapidly; it quickly becomes dry in hot weather.

To do a clay test, squeeze a ball of moist soil in your hand. If it forms a firm ball, it's clay.

Loam consists of a friable (or crumbly) mixture of sand, silt, and clay.

Clay soil has tiny particles that trap water and can make the soil waterlogged.

Sandy soil is quick to warm up in spring, is light and easy to manage, and is rarely waterlogged. However, it is a hungry, thirsty soil because water and dissolved nutrients drain through it before plants can use them.

A heavy, clay soil remains cold for longer in spring, and it is difficult to dig. It soon becomes waterlogged and airless in wet weather; yet it can bake rock hard in droughts. However, clay soil usually contains good quantities of vital plant nutrients.

Improving soil structure

The structure of both very heavy and very light soil can be greatly improved by adding organic matter.

Fibrous organic matter helps to break up clay soil, making it easier to dig, and it encourages soil particles to stick together so that drainage is improved. In free-draining soils, it acts like a sponge, soaking up moisture and holding on to it so that it remains available to plants. (For more about organic matter, see pages 36–39.)

Cultivation

Digging and forking are cultivation techniques that involve turning over and mixing layers of soil. This helps to break up the hard surface soil cap to let in air and moisture. It allows heavy, sticky soil to be broken down by exposing it to the weather; it incorporates organic matter; and it breaks up any hard layers of soil that have formed below the surface.

However, cultivation does have its drawbacks. Carelessly done, it can damage soil structure and cause compaction on heavy soils; it can also bring buried weed seeds up to the surface where they can germinate.

Quick Tip

Walking a plank

Clay soil is easily compacted when wet. Avoid walking on wet clay soil and taking heavy equipment, such as wheelbarrows, across it. Where you cannot avoid it, put a plank down to walk or push a wheelbarrow on—it will help to spread the load and limit the damage.

CULTIVATING YOUR SOIL

You will find these tools essential for soil cultivation.

Tool	Use
Spade	For digging: Keep the blade clean and sharp so that it slices down into the soil with minimum effort. Stainless steel spades are easier to use because the soil doesn't stick to them; however, they are more expensive to buy.
Fork	Good for easing out perennial weeds without breaking their roots and for lifting mature vegetables.
Rake	Breaks the soil surface down into really fine crumbs and levels it for seed sowing and planting; also removes surface stones and weed debris.
Trowel	For digging individual planting holes or removing deep-rooted weeds.

EARTHWORMS

The presence of earthworms will greatly improve the structure of your soil. They make burrows, which help to bring air into the soil and allow water to drain away. These burrows may extend as far as 6 feet (2 m) below the soil surface.

Earthworms eat organic matter such as dead leaves, rising up to the surface and dragging the leaves down into their burrows. They also ingest soil as they burrow through it, depositing the sifted remains as casts either on the soil surface or within the burrow. These habits incorporate large amounts of surface organic matter into the soil and begin the process of breaking it down; they also mix up the layers of soil.

Earthworms can be encouraged by spreading large amounts of organic matter, such as compost and leaf mold (see pages 36–37), on the soil surface. They are usually particularly abundant in no-dig plots (see pages 42–43) because of the amount of organic matter used. In fact, they will do the soil mixing and "digging" for you.

Worms sold as bait in fishing stores are night crawlers. Don't be tempted to buy these worms to add to garden soil; they don't do the same job as earthworms.

Enriching your soil

Organic matter is a valuable addition to almost any soil; however, you'll need a lot of it for even an average-size vegetable garden. A compost pile is one way to obtain organic matter—for free—but there are other ways of obtaining useful organic matter, too.

OTHER SOURCES OF ORGANIC MATTER

Depending on where you live, you may be able to obtain other useful organic products.

- Mushroom compost is rotted horse manure previously used for growing a crop of mushrooms. Lime is used in the mushroom-growing process, so it is not suitable for alkaline, chalky soils.
- Spent hops are available cheaply or free from breweries. They are difficult to handle because they are wet, but they will give your garden a distinctly interesting aroma when fresh.
- If you live near the coast, you can collect seaweed, which is rich in nutrients. It is wet and bulky, and it can attract flies unless covered, so add it to the compost pile in small quantities.

By its nature, organic matter is bulky, often making it difficult to transport. However, if you can overcome that problem, there are useful sources that can be valuable for improving your garden soil.

Compost. Homemade compost is the primary source of organic matter for most gardens. It helps dispose of waste plant material, and it is on-site, ready to use. (For making compost, see pages 38–39.)

Leaf mold. Because they take longer to break down, you should compost fall leaves on their own instead of adding them to the compost pile. You can make a standard compost pile for them (see page 39), but a simple way to compost leaves is to place them in plastic garbage bags with a few layers of garden soil. Tie the neck of the bag when it is full, puncture the sides of the bag several times with a garden fork to provide air holes, then leave the bags in an out-of-the-way corner for six months to a year until the mixture is dark brown and crumbly.

Fall leaves are composted in a separate pile on their own and will eventually turn into leaf mold.

Manure. Animal manures are excellent soil additives, providing useful quantities of plant nutrients, as well as having a beneficial effect on soil structure. Allow manure to rot down before you use it in the garden. Fresh manure can scorch plant roots if it comes into contact with them. It also uses nitrogen as it starts to decompose and will take that nitrogen from the soil, stealing it from the plants. Stack manure into a pile and allow it to rot down, or add it to the garden compost pile.

Horse manure is probably one of the most available types, and it tends to rot down more quickly than farmyard manures from cows and pigs.

Poultry manure is lightweight but caustic and will need to be well rotted before you can use it, so add it to the compost pile. It can be extremely smelly, and because it may come from animals raised in crowded, unethical conditions, you may also have moral objections to using it.

Manures are often mixed with the animals' bedding. Straw is much better than wood shavings, which will take a long time to decompose.

Using organic matter

It is usually best to make a compost from organic matter before using it. However, you can use fresh organic matter by spreading it on a cleared vegetable plot in the fall, because it will have time to rot down before sowing and planting in the spring.

You can add organic matter to the soil in three ways: place it in the base of a trench and cover with soil; mix it into the soil with a fork or spade; or apply it as a surface layer (called a mulch), which will be taken down into the soil gradually by earthworms. Placing it in the bottom of a trench is a good method for thirsty plants with deep roots, such as scarlet runner beans, where it will form a spongy moisture reservoir. Mix the organic matter with the soil if you want to get it to the area quickly where plants can take advantage of it. If you spread organic matter as a mulch, earthworms will do the same job, but they take more time. Mulching also suppresses weed growth, retains soil moisture (if the soil is already moist), and prevents an impenetrable crust or cap from forming on the soil surface.

Green manure plants have been chopped down and left to wilt. They will be dug into the soil, where they will add nutrients, which will enrich it.

Green manure

Plants that are grown specifically to be dug into the soil are known as green manure. These plants are useful as a cover crop where an area of the vegetable plot is left bare for several weeks because they help prevent weeds from taking over and, when dug in, they enrich the soil for the next crop.

Sow green manures in late summer and early fall, and cut them down in spring; or sow in early spring and cut down as the space is needed. Dig the plants in while they are young, before they flower, to prevent the plants from self-seeding and spreading new plants.

PLANTS FOR GREEN MANURE

Here are the most popular plants for green manures:

- Legumes (members of the pea and bean families) because they have the unique ability to take nitrogen from the air and convert it into a form that is usable to plants. This is known as nitrogen fixing.
- Alfalfa (lucerne), clover, agricultural lupin, vetch, and other nitrogen-fixing plants. Others such as buckwheat, rye, oats, millet, and mustard.

Quick Tip

Buying manure

Because most animal manures are so bulky, several proprietary, prerotted, bagged manures are available from garden centers. They are more expensive but easier to transport.

Making your own compost

Compost adds organic matter to your soil. This matter will supply essential nutrients, regulate moisture, improve soil texture, and encourage beneficial microorganisms. Making your own compost is easy—and it also helps to dispose of garden waste.

Compost is simply partially rotted plant and animal matter. When exposed to the right conditions, the original constituents will decompose until they become unrecognizable, forming a dark, moist, crumbly material with a pleasant earthy smell. If left alone, the matter will eventually turn to compost over several years. However, if it is encouraged to break down in the correct way, it is possible to have compost suitable for enriching your soil after only a few months.

The process of decomposition is carried out by microorganisms (see pages 32–33), and it requires air, moisture, and warmth. Air helps to break down the material—a process known as aerobic decomposition. Airless, or anaerobic, decomposition means slimy, evil-smelling compost, at least in the short term. To allow air to circulate, mix dense materials that will form a solid mass, such as grass, with open material, such as prunings and plant stems, or chopped straw.

The plant material added to the pile usually supplies enough moisture. However, in dry weather, you may need to water the pile; use a watering can or hose fitted with a rose.

As they work, microorganisms will usually create the warmth that is necessary for the decomposition process. However, if a new pile is slow to build up heat, you should add a compost accelerator, such as ammonium sulfate (available in garden centers), or a layer of fresh farmyard

Creating compost

You can make your own compost in a few easy steps. Turning the compost isn't essential, but it speeds up the process by adding air and spreading the heat more evenly (the heat often concentrates in the center of the pile).

In rainy climates, keep excess water out of the pile—too much moisture lowers the temperature and excludes air. A protective cover will keep out excess moisture as well as hold in heat.

1 Build up the first layer of garden waste. Keep adding to the pile until the layer is 12–18 inches (30–45 cm) deep.

2 Cover the waste with a layer of garden soil about 3 inches (7.5 cm) deep. Continue the layers as you build up the pile.

manure. Both of these supply the nitrogen that is necessary for the microorganisms to thrive.

The compost pile

At its simplest, a compost pile is just that—waste material piled up in one place. By banging four sturdy corner posts into the ground and securing chicken wire around them, you can help to keep the pile tidy and manageable; however, wooden planks nailed to the posts instead of the chicken wire will look better and encourage faster decomposition by holding in any warmth. Enterprising gardeners can use other available materials, including bricks, concrete blocks, plastic sheets, old pallets, and various other supplies. For the average garden, a compost pile of 3 cubic feet (1 cu m) is a suitable size.

Proprietary compost containers are available in a range of sizes and styles, but make sure they are large enough to be practical. You can make one from a garbage can. It will need holes in the sides to allow air to reach the decomposing material. Remove the bottom to allow worms to enter the pile to help the decomposing process.

COMPOST MATERIALS

All organic matter—material that was once alive—can in theory be composted. However, some waste is better left out of a compost pile. A mixture of different materials will help air to circulate and provide both carbon and nitrogen.

ADD

- In the fall, plant debris from borders and the vegetable garden.
- Grass clippings not treated with selective weed killer (but mix it with bulky waste first).
- Damaged fruit and vegetables.
- Fruit and vegetable trimmings, such as peels, from the kitchen.

Add with care

- Tough prunings and woody stems; shred these before adding to the pile—or they will rot slowly.
- Annual weeds before they go to seed—the seeds do not decompose.
- Fallen leaves: These take time to rot and are best composted as leaf mold (see pages 36–37).

AVOID

- Perennial weeds or invasive plants: Adding a few parts of a plant, such as root from bindweed, can cause a garden infestation when the compost is spread.
- Diseased plants: Some parts of a pile may not reach a temperature that kills all disease spores. Diseases such as clubroot on brassicas, halo blight on beans, potato blight, and white rot on onions can spread in compost. Burn affected plants.
- The first two or three grass clippings from lawns treated with selective weed killer. Some plants, such as tomatoes, are affected by even a trace of the weed killer.
- Cooked food and meat products: These attract vermin such as rats.

3 Turn the compost pile—sides to middle and top to bottom—when it is half full and again when it is almost full, or about every three months.

4 When the pile is full, cover it with a piece of old carpet or a sheet of strong black plastic, but check occasionally to ensure the pile does not become too dry.

5 Once the pile is full and rotting down, start another one—this will allow time for the first pile to mature.

Digging when and how

Few things are more satisfying than the sight of a freshly dug vegetable plot—and digging provides a whole range of benefits for your vegetable plants.

IS DIGGING FOR YOU?

PROS

- Breaks up compacted soil layers and improves aeration and drainage.
- Removes roots of old crops and weeds, which makes sowing and planting possible.
- Kills annual weed growth by burying the weeds.
- Mixes organic matter into the root zone of the plants.

CONS

- Hard work.
- Can damage the soil structure, especially on heavy clay soils.
- Digging can bring annual weed seeds buried deep in the soil up near the surface, where they can germinate.

One way to look at digging is to think about it as healthy exercise rather than hard work. Why pay to go to the gym when you can achieve the same result in your own garden for free? The best way to tackle the job is to do a little at a time instead of trying to do it all at once—and use a well-balanced, comfortable spade.

When to dig

Start digging as soon as you clear any crops in the fall. Dig the area over in small sections, as space becomes

Single digging

The simplest and most common method of preparing a plot is single digging. Start by marking the center of your plot with string tied to stakes. It will be a guide for your first trench. As you dig the soil, turn over each spadeful as you toss it into the previously dug trench, thereby burying any surface weeds.

1 Dig the first trench 1 foot (30 cm) wide and the depth of the spade's blade; store the soil in a wheelbarrow.

2 Scatter a layer of compost over the bottom of the trench to help improve the quality of the soil.

vacant. Leave the soil in rough, sizable clods. This exposes the maximum surface area to the weather, particularly to the effects of repeated freezing and thawing, which will break the clods down into small particles, thereby doing much of the hard work for you. The earlier you complete the digging in the fall or early winter, the more time the weather will have to do its work.

In spring, just before sowing and planting, you may need to turn the soil over again with a fork to break it down further. Any remaining clods will usually shatter easily if struck sharply with the back of the fork. On light soil, you may need to only rake the soil to give it the fine, friable (crumbly) texture needed for sowing.

DOUBLE DIGGING

Double digging, also known as trenching, is harder work than single digging, but it can provide worthwhile results—yields can be improved by 30 percent or more.

The benefits of double digging last for several years. It is worth doing the first time a new plot is dug, then every four or five years.

Take the soil from a trench as you would with single digging (see below), but make it 2 feet (60 cm) wide. Fork over the base of the trench another spade-depth deep and incorporate compost before soil from the next trench is thrown into it, thereby breaking up the consolidated area (the pan) that forms below the normal digging level. This will allow the plant roots to penetrate more deeply and improves the plants' water uptake, which increases the yields.

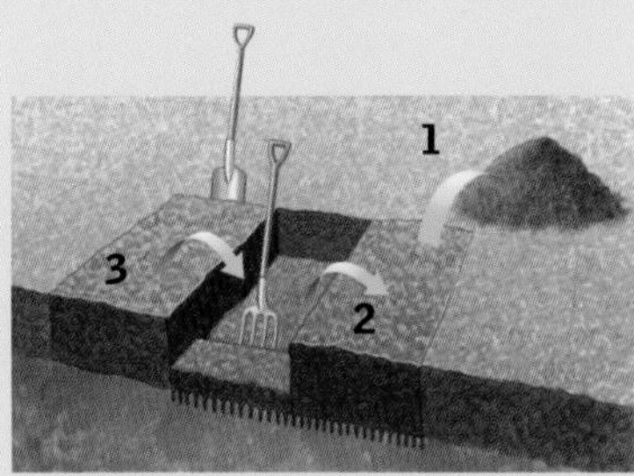

When double digging, be careful not to mix the lower infertile soil with the topsoil in which the plants grow.

How to dig

A spade or shovel is the normal tool used for digging, but some people find a fork easier to use, especially on heavy soil. Stainless steel spades are expensive, but they have a long life and often make work easier because the soil slides off the blade cleanly.

When turning a spadeful of soil over, keep one hand low on the shaft, near the blade, to provide yourself with the maximum leverage. Avoid overloading the spade with too much soil, which will make digging more difficult. Tools with extra-long handles are available from garden centers; these can be gentler on the back.

Before you begin to dig, warm up with stretching exercises to avoid injury. As you dig, straighten up and stretch the spine backward frequently. You can also avoid injury by starting off gently, digging 20–30 minutes at a time, then build up to about an hour.

3 Dig another trench next to the first one, turning the soil over into the neighboring trench. Continue to the end of the plot.

4 Finish off the last trench with the soil stored in the wheelbarrow.

Quick Tip

Too wet?

Don't attempt to dig when the soil is wet, because this will damage the structure of heavy soil by compacting it further. You should be able to walk on the soil comfortably, with only a little of it clinging to the soles of your boots.

No-dig gardening

Anyone who has labored to dig over a large vegetable plot will be attracted to the ease of the no-dig system. Many enthusiasts feel it is a growing system that is closer to nature—where regular digging is unknown.

IS THE NO-DIG SYSTEM FOR YOU?

PROS

- Avoids the hard labor of wielding a spade.
- Does not upset the natural balance of soil organisms that can be caused by digging.
- The soil structure is not compacted because the soil is not trampled on.

CONS

- May not be suitable for heavy soil such as clay.
- Weeds may be a problem in the first few years.
- Large quantities of good-quality compost will need to be transported and spread.

Instead of the soil of a bare plot being turned over in the fall, in the no-dig system layer of rotted organic matter, such as compost or manure, is spread over the surface. Earthworms gradually pull this compost layer down and mix it up with the topsoil, which improves the fertility of the soil.

This layer of mulch will protect the soil surface from sun and wind, thereby keeping it moist and helping to even out temperature fluctuations. This helps microorganisms in the soil (see pages 32–33) to flourish. The mulch will also help to protect the soil from beating rain, which can spoil the structure of the soil and form a hard, impenetrable cap on the surface.

In the spring, you can sow seeds directly onto the mulched surface and, ideally, cover them with another layer of organic matter.

Before you get started

Plan and prepare ahead. Start by obtaining enough good-quality organic matter for the size of your plot. Few gardens are able to supply a sufficient quantity of compost, so you'll need to find a bulk supplier of manure or other organic matter—preferably one who can deliver to your garden. Remember that materials

Sturdy black plastic covers an area of weeds. Without sunlight, they will die in a few months, and you can start a no-dig plot.

Steps to no-dig gardening

Although not essential, most plots will benefit from a low border of planks or bricks set around the edge to keep the deep mulch in place, particularly because it builds up over several years. A system of pathways or planks on the beds is necessary to avoid walking on the soil and compacting it.

1 In the fall, clear the plot of weeds, using a fork to lift out any perennials. If there are many weeds, cover the plot with sturdy black plastic from early spring to late fall. Remove the plastic; rake off and dig up the dead weeds and roots. Or use a weed killer such as glyphosate.

2 You can use naturally rot-resistant wooden planks or planks treated with a preservative to hold the compost in place. Nail them to stakes driven into the ground. Leave pathways between the beds to avoid stepping in the soil.

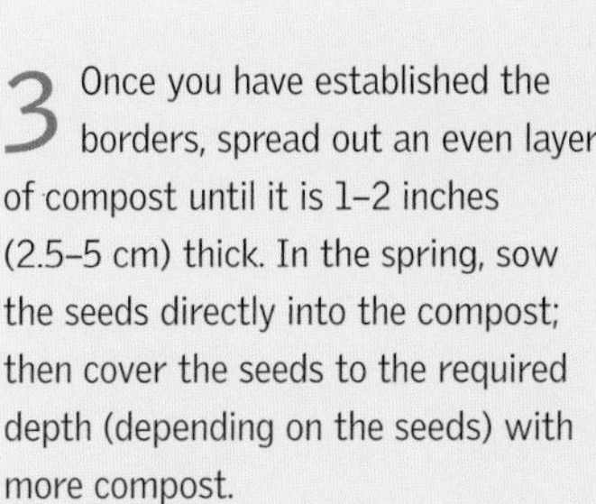

3 Once you have established the borders, spread out an even layer of compost until it is 1–2 inches (2.5–5 cm) thick. In the spring, sow the seeds directly into the compost; then cover the seeds to the required depth (depending on the seeds) with more compost.

that are not rotted, such as fresh straw, will take nutrients out of the soil, so they are not recommended.

A small-plot alternative

For a plot less than 5 feet by 15 feet (1.5 m by 4.5 m), after clearing the weeds in the fall (see box, left), spread layers of wet cardboard or newspaper over the area; then build up alternating layers of compost and grass clippings with shredded newspaper or chopped leaves until the layers are 6 inches (15 cm) deep. Let the bed decompose over the winter, and it will be ready for planting in spring. After the growing season, fork over the bed, incorporating some of the underlying soil into the organic matter on top.

Does it work?

No-dig gardening is most successful on soil with a good structure, where plenty of organic matter is available, and many gardeners have obtained good results. If weeds are a problem, you'll need to persevere in the first few years. Once the original weed seeds have sprouted, new ones are not brought up with digging, so the problem will lessen with time.

One of the benefits of digging is that it introduces air into the soil, and heavy soil can begin to suffer from lack of aeration after a few years of no digging. If you have heavy soil, this system might not be right for you.

Quick Tip

Pathways

When you plan the borders, make sure the pathways are large enough to fit a wheelbarrow—you'll need it to transport the compost.

Vegetables in containers

There's a surprising number of vegetables that can be grown successfully in containers. If you don't have a large garden, containers are a great way to maximize your use of space.

Ask most gardeners what type of vegetables can be grown in containers and they will usually come up with tomatoes and, after a little thought, perhaps peppers and eggplants. After that, they normally run out of ideas. However, there are plenty more crops that can be grown successfully in pots, grow bags, and even window boxes and hanging baskets—these are ideal for people who have patio gardens.

Types of container

Plastic and clay pots. The larger the pot, the less frequently it will need to be watered. The minimum practical-size container for most vegetables is 8 inches (20 cm) deep, but 12 inches (30 cm) deep is better. Make sure there are adequate drainage holes.

Window boxes. Many seed catalogs have a section for baby or miniature vegetable varieties, several of which are good for window boxes. Carrots (especially round-rooted varieties), radishes, and greens are all worth trying, as well as some compact herbs, such as thyme, basil, marjoram, chives, and parsley.

Hanging baskets. Special basket varieties of tomatoes make a colorful feature, particularly with a few thyme or rosemary plants tucked in among them. You could even try a malabar spinach in a basket. If you are growing vegetables in hanging baskets, remember that you will need to water them frequently.

Grow bags. Usually used by nurseries and greenhouse growers, these plastic bags (with drainage holes) are now available to the home gardener. They

Planting vegetables in a window box

Choose compact cultivars to grow in window boxes. If planting perennial herbs, ensure that there is proper drainage to avoid waterlogged plants in winter.

1 Carefully remove transplants from the tray or pots; make sure you avoid damaging their roots.

2 Leave enough space between plants to allow room to grow—the spacing will depend on the vegetable type.

Quick Tip

Feeding time

Plants need feeding as they develop because there is a limited nutrient supply in the potting mix. Apply a liquid feed every 7 to 14 days, or use granular, powder, or slow-release fertilizers (see pages 88–89).

Supporting container-grown vegetables

Some vegetables need a large container and require some type of support for climbing, such as peas and pole beans.

1 Place a layer of stones or broken pottery over the drainage holes, half fill with compost, then add a suitable potting mix. Use a dibble to make seed holes for peas or beans.

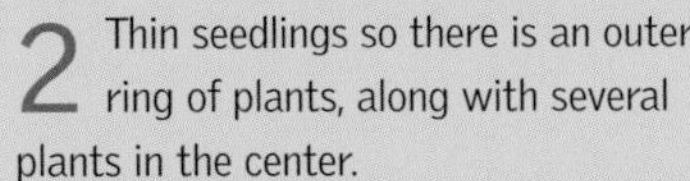

2 Thin seedlings so there is an outer ring of plants, along with several plants in the center.

3 Before the seedlings begin to climb, add supports by pushing bamboo canes into the soil (avoid disturbing the plants) and securing the top ends together with twine, forming a tepee shape. Encourage the plants to climb around the canes while they are young.

hold a limited depth of potting mix, so these also need frequent watering; otherwise, they are convenient to use. Most of the crops in *What Vegetables Can I Grow?* (right) are suitable for growing in a grow bag—even potatoes can be grown in one, although the yield may be small.

Preparing the containers

Good drainage is important for all container-grown plants, so check that there are plenty of drainage holes. (It is easy to add more holes to plastic pots by drilling them with an electric drill.) Raise containers off the ground on pot feet or bricks to allow water to flow through the holes freely. Cover the base of the container with pieces from broken clay pots or large stones in a layer 1–2 inches (2.5–5 cm) deep.

Fill the container with either a soil-based potting mix or a soilless mix. Soil-based mixes hold moisture well and have a higher level of nutrients than soilless types; they also make the container more stable and are less likely to blow over. However, they are heavy, making the bags of potting mix awkward to transport and large containers difficult to move once they are filled. Both potting-mix types provide good results, so the choice is a matter of personal preference.

Always moisten soilless mixes before use. When using it in small containers, such as hanging baskets, grow bags, and window boxes, mix in some moisture-retaining granules (available from garden centers), because these cut down the amount of watering needed and protect plants from drying out.

After planting, cover the surface of the potting mix with gravel or shredded bark mulch to help cut down moisture loss. Keep the potting mix just moist at all times; in sunny or windy weather the containers may need watering twice a day.

WHAT VEGETABLES CAN I GROW?

You should avoid growing some vegetables in containers because they need a lot of space and a long growing season for a good yield, such as Brussels sprouts and asparagus, or have long, deep roots, such as parsnips and salsify. However, you may have better luck with some of these:

- Baby beets
- Carrots (short-rooted types)
- Cucumbers
- Eggplants
- Pole beans
- Herbs
- Kohlrabi
- Lettuce and other greens
- Melons
- Peas
- Peppers
- Potatoes (new)
- Radishes
- Summer squash
- Tomatoes

3 Sowing and planting

The really exciting part of vegetable growing is witnessing the conversion of a packet of dry, shriveled-looking seeds into rows of vigorous, healthy plants. It is important to remember that vegetable plants are at their most vulnerable stage when they are young and need special care. The following pages contain advice to help you give your seedlings and young plants the best possible start, whether you are sowing them directly in the vegetable plot or in containers for transplanting—or if you are bypassing the sowing stage altogether and buying young plants.

Some young plants will benefit from a protective cover, whether provided by cloches, a cold frame, or a greenhouse.

A planting strategy

Careful planning is the best way to get the most from your vegetable garden. Many gardeners don't have the space—or time—to grow everything they would like, so it's a matter of establishing your priorities before you start buying tempting packets of seeds!

The following questions will help you get a better idea of your requirements and limitations so that you can plan your crops effectively:

GUIDE TO VEGETABLE YIELDS

The following yields are for planting a row 3 feet (1 m) long.

Vegetable	Yield
Bean, pole	13 pounds (6 kg)
Bean, snap	3 pounds (1.5 kg)
Beet	5 pounds (2.5 kg)
Broccoli, sprouting	2 pounds (1 kg)
Brussels sprout	4 1/2 pounds (2 kg)
Cabbage	7 pounds (3.2 kg)
Carrot	7 pounds (3.2 kg)
Cauliflower	4 1/2 pounds (2 kg)
Celery	3 pounds (1.5 kg)
Chinese cabbage	3 pounds (1.5 kg)
Leek	7 pounds (3 kg)
Lettuce	2 pounds (1 kg)
Onion, bulb	5 pounds (2.5 kg)
Parsnip	7 pounds (3 kg)
Pea	4 1/2 pounds (2 kg)
Potato	9 pounds (4 kg)
Scallion	12 ounces (340 g)
Rutabaga	4 1/2 pounds (2 kg)
Squash	9 pounds (4 kg)
Spinach	2 pounds (1 kg)
Sweet corn	2 pounds (1 kg)
Tomato	7 pounds (3 kg)
Turnip	4 pounds (2 kg)
Zucchini	6 1/2 pounds (3 kg)

Pole beans will produce a much greater yield than bush beans.

What do you want from your vegetable garden? You should think about the reasons you want to grow vegetables. You may be determined to grow all the vegetables necessary to supply your household needs so you can be sure of enjoying fresh, healthy, organically grown produce at all times. Or perhaps it's the fun and challenge of actually growing the crops that appeal to you most—and the harvest is a welcome bonus. Some gardeners are content to continue buying reasonably inexpensive staples, such as potatoes, at the grocery store, and concentrate on growing the more unusual and exotic vegetables that are expensive or difficult to find.

How much space do you have? This is a limiting factor for many gardeners. If you want to get the most out of a small area, concentrate on the crops that produce the biggest potential harvest per foot (m) of row. In the *Guide to Vegetable Yields* (left), these weights are only approximate. The actual yields vary considerably, according to your soil type, climate, and expertise. However, the chart will enable you to compare the different crops. If space is limited, for example, pole beans will be a better option in your garden than spinach.

It's also useful to know how long a crop will occupy the ground (see *Sowing to Harvest Times,* below); you can grow a whole series of short-term crops, such as lettuce and radishes, in the time it takes Brussels sprouts or winter cabbage to mature.

How much time do you have? If you are trying to grow vegetables as part of a busy working and family life, you probably won't have as much time for growing vegetables as someone with plenty of time on his or her hands, who sees vegetable gardening as a serious hobby. You should be sensible about the hours you can put in and choose crops that are easy to care for instead of labor-intensive ones if you have little time on your hands.

Be realistic about your capabilities. If you are new to vegetable growing, you can build your confidence with easy crops, such as lettuce, carrots, and beans, before trying the challenge of eggplant or cauliflower.

What about the family? Consider how many people you are growing for—there's no point in producing dozens of zucchini, tomatoes, or lettuce if there are just two of you to eat them. And don't forget people's likes and dislikes, too. It is surprising how many gardeners grow Brussels sprouts or parsnips, although no one in the family will eat them.

SOWING TO HARVEST TIMES

The chart below provides the average length of time you will need to wait between sowing seeds and harvesting your vegetables.

Short-term crop	Time
Asparagus pea	8 to 10 weeks
Bean, French	8 to 12 weeks
Bean, runner	12 to 14 weeks
Beet	12 to 16 weeks
Broccoli	12 to 16 weeks
Cabbage, Chinese (and Asian greens)	10 to 14 weeks
Carrot (early)	12 to 16 weeks
Corn salad	16 weeks
Cucumber	12 to 14 weeks
Fennel	10 to 14 weeks
Kohlrabi	8 to 12 weeks
Lettuce	6 to 14 weeks
Mesclun	3 to 8 weeks
Okra	16 weeks
Potato (early)	13 to 16 weeks
Radish	3 to 12 weeks
Scallion	10 weeks
Spinach	8 to 14 weeks
Sweet corn	14 weeks
Swiss chard	12 weeks
Tomato	16 weeks
Turnip	6 to 12 weeks
Zucchini and summer squash	10 to 14 weeks

Medium-term crop	Time
Bean, fava (and soy)	14 to 26 weeks
Carrot	16 to 20 weeks
Cabbage (summer and fall)	20 to 26 weeks
Cauliflower (summer)	20 to 26 weeks
Celery	18 to 30 weeks
Eggplant	20 weeks
Herbs	12 to 18 weeks
Pea	12 to 32 weeks
Peppers	18 weeks
Potato	20 to 22 weeks
Potato, sweet	18 to 24 weeks
Pumpkin and winter squash	10 to 19 weeks
Rutabaga	20 to 24 weeks
Salsify and scorzonera	25 weeks
Shallot	18 to 26 weeks
Tomatillo	18 weeks

Long-term crop	Time
Artichoke, globe	8 months
Artichoke, Jerusalem	40 to 50 weeks
Asparagus	12 months
Broccoli, sprouting	40 weeks
Brussels sprout	28 to 36 weeks
Cabbage (spring)	30 to 36 weeks
Cauliflower (spring)	40 to 46 weeks
Celeriac	30 to 35 weeks
Garlic	24 to 30 weeks
Horseradish	28 to 30 weeks
Kale	30 to 35 weeks
Leek	30 to 45 weeks
Onion, bulb	22 to 46 weeks
Parsnip	34 weeks
Rhubarb	15 months

Asparagus needs to grow a considerable length of time before you can harvest the spears.

All about seeds

Seeds are plants in waiting. All they need are the right triggers, such as moisture and warmth, to start growing.

A seed contains an embryonic plant in a dormant state, plus a reserve of energy to tide the new seedling over until it has developed sufficiently to fend for itself. The seed will remain dormant, protected by its outer casing, until the germination process is triggered by both moisture and warmth.

Importance of size

Once you open half a dozen packets of vegetable seeds, you will appreciate how widely they vary in size and appearance, and this will dictate how you sow them. Big, chunky runner bean seeds, for example, are easy to place individually at the correct spacing. However, tiny carrot seeds must be sown in a thin stream, and the resulting seedlings need to be thinned out to the right spacing later.

Seed size also affects sowing depth. Food reserves in the seed keep the seedling going from the moment of germination until the seedling breaks through the soil surface into the light. The larger the seed, the more reserves it contains. If a tiny seed is sown too deeply, its meager food supply will run out before it manages to fight its way up through the soil.

Buying seeds

Seeds are available from every garden center in the spring, but a much bigger selection is available from mail-order catalogs and Internet sites that specialize in selling seeds. The seed catalogs usually appear in late fall or early winter, and they are nearly always free and contain a wealth of information. Look for advertisements in gardening magazines; once you're on the mailing list, the catalog will usually keep coming every year.

What's on the packet?

Many seed packets have a color picture on the front of the variety they contain—these pictures are always useful guides. However, you shouldn't reject packets from seed companies that don't produce color pictures. These companies often stock less common varieties, and they may also provide more seeds in a packet, so you'll get more for your money.

Along with the type of vegetable, the seed packet should also provide a variety name, such as the bean 'Romano', the beet 'Boltardy', or the lettuce 'Buttercrunch'. There are international standards for plant names to ensure that the same variety is not

CHECKING SEEDS FOR VIABILITY

If you have seeds that are a few years old and you're not sure if they are worth sowing, you can try this test:

Place a folded paper towel in the base of a wide-mouth cup or dish and moisten it. Place 10 seeds on the moist paper towel, put the dish in a plastic bag, and seal it. Place the dish in a warm, dark place; a 70°F (21°C) temperature is ideal.

Check every other day that the paper towel is still moist, and after 10 days, count the number of seeds that have germinated. If the number is five or less, throw the seeds away. If it is six or seven, sow the seeds only if they are expensive or difficult to replace. If 8 to 10 seeds germinate, they are fine.

A GUIDE TO SEEDS

As a rough guide, you can divide seeds into large, medium, and small types. Remember, the sowing measurements are only a guide—no one expects you to get the depth exactly right.

Size	Small	Medium	Large	Extra large
Description	Seeds that are difficult to handle individually, such as carrot, leek, lettuce, and onion.	Most vegetables, such as the cabbage family, tomatoes, and parsnip.	Those that can be handled individually, such as beans, peas, sweet corn, and zucchini.	The largest seeds, such as runner and fava beans.
Sowing instructions	Sow small seeds ¼ inch (6 mm) deep.	Sow medium seeds ½ inch (12.5 mm) deep.	Sow 1–1½ inches (2.5–3.75 cm) deep.	Plant 2 inches (5 cm) deep in light soil.

available under several different names. The accepted way of writing a variety name is to enclose it between single quotation marks; however, this is not always practiced on seed packets or in catalogs.

Many varieties are labeled as "F1 hybrids." This means that they are the first generation of seeds from a deliberate cross between two different-named varieties. F1 hybrids are often more vigorous and produce heavier, more uniform crops. These seeds are usually also more expensive than "open-pollinated" varieties—plants whose flowers have been fertilized by those of the same variety while growing in the field.

Seed packets will usually inform you of the year the seeds were packed. There may also be instructions for sowing the seeds and growing the plants. However, these are often generalized, and you will probably need to adapt them for your particular garden, although some seed companies do provide detailed information on their packets.

The packet may sometimes say that it contains "treated" seeds. This means that the seeds are particularly prone to pest or disease attack, so they have been pretreated with a fungicide or pesticide for improved germination. The seeds are dyed to make this treatment obvious, and you should wear gloves whenever you handle them. If you want to use only organic gardening methods, you may prefer to avoid these seeds.

Storing seeds

If vegetable seeds are kept cool and dry, they can remain dormant but viable (capable of germination) for a number of years. However, for most vegetables, the fresher the seeds, the better the result. Old seeds germinate more slowly and in patches, and they may completely fail.

Store seeds in a cool, dark place, preferably in a sealed container with a sachet of silica gel to absorb any moisture. Also take note of the "best before" date, if there is one, which may be stamped on the packet. As a guide, five years is the maximum storage time for most vegetable seeds: onion, parsnip, and sweet corn have much shorter lives and will remain viable for only a year or two.

Quick Tip

Shallow truth

Lettuce is unusual in that the seeds need light to be able to germinate, so it is particularly important to avoid burying lettuce seeds too deeply.

Preparing your plot for sowing

Many vegetable crops are sown outside, directly in the positions where they will mature, so it's worthwhile spending some time getting the vegetable plot into the ideal condition for the seeds.

Most vegetables are sown in spring (although there are some vegetables sown outdoors in summer and fall). For these springtime sowings, prepare the soil in your vegetable plot in the fall (see pages 30–43), so that winter frosts can help loosen the soil before sowing time arrives. However, you'll still have to add some final touches.

Reasons for a fine tilth

The object of working the soil for spring sowings is to break it down to a fine tilth—that means reducing the texture to small, even crumbs. If you sow seeds into rough soil full of clods, the seeds will end up at varying depths and not always with good access to soil moisture. This will lead to uneven germination—not to mention the practical difficulties of trying to draw a straight furrow in lumpy soil.

Seeds are much easier to sow in a fine, crumbly soil where they can be covered to a consistent depth. The seeds will germinate much

STONY SOIL

Stony soil can be a nuisance because stones can make it difficult to draw a furrow and sow evenly. However, if you rake away stones too energetically, you may bring more stones from below the surface up to the top.

Lightly rake the uppermost stones from the soil surface, gathering them with short strokes. Pick the stones off the soil and save them for another use, such as making a path.

Preparing the surface

If you dug over your plot in the fall (see pages 40–41), you may need only a rake to prepare the surface of your soil for sowing. Alternatively, you may need to turn the plot over with a garden fork and break up large clods into a suitable size for raking. If the soil is wet, wait until it has dried. When you can walk over the soil without it clinging to your boots, you know it's ready for you to start work.

1 If necessary, turn over the soil and break up any large clods, using a fork or a hoe; then begin leveling the soil with a rake.

Quick Tip

Frosty surprise

Don't be tempted to start work too early in the year. An early warm break in the weather that makes you think spring is here can be followed by a return to winter conditions. Be guided by the average dates of the last frost in your particular region.

more rapidly and consistently, and the seedlings will be able to push straight up through the soil crumbs instead of having to find their way around the clods.

When to prepare

If the soil is wet, don't try to prepare it for sowing; it won't break down properly. You should wait until there are several fine, dry days, preferably with a brisk wind, which will help dry out the surface.

If you have a heavy soil, such as clay, that is always wet and difficult to work in spring, you can use cloches from late winter onward to cover an area where you want to sow early crops. This will keep the soil dry and allow you to rake it down for sowing earlier than normal in the spring.

Assessing the soil

The amount of work needed to get soil in the right condition for sowing varies from garden to garden and from year to year. If you finish all your fall digging on time, have a reasonably light soil, and have a winter with a lot of freezing and thawing to help break up the soil, you may need only a rake to prepare the surface for sowing. If you're not so lucky, you may need to turn the plot over with a garden fork to break up large clods into a suitable size for raking, but even this should be fairly light, quick work.

Creating a fine tilth

Once all the clods are broken down to pieces no bigger than the size of a fist, it's time to start raking. Raking removes stones and the remains of weeds, reduces the soil to fine crumbs, and levels the surface of the plot. It is something of an art, but it's an art that's easily achieved with practice.

After leveling, it's a good idea to firm the bed, particularly if the soil is light in texture. You can do this simply by treading across the soil, using a rapid, shuffling gait that may bring a few strange looks from the neighbors but that is efficient at firming the entire soil surface evenly.

Once the plot is leveled and firmed, it's time to use a metal rake to achieve the final fine tilth. Work the rake lightly, with long, sweeping strokes. Break up any stubborn remaining clods with a quick or solid blow from the back of the rake.

USING RAKES

Ideally you should have two rakes: a wide, wooden one for leveling (but these are hard to find) and a smaller, metal one for creating a tilth and covering seeds. The secret of raking soil to a level is to handle the rake lightly. Let the rake almost float over the soil as you pull and push it in sweeping strokes while holding it at a low angle to the soil surface. Don't be tempted to dig the rake in or push down on it while raking—you'll only make troughs and hills that will be difficult to level out. Rake in several different directions for a good finish.

2 As you level the soil, you can break up any large clods of soil into tiny pieces with the back of your rake, using a good sharp wallop.

3 After leveling the soil, firm it by treading across the plot. However, for heavy soil, firm lightly with the palm of your hands instead.

4 Create the final fine tilth with a rake, using long, sweeping strokes and applying light pressure until all the soil is ready for sowing.

Sowing seeds outdoors

Many vegetables are sown directly outdoors, where they will grow and can be harvested. Sowing in rows is the most common method, but there are other ways that can sometimes work better.

The usual way to sow seeds is in parallel rows across the vegetable garden. Mark out the position of the first row with a garden line—a piece of twine stretched taut between two sticks. For a shorter row, you can use a length of wood as a guide.

Making a furrow

Use the corner of a draw hoe to pull out a furrow. To make sure the row is straight, place one foot on the line to hold it in the correct position as you make the furrow. (For the correct depth of the furrow, see pages 50–51.)

Using the corner of a draw hoe, pull out a shallow furrow in the soil along a taut garden line. Try to keep the furrow an even depth.

If the soil is dry, water the base of the furrow before sowing. Take care to use a gentle stream of water. You can use a light dribble from a hose or create a gentle stream by putting your thumb partially over the spout of a watering can.

Sowing seeds in a furrow

Try to space the seeds evenly as you sow them along the furrow. You can tip some seeds out into the palm of one hand and take pinches of them to sprinkle along the row, or you might prefer to tap them carefully straight out of the packet. (Creasing the edge of the packet to form a funnel will give you more control over the flow of seeds.) Some people prefer handheld seed sowers, which can be bought inexpensively from garden centers or mail-order catalogs.

Sow the seeds evenly along the length of the furrow, whether you tap them straight out of the packet or use another method.

Use whatever method you feel most comfortable with, as long as you're able to sow the seeds thinly and evenly. Small seeds, such as carrots and lettuce, are usually sown this way—completely along the length of the row—and the seedlings are then thinned out to the correct spacing later.

Larger seeds are easier to handle, so you can sow them at their final spacing from the beginning—this is known as sowing at stations, and it uses fewer seeds. You can use this technique for crops such as French beans, parsnips, and beets. To allow for germination failures, sow three seeds at each station—weed out the surplus seedlings later.

Another method is to sow seeds at half their final spacing—for example, if you are growing beans 6 inches (15 cm) apart, sow the seeds 3 inches (8 cm) apart; then remove the surplus seedlings later. These extra seedlings

To make a double row, use the full width of the blade of a draw hoe to make a wide furrow in the soil. Alternatively, you can use a spade to lift out the soil.

Sow the seeds in two rows along each side of the furrow. Alternatively, you can broadcast, or scatter, the seeds over the base of the furrow.

are often useful for transplanting to fill up any gaps in the rest of the row.

Once the seeds are sown, cover them with soil as soon as each row is completed. Use a metal rake to pull the soil back to fill the furrow evenly, being careful not to disturb the seeds. Finally, firm the soil, either by walking along the furrow or tamping it down with the back of the rake. Label the row with the variety and the date of sowing, and move the garden line into position for the next row.

To make a shallow furrow for small seeds, lay a rake along the soil where you want your row to grow. The handle of the rake will leave a depression that you can use as a furrow.

Other ways of sowing

Sowing in furrows across the vegetable garden is convenient, but there are other methods that can work better.

Short rows. It is often impractical to harvest and use a whole, long row of a single crop, such as lettuce, before it goes to seed; in these cases, it can be more sensible to sow short rows. You should consider splitting a row into three sections and sowing them with different vegetables—for example, one-third with lettuce, one-third with radish, and one-third with scallions.

Wide rows. Peas are usually sown in furrows about 6–8 inches (15–20 cm) wide. Use a garden line or length of wood to guide a draw hoe or spade to make the furrow. You can broadcast the peas over the base of the furrow or sow them in two rows (see above). You can also use these wide rows for patches of lettuce and mesclun crops.

Broadcast. Instead of sowing seeds in furrows, you can broadcast them by scattering the seeds over an area of soil in the same way you would sow a lawn. Some crops, such as lettuce, are sown with this technique in little square beds, but it makes controlling weeds difficult. As an alternative to broadcasting, sow seeds in closely spaced, short rows within the beds. It is then easy to distinguish between crop seedlings and weed seedlings when they emerge, and you can use the hoe or hand weed until the crop plants grow large enough to cover the whole bed.

Individual spacing. You can sow large seeds—pole beans, for example—by simply pushing them into the soil instead of drawing a furrow, which can save time. You can use a dibble to make the hole for the seeds, but first mark the depth on the dibble so that you can be sure that you sow the seeds at the correct depth.

Hill. Squashes do well when they are sown on a little hill of soil. The necks of the plants are prone to rot if they are surrounded by moisture, and sowing on a hill ensures the water can drain away from the stems. Draw the soil up into a mound, and sow three seeds into the top of the hill. Make a moatlike channel circling around the base of the hill, which will divert water to the roots, where it will be needed.

When hilling seeds, draw the soil up into a mound about 4 inches (10 cm) high and 8 inches (20 cm) across; then sow three seeds into the top of the hill.

Special sowing techniques

Seeds usually germinate easily, but there are times when a little extra help is required. There are several ways of making sure you get the best results from your sowings.

For seeds that are slow or difficult to germinate try a technique known as fluid seeding. It is also a good technique if you are sowing early in the spring, when weather and soil conditions are unpredictable.

The technique involves first pre-germinating the seeds in a warm place indoors and then mixing them with a carrier gel before "sowing" them in the garden. Because germination has already taken place, the seeds grow quickly, even if in cold soil. Fluid sowing is useful for slow-germinating seeds, such as parsley, parsnips, and celery, and in short-season areas, for carrots and other root crops, lettuce, and cabbages.

Steps to fluid seeding

To prepare the seeds first line the inside of a plastic sandwich container with paper towel. Moisten the paper towel thoroughly before scattering the seeds thinly over it. Cover the container and keep it at 70°F (21°C). Check the container every couple of days; as soon as most of the seeds show signs of germination, it is time to sow them. The emerging roots should be only just visible (you will need a magnifying glass for small seeds); if they are allowed to develop too far the process will fail.

Make a gel to carry the seeds. Use a wallpaper paste (choose a fungicide-free one) diluted 50 percent with water, or mix 2–3 tablespoons (30–45 ml) of cornstarch with 1 pint (475ml) of boiling water and allow it to cool. Make the gel thick enough so the seeds remain suspended and don't sink.

Wash the pre-germinated seeds off the paper towel into a sieve with a gentle stream of water, and then stir them into the gel with your fingers until they are well distributed. Put the gel into a plastic bag, snip off one corner, and squeeze the gel into an already prepared, moistened furrow. Cover the seeds, as usual.

Pelleted seeds

Seeds that are individually coated with a clay compound that sets hard are

Stale seedbed

This technique helps to prevent annual weeds from swamping your seedlings. Allow weed seeds buried in the top of the soil to germinate, then destroy them before planting vegetable seeds. When you destroy the weeds, be careful to do so in a way that does not disturb the soil any further. Once the vegetable seedlings emerge, they should have much less competition from weeds.

1 Prepare the seedbed about two to three weeks before you want to sow your vegetables, then wait.

2 Within a short time there will be a flush of weeds from the seeds that have been brought close to the surface by your cultivation.

To use a seed tape cut it to the appropriate length, place it at the bottom of a furrow and cover it with soil.

known as pelleted seeds. The hard coating makes the seeds larger and evenly rounded, so they are easier to handle and space accurately. Some seed coatings also include nutrients or fungicides. Pelleted seeds do not necessarily germinate more quickly—in fact, they may germinate more slowly. Keep the soil moist after sowing to allow the clay coat to break down.

Seed tapes

Small seeds are sometimes glued onto long, thin strips of paper at the correct spacing—these are called seed tapes. Simply lay a length of tape along the base of a furrow and cover it with soil. The paper will rot away, and the seedlings will emerge perfectly spaced and in nice straight rows.

You can make your own seed tape using strips of 1 inch (2.5-cm)-wide plain paper, such as photocopy paper or newspaper. Make a glue by mixing together flour and water until the mixture is the consistency of gravy. Use a small artist's paintbrush to dab a dot of glue at regular intervals along the paper at the appropriate spacing for the seeds; gently place the seeds on the glue. Allow the glue to dry.

Catch crops

Some crops are slow to germinate and develop. To make maximum use of space in your vegetable garden you can plant quick-growing "catch crops" in between them. You'll harvest the quicker-growing crop before it starts to compete with the slower one.

A classic combination is parsnips and radishes. Parsnips can take 28 days to germinate, whereas radishes need less than a week. Sow the parsnips at appropriately spaced stations (see pages 54–55) and sprinkle radish seeds in a furrow in between each station. Cover the seeds, as usual. You will be able to start eating the radishes before they interfere with the parsnip seedlings. The radishes will also help prevent a crust from forming on the soil, which will allow the germinating parsnips to push through more easily.

Other slow-germinating crops include beets, Swiss chard, endive, leeks, onion,s and parsley. For catch crops, try spinach and lettuce. You can also try succession planting (see page 18).

HOT WEATHER TIPS

Most seeds need warmth to germinate. However, for many vegetables, germination will be hampered if temperatures reach above 86°F (30°C). Lettuce seeds are especially vulnerable. They become dormant at soil temperatures above 78°F (25°C).

The timing of sowing is essential; for example, sow lettuce seeds in the early afternoon during hot spells, so that the critical germination process is most likely to take place during the coolness of nighttime. You should water the bottom of the seed furrows immediately before sowing to keep the temperature down.

The best way to resolve the problem in consistently hot areas is to pre-germinate the seeds under controlled, cooler conditions indoors and then use either the fluid-seeding technique or transplant the seedlings (see pages 68–69).

3 Careful hoeing, using a sharp blade that slices off the weeds at the soil surface, will kill the weeds, or use a flame gun or herbicides.

4 As soon as the weeds are gone, you can sow the vegetable seeds with as little soil disturbance as possible.

Quick Tip

Marker crops

The catch-crop technique is useful as a marker to show where a slow-germinating row has been sown. You'll appreciate this marker when you need to weed between the rows before the slow-growing seedlings appear.

Care after sowing

A newly emerged seedling is very vulnerable, but a little special care will ensure that it soon develops into a strong and healthy young plant.

During the first stage of the germination process, the seed absorbs water from the surrounding soil, which softens the seed coat so that the young root can emerge. Part of the reason for breaking the soil down into fine crumbs is to ensure that the seed will be in contact with sufficient soil moisture for this process to happen. The process can take from one day or two to several weeks, depending on the type of seed.

The emerging seed

Once the seed absorbs enough water, and if the soil temperature is suitable, an embryonic root known as the radicle will grow. No matter which way the seed is positioned, the radicle grows downward, guided by a positive response to gravity. Fine root hairs develop on the rapidly growng root, and these absorb water and minerals from the soil. The root helps to anchor the plant in the ground.

Shortly after root growth begins, the seed's shoot starts to develop. The tip of the shoot—the plumule—is held between two bulky seed leaves, or cotyledons, which help to protect the plumule as it pushes through the soil. The shoot responds to gravity, but with a negative response, growing in the opposite direction to gravity.

While the seedling is growing up through the soil, it relies on the food stored in the seed leaves. The leaves start to photosynthesize to make energy from sunlight only when the seedling breaks through the soil surface. Bury a seed too deeply, and its food supply may run out before the seedling reaches the surface.

Seedlings can push past small obstacles in the soil. However, if they hit a larger obstacle, such as a stone, they have to find a way around it before they can continue toward the surface. A fine, light, crumbly soil, free from stones and other debris, makes life easier for the seedlings, helping them to reach daylight quickly.

Providing the right conditions

Make sure you keep the soil moist, but not flooded, at all times after sowing. Watering the furrow before sowing is the best way to supply moisture, but if conditions are extremely dry in the following days, additional watering may be necessary before the seedlings emerge.

Be sure to water using a watering can with a rose or a sprinkler to give a fine spray; a jet of water is likely to wash the seeds out of the soil. Heavy droplets can also cause the surface layer of soil to form a hard crust as

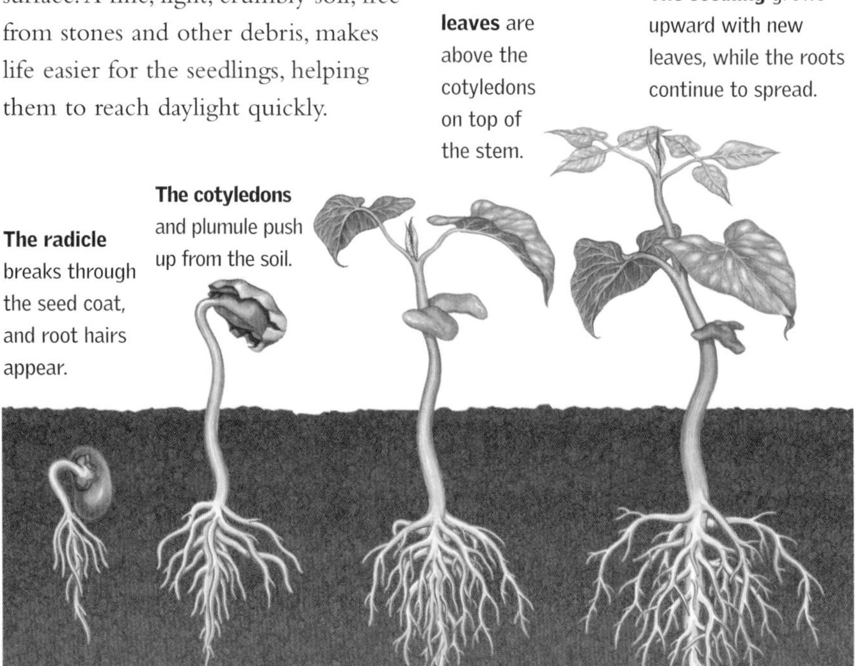

The radicle breaks through the seed coat, and root hairs appear.

The cotyledons and plumule push up from the soil.

The first true leaves are above the cotyledons on top of the stem.

The seedling grows upward with new leaves, while the roots continue to spread.

Thinning

Seedlings will need thinning once they are large enough to handle easily but before they start to crowd one another. Select the strongest seedlings to leave in place at the appropriate spacing, and carefully remove all the others.

1 If your plants are not growing closely together, you can slice off the extra seedlings with a sharp hoe blade.

2 To remove nearby seedlings, hold the remaining plant with a finger at each side; push down as you tug away the others.

3 You can use the extra thinnings by carefully planting them in a less crowded area in the plot. You should hold them by their leaves.

4 After thinning, water the seedlings using either a watering can with a fine rose or a fine spray from a hose.

it dries, which the seedlings might not be able to penetrate. Crusting is a particular problem on fine, silty, or clay soil. Covering moist soil with finely shredded bark, a single sheet of wet newspaper, or a floating row cover will help keep the moisture in and prevent a crust from forming. Make sure you remove the paper or row cover once the seedlings emerge, before it restricts their growth.

Soil temperature is more difficult to control than moisture, so getting the timing of sowing right is the most important factor. If a sudden, unexpected cold spell arrives after sowing, you can use floating row covers, cloches, or plastic tunnels to protect the seedbed from the worst of the weather.

After germination, continue to keep the soil moist, but make sure you still use the fine spray to avoid damaging the young plants.

Thinning

Seeds are sown relatively thickly to allow for inevitable germination failures. Once the seedlings are through the soil, they will grow quickly and you will soon find them competing for space. At this point, the young plants usually require thinning to the recommended spacing.

It is often a good idea to carry out thinning in two stages. If the final spacing required is 6 inches (15 cm), thin the seedlings first to 3 inches (8 cm) apart, then to their final spacing a few weeks later. This helps to avoid gaps in the row where selected seedlings have died.

PEST CONTROL

Some pests are attracted to plants by the scent produced by their bruised foliage; this is how the carrot fly, for example, finds its targets. Thinning out seedlings will release a strong scent, so you should do your thinning shortly before dusk, giving the adult flies minimal time to track down the source.

You can help disguise the scent by growing a strong-smelling herb, such as rue or chamomile, near your plants. However, don't grow parsley, which is related to carrots and is also attractive to carrot flies.

A guide to sowing seeds

This chart is a quick at-a-glance guide to basic sowing information. For detailed information, see the full entries for each vegetable.

Vegetable	When to sow	Spacing (between rows)	Spacing (within rows)	Comments
Arugula page 132	Early to mid-spring; again in late summer	6 in. (15 cm)	1–6 in. (2.5–15 cm)	Close spacing provides baby leaves for harvesting.
Beet pages 194–95	Early to late spring; again in midsummer	18 in. (45 cm)	4–6 in. (10–15 cm)	Intensive spacing: sow thinly over a 15–18 in. (30–45 cm)-wide bed.
Broccoli rabe page 175	Early to mid-spring	18 in. (45 cm)	6 in. (15 cm)	Or broadcast seeds in wide rows; thin to 3 in. (7.5 cm) for intensive spacing.
Bush bean pages 148–49	After all danger of frost is past	18–30 in. (45–75 cm)	6 in. (15 cm)	Intensive spacing: 6 in. (15 cm) apart on center.
Carrot pages 192–93	Early spring to late summer	6–12 in. (15–30 cm)	2–4 in. (5–10 cm)	Sow seeds every 3 weeks if you want a succession crop.
Celeriac page 201	Early spring	24 in. (60 cm)	8–10 in. (20–25 cm)	Intensive spacing: 12 in. (30 cm) apart on center.

Vegetable	When to sow	Spacing (between rows)	Spacing (within rows)	Comments
Chicory page 134	Early to mid-spring; again in midsummer	18–24 in. (45–60 cm); for grumolo, 12 in. (30 cm)	10–12 in. (25–30 cm); for grumolo, 6–8 in. (15–20 cm)	In hot-summer areas, sow to avoid leaves maturing in peak heat.
Kohlrabi page 179	Mid-spring to late summer	12–36 in. (30–90 cm)	6 in. (15 cm)	Sow seeds every 2 weeks for a succession crop.
Lettuce pages 128–31	Early spring until fall	18–24 in. (45–60 cm)	6–12 in. (15–30 cm)	Try to time the sowing to avoid the hottest periods of the summer.
Melon pages 234–37	After all danger of frost is past	4–6 ft. (1.2–1.8 m); for watermelon, 5–7 ft. (1.5–2.1 m)	4–6 ft. (1.2–1.8 m); for watermelon, 5–7 ft. (1.5–2.1 m)	In short-season areas, you can raise seeds under cover.
Mesclun pages 136–37	Early spring until fall	3–6 in. (7.5–15 cm)	Sow lightly	Alternatively, you can broadcast seeds lightly over a wide row.
Okra pages 220–21	In long-season areas, 2 to 4 weeks after last spring frost	18–36 in. (45–90 cm)	12–24in. (30–60 cm)	In long-season warm-summer areas, only direct sow.
Onion pages 158–61	Early to mid-spring or fall	12–18 in. (30–45 cm)	4–6 in. (10–15 cm)	For scallions, sow seeds thinly and harvest without thinning.
Parsnip page 197	Early spring	18–24 in. (45–60 cm)	4–6 in. (10–15 cm)	In mild-winter areas, sow in late fall for a spring harvest.
Pea pages 144–47	Early spring; again in late summer or fall	24 in. (60 cm)	4–6 in. (10–15 cm)	Choose different varieties to harvest over a longer period. *(Continued)*

By knowing the correct sowing times, you'll have a bountiful vegetable garden such as this one with Swiss chard and cabbage.

Vegetable	When to sow	Spacing (between rows)	Spacing (within rows)	Comments
Pole bean pages 150–51	After all danger of frost is past	Double rows: 2 ft. (60 cm) apart, 5 ft. (1.5 m) between rows	6–9 in. (15–23 cm)	Or sow 6 seeds per hill at the base of stakes or tepee poles; thin to 2 to 3 plants per stake.
Pumpkin and winter squash pages 228–33	Early summer, after all danger of frost is past	5–6 ft. (1.5–1.8 m)	6 ft. (.18 m); compact varieties, 2–4 ft. (60–120 cm)	In short-season areas, you can raise seeds under cover.
Radish page 196	Early spring through to fall	6 in. (15 cm)	2–4 in. (5–10 cm)	You can sow seeds in succession throughout the season.
Salsify and scorzonera page 202	Early spring	15–18 in. (38–45 cm)	4–6 in. (10–15 cm)	In hot-summer mild-winter areas, sow seeds in late summer.
Spinach pages 138–39	Early spring; again in mid- to late summer	18 in. (45 cm)	4–6 in. (10–15 cm)	You can sow seeds later to overwinter for a spring harvest.
Sweet corn pages 240–43	After danger of last spring frost is past	36 in. (90 cm)	3–4 in. (7.5–10 cm)	Plant in blocks of at least 4 rows to ensure pollination.
Swiss chard pages 140–41	Early spring and again in mid- to late summer	12–24 in. (30–60 cm)	6–12 in. (15–30 cm)	Less likely to bolt than spinach during hot weather.
Turnip pages 198–99	Early spring and again in midsummer to fall	18 in. (45 cm)	1–6 in. (2.5–15 cm)	Space close to harvest greens; use wider spacings for roots.
Zucchini and summer squash pages 226–27	Early summer, after all danger of frost is past	24–36 in. (60–90 cm)	24–36 in. (60–90 cm)	In short-season areas, you can raise seeds under cover.

Starting transplants

While many vegetable crops are left to mature where they are sown, others are moved to new positions as young plants. There are several reasons why this may be a good idea—and there are some occasions when it is a bad one.

PROPAGATORS

Heated propagators are special units for raising seeds and cuttings; they supply a gentle warmth to the seed-starting mix, which helps ensure quick, even germination and rooting. An electric cable runs through the base of the propagator and can be thermostatically controlled to achieve the ideal level of heat. Seed flats filled with seed-starting mix and sown in the traditional way are placed on top of the heated base.

Some propagators are supplied with their own covers to keep humidity levels high; if not, you should fit each flat with its own individual plastic propagator top.

Starting plants off in one spot and moving them to another saves wasting space in the vegetable garden. Brussels sprouts, for example, need plenty of space as they mature, but as seedlings and young plants, they are happy growing close together. Starting them in a separate seedbed allows the area earmarked for their final positions to be used for a fast-growing crop while the sprouts are still in their early stages. (For more information about sowing in seedbeds, see pages 66–67.)

Starting under cover

Sometimes seeds are sown indoors, in a heated propagator or greenhouse, or under cover outdoors earlier than they can be sown outside, and then transplanted to their final growing position. This gives the plants a good start, and in cooler areas, it enables

You can sow large seeds in individual compartments in a seed flat filled with a sterile seed-starting mix.

Growing seedlings don't need such a humid atmosphere—too much humidity encourages fungus diseases such as damping-off.

When pricking out, handle the seedlings by their seed leaves (the first, expendable, pair of leaves that open). Never touch the stems.

earlier harvesting than would otherwise be possible. Starting seeds under cover is also good for seeds that are difficult to germinate, such as celery, and for types that are difficult to find or are expensive. When sown in containers under cover, it is easier to provide them with the best conditions for germination than when sown outside.

Sowing in containers

You can sow seeds for transplanting in flats or pots, according to the type of plant and the size of seeds. Use a sterile seed-starting mix to avoid problems with weeds and soil-borne pests and diseases often found in garden soil. Fill the seed flat or pot evenly, pushing the mix out to the corners of the flat, and level it off and firm it with a presser. Water the mix, using a fine rose on the watering can; then allow it to drain for an hour or so before sowing.

Space large seeds by hand; shake out smaller seeds thinly and evenly over the surface of the mix. Cover the seeds with more seed-starting mix to the recommended depth; you can shake the mix through a small garden sieve for an even distribution. Cover the containers with plastic propagator tops, a sheet of glass, or an upturned seed flat to keep in the moisture and warmth. Add a sheet of newspaper on top of a transparent cover.

Keep the seeds in an even warmth (check the packets for the suggested germination temperature) and keep the mix just moist. Once the first seedlings appear, remove the newspaper or upturned flat to allow light to reach the plants; when the first seedlings reach the glass cover, remove that, too. Propagator tops have extra headroom, so they can be left on the flats or pots for longer, but when all the seedlings appear, open the ventilators or prop the cover up for good air circulation. When watering is necessary, use a fine rose to avoid damage and keep the mix moist, never wet.

Pricking out

If the seeds were well spaced or individually sown, the young plants may be able to remain in the same containers until it is time to plant them in their final positions. However, most seedlings will need replanting to give them more room to develop, and this is known as pricking out. They can be spaced farther apart in another tray or moved to individual pots.

Prick out seedlings as soon as they are large enough to handle. Use a dibble to lever the roots carefully out of the mix; you may need to lever up a small clump of seedlings and gently untangle the roots. Make a hole with the dibble in the new container of seed-starting mix; then lower the seedling into it, making sure the roots make contact with the base of the hole and are not dangling in midair. Firm the seedling in gently.

When the container is planted, water it, using a fine rose, and put it in a well-shaded place. The seedlings often droop after pricking out, but after a few hours they should recover and you can bring them into the light.

TRANSPLANTING PROBLEMS

Transplanting often involves damage to the roots and gives the plants a slight "check," or pause, to their growth. For this reason, it is not a good idea to transplant root crops, such as parsnips, salsify, scorzonera, and carrots, because any damage to the young root will cause it to be misshapen at maturity.

Root disturbance can also cause susceptible crops to bolt, or run to seed, prematurely—Florence fennel, spinach, lettuce, and Chinese cabbage are often affected in this way.

However, it is still possible to transplant these difficult plants. You can sow individual seeds in soil blocks or in fiber pots, which can be planted in their entirety to avoid root disturbance.

Starting transplants in seedbeds

You can sow vegetables that don't need the extra protection of a greenhouse in an outdoor seedbed; then transplant them to their final positions at a later date.

BEATING THE COLD

In cold areas, cover the seedbed with cloches or similar devices in late winter. This will keep off the rain and snow and allow the soil to dry out and warm up more quickly, so it can be prepared for sowing earlier in the following spring. It is also possible to make a seedbed within a cold frame, sowing directly into the soil. This will give the seedlings maximum protection in the early stages of growth, when they are at their most vulnerable. Harden off seedlings raised in a cold frame before transplanting them (see pages 68–69).

There are two main vegetable candidates for sowing in a seedbed: the members of the brassica, or cabbage, family—particularly those that mature in the winter and spring—and leeks. Sowing them in seedbeds avoids wasting space in the garden. (For vegetables that shouldn't be transplanted, see page 65.)

Determining the size of the bed

The size of your seedbed will depend on the number of plants you intend to grow. As a rough guide, most cabbage-family plants will require a final spacing of about 24 inches (60 cm) apart. You can thin seedlings in the seedbed to 2 inches (5 cm) apart and grow them in rows 6 inches (15 cm) apart. This means that a seedbed row 24 inches (60 cm) long should provide enough young plants for a crop row that is 24 feet (7 m) long.

Preparing the soil

You should prepare the soil as you would for sowing into the vegetable garden (see pages 52–53). An

Making a seedbed

Ideally, choose a site where the seedbed will be in a sheltered position. The soil should be fertile and easily worked so that you can prepare a fine tilth.

1 To mark out the area for your seedbed, you can use twine held in place by stakes at each corner.

advantage of a seedbed is that it is a small area, which is much easier to get it into an ideal condition for raising seedlings. Add plenty of well-rotted compost or similar organic material in the fall, and rake the soil to a fine tilth in early spring. Cabbage-family plants prefer a firm soil, so remember to tamp the seedbed area thoroughly.

Sowing the seeds

Because the seedbed is usually small, it is not normally necessary to use a line for sowing. Instead, press the handle of a hoe or rake into the soil to make a furrow. On heavy soil, this may compress the soil too much; instead, lay a tool handle on the ground as the guide and pull out the furrow with a hoe in the usual way.

Sow the seeds thinly along the furrows. Because the seedlings will be transplanted, some root damage is bound to occur, but thin sowing will help prevent a tangle of roots and keep the damage to a minimum.

When sowing several different types of cabbage-family plants, label each furrow as soon as it is sown. Trying to distinguish between rows of almost identical-looking cabbage, cauliflower, and Brussels sprout seedlings is not easy.

Caring for the seedlings

Cabbage-family plants will usually germinate within 7 to 14 days; leeks take a little longer at 21 to 25 days. Once the seedlings emerge, keep the soil moist by watering through a fine rose. The object is to keep the young plants growing without an interruption to their growth.

When cabbage-family seedlings are large enough to handle, thin them to 1–2 inches (3–5 cm) apart. Slender leek seedlings do not usually need thinning as long as they have been sown reasonably thinly.

Cabbage-family plants will be ready for transplanting after five to seven weeks, when the plants are about 4–6 inches (10–15 cm) high. Try not to delay any longer; the larger the plants, the more of a stunting in growth they will receive. You can transplant leeks when they are about 6–8 inches (15–20 cm) tall—usually about 8 to 10 weeks after sowing—when their stems are about half the thickness of a pencil.

BUYING TRANSPLANTS

If you don't have the space or time to raise your own plants from seeds, you can buy young plants for transplanting from garden centers and mail-order suppliers. They are available either as bare-root plants that have been lifted from the open soil or plug plants, or (more expensively) as plants growing in containers of various sizes.

Make sure that bare-root plants look fresh and healthy, and that their roots have been carefully wrapped to protect them from drying out while you bring them home. As soon as you get home, dunk them in a bucket of water and plant them without delay.

When buying cabbage-family seedlings, be aware that you can import incurable club-root disease into your garden. If possible, always raise your own seedlings. If you buy transplants, ask your supplier if they have been raised in sterile mix. If not, you shouldn't buy them.

2 After preparing the soil, lay the handle of a garden rake or fork on the ground and step on it to form the furrows.

3 Sow the seeds thinly along each furrow. Remember to label each furrow so you can identify the young seedlings.

4 Cover the seedlings with a thin layer of soil; without pushing it down, use a rake to move the soil at right angles to the furrow.

Planting out transplants

It's important to plant out young vegetables as soon as they are ready—a delay could reduce both the quality and quantity of the harvest. You also need to take steps to reduce the stress on transplants as much as possible.

If you delay the transplant of cabbage-family plants for only two or three weeks, you will reduce both the yield and the quality of the crop, because of the greater stress suffered by larger transplants. (To determine when they are ready for transplanting, see pages 66–67.) This is also true for other vegetables that have been grown under cover, although some vegetables, such as leeks, are less sensitive to transplanting.

Hardening off

If young plants have been raised under cover indoors, in a greenhouse, or in a cold frame, they must be hardened off—gradually acclimatized to the cooler temperatures in the open garden—before they will be ready for planting in their final positions. Moving them straight from a warm environment to one that is several degrees colder will seriously affect their growth, sometimes to such an extent that you will lose any advantage of an early start.

Hardening off should take about two weeks. First increase the amount of ventilation the vegetables receive under cover; then move them to a sheltered position outside during the day, bringing them under cover again in the evening. After a few days, you can leave the plants in a sheltered spot outside all day and night; finally, move the plants from the shelter to an open position just before planting.

A cold frame is a useful adjunct to a heated greenhouse. Young plants can start their hardening-off process in the closed frame, with more ventilation given day by day until the frame sash is left open entirely.

Choosing the day

The ideal weather for transplanting is overcast and still; a hot, sunny, breezy day will make it difficult for plants to recover from the inevitable wilting when they are newly planted. Wait a few days for better conditions, if possible, or tackle the job in the evening when it is cooler.

Preparation for planting

You should thoroughly prepare the designated area for planting. Although the soil does not have to be as fine as the tilth needed for sowing seeds, it should be raked down well and the soil should be crumbly to allow the plants to grow quickly.

Before transplanting, water the young plants thoroughly a few days beforehand, ensuring the water penetrates to the plants' full rooting depth. This will help to reduce root damage when lifting the plants.

Before lifting the plants or knocking them out of their pots, make sure you have everything ready for planting—for

Planting out

Before starting, dig a hole the appropriate size for each vegetable plant with a trowel. Once a row has been completely planted, water the row, providing enough water to penetrate the whole rooting area.

1 Loosen the soil in the pot or flat by tapping the container. Tilt the container upright to help ease the plant out, and gently handle the plant by the soil ball, not by the stem.

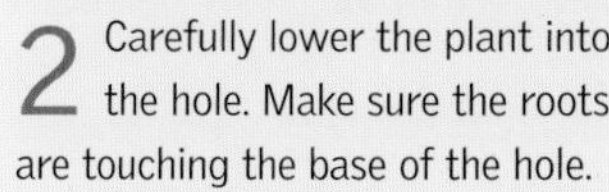

2 Carefully lower the plant into the hole. Make sure the roots are touching the base of the hole.

3 Fill in the hole with good-quality soil, and firm in the soil with the heel of your hand or by treading. Test that the plants are firm enough by tugging gently at a leaf—there should be no movement of the plant in the soil.

example, put a straight line in position ready for the first row.

Preparing potted transplants

If a vegetable plant has been raised in an individual pot, you should remove it from its container by turning the pot upside down; then, with the plant stem between your index and second fingers, rap the top edge of the pot firmly on a hard surface. This should enable the root ball of the plant to slide out with minimum disturbance to the roots.

If young plants have been raised in flats, loosen the potting mix by shaking the flat firmly from side to side and tapping the base on a hard surface. Then pry up a section of the mix and carefully separate the plants, teasing the roots apart.

Preparing seedbed transplants

Try to minimize the time the seedlings are out of the soil. If you are lifting young plants from a seedbed, don't lift all the seedlings at once. Take only as many as you can plant and water within 20 minutes or so; then return for another batch.

To lift the plants, push a fork deeply under the row of transplants and lever them up carefully. When transplanting cabbage-family plants, you should handle them by their leaves to separate the individual plants, teasing the roots apart while trying to retain as much of the soil clinging to the roots as you can. Lay the plants in a flat and cover them with a damp burlap bag or newspaper until you can plant them in their new positions.

CARING FOR TRANSPLANTS

The transplants will flag at first, but they will soon recover if they receive enough water. If the transplanting day is sunny, lay a floating row cover or single sheets of newspaper over the top of the plants to shade them until the evening. To get the plants off to the best possible start, give them an application of a balanced liquid fertilizer immediately after planting. Continue to water as necessary over the following days.

A guide to transplanting

The following pages provide a quick reference on information for transplanting. For more detailed information, see the full entries for each vegetable.

Vegetable	When to sow	When to transplant	Spacing (between rows)	Spacing (within rows)	Comments
Broccoli page 174	Late winter to early spring; again midsummer to early fall	Mid-spring and late summer to late fall	24 in. (60 cm)	18 in. (45 cm)	Sowing and cropping time vary according to climate.
Brussels sprouts pages 172–73	Early to midsummer	Mid- to late summer	18 in. (45 cm); for tall varieties, 24 in. (60 cm)	18 in. (45 cm); for tall varieties, 24 in. (60 cm)	In warm-summer areas, do not sow until peak summer temperatures have passed.
Bush bean pages 148–49	Mid- to late spring under cover	Early summer, after all danger of frost is past	18–30 in. (45–75 cm)	6 in. (15 cm)	Sow for transplanting only in short-season areas—otherwise, sow direct.
Cabbage pages 170–71	Early spring to midsummer	Mid-spring to late summer	18 in. (45 cm); for small heads, 12 in. (30 cm)	18 in. (45 cm); for small heads, 12 in. (30 cm)	With the right varieties, you can grow cabbages all year round.
Cauliflower pages 176–77	Early spring to early summer	Mid-spring to midsummer	24–36 in. (60–90 cm); intensive spacing, 18 in. (45 cm)	15–24 in. (38–60 cm); intensive spacing, 18 in. (45 cm)	Sowing and cropping times vary according to climate and variety.
Celeriac page 201	Early spring	Mid- to late spring	24 in. (60 cm)	8–10 in. (20–25 cm)	Can also plant 12 in. (30 cm) apart on centers.

Vegetable	When to sow	When to transplant	Spacing (between rows)	Spacing (within rows)	Comments
Celery page 200	Late winter to early spring	Mid- to late spring	24 in. (60 cm)	9–12 in. (23–30 cm)	Can also plant 12 in. (30 cm) apart on centers.
Cucumber pages 224–25	Early to mid-spring under cover	After danger of frost is past; in greenhouse, mid- to late spring	12 in. (30 cm)	12 in. (30 cm)	Can sow outdoor cucumbers three plants to a hill, with hills 3–4 ft. (90–120 cm) apart.
Eggplant pages 218–19	Early to mid-spring under cover	Early to midsummer, after all danger of frost is past	18–24 in. (45–60 cm)	18–24 in. (45–60 cm)	In cool-summer areas, you can grow eggplant to maturity in a greenhouse.
Florence fennel page 203	6 to 8 weeks before last expected spring frost	2 weeks before last expected spring frost	10–12 in. (25–30 cm)	10–12 in. (25–30 cm)	Protect them if temperatures drop below 25°F (-4°C).
Kale and collards page 178	Early spring to midsummer	Mid-spring to late summer and early fall	18 in. (45 cm)	12–18 in. (30–45 cm)	In hot-summer areas, plant kale only in late summer.
Kohlrabi page 179	Early spring, midsummer; in hot areas, early fall and early winter	Mid- to late summer or mid-fall to early winter	12–36 in. (30–90 cm)	6 in. (15 cm)	Can sow seeds throughout the winter in temperatures above 40°F (4.5°C).

(Continued)

Vegetable	When to sow	When to transplant	Spacing (between rows)	Spacing (within rows)	Comments
Leek pages 164–65	Late winter to early spring; in mild-winter areas, midsummer	Late spring to early summer; in mild areas, late summer and fall	12–18 in. (30–45 cm)	4–6 in. (10–15 cm)	Can sow indoors 10–12 weeks before outdoor-planting date.
Lettuce pages 128–31	Late winter to early spring under cover	Mid-spring	18–24 in. (45–60 cm)	6–12 in. (15–30 cm)	When you transplant, minimize root disturbance.
Melon pages 234–37	Mid-spring under cover	Late spring to early summer, after all danger of frost is past	4–6 ft. (1.2–1.8 m); for watermelon, 5–7 ft. (1.5–2.1 m)	4–6 ft. (1.2–1.8 m); for watermelon, 5–7 ft. (1.5–2.1 m)	In cool-summer areas, choose early ripening varieties.
Okra pages 220–21	2 to 4 weeks after spring frost; early to mid-spring under cover	Early to midsummer, after all risk of frost is past	18–36 in. (45–90 cm)	12–24 in. (30–60 cm)	In long-season warm-summer areas, make successional sowings for fall harvest.
Onion pages 158–61	Mid- to late winter under cover; fall if overwintering	Spring or fall	12–18 in. (30–45 cm)	4–6 in. (10–15 cm)	Choose the correct varieties for fall sowing.
Pepper pages 214–17	Early spring under cover	Late spring	24–36 in. (60–90 cm)	15–18 in. (38–45 cm)	In cool-summer areas, you can grow peppers to maturity in a greenhouse.

Vegetable	When to sow	When to transplant	Spacing (between rows)	Spacing (within rows)	Comments
Pole bean pages 150–51	Mid–late spring under cover	Late spring to early summer, when all danger of frost is past	Double rows: 2 ft. (60 cm) apart, 5 ft. (1.5 m) between rows	6–9 in. (15–23 cm)	In mild-winter areas, plant again in late summer for a fall harvest.
Pumpkin and winter squash pages 228–33	Mid-spring under cover, after all danger of frost outdoors	After all danger of frost is past	5–6 ft. (1.5–1.8 m)	6 ft. (1.8 m); for compact varieties, 2–4 ft. (0.6–1.2 m)	In short-season areas, raise seeds under cover.
Sweet corn pages 240–43	Mid-spring under cover	After all danger of frost is past	3 ft. (90 cm)	10 in. (25 cm) to 24 in. (60 cm), depending on the variety	Can sow short types in double rows 12 in. (30 cm) apart, 36 in. (90 cm) between rows.
Tomatillo pages 212–13	Late spring to early summer; under cover, early to mid-spring	Mid-spring to early summer	2–3 ft. (60–90 cm)	2–3 ft. (60–90 cm)	In cool-summer areas, grow to maturity in a greenhouse.
Tomato pages 206–11	Mid- to late spring; early to mid-spring under cover	Mid- to late spring and early summer	2–4 ft. (0.6–1.2 m)	2–4 ft. (0.6–1.2 m)	In cool-summer areas, grow to maturity in a greenhouse.
Zucchini and summer squash pages 226–27	Mid-spring under cover, after all danger of frost outdoors	After all danger of frost is past	2–3 ft. (60–90 cm)	2–3 ft. (60–90 cm)	To establish transplants, cover with a tunnel or floating row cover.

Extending the growing season

If the growing season is too short for all the crops you would like to grow, there are methods you can use to lengthen it, from simply mounding soil over potato shoots to protect them from late-spring frosts to creating an indoor space to start seedlings.

FLOATING ROW COVERS AND FILM

These protective materials are made either from a lightweight, woven fabric or from a clear, perforated plastic film. You can lay them on top of growing crops without damaging them. Both types allow moisture and air through to the plants while providing a degree of protection from cold weather, as well as from insects and animals.

You should anchor a floating row cover or film securely around the edges by digging them into the soil or weighing them down with stones. Although they stretch to an extent to accommodate growing crops, you will need to adjust them occasionally to prevent damage to the plants.

In cool and temperate regions, you can extend the season by sowing seeds and growing seedlings early in the year, before spring arrives. However, warm-season vegetables, such as tomatoes and peppers, will not survive even a slight frost, and in many places, frosts occur into mid-spring. Yet, if sowing seeds is delayed until all risk of frost has passed, the remaining season may be too short to allow the plants to reach maturity.

The answer is to provide protection to allow the seedlings to thrive. Even crops that are not frost tender can benefit from being started under protection; the warmer conditions allow faster growth, giving plants under cover a head start over those sown outside, leading to earlier crops.

Areas where spring comes late often have to suffer the double blow of fall and winter arriving early, too. However, plants that have not finished producing their yield by the time the fall weather arrives can often be safeguarded against early frosts, wind, and rain by using movable forms of protection, such as cloches and floating row covers. The extra days gained can make all the difference to your final harvest.

Simple forms of protection

If the forecast of a late, sharp spring frost takes you by surprise when potato shoots are thrusting through their ridges or tender seedlings are beginning to show in their furrows, don't panic. You can protect early potatoes by hilling them every two or three weeks once the shoots appear. Carefully pull the soil over the top of the shoots with a draw hoe. This will protect them from frost damage, and the shoots will soon push their way through the soil. Alternatively, you could use single sheets of newspaper or a floating row cover laid over the

Piles of loose dry straw, leaves, or compost can provide some insulation against cold weather in the fall.

A floating row cover can be stretched over vegetable plants, such as these carrots, to provide protection from cold weather.

top of the shoots; this method also works well with newly germinated seedlings. Weigh down the edges of the paper or row cover with soil to prevent it from being blown away.

The shoulders of root crops such as rutabagas, parsnips, and carrots can be damaged by exposure to hard frost at the soil surface. Heaping dry leaves, straw, or compost over the rows before cold weather sets in will give them protection, and it will make it easier to dig the crops up in freezing spells.

Heavy clay soil takes a long time to dry out and become fit to break down for sowing seeds. You can speed up the process of preparing the soil by covering it with cloches or sheets of sturdy black plastic from mid-winter onward. This will keep off the rain and snow, allowing the soil to dry out and warm up. Black plastic is particularly good at retaining warmth.

Cloches

Early cloches were bell shaped and made from heavy glass to fit over individual plants. Nowadays, cloches are available in many different types and styles. They are normally shaped so that they can be placed end to end to form a continuous cover over a row of plants.

Glass cloches provide excellent shelter from cold and wet weather, and they can raise the temperature of the air considerably, as long as the ends of the rows are blocked. They are also stable. However, glass has a number of drawbacks; it is fragile, dangerous when broken (a point to keep in mind if there are young children in the garden), expensive, and heavy to move around. Cloches made from corrugated or sheet plastic are much cheaper and easier to move, but not quite as effective at trapping warmth; remember that they need to be firmly anchored in place.

Cloches may be barn shaped, tent shaped, or semicircular. Check how much headroom the different types provide and whether it is sufficient for your plants.

Setting up an indoor space

Gardeners living in a region with a short growing season can still grow plants with a long growing season by starting them indoors, as long as they are provided with the correct conditions. The soil temperature needs to be warm enough for the seedlings to germinate—this will depend on the type of vegetable you are growing—and you need to keep the soil moist.

Light is vitally important. If you don't have enough room on a sunny windowsill, position a table near the window. Alternatively, clear a space elsewhere in the house, perhaps in the basement, and provide light for the plants by suspending a fluorescent workshop light over the plants. By using linked chains to support the light, you can adjust the height of the light so that it remains 2–4 inches (5–10 cm) above the seedlings.

Avoid starting the seeds too soon, or you could find the seedlings will become too leggy and rootbound to transplant to a bed outdoors. For more about sowing seeds indoors, see pages 64–65; for growing plants in a greenhouse, see pages 78–81.

PLANTS FOR INDOORS

The following plants are among the easiest ones that you can start off indoors:

Broccoli	Cucumber
Brussels sprout	Leek
Cabbage	Lettuce
Cauliflower	Onion
Chive	Tomato

Quick Tip

Light fantastic

If your row of cloches are within reach of an electrical outlet, you can add extra warmth by running two lines of outdoor Christmas lights inside the row of cloches, one along each side. The heat from the bulbs lifts the temperature a few degrees.

Tunnels and cold frames

Structures in the vegetable garden, such as tunnels and cold frames, provide more facilities for raising tranplants—or even for growing crops until they reach maturity.

COLD-FRAME VEGETABLES

You can grow the following vegetables to maturity in a cold frame:

early carrots
winter lettuce
spring lettuce
cucumbers
some melons

Sometimes plants growing in their permanent planting positions will need protection to help them survive a late frost in the spring or an early one in the fall. The same methods for providing this type of protection can also be used to harden off transplants (see pages 68–69).

Tunnels

One type of versatile product for the garden is a tunnel made from polyethylene sheeting. Tunnels are easily obtained, lightweight, and simple to work with. Although they do not have a long life (two or three years), they are inexpensive to replace.

Polyethylene sheeting is often used to form long, low tunnels that are about 12–24 inches (30–60 cm) high, and these can be used as a type of cloche (see page 75). You can easily construct a low tunnel yourself by driving a series of metal hoops into the ground, then stretching the polyethylene over them and securing it in place with twine or more metal hoops. Form the ends of a cloche by gathering together the polyethylene and tying it to a stake. To ventilate the tunnel, simply push the polyethylene up at the sides.

You can create a tunnel for any size that is required, whether it is to cover a single row of seedlings or a whole patch of early lettuce crops—you can even construct it as a walk-in tunnel

Quick Tip

Make a cold frame

You can build a cold frame using an old window from a junkyard. (If you're not sure if it has lead paint, paint over it with an exterior paint.) Make the base from wood the size of the window, with a height of about 2 feet (60 cm) at the back, sloping to 18 inches (45 cm) at the front.

that is large enough to work in. Walk-in polytunnels are available as self-assembly kits of steel hoops and heavy-gauge polyethylene that has been stabilized against ultraviolet light to improve the length of its life.

Walk-in tunnels are less expensive and easier to put up than a glass greenhouse, but they have their drawbacks. They are not suitable for exposed windy sites because strong winds can distort the framework. And while they can be heated, they are not as efficient at keeping the heat in as a greenhouse, and condensation can be a problem because ventilation is limited to the ends of the tunnel.

The cold frame

A cold frame is often used unheated—it is a little like a large cloche built in a permanent position—but it also can be heated and used as a hotbed. A traditional cold frame has a base of bricks or wood. The base is slightly higher at the back than the front, and it is covered by a sloping glass top, known as a sash. The slope ensures the frame receives the maximum sunlight, and it also sheds rainwater effectively. Modern frames may be made from metal or plastic, and they often have two sloping roof sides rising to an apex, somewhat like a miniature greenhouse.

Cold frames are ideal for vegetable plants that do not need the full protection of a heated greenhouse, and they are perfect as a halfway stage for vegetables being hardened off before being transplanted. They can be heated, either with small electric or paraffin heaters or with soil-warming cables.

SOIL-WARMING CABLES

During the plant-growing process, germination requires higher temperatures, and this heat can be supplied effectively by soil-warming cables (available at garden centers), a convenient and economical way of providing "bottom heat."

Fill a frame or box with about 2 inches (5 cm) of sharp sand (also used for laying walkways) and lay the cable on top, running it back and forth in loops about 3 inches (8 cm) apart. Cover it with another 2 inches (5 cm) of sand, and place the trays and pots on top for sowing. You should use a thermostat, which will keep the heat set at a predetermined temperature.

Plant-heating mats, also available at garden centers in a range of sizes, are easier to use. Simply place pots and trays of potting mix directly on top of the mat.

To provide ventilation in the cold frame, prop open or remove all or some of the sashes. When purchasing a cold frame, look for one with sashes that are hinged and fitted with a stay to hold them open—the sashes can be heavy and unwieldy to move around.

You should position your cold frame in a sunny but sheltered site, so that the sloping side receives the maximum sunlight. On cold nights, you can place a layer of old carpet, burlap, or a similar material over the sashes for extra insulation.

The polyethylene sheeting on this tunnel is stretched over a tentlike frame. Push back the plastic to allow ventilation or if the plants become too hot.

Starting plants in a greenhouse

A greenhouse is perfect for raising plants that benefit from an early start. While the weather outside is still too chilly for sowing, strong seedlings can develop in the warmth of a greenhouse.

A greenhouse can be an expensive purchase, but it enables you to achieve more from your vegetable garden. Apart from early seed sowing to raise your own transplants, you will be able to grow out-of-season crops, such as winter lettuce, spring carrots, and early summer snap beans. In cool or unpredictable climates, you can use a greenhouse to successfully grow heat-loving crops, such as tomatoes, eggplants, and melons.

There is a choice of greenhouse shapes and styles. Buy as large a model as your budget can afford—while keeping heating costs in mind—and position it in an open, sunny site that is convenient to the house and that preferably has access to the water and electricity supply.

The greenhouse effect

A greenhouse is always a few degrees warmer than the outside temperature, even if it is unheated. This is partially because it is an enclosed space that is sheltered from wind and weather. It is also due to the "greenhouse effect," where light, as short-wave radiation, passes through the glass panes and is converted into infrared waves, or heat, within the greenhouse. Glass is far less permeable to the longer-wave infrared, so the heat is trapped within the greenhouse, steadily building up as more light waves continue to come through the glass.

MOVING AIR

Ventilating a greenhouse is important because plants thrive in a "buoyant atmosphere"—an area with good air movement. An automatic vent opener, which is controlled by the greenhouse temperature, will help to achieve the correct balance between warmth and ventilation. In windy weather when you shouldn't open the vents, use an electric fan (with the heater off) to keep the air circulating.

Quick Tip

Playing safe

Use a qualified electrician to set up the electricity supply to a greenhouse. The damp atmosphere and frequent use of water in a greenhouse make it vital that the electricity is installed correctly to prevent the danger of electric shock.

CHOOSING A GREENHOUSE

Framework	Pros	Cons
Timber	Some gardeners prefer its traditional appearance. Western red cedar has a natural resistance to rot and insect attack.	Needs regular maintenance to ensure a long life. Cedar is expensive; softwoods do not last many years.
Aluminum	Strong, durable, and maintenance free. Those with a powder coating come in a range of colors.	Plain, uncoated ones are not attractive.
Plastic (PVC)	Maintenance free and retains heat well.	Does not have the strength of aluminum or timber.
Cladding	**Pros**	**Cons**
Glass	Looks attractive and provides the best light transmission. Strengthened tempered glass is the most durable type.	Breakable; dangerous if you have small children. Tempered glass is less dangerous, but is the most expensive cladding material.
Rigid plastic sheets (acrylic or polycarbonate)	Inexpensive. Much lighter in weight than glass, so the greenhouse frame does not have to be as sturdy, which will reduce costs further.	Not as attractive as glass.

The temperature in an unheated greenhouse will still fall to low levels on cold nights or on dull winter days when there is no sun to warm it. Fortunately, many vegetable plants don't need frost-free conditions. Young cabbage-family plants, lettuce, peas, carrots, and leeks, for example, benefit from the warmer conditions in the greenhouse on sunny days, but will not be harmed if the temperature drops to freezing occasionally.

If starting tender plants—such as eggplants, beans, peppers, squashes, cucumbers, melons, zucchini, sweet corn, and tomatoes—in an unheated greenhouse, don't sow them too early; just one frost could kill the seedlings. You don't need to sow early to gain an advantage. Greenhouse-raised plants will still be more advanced than those grown outside, even if they are both sown at the same time.

Heating the greenhouse

Providing heat in the greenhouse will allow you to grow a wider range of vegetables and to start them earlier. Electricity is the most convenient form of greenhouse heating. Electric heaters have thermostats that save wasting fuel and protect against an unexpected frost. The heat is clean and dry, providing a good growing atmosphere, especially if you use a fan to circulate the heat.

If there is no electricity supply to the greenhouse, choose between gas and kerosene (paraffin). Gas heaters are best. Less expensive kerosene heaters are basic. They need to be lit and inspected daily, are rarely controlled by a thermostat, and produce water vapor, which can encourage fungus diseases. If not maintained, they can also release damaging fumes.

Care of young plants

Keep seedlings growing without a check until they are ready for planting in their permanent positions (for sowing and pricking out, see pages 64–65). Make sure they have plenty of space and light; overcrowded plants are pale, spindly, and weak, and they will take longer to become established after transplanting. Crowded plants are also more prone to attack by fungal diseases, because when overcrowded, they create a humid atmosphere.

REDUCING HEAT COSTS

Heating can be expensive, but there are several ways to keep the cost down:

- You can line the interior of the greenhouse with bubble polyethylene to insulate it. Take the lining down as soon as it is no longer needed, because it cuts down the amount of light entering the greenhouse.
- Heat only a small area of the greenhouse, sectioning it off with polyethylene sheeting. Alternatively, a large, enclosed heated propagator may be sufficient for your needs.
- To avoid wasting fuel, use a form of heating that can be thermostatically controlled.

Maturing plants in a greenhouse

Some regions are just not warm enough to enable you to grow reliable crops of heat-loving vegetables outside. However, if you give these plants the shelter of a greenhouse, it will be a different story.

LIGHTEN THE DARKNESS

A greenhouse may provide the warmth that is missing from our gardens in winter, but there is another vital ingredient for good plant growth—light. Out-of-season vegetables will rarely be as good as those grown in the main growing season, because the lack of light in short winter days limits their development.

In the greenhouse, natural daylight can be supplemented with artificial light to improve the development of vegetables. Ordinary lightbulbs are not suitable; special plant-growing lamps provide just the right type of light for growth but are relatively expensive. Compact fluorescent bulbs are a useful alternative. Suspend the bulbs above the plants, about 4 inches (10 cm) over the top of the crop. Use the artificial light to supplement daylight, providing plants a total of 8 to 10 hours of light per day.

Although a greenhouse is useful for starting crops early, when conditions outside are far too cold for sowing seeds, the benefit of a greenhouse is probably most truly appreciated in the cool-weather areas. There are several vegetables that won't thrive in cool conditions, and in these regions, they will provide a good, reliable harvest only if they are grown under cover for the whole of their lives.

Native heat lovers

The heat-loving vegetables originally from hot-weather regions, such as South America and Africa, will thrive in a greenhouse. While many varieties will provide a reasonable harvest outside in a good summer, you can obtain the largest and best-quality harvests by growing these plants in a greenhouse.

Probably the favorite vegetable for growing in a greenhouse has to be the tomato. Tomato plants are reasonably compact, not too difficult to grow, and provide a rewarding harvest. Peppers are probably next in order of popularity, followed by eggplants and melons. The more exotic vegetables, such as tomatillos and okra, are the province of the more adventurous gardener.

Out-of-season crops

Greenhouses can also provide us with the luxury of out-of-season crops. Even a humble lettuce becomes a treat when it is freshly harvested in the middle of winter, and a picking of snap beans in early spring is a delightful foretaste of the summer crop to come. These out-of-season crops will make good use of the greenhouse at a slack time of year.

Greenhouse borders

You can grow plants in containers in the greenhouse or grow them in a soil border if there is one. Plants grown in the border will have a free root run and are less likely to suffer from water shortages. This is particularly important for tomato plants, because water stress when the fruit is forming can result in blossom-end rot. Growing plants in the border also saves spending money on potting mix and containers.

However, border soil will need replenishing with organic matter, such as well-rotted compost or manure, every year, plus an application of a general fertilizer before planting in spring. If the same crop is grown in the border for several years, there could be a buildup of specific pests and diseases, which means it will be necessary to replace the soil.

Greenhouse containers

Containers, such as tubs or large clay or plastic pots, filled with potting mix can be used for greenhouse vegetables. However, you can also use grow bags by buying bags of potting mix and punching a few drainage holes in the sides that will be facedown, then cutting slits in the top faces to insert the plants.

Because the containers and grow bags have a relatively small volume of compost that soon becomes filled with roots, plants grown in them are prone to drying out. All container-grown vegetables will need careful watering, as often as twice as day in hot weather.

Providing support

Virtually all greenhouse vegetables will need some form of support as they grow to prevent them from flopping over and to keep the crop accessible and free from damage. Provide bushy plants, such as peppers, tomatoes, and eggplants, with a tall cane and gently secure them with soft twine as they grow.

Another method is to tie a length of twine to either a piece of bent wire pegged firmly in the soil or around the base of the stem, just below the bottom leaf. Attach the other end to a metal eye or hook on the greenhouse roof immediately above the plant; make sure the twine is just taut. As the plant grows, gently twist the main stem around the twine. This is a good method for plants in grow bags on a firm floor, where there is nowhere to secure a stake in the ground.

VEGETABLES FOR THE GREENHOUSE

The following crops can be grown in the greenhouse—sowing them directy in the border or in containers.

	Directions	Varieties
Snap bean	Sow in containers with bottom heat in mid-winter and transplant to the border or grow bag when approximately 4 in. (10 cm) tall.	'Blue Lake 274' is a good compact variety.
Carrot	Sow in early fall for a winter crop, or from mid-winter to spring for harvesting in early summer.	Choose short-rooted varieties, such as 'Red-Cored Chantenay' or round-rooted types such as 'Orbit' or 'Tumbelina'.
Lettuce	Sow from fall to early winter for harvesting in winter and spring. Sow seeds in soil blocks or fiber pots to prevent root disturbance when transplanting.	Choose a variety specifically bred for winter greenhouse harvesting, such as 'Grand Rapids'. Plants won't form a firm heart.
Potato	Plant two tubers in a grow bag or one in a 12-in. (30-cm) pot of potting mix in late summer for a winter harvest or mid-winter for a late spring crop.	Choose an early (fast-maturing) variety, such as 'Irish Cobbler' or 'Norland'. Don't expect a big yield.
Scallion	Sow thinly in early fall for a spring crop.	'White Lisbon' is one of the most popular and reliable varieties.
Radish	Sow in early fall or from late winter to mid-spring; they should be ready to eat in 4 to 8 weeks.	Any variety can be used.

You can also grow vining plants, such as melons, up twine or wires secured to the roof, using two or three horizontal wires about 10 inches (25 cm) apart, along which you can train the fruit-bearing side shoots.

4 Making your vegetables grow

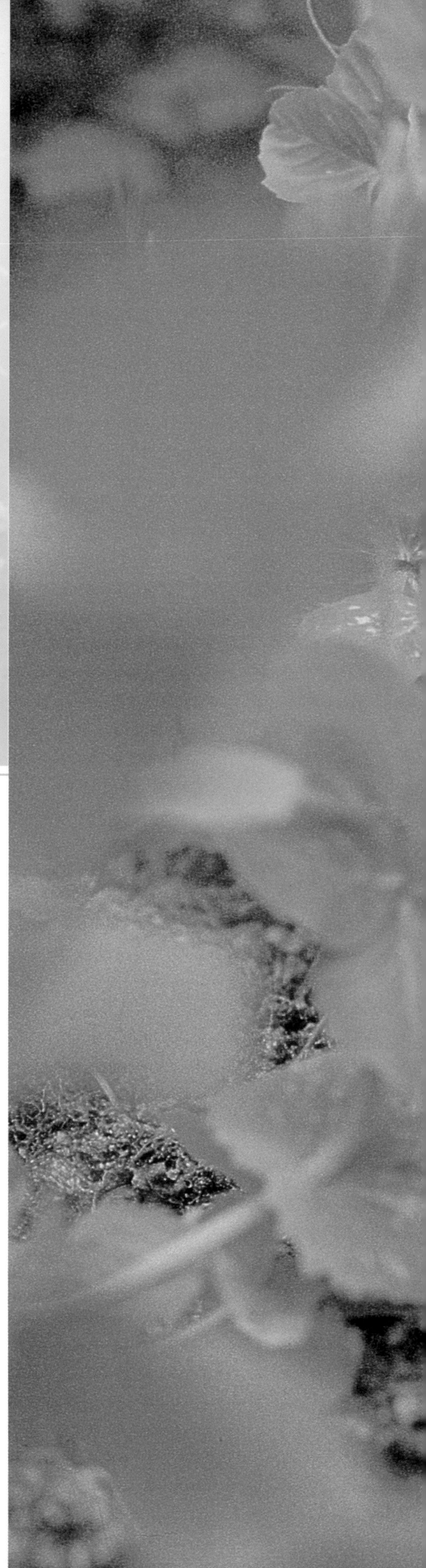

You've planned, dug, sown, and planted, and now you can feel a great satisfaction as you survey your vegetable garden filled with healthy young plants. It's a great achievement, but now is not the time to let your guard down. It's up to you to keep those plants growing well until harvesttime.

Your vegetables will need watering, feeding, and supporting as they grow; they will also need your help to battle against weeds, pests, and diseases. Make sure you spend a few minutes each day walking around your plot to see what needs to be done.

Make it a daily routine to inspect your garden and perform any necessary tasks. By taking early action, you'll keep work to a minimum.

Watering vegetables

All plants need water to grow, and sometimes natural rainfall just isn't enough. Watering your crops can make all the difference to the eventual harvest, but it's important to know when and how to water to get the best results.

Without a water supply, many of a plant's natural processes are impossible. Germination, the beginning of a plant's life cycle, is triggered when the dormant seed absorbs moisture from the soil. As the plant grows, it will need water for photosynthesis, for respiration, and to dissolve and transport nutrients. Without water, plant cells become limp. The plant can no longer stand up or hold out its leaves to capture sunlight's energy, or to keep itself cool in hot temperatures.

How plants get water

A plant absorbs water from the soil, where it is held in gaps between the soil particles (see pages 34–35). The water is absorbed by tiny, delicate root hairs that fringe the roots, and it is continually pulled up through the plant by the power of transpiration (where water vapors pass through the stomata, or pores, of the leaves).

Because moisture is lost to the air through the leaves, plants with large surface areas of leaf lose water faster than those with narrow, needlelike leaves. Most water is lost when the weather is hot and sunny, and also when it is windy—moving air whips moisture away from the leaves quickly.

As long as there is sufficient water in the soil to replace the moisture that is lost, no harm is done. But sometimes plants can't keep up with the demand. This is usually because there has been no rain to replenish the soil water. However, it can also be because the delicate root hairs have been damaged and they are not able to do their job properly. This is why when it comes to watering transplants, they need careful attention until the roots have had time to reestablish themselves.

> *Quick Tip*
>
> **Sweet tomatoes**
>
> Watering tomato plants frequently will increase the total yield, but the flavor of the fruit will suffer. Once plants are flowering, water only as necessary to keep the soil just moist—then you will be able to enjoy the sweetest fruit with the richest flavor.

Water conservation

Much of the water in the soil goes to waste, either draining away before plants can tap into it or evaporating from the soil surface. Whatever you can do to prevent this waste will save you time and energy, as well as conserve the water supply. There are several methods that you can use:

To determine if your plants need watering, you can carefully dig a hole a few inches deep—be careful not to disturb the plant's roots—then check the soil.

Improve the soil. You can dig in bulky organic matter, such as garden compost or manure, to improve the soil structure and its capacity to hold water (see pages 36–39).

BEST TIMES TO WATER CROPS

Root vegetables	Leaves and shoots	Fruit, pods, and seeds
Beet, carrot, parsnip, potato, radish, rutabaga, salsify, scorzonera, turnip	Asian greens, cabbage-family plants, celery, chicory, endive, lettuce, radicchio, spinach, Swiss chard	Peas, beans, eggplants, peppers, squash, sweet corn, tomato, zucchini
Extra water promotes leafy growth on root crops but not root growth. Water as needed while plants are young to help them grow steadily. After a prolonged dry spell, heavy rain or watering can cause roots to split, so water occasionally during a drought to prevent this damage. Potatoes respond well to watering when the tubers are forming (when flowering starts); you can increase both size of tubers and the overall yield. For the best response from early crops, wait until the tubers are marble size before watering.	For the best-quality harvest, do not allow this group to suffer a water shortage at any stage of growth. The best response to watering comes about 10 to 20 days before the crop will be ready for harvest, so if water is in short supply, this is the time to apply it. Give only enough water to moisten the top 12 inches (30 cm) of soil; too much water can cause maturing lettuce and cabbage heads to split. Widely spaced winter cabbage-family plants, such as Brussels sprouts, are unlikely to need watering.	A bountiful harvest will rely on watering at the right time. Water after transplanting, but unless conditions are so dry that the plants begin to wilt, do not water again until flowering begins. Watering too early will encourage leaf and shoot growth at the expense of flowers, which reduces yields. Once flowering starts and while fruit are developing, watering increases the numbers of flowers, the percentage of flowers setting fruit, the number of seeds per pod, and the overall yield (but see *Sweet tomatoes,* opposite).

Mulch. When the soil is moist—in the spring or after a thorough watering—you can mulch the surface to block evaporation by using compost, store-bought mulches, or black plastic sheeting. Straw and grass clippings are sometimes recommended, but unrotted materials such as these are best applied where there are no growing vegetables, because they take nitrogen from the soil as they rot down. You can sprinkle a nitrogen-rich fertilizer, such as blood meal, on the soil before you apply the mulch.

Control weeds. Weeds steal water from vegetables. Deal with them often and while they are still small, using a sharp hoe to slice the weeds off at the soil surface. Avoid disturbing the soil to prevent turning up new weed seeds.

Plant at the correct spacing. If you leave the recommended amount of room between neighboring plants, they won't compete for water.

Provide a free root run. Cultivate the soil deeply, breaking it down to a fine crumbly texture, which will allow the roots to extend freely in their search for moisture. Because many gardeners dig to just one spade's depth year after year, a hard, impenetrable layer (known as a pan) can form just below this depth. Double digging (see pages 40–41) every four to five years will overcome this problem.

Do I need to water?

Most gardeners water crops on a haphazard basis—the soil looks a bit dusty on the surface, and it hasn't rained for a few days, so it's probably time to get the hose out. However, it is best to be a bit more scientific about it. The truth is that water is a limited resource and it's important that we don't waste it—or waste our time applying it. And water applied at the wrong time can actually harm the crops we are trying to help.

If you think your plants may need watering, dig a hole a few inches deep with a trowel to see what conditions are like in the plants' root zone. If the soil below is dry, it might be time to water. Check with the chart (above) for the most efficient times to water different types of vegetables plants.

Plants need moist soil to germinate and must be watered after transplanting (about 10 ounces/300 ml of water per transplant). Or water only when the soil is dry, applying 2–4 gallons per square yard (9–18 liters per sq m).

The exception is plants growing in containers, such as tomatoes and peppers, which have restricted root space. They will need more frequent watering than those grown in open ground or soil borders.

Watering systems

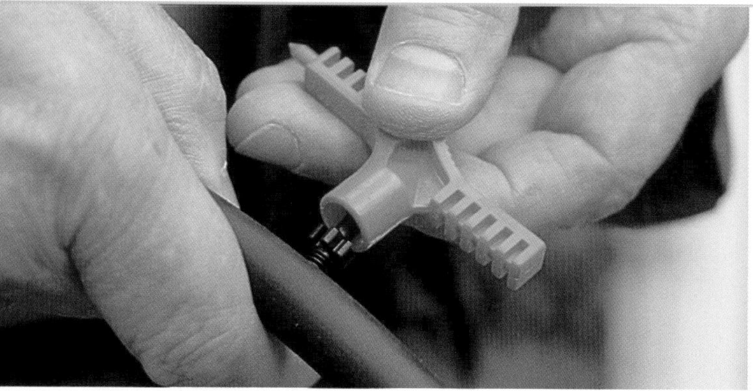

Watering plants can seem like a lot of work, but there are plenty of methods to make it quicker, easier, and more efficient. The one that is right for you will depend on the size of your garden, your climate, and your budget.

Using a watering can may be acceptable for a small area, but it will soon become a trial in a large garden, especially in a dry climate, where watering is a regular chore. For effortless watering, you can install a fully automatic system that will look after the garden's water needs even when you are away—but it will be comparatively expensive.

The watering can

For small vegetable gardens and containers, a watering can is sufficient. Choose a watering can that is nicely balanced, easy to carry, and has a long spout for a good reach. It may be made of metal or plastic; although plastic is lighter and cheaper than metal, it has a shorter life. The most popular sizes are 1 gallon (4.5 liters), 1½ gallons (7 liters), and 2 gallons (9 liters). Large cans will cut down the number of trips you need to make to the faucet and back, but they can be heavy when full, so you may need to compromise.

To break up the water into a shower of droplets, all spouts should be able to be fitted with a rose. Like the cans, the roses may have a metal (brass) or plastic face. Use the rose faceup for the gentlest shower; turn it facedown for a soaking.

Hose

A hose enables you to apply large quantities of water with less effort than a watering can. To prevent water from siphoning back into the water supply, you may have to attach a special valve to the faucet to prevent backflow. In a drought, there may be restrictions on watering your garden. You may be allowed to water your vegetables with a hose only on certain days of the week or at certain times of the day.

There are many types of hose, so shop around to see what best meets your needs. There are anti-kink hoses, hoses that flatten for easy storage, through-flow hoses that can be used even when they are partly stored on a reel, and coiled hoses that take up less space. The diameter of the hose also varies; the larger the diameter, the more water the hose delivers, and the further from the faucet you can use it without losing pressure.

You should fit a hose with a device to break up the water into droplets. Wand attachments come in a range of styles and patterns and allow you

CHOOSING A WATERING METHOD

Before deciding which method of watering is right for you, ask yourself these questions:

- How large is your vegetable garden? A watering can will suffice for a small garden; a hose or automatic watering system is preferable for a large garden.
- How much time do you have? Watering the garden with either a watering can or hose will be time-consuming; an automated system won't.
- What is the climate like in your area? If there's plenty of rain, you won't need to water nearly as much as if you live in a hot, arid region.
- How much money are you prepared to spend? A hose will cost only a fraction of the price of an automated system.

to water close to soil level to avoid wetting the foliage, and they are also useful for reaching hanging baskets. Among the most useful are those that have a water-stop connector to enable you to turn the hose off at the delivery end, without trailing back to the faucet. Make sure that the hose and all the connectors are of good quality and correctly fitted; otherwise the hose may burst apart at the connectors when the water-stop valve is used.

Sprinklers are useful for watering vegetable gardens, and they come in a number of patterns to suit different plots. However, because they throw water droplets into the air, they lose much of their water by evaporation before they reach the soil, especially in dry, arid climates. They are the least efficient method of watering.

Automatic watering systems

Systems that automatically water your garden can be an efficient way of watering—not only efficient in time but also in the amount of water used. You can buy a complete kit from a garden center. It contains a pressure regulator; a length of supply hose that connects to the faucet; microtubing to take the water from the supply hose to the plants; and drippers, sprinklers, or a soaker hose for the final delivery of water to the plants.

A basic system can be set up and operated by turning the faucet on and off, or it can be fully automated by adding an automatic timer. This is programmed to switch on and off at set hours, and will continue to water the garden while you are away from home. You can also set it to turn on at night, so that water is not wasted through evaporation.

Before buying your watering system, contact your water-supply company to see which regulations and requirements may apply to its use.

A wand attachment is ideal for watering vegetables. Try to avoid getting water on the leaves, which can spread disease.

THE SOAKER HOSE

A different type of "sprinkler" is the soaker hose or drip tubing. One type is a porous hose that leaks water gently along its length and can be laid along rows of vegetables or buried just beneath the soil surface.

Another type is a soft hose perforated at intervals on one side. It lays flat on the soil surface (or under a light mulch) when not in use; it becomes rounded and emits water once the tap is turned on. It is available in single or double tubes; set it hole-side down.

A soaker hose is an efficient way of applying water because little water is lost through evaporation into the atmosphere.

Quick Tip

Getting connected

You should invest in good-quality connectors for your garden hose. Simple brass or plastic push-click connectors are much quicker and easier to use than connectors that screw together.

Feeding your plants

Vegetables need a range of nutrients to grow and develop. These nutrients are available in the soil, but sometimes not in the right quantities for the best growth. Fertilizers can help to make up for any shortfall. Nutrients are absorbed through the plants' roots and, to a much lesser extent, through their leaves.

Nutrients in the soil are often in short supply where vegetables have already grown. Different soils have varied amounts of nutrients, and vegetables require a range of nutrients. Your plants may indicate a deficiency (see *Nutrient Deficiencies,* right) or test your soil (see pages 32–33).

Fertilizers

You can apply fertilizers to increase nutrient levels. Organic fertilizers come from something that once lived, such as fish emulsion or bone meal, or that occurs naturally, such as rock phosphate or rock potash; artificial fertilizers are manufactured. Commercial organic fertilizers are available, such as alfalfa meal, bat and bird guano, blood meal, composted manure, and kelp emulsion.

Some organic gardeners use all types of "something that has once lived" fertilizers; others have ethical concerns about using by-products of animal slaughter, such as bone meal or blood, fish, and bone. All fertilizers are broken down to identical chemicals.

Formulations

Fertilizers, whether synthetic or organic, may contain a single plant nutrient (straight fertilizers) or a combination of nutrients (compound fertilizers). Straight fertilizers include ammonium sulfate (a nitrogen source) and superphosphate (a phosphorus source). Compound fertilizers usually consist of nitrogen, phosphorus, and potassium (N, P, and K) in varying proportions. These proportions are given on the package—NPK 7-7-7 is a balanced fertilizer, while NPK 5-5-10 has a greater amount of potash. Some compound fertilizers also contain trace elements—such as iron and boron—which are needed in only tiny amounts.

Quick Tip

Hand protection

Wear gloves when you apply powder or granular fertilizers because they can irritate the skin. It is important to make sure that cuts and scratches on your hands are covered up.

NITROGEN REQUIREMENTS

Some vegetables are more likely to need fertilizer applications.

High	Medium	Low
Beet	Asparagus	Lima beans
Brussels sprouts	Eggplant	Carrot
Cabbage	Lettuce	Cucumber
Cauliflower	Onion	Parsnip
Celery	Peppers	Peas
Leek	Snap beans	Radish
Potato	Squash	Rutabaga
Spinach	Sweet corn	
Swiss chard	Tomatoes	

Compost tea

Adding compost to your soil will improve its nutrient content. Watering plants with compost tea will supply nutrients more quickly. To make this tea, place well-rotted compost in a bucket of water and leave it to soak for several days; then strain it through cheesecloth. Use one part compost to between five and eight parts of water. You can put the compost inside burlap and suspend it in the water to avoid having to strain the liquid.

Applying fertilizers

You must apply fertilizers carefully. A dry nonorganic fertilizer can damage or kill plants if it coats the foliage and buds, or granules lodge in the growing points. Too much fertilizer will harm the plants. Fertilizers come in three forms: powders, granules, or liquids.

Powder and granular fertilizers. Some powder fertilizers dissolve in water, but others, especially organic versions, are spread on the soil, as are granular fertilizers. You can apply a side-dressing of fertilizer by spreading it in a band around the plant or alongside it, but not too close to the stem; work it into the top few inches of soil, using a rake or hoe. Choose a still day so that the fertilizer is not blown away.

Follow the package instructions for application rates. If rates are given as ounces per square foot (or grams per square meter), measure out a square foot on a patch of soil, weigh out the quantity of fertilizer, and spread it as evenly as possible. This will give you a visual idea of the correct application rate. If rain does not follow within two or three days, water it in enough to moisten the soil—don't flood it.

Liquid fertilizers. The nutrients in liquid fertilizers are more quickly available to the plants. Most liquid types must be diluted before use; follow the directions carefully. You can apply it with a watering can, but for large areas, a dilutor attachment that fits on the end of a hose is useful.

Some chemical liquid fertilizers are made to be absorbed by the plants' foliage. These are useful as a tonic for nutrient-deficient plants. You can also use a kelp or fish emulsion spray or compost tea as a foliar spray to supply trace elements. Or try one of the best organic foliar sprays—a 50/50 ratio of fish and kelp emulsions.

Slow-release fertilizers. Most organic fertilizers slowly release their nutrients, so that the effects of one application last throughout the growing season. Some chemical fertilizers are made to be released slowly. The rate of breakdown is controlled by soil moisture and temperature, so that the warm, moist conditions that promote growth also allow nutrients to be released. Slow-release fertilizers are less likely to scorch plant roots.

Fertilizers and pollution

The overuse of fertilizers leads to the pollution of groundwater and rivers, with nitrogen stimulating excessive growth of algae and water weeds. Pollution from gardens is small but significant, particularly on light, free-draining soil. Runoff from compost piles and misuse of compost tea can contribute to water pollution. Apply fertilizers only when necessary. Use slow-release fertilizers when possible.

NUTRIENT DEFICIENCIES

A lack of nutrients can show up as symptoms in vegetables.

Boron: Growing points blacken; hollow stems in cabbage-family plants. Beets form cracks and canker spots; celery has a black heart. On sweet corn, foliage forms white stripes; cobs are stunted.

Calcium: Young leaves curl; growing tips blacken. Tomatoes and their relatives develop blossom-end rot; tip burn occurs on lettuce; browning occurs inside Brussels sprouts.

Iron: Leaves turn yellow or pale between bright green veins. Young leaves are affected first.

Manganese: Mottled yellowing between veins, with dead patches on leaves. Brown areas may form on seed leaves of peas and beans. It occurs on beans, beet, spinach, peas, and cabbage-family plants.

Magnesium: Leaves yellow between veins (interveinal chlorosis), showing on older leaves first. It is common on lettuce, potatoes, and tomatoes.

Molybdenum: Leaves are thin and straplike, and growing points die. Known as whiptail on cauliflower.

Nitrogen: Small leaves, pale, yellowed, or with blue or red coloration; stunted plants; poor performance. It is common on cabbage-family plants.

Phosphorus: Stunted growth; blue or bronze tints on older leaves.

Potassium: Older leaves turn pale, with brown scorches at margins; sometimes brown spots on leaves.

Supporting the plants

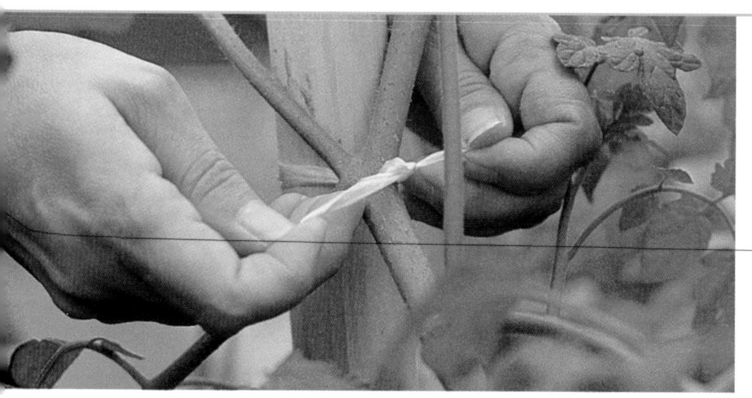

Some vegetables are climbers, some scramble and sprawl, and some may be blown over in windy gardens. All of these plants will benefit from a sturdy support system to make sure they produce the maximum yield and are easy to harvest.

VINING PLANTS

You can grow cucumbers, squashes, and melons trained up trellises or tepees of canes outdoors. The fruit of melons, and sometimes squash, are relatively heavy, and they often need the support of individual "hammocks." Old panty hose cut into strips of a suitable length provide the perfect material for these hammocks.

In a greenhouse, train these plants up strings suspended vertically from the roof (see pages 80–81).

Most of the vegetables that we commonly provide with support, such as beans and peas, would still thrive if left on their own, romping over the ground and only scrambling up trees or bushes when they happened to come across them. However, training them upward makes sure that the crops they carry are less likely to be misshapen, spoiled by soil contact, or eaten by pests, such as slugs and snails.

The crops will also be much easier to find and pick during harvesttime. Searching through the tangled growth of unsupported pea plants looking for ripe pods can be a backbreaking job. There are a variety of supports, and the ones you choose will depend on the vegetables that need them.

Poles and canes

Perhaps the vegetable best known for needing support is the pole bean. These plants will climb 10 feet (3 m) or more quite easily, twining their supple stems around anything upright. One of the best ways to support a number of plants is to set bamboo canes or sturdy bean poles in a double row, leaning them together at the tops and tying them with twine. To keep the structure secure, lay a row of canes along the ridge at the top, tying these firmly in place. Space the canes 6 inches (15 cm) apart if possible, so that you have one cane per plant. If you have a lot of beans, this can be an expensive option, in which case, space the canes more widely and run twine horizontally between them to help support the plants. A tepee is a more suitable option if you are growing only a few plants.

Climbing beans like to cling to a rough surface, which is why bean

To make a tepee, tie together a half-dozen or so canes firmly at the top.

Quick Tip

A twisting tale

At planting time, twist the tips of pole beans around the base of the supports in the direction they grow—counterclockwise (clockwise if looking down on the top of the bean from above). Twist them the wrong way and they'll just unwind.

poles complete with bark are often preferred to smooth, shiny bamboo canes. However, if beans have trouble clinging to canes, wrap a little garden twine around the base of the canes to give the shoots a grip. Once they get started, they won't look back.

Pea sticks

The ideal support for scrambling peas, which cling tightly with tendrils, are pea sticks—twiggy, branching stems of shrubs, such as hazel. Cut these in winter and trim them to 3–4 feet (0.9–1.2 m) high. Push them firmly into the soil every 12 inches (30 cm) or so along the row.

Pea sticks will provide excellent support for your peas while also looking attractively rustic. Smaller versions are useful to support lower-growing plants, such as bush beans.

Netting

Plastic netting that is stretched taut between supporting canes or poles is particularly useful for peas. When used for taller plants, such as climbing beans, it needs sturdy supports; the netting provides a great deal of wind resistance when covered in plant growth, so it can be easily blown over.

It is often difficult to free the netting from the remains of plant growth at the end of the season, making it awkward to use again. You can try burying the whole bundled net in a compost pile, the theory being that the plant remains will rot away while the plastic netting won't. In practice, you may not get the results you desire.

A tepee is ideal for supporting beans. They are useful when you want to grow only a small number of plants.

THE BENEFICIARIES

There are several types of plants that can benefit from support:

- Climbers and scramblers, such as pole beans, peas, cucumbers, and melons.
- Bushy plants with weak stems, such as tomatoes, peppers, and eggplant, which tend to lie down under the weight of their crop.
- Sturdy-stemmed plants that are exposed to winter winds, such as all the winter cabbage-family plants—strong winds can topple them.
- Smaller plants, such as bush beans or asparagus peas; twiggy sticks can help to keep the beans off the soil, where they could rot or be nibbled by pests.

Stakes

Some varieties of plants, such as tomatoes, peppers, and eggplants, are stocky enough to be self-supporting, but the majority need help to keep them upright and ensure that the crop is accessible and clear of the ground. A sturdy bamboo cane or stake, pushed several inches into the soil 4 inches (10 cm) away from the main stem, is sufficient. Tie the plant to the cane with twine in a figure-eight loop or use plastic-covered twist ties. In a greenhouse, strings can be used to support tomatoes.

In exposed, windy gardens, tall winter cabbage-family plants, such as Brussels sprouts, may be blown over. You can provide support by driving a short, stout stake firmly into the soil 10 inches (25 cm) from the main stem on the windward side of the plant, so that the plant is blown away from the stake rather than into it.

Understanding weeds

Weeds don't just make the garden look untidy—they can also have a significant effect on the quality and quantity of your vegetable harvest.

Quick Tip

Telltale weeds

Some weeds can provide useful information about your soil. Sorrel and plantains prefer acidic conditions, but poppies and pansies like chalky soil. Docks indicate that you have a rich, fertile soil; clovers are a sign of poor fertility.

A weed is simply a plant in the wrong place. Weeds are often wild plants, but they can also include cultivated plants that have spread and are growing where they aren't wanted.

Why weeds matter

Weeds will compete with vegetable plants for water, nutrients, light, and space—all the essentials of plant life. If allowed to grow uncontrolled, they will usually win—vegetable plants are often crowded out. Apart from their competitive effects, weeds can harbor pests and diseases; slugs and snails, for example, find the lush growth of weeds a perfect habitat from which to make their nighttime forays to devastate vegetables. Several weeds carry virus diseases, showing no symptoms themselves, but they are spread by insects to cultivated plants.

Annual weeds, such as shepherd's purse, don't have an extensive root system, because they need to last only the one season.

Large taproots or rhizomes on perennials, such as dandelion, have a long, sturdy root system to survive for years.

Perennials that grow on stolons, such as creeping buttercup, can spread quickly over a wide area.

Rampant weed growth makes harvesting a tiresome job.

Do weeds have any redeeming features? Wild plants do because they provide food and habitats for a wide range of welcome wildlife. Allowing a corner of your garden to go wild encourages all sorts of creatures, many of which will be your garden's allies, or at least it will be interesting and fun to watch. However, keep weeds out of the vegetable plot if you want the best from your plants.

Where weeds come from

Turn over a piece of soil and within days weeds start to cover its surface. How do they get there? Any area of fertile garden soil is filled with thousands of weed seeds. They may have been shed from previous weeds that grew and flowered, they may have blown in on a breeze, or they may have been carried in by birds and other wild creatures—or even by you, on the soles of your shoes.

These seeds may lay dormant for years, so that the stock in the soil builds up all the time, waiting for the right conditions to germinate. Plants bought from garden centers or given by friends all contribute fresh stocks of seeds in their soil, and they often bring along a quota of vigorously growing weed seedlings, as well.

Good gardeners compost their garden waste, and much of that waste is likely to consist of weeds. Dumping flowering weeds in the compost pile will lead to you spreading weed seeds around the garden later, too. The weeds themselves usually die as they are smothered in the compost pile, but their seeds are tougher. Even the best-made compost pile will not heat up sufficiently to kill all weed seeds, so by spreading compost over your vegetable plot, you may be distributing weeds.

Dealing with weeds before they start flowering is the best way to cut down the number of seeds in the compost pile. Take care to use the correct composting techniques so there is sufficient heat to kill them (see pages 38–39). However, even if a few weeds are spread with the compost, the benefits provided by the compost far outweigh the inconvenience of the weeds.

Stems that creep below the ground, such as bindweed, are some of the most difficult weeds to eradicate.

Weed wake-up call

Weed seeds are usually small, with little food reserves for the young plant. Most types need to be fairly near the soil surface before the seedlings have a chance of survival; if the seeds are buried too deeply, the germinating seedling runs out of steam before it can get into the light and start fending for itself. For this reason, most deeply buried seeds remain dormant. However, once they are brought closer to the surface, they will receive the right signals to start their growth. This is why any soil cultivation is usually soon followed by a good crop of young weeds.

ANNUAL OR PERENNIAL WEEDS?

There are many different weed species that might invade the vegetable garden, but they can easily be divided into two main groups: annual and perennial. Annual weeds germinate, flower, produce seeds, and die in one season—although some types survive two seasons. Shepherd's purse and lamb's quarters are two successful examples. Annual weeds are easy to manage as long as you deal with them before they flower and seed.

Perennial weeds may continue for a number of years. They can regrow from their roots even when the parts above the ground have been destroyed—sometimes several times. Several types of perennials produce food-storage organs, such as large taproots or rhizomes, to keep them going through periods of poor growing conditions. For example, dock grows deeply into the ground and can be difficult to dig up.

Some perennials produce new plants on stolons, which creep along the ground and root as they go. One extremely invasive type of perennial is bindweed, which has stems that creep below the ground. If these stems are broken, every minute piece that remains is capable of growing into a new plant.

Controlling weeds

Early action is the key to weed control. Never let weeds get the upper hand, because they will be much more difficult to remove if they become well established.

HERBICIDES

Many gardeners choose not to use chemical herbicides, but they can be valuable in clearing a plot containing difficult perennial weeds, especially if you are unable to hand-dig the plot. An effective chemical option is glyphosate. It is absorbed and distributed around the plant, killing the roots as well as the top growth. Herbicidal soap, based on fatty acids, is an organic option for killing the top growth of weeds, but it does not destroy the roots.

When using herbicides around a growing crop, remember that one slip of your spray wand means you may kill crops instead of the weeds. Even herbicidal soap will kill vegetable plants if sprayed on them by mistake.

Apply all herbicides with care, following the manufacturer's instructions exactly. For the best results, choose a dry day with light air movement to avoid spray drifting into other areas.

The longer weeds remain in place, the more time and physical effort will be neccessary to remove them, especially if you allow them to spread. You should always try to remove weeds before they form their seeds.

Weed prevention

There are many methods you can use to help prevent weeds from becoming a real problem.

Clear the ground. When starting a new vegetable plot, make a real effort to get rid of all the perennial weeds. Dig up and remove as much of the roots and stems as possible. If the plot is extremely weedy, you can kill the weeds with a mulch or herbicide (see *Herbicides,* left) before you start.

Cultivate carefully. Remember that soil cultivations bring new weed seeds up near the surface where they can germinate. The no-dig method helps avoid this problem (see pages 42–43), or you can use the stale seedbed technique (see pages 56–57) to cope with the weeds that arise. Always keep soil disturbance to a minimum when carrying out routine care, such as hoeing around established plants.

Rotate crops. Some vegetables are much more able to compete with weeds than others. Potatoes, for example, crowd out weeds far more efficiently than onions. Rotating these crops around the plot ensures that weeds are less likely to build up in one particular area.

Mulch. Cover up bare soil to prevent weeds from getting a foothold by depriving them of light. You can use organic mulch, such as rotted compost, or inorganic mulch, such as black plastic sheeting. You can cover a whole bed with plastic sheeting, burying the edges to keep it in place. If you don't intend to plant the area for a while, pieces of old carpet can be used instead of plastic, although they tend to look even less attractive.

Organic mulches are easy to spread between the rows after you plant the vegetables. The mulch should be a minimum of 1 inch (2.5 cm) deep, but preferably 3 inches (7.5 cm) deep, to suppress weed growth.

Grow green manure. If you have a spare piece of ground that you don't intend to grow vegetables in for a while, sow a green manure or cover

If you use plastic sheeting as a mulch, you can cut slits into the plastic through which you can plant your vegetables.

crop such as rye or buckwheat. Sown thickly, these prevent less desirable weeds from colonizing the soil.

Target fertilizer applications. If you broadcast fertilizers over the whole area, weeds will benefit from them, too. If you can, apply fertilizers more selectively near the vegetables.

Weed control

Vegetables and weeds that germinate together can coexist for a while; it usually takes about two to three weeks before the weeds start to compete with the vegetables. However, it is easier to keep the weeds under control if you take action against them beforehand.

Hoeing. One of the best methods of weed control is hoeing—it is effective and is not too strenuous. Use a Dutch or stirrup hoe, and keep the blade sharp. The trick is to push the blade along the soil surface, severing the weed stems from their roots—don't try to dig the weeds up with the hoe. Disturb the soil as little as possible.

Hoe on a sunny day when the soil surface is dry; then the weeds can be left on the surface where they will quickly shrivel up. If the soil is moist, they may re-root. Hoeing works best when the weeds are small. You will need to take care when hoeing near vegetable seedlings because it's easy to slice the vegetable plants off along with the weeds.

Although hoeing weakens deep-rooted perennials, they will probably need to be hoed off several times before they die. Weeds such as annual grasses are difficult to control with a hoe because they don't separate easily from their roots.

Hand cultivators. These tools, usually with three or five tines, don't work as well as a hoe. They are pulled through the soil and loosen the whole weed, complete with root, which must be removed. By disturbing the soil surface, you may encourage more weed seeds to germinate.

Hand weeding. You can pull weeds out of moist soil or loose mulches by hand. It is a satisfying job but can be backbreaking over a large area. You should pull the weeds out with their roots and remove them from the site; if left lying on the soil surface, they could grow again. Where weeds are large, use a hand fork, trowel, or garden fork to pry them out of the soil. Again, soil disturbance will tend to encourage more weeds.

CLEARING A PLOT

You can cover a weedy plot with black plastic mulch or old carpet to kill the weeds by depriving them of light. Where weeds are already established, leave the mulch in place for at least a whole growing season to be effective. After you remove the mulch, make sure that you dig out any perennial weeds that are still alive.

Although a flame gun is a quick and effective way to kill weeds on a spare piece of ground, it is less suitable for using between crop rows because of possible accidental damage to the vegetable plants. Use a shield on the gun to direct the flame where you want it. Make one pass to wilt the weeds; then take a second pass to burn up the top growth.

Perennial weeds may need more than one treatment to get rid of them, or you can use a fork to remove their roots once you destroy the top growth.

Tug a small weed from the base of the stem. Hand weeding is the best option to avoid accidental damage to nearby vegetables.

Preventing pest problems

An inevitable part of growing plants is an attack by pests, and sometimes vegetables seem to be especially prone to attack. However, there are several simple ways to protect your crops.

A pest is any creature that has a detrimental effect on a vegetable crop. It may be as large as a deer, or a tiny mite that's hardly visible to the naked eye. Sometimes a pest will interfere with the plant's development, weakening it so that it is unable to carry a good crop; other times the pest directly damages the crop itself.

The amount of damage varies, from a few minor blemishes to total destruction. The majority of vegetable pests are insects, although mammals, birds, nematodes, and mollusks all make their own contributions.

Pest prevention

Be prepared for inevitable visits from pests by making it harder for them to build up to damaging numbers.

Provide good growing conditions. Sturdy, healthy plants may be no less likely to be attacked by pests, but they

CONFUSE THE ENEMY

Several pests, such as carrot fly and onion fly, search for plants by smelling their scent. Avoid bruising or handling the foliage of the plants, and perform thinning or weeding operations late in the day to give the flies minimal time to track the vegetables down. Grow carrots and onions next to each other, or alongside a strong-smelling herb, such as tansy or garlic, to send out confusing scent signals.

Laying shiny aluminum foil alongside rows of lettuce can trick aphids by dazzling them, so they don't land on the plants. Birds are also deterred by shiny, moving objects, such as strips of foil or old CDs suspended from a string.

PLANTS TO ATTRACT BENEFICAL INSECTS

Growing these plants near your vegetables can attract pest-controlling insects, including lacewings, ladybugs, and hoverflies.

Achillea filipendula (fern-leaf yarrow): Tall perennial with aromatic, ferny leaves and broad clusters of yellow flowers.

Anthemis tinctoria (golden marguerite): Perennial evergreen, with feathery foliage and golden daisy flowers.

Calendula officinalis (marigold): An easy-to-grow hardy annual with bright orange daisy-type flowers carried over a long season.

Coriandrum sativum (coriander): Carries heads of small white flowers, which set edible coriander seeds.

Fagopyrum esculentum (buckwheat): Fast-growing, medium-height plant with white flowers, popular with hoverflies. Grow it as a green manure.

Foeniculum vulgare (fennel): Tall herb with threadlike foliage.

Melissa officinalis (lemon balm): An herb with lemon-scented leaves.

A walk-in cage with a roof is ideal for keeping larger animals, including birds, away from your vegetables.

are able to manage the attack better. A strong plant can shrug off a pest infestation that would have a serious effect on a weaker specimen.

Keep the vegetable garden tidy. Weeds, leaf litter, and general plant debris often provide hiding and breeding places for a whole variety of plant pests, but particularly for slugs and snails. A wild area is good for encouraging beneficial species, but keep it to a specific part of the garden, away from the vegetable plot.

Inspect plants frequently. Pest species usually build up on plants quickly. Inspect your plants every two or three days. Look for anything unusual—a plant that is not keeping up with the others, the odd yellowing leaf, or a few little holes in the foliage.

If you see something peculiar, investigate it right away. Check the growing tips of the plants and the undersides of leaves for insects; look for the slimy trails of slugs and snails or wilting leaves that signify root damage. A pest attack in its earliest stages is simple to manage—you may need to only pick off a leaf or pinch out a growing tip to literally "nip it in the bud."

Remember also to inspect new plants for pests before buying them or planting them out.

Grow resistant varieties. Most seed catalogs feature varieties bred for their resistance to certain pests and diseases. For example, the carrot 'Flyaway' is less likely to be attacked by carrot fly (carrot maggot) than other varieties. The lettuce 'Avondefiance' is resistant to the lettuce root aphid.

Time your sowings carefully. Once you know the peak season for a particular pest, sow seeds early or late to avoid the crop developing during that season and decrease the chance of it being adversely affected.

Make use of barriers. Deter animals by using physical barriers. To keep deer out of your garden, erect a fence 8 feet (2.5 m) high—they can leap over lower fences. Keep out burrowing animals, such as rabbits, by burying the bottom 12 inches (30 cm) of fencing below ground, turning it up in a U-shape on the outside edge of the fence.

You can construct a walk-in cage around the vegetable garden using sturdy stakes and small-mesh netting to completely enclose the area—this is a sure way of keeping larger pests away. In areas where snow is likely, replace the top netting with one of a larger mesh for the winter, or the weight of snow may damage the cage.

Keep out insects, slugs, and snails. You can also keep smaller creatures at bay by using physical barriers. You can erect fences of polyethylene, floating row cover, or fine-mesh netting about 2–3 feet (60–90 cm) high around blocks of carrots to keep out carrot fly, which flies close to the ground to seek out target plants by smell. This type of barrier will also make a good deterrent against slugs and snails.

Cloches and floating row covers are a boon for keeping plants safe from a wide variety of pests, especially when the plants are young. You can cut off the bases of empty, large plastic soda bottles and use the top sections (minus the screw caps) to make individual plant covers.

When planting out cabbage-family plants, surround each plant with a disk of material, such as cardboard or felt, to prevent the cabbage root fly from laying its eggs by the stem. Commercial cabbage-family collars are also available and are easy to use.

Surround the stems of transplants with a collar of aluminum foil to prevent them from being eaten by cutworms. These emerge at night and play havoc with many crops.

Controlling pests

No matter how good your preventive measures are, it is impossible to keep your vegetable garden free of pests. Once they appear, you need to take swift action to limit the damage.

PESTICIDES

Although there are some organic pesticides, most are inorganic. All the pesticides available today have to pass stringent tests to ensure that they will not harm the user—as long as they are used as instructed. However, most gardeners usually want to avoid using pesticides. One of the main reasons people give for growing their own vegetables is that they want to be sure they are free from pesticide residue.

If all other measures have failed, look for environment-friendly products that have a low toxicity and break down rapidly after use. Among the safest ones to use are those based on fatty acids or insecticidal soap; rotenone and pyrethrum are short-lived insecticides of plant origin. If you use pesticides, remember that even "safe" pesticides can be harmful to beneficial insects and fish, and they must be used with care.

When a problem arises, you'll need to decide which steps to take. If the vegetable in question is near maturity, it may be that no action is necessary—the pest may not have time to damage it. However, more often than not, you will have to do something to prevent the harvest from becoming severely damaged.

Pest control measures

There are many ways to control pests in the garden. A combination of these measures will keep your plants healthy.

Handpicking. If you spot an infestation early enough, you may be able to pick off the pests, or infested leaves or shoots, by hand and destroy them. Caterpillars are easy to pick off when there are only a few of them, and aphids start off clustered on just one shoot—although they soon spread.

Spraying with water. A strong jet of water from a hose will be enough to dislodge pests from plants. However, be careful that the jet of water is not so strong that it damages the plants.

Repellents. Many repellents rely on the pests' sense of smell, using extracts of citrus, garlic, or other deterrent plant oils. Slug and snail repellents use substances that make it uncomfortable for the creatures to crawl over them, either because they are irritating or dry up their slime or, in the case of copper tape, contain an electric current.

Make your own slug trap by sinking a plastic container into the ground and filling it with beer. Keep the top rim just above soil level to avoid trapping useful ground beetles.

Trapping. There are many types of traps for pests, from yellow, sticky strips of cardboard to snare insects to specialized animal traps to capture woodchucks and raccoons. If you decide to use live mammal traps, it is essential that you inspect them at least twice a day. You will also have to decide what to do with the animals once they are trapped. Wildlife experts don't recommend releasing them into the wild, because they have trouble adapting to new surroundings.

Sticky traps are strips of cardboard or plastic coated with a non-drying glue; they are yellow, because this color attracts whitefly. They are useful in greenhouses, but not outdoors because you can trap beneficial insects. Sticky traps are not a complete control, but they keep whitefly numbers down.

Slug and snail traps are sunk into the ground just above soil level and baited with beer or a special slug attractant, which drowns the slugs and snails. Commercial traps are designed to make disposing of the remains less unpleasant.

Biological controls. You can use the natural enemies of some pests to help control their numbers. The first step is to recognize and encourage the useful creatures that already occur in the garden—insects, such as ladybugs, lacewings, syrphid flies, rove beetles, and centipedes, as well as creatures, such as bats, frogs, toads, and lizards. You can provide suitable food sources and habitats to help these species proliferate in your garden. Grow the right wild plants as a food source, create a pond, put up nesting boxes or winter shelters—even a pile of stones or logs in a corner of the garden. Although your wildlife areas may harbor a few plant pests as well, the good creatures should outnumber the bad ones. If you are considering using chemical pesticides, remember that most of them are indiscriminate; they kill the beneficial insects along with the harmful ones.

For tailored biological controls, you can import pest predators and parasites into the garden (see *Common Biological Pest Controls,* right). A useful biological control for the vegetable garden is a bacterium, *Bacillus thuringiensis* (also known as Bt). It is available as a powder containing spores and toxins, which is mixed with water and sprayed onto the plants. *Bacillus thuringiensis* var. *kurstaki* kills caterpillars (including nonpest species of butterflies and moths); *Bacillus thuringiensis* var. *san diego* kills Colorado potato beetle larvae. When the bacterium is eaten, it attacks the caterpillar's or beetle's digestive system, rapidly stopping it from feeding and eventually killing it.

COMMON BIOLOGICAL PEST CONTROLS

Biological controls are available from speciality suppliers, usually by mail order, for specific pests. Follow the supplier's instructions carefully—some are for outdoor use, but others are only suitable for use in a greenhouse.

Aphids
Aphidius
Aphidoletes aphidomyza
Chrysoperla (lacewing)
Hippodamia (ladybug)

Red spider mite
Phytoseiulus persimilis

Vine weevil
Steinernema kraussei (nematodes)

Whitefly
Delphastus
Encarsia formosa

Mexican bean beetle
Pediobius foveolatus

General pest control
Podisus (spined soldier bug)
Tenodera (praying mantis)

Caterpillars
Bacillus thuringiensis

A wildlife pond, even a small one, is one way to encourage beneficial ceatures, such as frogs, to make your garden their home.

Understanding plant diseases

Plant diseases can have just as much of a harmful effect on vegetable yields and quality as pests, but good growing techniques will help to keep these afflictions at bay.

Plants are vulnerable to diseases mostly caused by fungi and viruses. However, there are a few bacterial infections that attack plants, and they produce similar symptoms to those of fungi.

Fungi diseases

Because fungi have no chlorophyll, they cannot manufacture food from sunlight, as plants do, so they must obtain their food from other sources. Many of them will tap into the food supply provided by plants.

Some types of fungi grow only on dead plant material, and they are valuable for breaking down plant debris into humus. Other fungi need living plant tissue to survive; these fungi can certainly damage plants, but they don't usually kill them, because this is counterproductive to their needs. There are relatively few of this type, but powdery mildew is one that often causes problems for gardeners.

The largest, and most troublesome, group consists of fungi that will grow on either living or dead tissue; they will continue to obtain nourishment from a plant even if they kill it and there is nothing to hold them back once an infection is under way.

Fungi produce wide-ranging, threadlike structures called hyphae, which act much like a plant's root system, and they can spread effectively through plant tissues or soil. The hyphae extract nutrients from the plant, either debilitating it or causing a more serious breakdown of the plant material until it becomes a mushy mass. Instead of seeds, fungi reproduce by spores, which can persist in a dormant state for many years until conditions are right for them to start to grow.

Viral diseases

Viruses are tiny organisms that can cause a huge range of symptoms in plants. Most familiar are the yellow mottling, streaking, or mosaic patterns on foliage, and the malformation of leaves and shoots, which can be curled, twisted, or crinkled.

Apart from the obvious symptoms, viruses can cause a general reduction in the health and vigor of affected plants, reducing crop yields severely. Viruses are difficult to control; while fungus diseases can be prevented or cured by fungicides, there are no chemicals that will have the same effects on viruses.

FROM THE APHID'S MOUTH

Viruses are spread from plant to plant by touch or through knives or pruners that have been in contact with infected plant material. However, the most common means by which viruses are spread is aphids.

An aphid actually injects a dose of disease into the sap of a plant with its piercing mouthparts when it moves from feeding on an infected plant to a healthy one. Viruses that affect crop plants can also exist in weeds, which may show no symptoms but form a source of infection for future crops. (For prevention and control, see pages 104–5.)

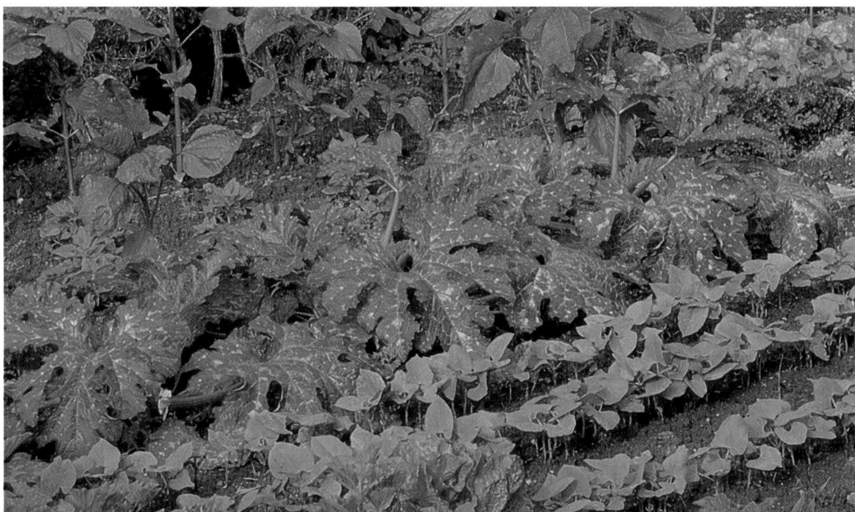

Powdery mildew occurs late in the season. It spreads by spores, so destroy the plants after harvesting so it won't recur in the spring.

Bringing diseases into the garden

There is a depressingly long list of ways in which plant diseases can sneak into the vegetable garden and attack the plants. There are some diseases we can do little about, but there are others that we have some control over.

Disease spores can literally arrive in the garden on a wind; they may also come in on new plants or plant material from garden centers or other gardens. They could be in the soil around the roots of a plant, or carried in the soil on the soles of your shoes. Several diseases may already be present in the seeds you sow.

Once a plant has been attacked by disease, the debris from that affected plant is a potent source of infection. There may be fallen leaves left lying on the soil surface, scraped up into a pile at one end of the vegetable plot, ready for disease spores to be blown around the garden; or they can be carried in water splashes onto new plants. Diseased plant remains put on the compost pile will contain spores that are resistant to the composting process, so spreading the compost will also spread the disease.

Diseases that survive in the soil can be persistent—clubroot disease can remain dormant for over 20 years. In these cases, you'll need to live with the disease and reduce its effects—but you won't be able to eradicate it.

Blossom end rot on the bottom of tomatoes occurs when insufficient water leads to a calcium deficiency; it is not caused by disease.

PLANT DISORDERS

Although a plant may look as though it is suffering from a disease, it doesn't necessarily mean it has been attacked by a disease-causing organism. Nutrient deficiencies in the soil can create a range of symptoms, such as pale, mosaic-patterned leaves and blossom end rot on tomatoes—a hard, brown, sunken patch at the base of the fruit that is caused by a lack of calcium and too little water.

Wilting plants may be caused by drought or waterlogging; low temperatures or cold winds can blacken leaves or turn their edges brown. Greenback on tomatoes—a hard area on a part of the fruit that remains green and fails to ripen—can be the result of too much sunlight. Keep these types of disorders in mind when checking plants for symptoms of disease.

Quick Tip

Don't spread it

Don't try to propagate from a diseased plant. Viruses are present throughout the whole system of an infected plant; propagating from even apparently healthy parts of the plant by cuttings, division, or tubers will mean the new plants are infected, too.

Controlling plant diseases

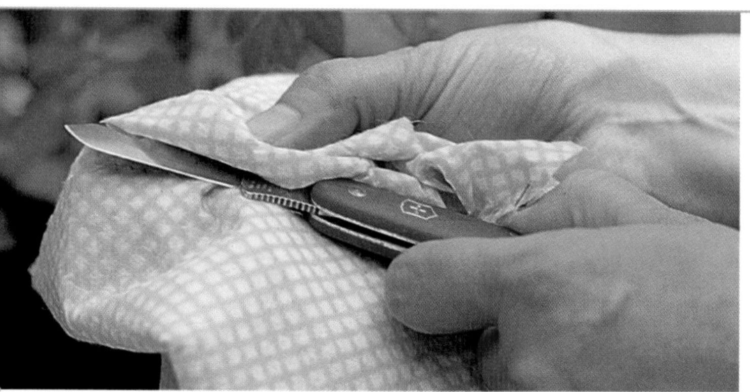

Outbreaks of plant disease are often due to poor cultivation techniques in the garden. Fortunately, there are some simple steps that you can take to reduce the risk.

Where plant diseases are concerned, it is easier to prevent an outbreak than it is to cure one once it has become established. Here are some commonsense rules to follow to prevent diseases.

Practice good hygiene. This is the first essential step when trying to maintain a healthy vegetable garden. Always clear up any plant debris promptly, especially if a crop has been suffering from some type of ailment. Diseased plant material is best burned, but if that isn't allowed in your area, you should dispose of the diseased material in sealed plastic bags, along with your household trash.

Make sure you always keep your gardening equipment clean. Wash pots and seed trays in hot water at the beginning of the season, and occasionally wipe over the blades of knives and pruners with a garden disinfectant. Use a sterile mix or growing mix for raising plants.

Provide the right conditions for rapid growth. Sowing or planting vegetables too early, when the soil is wet and cold, will increase the amount of time they take to become established, leaving them more prone to attack by disease organisms. The same applies to trying to grow plants that are not suited to your particular climate. It's always an enjoyable challenge to see how far you can push the boundaries, but a plant that thrives in hot, dry conditions will be more prone to problems in a chilly, damp area—and vice versa. You can try it, but be prepared for disappointments.

If you want to get an early start with your vegetables, try raising the plants in containers in a cold frame, a greenhouse, or under lights indoors. You should only set them outside once growing conditions are more suitable for the plants.

Plant healthy stock. If you can, raise your own plants from seeds sown in sterile mix and clean seed trays. Buy the seeds from a reliable source, too—some plant diseases are seed borne. If you have limited space to raise your own plants, cabbage-family plants are probably the most important ones to concentrate on. It's easy to import clubroot disease with newly purchased cabbage-family seedlings—and once you have clubroot in the soil, it is there for good.

DISEASE CONTROL

There are not too many options for controlling diseases once they have broken out. Diseases develop fast, so prompt action is essential.

Remove and destroy affected parts as soon as you notice signs of disease and destroy them, preferably by burning. This will help to prevent the disease from worsening on the affected plant, and will also help to prevent it from spreading to other plants. If a plant is badly affected, destroy the whole plant.

You can use fungicides to help prevent diseases. Two fungicides for organic use are copper and sulfur. You can also use fungicidal soaps to prevent diseases or a homemade baking soda spray to prevent powdery mildew on vine and other crops. To make the spray, add 1 tablespoon (15 ml) of baking soda to 1 cup (235 ml) warm water. Stir until the baking soda dissolves; then add 1 tablespoon (15 ml) of vegetable oil and mix. Add the solution to 1 gallon (3.75 liters) of warm water; mix. Apply it with a sprayer immediately.

If you have to purchase vegetable plants, you should make sure you buy them from a reputable supplier whose stock looks healthy and well maintained. If certified disease-free stock is available (as with seed potatoes, for example), buy only that type. At least you'll know that you're starting out with healthy plants.

Make conditions unfavorable for diseases. Some plant diseases need specific conditions to thrive, and you can manipulate these to your advantage. Clubroot, for example, requires an acid soil, so reducing soil acidity by adding lime to your cabbage-family plot will help keep clubroot away. Conversely, potato scab likes alkaline soil, so make sure you don't lime the area where you plan to grow potatoes.

Rotate crops. Growing the same type of vegetables in the same patch of soil year after year will give disease organisms the ideal opportunity to build up. Following a crop-rotation plan (see pages 18–19) will help to avoid this, particularly where the diseases are soil borne.

Avoid overcrowding. Most diseases thrive in a humid atmosphere—the same type of setting that is created by overcrowded plants. Thin seedlings out as soon as they can be handled easily, and make sure the plants are set out at the recommended spacings. A good airflow is essential. Don't forget that weeds will create a humid microclimate around your vegetable plants, too—another good reason for getting rid of them.

Keep the plants happy. Keep your vegetable plants growing strongly by practicing good growing techniques. Putting plants under any type of stress—whether it's by overcrowding, a lack of nutrients, too high or too low temperatures, or a lack of water—will make them less able to withstand a disease attack.

Water carefully. Because many plant diseases like humid conditions, take extra care when watering. Don't splash water around too freely when it's not really necessary. Overhead watering, particularly in cool conditions where moisture stays on the leaves, is much more likely to promote disease than applying water direct to the soil. Water splashes may also carry disease spores from one plant to another.

Be aware of the weather. Certain weather combinations create the ideal conditions for various diseases. Warm, wet summers, for example, are ideal for potato blight to develop, whereas warm, dry conditions are favorable for powdery mildews. Downy mildew on lettuce tends to appear in cool, damp weather, which is also loved by gray mold disease, especially in greenhouses. By knowing which diseases are most likely to appear and by keeping a close eye on plants, you can take action as soon as a problem arises.

Control aphids. One of the best steps you can take to prevent the spread of virus diseases (see pages 100–1 and pages 104–5) is to keep aphids under control.

Grow resistant varieties. You can look through seed catalog descriptions for details on resistant varieties.

Use fungicides. Unlike insecticides, fungicides can have a preventive effect by coating the leaves of plants to stop disease spores from germinating. (See *Disease Control,* left, for more information about fungicides.)

Provide proper spacing between your vegetable plants—this is especially important in hot, humid areas to help prevent disease.

Identifying pests

Soil pests

Includes: Cutworm, millipede, wireworm

Symptoms: These pests feed on the roots or stems of plants, causing the leaves to turn yellow and wilt; young plants often die. The stems of seedlings and transplants may be severed at soil level. Pest larvae are responsible; look for curled white or brown grubs in the soil. Adult millipedes also cause the damage.

Prevention and control: Dig soil in fall and winter to expose the pests to birds and the weather. Keep vegetable plants weed free to discourage adults from laying eggs. Clear away plant debris. Use collars against cutworms.

Chemical control: None.

Beetles

Includes: Asparagus beetle, Colorado potato beetle, flea beetle, Mexican bean bug, pea and bean weevil, Japanese beetle

Symptoms: Beetles feed on leaves and stems of plants; some species, such as striped cucumber beetles, have larvae that are soil pests.

Colorado potato beetles are a serious potato pest, rapidly devouring foliage and stems; flea beetles attack young seedlings, often cabbage-family plants, biting small holes in the leaves; pea and bean weevils eat the leaf edges of pea and bean plants. Asparagus beetles eat foliage and distort young shoots.

Prevention and control: Encourage rapid growth of vulnerable seedlings and young plants by providing the correct conditions. Handpick beetles where seen. Remove plant debris, which shelters adults and allows them to overwinter.

Chemical control: Bifenthrin, rotenone, pyrethrins.

Flies

Includes: Cabbage root maggot, carrot maggot, celery leafminer, onion maggot

Symptoms: Cabbage root maggot attacks all cabbage-family plants; the first sign is often wilting of lower leaves in warm weather. Small white larvae feed on roots, which checks or kills plants.

Carrot maggot feeds on roots of carrots, celery, parsley, and parsnips; leaves on affected plants have a red tinge. Celery leafminer attacks the leaves, causing patchy white areas, and weakens plants. Onion maggot attacks stems and bulbs; plants will rot.

Prevention and control: Dig soil in fall and winter to expose pests to birds and the weather. Clear away plant debris, which gives cover for adults. Destroy affected leaves on celery.

Protect cabbage transplants by placing a cardboard or fabric disk around stems.

Carrot maggot find carrots by smell, so avoid bruising the foliage; sow seeds thinly to reduce hand thinning. Sow late in the spring or early summer to avoid worst attacks. Lift and store mature carrots.

Chemical control: None.

Caterpillars

Includes: Cabbage looper, imported cabbage worm, corn earworm, pea moth

Symptoms: Cabbage caterpillars reduce healthy cabbage-family plants to lacework in a few days.

Pea moths feed on the developing peas that are unseen within the pod. Corn earworms tunnel into the tips of ears of sweet corn.

Prevention and control: Inspect the undersides of cabbage-plant leaves for egg clusters; destroy affected leaves. Pick or hose off caterpillars as they appear. Cover cabbage-family plants with floating row covers or grow in a fruit cage to keep butterfly eggs off.

Sow peas early or late to avoid plants growing during the peak caterpillar season.

Plant sweet corn varieties with tight husks that earworms cannot penetrate. Apply BTK or mineral oil to the tip of ears when silks start to dry.

Try *Bacillus thuringiensis* (Bt), a biological control for caterpillars.

Chemical control: Bifenthrin, rotenone, pyrethrins.

The following chart lists some of the major pests that are fond of vegetables. In addition to the preventive and control measures listed here, if all else fails, some gardeners may want to use chemical pesticides (see pages 98–99)—always follow the product label exactly.

Mammals and birds	Aphids	Greenhouse pests	Slugs and snails
Includes: Armadillo, cat, deer, groundhog, mouse, vole, rabbit, raccoon, woodchuck **Symptoms:** Deer, rabbits, and woodchucks eat almost anything green; raccoons like sweet corn. Armadillos dig up large areas of soil. Mice and voles eat seeds, especially peas and beans, and stored produce. Cats foul beds. Many birds are useful pest predators, but starlings and blackbirds attack lettuce and cabbage-family plants in spring, and jays steal peas and beans. **Prevention and treatment:** Put down traps for mice and voles; keep garden clear of debris that provides shelter. Put up fencing to keep out larger mammals and birds (see pages 96–97). Various scaring devices can be used to deter them, and netting or floating row covers help to protect vegetables. Cover freshly prepared seedbeds with plastic netting to prevent cats from digging or keep soil moist. Repellents may have some affect against these pests. **Chemical control:** None.	**Includes:** Black bean aphid, cabbage aphid, mealy cabbage aphid, potato aphid **Symptoms:** These small insects are often green or black but may be gray, brown, or pink, depending on species. All are sapsuckers: They weaken plants, make crops unpleasant to eat, and spread virus diseases. They develop in dense colonies on shoot tips and leaves and reproduce rapidly. Females give birth without mating, but there are also winged females that do mate. Aphids exude a sticky honeydew when feeding. **Prevention and control:** Clear plant debris promptly, especially old cabbage-family plants, where aphid eggs overwinter. It is impossible to keep aphids out of a garden, so be vigilant and deal with outbreaks as soon as they occur. Pick off and destroy the infested shoots and leaves, or knock the aphids off plants with a strong spray of water. In greenhouses, you can use biological controls. **Chemical control:** Bifenthrin, fatty acids, rotenone, pyrethrins.	**Includes:** Red spider mite, whitefly *(Note: These pests are not limited to the greenhouse.)* **Symptoms:** Red spider mite infests tomatoes, cucumbers, eggplants, and peppers, causing white flecks on the leaves and webbing at tips. Look for tiny orange mites. Whiteflies look like tiny white moths; they like cucumbers but attack all greenhouse plants and cabbage-family plants outdoors. They cluster on the undersides of leaves and rise up when plants are disturbed. Both pests are sap suckers and weaken plants. **Treatment and control:** Red spider mites thrive in dry conditions; keep atmposphere in the greenhouse moist to deter them. Try using the biological control *Phytoseiulis persimilis*, a predator. Use *Encarsia formosa,* a parasite, to control whiteflies. Yellow sticky traps help to keep numbers down. Clear away plants as soon as harvesting is over to reduce populations of both pests. **Chemical control:** Bifenthrin, pyrethrins, rotenone, fatty acids; for eggplants, peppers, and tomatoes, imidacloprid.	**Includes:** Banana slug, field slug, garden slug, garden snail **Symptoms:** Slugs and snails eat leaves and stems, leaving just a network of veins, with telltale slimy trails. Damage is generally done at night. Tender young plants are most at risk—seedlings may be entirely consumed overnight. **Prevention and control:** They are most evident in moist, warm weather. Keep areas surrounding the vegetable garden clear of weeds and debris because slugs and snails shelter there during the day. Use traps (see pages 98–99) and empty them regularly. You can hunt for slugs and snails at night, by flashlight, to remove large numbers; wear gloves to pick up slugs because slime is difficult to remove from your fingers. You can use a microscopic nematode, *Phasmarhabditis,* a form of biological control. To protect individual plants, surround them with a circle of diatomaceous earth or cover with plastic bottles. **Chemical control:** Aluminum sulfate, metaldehyde.

Identifying diseases

Blight

Crops affected: Potatoes, tomatoes

Symptoms: Blight favors warm, wet weather. It progresses rapidly on potatoes. First signs are dark blotches on the leaves, followed by rapid wilting and yellowing of foliage and stems; then a collapse of the plant, often in a few days. Spores wash down to infect the tubers, which develop a brown rot.

Blight is less dramatic on tomatoes but is serious, with leaves collapsing and fruit developing brown rotting patches.

A different organism is responsible for early blight, which causes brown spots on the leaves, but it is much less serious.

Prevention and control: Warnings are often given by official bodies when the right combination of humidity and temperatures can lead to a risk of blight.

If the disease is spotted on potato foliage, remove and burn the haulms (top growth). If you harvest the crop right away, the tubers may be unaffected. Destroy infected or suspect crop remains by burning, or bury them deeply and well away from the vegetable garden.

Greenhouse tomatoes are slightly less vulnerable to attack than outdoor ones.

Chemical control: Mancozeb, copper sulfate, copper oxychloride.

Blossom end rot

Crops affected: Tomatoes, peppers

Symptoms: A hard, sunken brown rot forms at the blossom end of the fruit, farthest away from the stem.

Prevention and control: This is a disorder caused by a shortage of calcium; it occurs when there is a water shortage at fruit development.

A plant that wilts while flowering and fruiting is liable to carry fruit with blossom end rot later on.

It mostly affects plants growing in small containers that dry out quickly. Keep the soil around the roots moist at all times. Add a handful of garden lime to the watering can occasionally.

Chemical control: None.

Botrytis (gray mold)

Crops affected: Many, especially lettuce and tomatoes

Symptoms: This fungus starts on dead tissue but spreads to live parts. It produces a fluffy gray mold growth; under this growth the plant tissue rots. It is most often found in greenhouses.

Prevention and control: It prefers cool, damp conditions.

Clear all dead and dying plant debris away. As soon as you see gray mold, cut out and destroy affected parts.

Keep greenhouses ventilated; avoid overcrowding of plants. Water early in the day, and do not splash water.

Chemical control: Copper sulfate can control an outbreak.

Clubroot

Crops affected: Cabbage-family plants

Symptoms: Plants wilt in warm weather; growth is stunted and may die. Roots swell and are distorted.

Prevention and control: Clubroot likes moist, acid soil. Lime the soil; improve drainage on heavy soils.

Grow plants from seeds; don't buy plants or accept them as gifts.

Dormant spores can persist for 20 years; no real benefit from crop rotation. There are no fungicide treatments.

If the garden is infected, raise plants in pots of sterile mix; plant out with roots in a good ball of mix.

Chemical control: None.

Damping-off

Crops affected: All seedlings

Symptoms: The seedlings collapse, sometimes with a lesion on stems. This often occurs in circular patches in seed flats.

Prevention and control: It thrives if crowded, such as in pots.

Clean flats and equipment at the start of season—use a disinfectant. Use sterile compost; sow seeds thinly. Keep flats ventilated when seedlings appear. Do not overwater.

Try a product with a beneficial soil fungi.

Chemical control: Copper sulfate and copper oxychloride when signs first appear.

The following chart lists some of the major diseases that attack vegetables. Preventive and control measures are listed below; however, as a last resort, some gardeners may want to use chemical fungicides (see pages 100–3).

Leaf and pod spots

Crops affected: Beans, cabbage-family plants, cucumbers

Symptoms: Anthracnose on beans causes sunken, reddish brown spots on pods and dark stripes on stems. Chocolate spot on broad beans forms brown spots on foliage and stems. Halo blight on beans causes dark spots surrounded by a pale ring.

Cucumbers with anthracnose have spreading spots on leaves and stems and sunken areas on fruit. Many organisms cause spots on cabbage-family plants.

Prevention and control: Practice garden hygiene; give plants a lot of space. Destroy affected leaves. Do not save seeds.

Chemical control: Mancozeb.

Mildew

Crops affected: Cabbage-family plants, peas, onions, lettuce, spinach

Symptoms: Powdery and downy mildew produce a white or gray mold, often in round patches, not as fluffy as mold.

Downy mildew appears on undersides of leaves in cool, damp conditions; powdery mildew forms on top in dry conditions.

Prevention and control: Look for mildew-resistant varieties. Do not overcrowd plants; do not overwater. Remove plant debris promptly.

Mildew appears late in season, so it may not need treatment.

Chemical control: Mancozeb (for downy mildew), green and yellow sulfur (for powdery mildew).

Root-knot nematode

Crops affected: Many, including carrots, lettuce, and onions

Symptoms: Irregular, lumpy galls or swellings on the roots; the plants are stunted, and the foliage may yellow.

Prevention and control: Remove and destroy all severely infected plants.

Rotate crops and plant nematode-resistant varieties. Apply beneficial nematodes to the soil before planting for a few months of control.

Chemical control: None.

Scab

Crops affected: Potatoes

Symptoms: Tubers have brown, roundish corky areas on the surface.

Prevention and control: Scab thrives in alkaline soil, so never lime before growing potatoes. The disease is worst on light, free-draining soils, which should have plenty of organic matter added.

Keep potato plants watered during prolonged dry spells.

Chemical control: None.

Virus

Crops affected: Cabbage-family plants, lettuce, potatoes, tomatoes

Symptoms: A streaking, mosaic, or mottling pattern on leaves, or malformed leaves with crinkled or rolled edges.

Common viruses include cauliflower mosaic, cucumber mosaic, lettuce big vein, tomato mosaic, and potato leaf roll.

Prevention and control: Aphids are the main way viruses spread, but any contact can transmit disease. Control aphids; keep tools and equipment clean.

Remove and burn affected plants as symptoms appear. Buy certified virus-free stock; look for virus-resistant varieties in seed catalogs.

Chemical control: None.

Wilt

Crops affected: Tomato- and cabbage-family plants

Symptoms: Fusarium wilt is the most common type. Young plants become pale and stunted; lower leaves yellow and wilt, sometimes on only one side of the plant. The symptoms move upward and plants may die. If you cut across the stem of an affected plant, there may be a brown stain.

Verticillium wilt causes similar symptoms but without one-sided effects. Wilt diseases are worst in hot weather.

Prevention and control: Wilt diseases stay in the soil, so if a garden is infected, grow resistant varieties. Clear away plant debris and rotate crops.

Chemical control: None.

5 Harvesting and storing

One of the major benefits of growing your own vegetables is that you can pluck them from the plant or take them out of the ground when they are absolutely at their peak and enjoy them ultra-fresh and bursting with nutrients.

Vegetables are usually at their best when eaten within minutes of harvesting, but you can also store many of them for later use. Knowing the right way to store them will ensure that the flavor, texture, and nutrient value of your vegetables are all preserved.

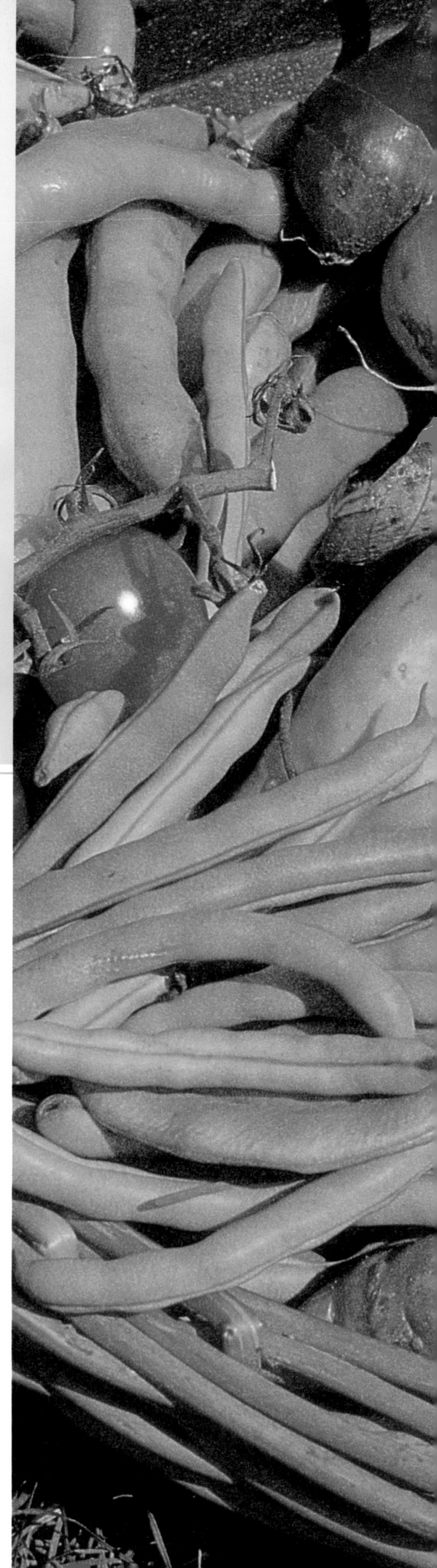

Harvesttime is the moment when you reap the benefits of all your hard work in the garden.

The right time to harvest

Relatively few of the vegetables we eat are grown until maturity. In fact, most of them are gathered young, when they are tender and sweet. To be able to achieve a balance between the greatest yields and the best-quality crops, it's important to understand when each type of vegetable is in its prime.

How and when a vegetable is harvested depends on whether it belongs in the leafy vegetable or fruiting vegetable group or if it is a stem or root.

Leafy vegetables

Among the leafy vegetable group are cabbage, kale, spinach, Swiss chard, lettuce, and other salad greens. You can grow some plants—cabbages and many lettuce varieties, for example—until they form a firm head. When the head is large enough, cut the whole plant.

To check that a lettuce heart is firm and dense and ready for harvest, press it gently with the back of your hand—don't pinch it with your fingertips, because you can bruise the leaves. Try to cut lettuce as soon as it reaches a usable size; if left too long, it will turn to seed.

You can eat summer cabbages as soon as they look large enough. Don't wait until they are enormous, because super-size heads can split and be ruined. Fall and winter cabbages are hardier than summer ones. Where winters are mild, you can leave many of them in the ground for harvesting throughout the winter. However, some varieties require that you cut and store them in a cool place before the worst of the cold weather arrives.

For other leafy vegetables, such as spinach, Swiss chard, kale, and some lettuce varieties, harvest gradually over the season. If you take just a few well-developed leaves from the outside of each plant per picking, the plants will continue to grow and crop.

Fruiting vegetables

Tomatoes, peppers, and melons are the obvious fruit, but this category also includes cucumbers, eggplants, tomatillos, okra, and squash, as well as the seed producers—peas, beans, and sweet corn.

Vegetable plants produce fruit, cobs, and pods for only

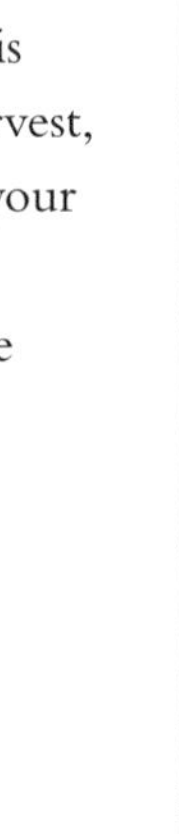

When to pick

Harvest times can vary widely according to the variety grown, so always check the seed packets for details.

Pick string beans before you can feel bumps in them, which are a sign that the beans are too ripe.

Leave tomatoes on the vine until ripe and ready to eat. They will develop more flavor when ripened on the vine.

STEMS AND ROOTS

You can enjoy new potatoes, baby beets, salad turnips, and young carrots at a relatively immature stage, so you can harvest root vegetables as soon as they become large enough. Otherwise, leave roots in the ground until the end of the season. In fact, some roots can remain there throughout the winter (see pages 116–17).

Kohlrabi—which is not a root but a swollen stem base—becomes tough and woody when it reaches about tennis-ball size, so harvest it while still young.

Harvest **celery** and **Florence fennel** when the heads reach a suitable size. Keep an eye on fennel—if left too long, it will turn to seed. You can keep some varieties of celery in the ground until mid-winter.

Asparagus shoots start to push their way through the soil in mid-spring; cut them when they are 6–8 inches (15–20 cm) tall, before the bud scales start to open. Continue harvesting for about eight weeks; then stop to allow the plants to build up their reserves for next year.

one reason—to contain seeds that will ensure the continuation of the species. As soon as some of the seeds are fully ripe, they send the parent plant a message, which signals the end of fruit and seed production for the season. For maximum crops, harvest frequently so that the seeds never have a chance to ripen and switch the production system off. (The exception is when a mature crop is required—haricot beans for drying, for example, or pumpkins for winter storage.)

Most pod and cob vegetables are eaten young, when tender and sweet. The first sign of ripening is when the sugars in developing seeds begin to turn to starch. This is familiar to anyone who has eaten corn or peas beyond their prime. The pods holding them become tough and fibrous. For French and string beans, asparagus peas, snap and snow peas, and others in which the pods are eaten, pick the pods while they will still snap cleanly, without any stringiness.

You should pick summer squashes and cucumbers while they are young and tender—and remember, the more you cut, the more new fruit will be produced. Allow winter squashes to ripen into the fall for the flesh to develop its characteristic sweetness—this is one case where you'll have to accept a lower yield. You should also allow tomatoes to ripen on the plant. However, for sweet peppers, pick the first fruit while still green to encourage heavier crops.

How to harvest

Gathering your crops is one of the most satisfying and enjoyable tasks in the whole process of vegetable gardening. By making sure you do the job properly, you'll also ensure a high-quality product with a long shelf life.

DIGGING AND LIFTING

A garden fork is more useful than a spade to pry crops from the ground, but be careful to avoid spearing them on the prongs. When digging crops, such as Jerusalem artichokes and potatoes, use the fork to loosen the soil; then work through the soil with your fingers to unearth the roots.

Main-crop carrots, parsnips, salsify, and scorzonera often have long roots, so push the fork down a good depth before levering it up, otherwise, you may snap the roots. In light soil, you can sometimes pull up these crops by hand. However, if the roots are shallow, such as those on radishes, loosening the soil with a fork is the safest option.

You can also use a fork to lift non-root crops that are partly buried, such as leeks, blanched celery, and onions.

Harvesting can be as simple as picking a few leaves off a plant, or it may require a knife for cutting or a fork for digging. No matter which method you use, it won't take much effort to harvest your crop.

Harvesting a leafy crop

A good, sharp knife is useful to cut many leafy crops cleanly, particularly those that form a heart or head, such as many varieties of lettuce and cabbage. You can also use a knife (or sharp scissors) to cut individual leaves of spinach, kale, or chard. You can pick leaves by hand, but you run the risk of tugging up the whole plant by the roots if you don't do so carefully.

Sprouting broccoli has a much longer cropping season if the young flowering shoots are cut high up so that several leaves remain at the base of the stems. New shoots will then grow from each leaf axil to multiply the harvest.

Wield the knife carefully when cutting asparagus. Harvest spears as soon as they are long enough, cutting the stems at soil level with a sharp

When picking a leaf by hand, hold the stem of the plant with one hand and pull carefully with the other.

blade. Be careful not to damage developing shoots close by, hidden below the soil. Special forked asparagus knives are available to make the job a little easier.

Cut and come again

You can grow many varieties of leafy vegetables as cut-and-come-again crops, including kale, salad leaves, Swiss chard, beet greens, and spinach. Harvest the plants leaving stumps about 1–2 inches (2.5–5 cm) high. A fresh flush of leaves will regrow and be ready for picking a few weeks later. In a good growing season, you may even be able to get a third picking from the same plants.

Handpicking

Pick most fruiting vegetables—peas, tomatoes, eggplants, peppers, and beans (see pages 110–11)—as they are ready. Always try to remove the entire pod or fruit cleanly; damaged crops don't keep for long after picking, and any portion left on the plant provides an entry point for disease. When pulling off peas and beans, hold the stem with one hand to make sure you do not loosen the plant in the soil as you tug.

Pick tomatoes with the spidery green calyx still attached; snap the fruit away at the knuckle that is found just along the stem. Use the fruit that come away without the calyx first, because they may not keep as long as those with the calyx intact.

Peppers and eggplants don't have a knuckle like tomatoes do, but they should also be picked with a short length of stem attached. You may need a sharp knife or pruning shears because the stems can be tough.

Pick Brussels sprouts as soon as the first buttons are large enough, starting at the bottom of the stem and moving upward. Remove old yellowed leaves for easier access and push the buttons off sideways. Leave the leafy tops on the plants to protect the maturing sprouts below them from the weather. As soon as you pick the last sprout, cut the tops and eat them, too.

Zucchini, cucumbers, and other squashes have sturdy, prickly stems, which should be cut with a sharp knife just below the base of the fruit.

Quick Tip

Extra pickings

After you cut a large head off a cabbage plant, leave the stalk in the ground and cut a shallow cross in the top. After a few weeks, another crop of leafy greens will sprout from each corner of the cut.

Keeping harvested vegetables fresh

It's not always practical or possible to eat harvested vegetables right away. In these situations, follow the appropriate storing method to slow down the inevitable fall in quality that occurs once a vegetable is harvested.

Spray beans and peas with fresh cool water to cool them quickly.

Being able to eat fresh crops as soon as you pick them is one of the joys of having a garden. As a rule of thumb, pick crops only when you want to eat them or when they are in danger of becoming overripe. The best place to store vegetables is in the ground or on the plant.

Once vegetables reach the point when they will start to spoil if left any longer, there is no choice. You'll have to harvest them, even if you already have all the beans or lettuce you need for the next few days. If you have a real glut (and it happens in even the best-planned gardens), you should consider a long-term storage method (see pages 116–23). However, for smaller surpluses, a few days' grace is usually all that is needed.

Stopping deterioration

Once vegetables are picked, their quality begins to deteriorate because they are cut off from their supply of food and water, and, therefore, have to start using up their own stores. Sugar will begin to turn to starch; the leaves will lose their crispness and become limp and wilted; and various microorganisms will begin to cause rotting in the plant tissue.

You can slow down or halt the deterioration process by carrying out the following simple steps:

Check for damage. Even if only slightly damaged, eat the produce right away. The disease-causing microorganisms will soon multiply in damaged areas—and they can spread to adjacent, undamaged produce, too.

Cool down the crop. It is extremely important to keep the temperature of your harvested crop low, because warmth can speed up the rate of deterioration. Try to pick vegetables for short-term storage early in the morning, while they are still cool and fully charged with moisture from the night. Bring them into a cool, shaded place immediately after picking, and spread the produce out instead of piling it up in a heap.

Reduce water loss. As soon as a vegetable is removed from the plant or the soil, it can no longer replace the moisture it loses by evaporation. Soft, leafy crops, such as spinach and lettuce—with their large surface areas—are affected most rapidly by moisture loss.

Water loss is accelerated by heat, so it is best to cool down susceptible crops quickly. You can spray leafy crops with freshly drawn cool water to help to rehydrate them, as well as bring the temperature down. You should use a gentle spray to avoid damaging the leaves. After cooling, shake or blot excess water from the produce and move it to a cool place, such as a pantry, root cellar, or refrigerator, to protect it from further moisture loss.

Wrap asparagus in a damp kitchen towel and store it in the refrigerator.

STORING VEGETABLES IN A REFRIGERATOR

The cool environment of a refrigerator is ideal for many vegetables, but be careful—some crops can be spoiled by low temperatures. You should never refrigerate tomatoes, for example, because it ruins their flavor, even if they are allowed to come to room temperature before being eaten. Keep them in a cool room or pantry.

Store squashes, peppers, and cucumbers in a refrigerator at 37–39°F (3–4°C) for two to three days, and keep all crops above freezing unless you first prepare them for freezing (see pages 118–19). Most refrigerators have a vegetable section that maintains higher humidity. You can also put produce in plastic bags or containers, or roll it up loosely in a damp towel. Check the produce often—high humidity encourages mold and rot.

Quick Tip

Protecting roots

Root crops are best left in the ground until needed. However, if you do have to lift them in advance, don't wash off the soil clinging to the roots until the last minute, because it protects them from drying out and wrinkling.

Long-term storage

It's always a bonus to save some of summer's bounty to enjoy through the leaner winter months. Some crops need only minimal preparation to stay in good condition for many weeks, well into the winter.

Crops that are natural storage organs—including roots (carrots and turnips), tubers (potatoes), and bulbs (onions)—are easy to store with a little preparation. Leeks and winter-hardy cabbage-family crops are also easy to store into winter.

Most of these crops will remain in good condition because they have natural protection against excessive moisture loss, whether it is their tough, waxy outer leaves; protective skins; or their small surface area in relation to their density. You can help prolong their useful life even further by taking extra precautions to prevent moisture loss. Remember that the crops chosen for storage should be healthy and undamaged. There are several storage options for these vegetables.

In the ground

Often the best way to keep crops in good condition is to leave them in their growing positions. However, there are drawbacks: Crops in the ground are prone to attack by pests and diseases, and depending on the climate, they can be damaged by excessive cold, rain, or wind. They can also be impossible to harvest where winters are harsh and the soil is frozen for long periods.

Because potatoes and sweet potatoes can be damaged by frost, harvest them well before the cold weather. They are also prone to slug damage if left in the soil too long.

Depending on the severity of the winter, roots such as beets, carrots, rutabagas, and turnips are usually sufficiently hardy to be left in the ground; however, some varieties are hardier than others, so check the seed packet. In cool areas, provide extra protection by piling straw or leaf litter over the rows once the leaves die down. Parsnips, celeriac, salsify, and scorzonera are the hardiest of the root vegetables, and they can usually remain in the ground throughout winter in milder areas.

A perfect place for storing parsnips and other root vegetables is in sand in a box.

Quick Tip

Stake sense

Brussels sprouts, winter cabbages, sprouting broccoli, and kale shrug off low temperatures. On exposed sites, tie these plants to a stout stake to keep them from being blown over by fall and winter winds.

STORING IN CLAMPS

A root clamp—a pile of roots covered in an insulating layer of straw and soil—is a traditional storage method.

Root clamps are seldom used now, but they are worthwhile if you have a lot of roots to store. Build a clamp in an unheated basement or garage, or in a sheltered spot in the open. Start with a 6-inch (15-cm)-thick layer of light soil, sand, or straw; then build a neat stack of roots on it, sloping the sides to form a conical pile about 30 inches (75 cm) high and the same across at the base. Cover the stack with a thick layer of straw; then top that with another 6-inch (15-cm) layer of slightly moist, sifted soil or sand, patting it down smooth with the back of the spade. Finally, pull a handful of straw through the soil at the top of the stack for ventilation.

The roots must be cold before they are piled up, so wait until early winter to build the clamp.

Take roots out through the side of the clamp, then replace the covering.

Leeks are another hardy crop that can often remain in place. However, where winters are long and harsh, lift a proportion of leeks, and all the root crops already mentioned, before the low temperatures arrive. Store them in boxes as described below—this way you can ensure that you'll have some vegetables available when the rest are frozen into the ground.

In boxes

Store roots in frost-free basements, sheds, or garages in boxes layered with moist soil or sand. Wooden boxes are best, but stout cardboard boxes will do. You should place them in their storage positions before filling—they may be too heavy to move afterward.

Store potatoes in strong paper bags—don't use plastic bags because they encourage rotting. Harvest potatoes on a dry day so they can be left on the soil surface to dry for a couple of hours after lifting and before bagging up. Close the tops of the filled bag and store them in a cool, dark place. Exposure to light causes potato tubers to turn green and produce poisonous, bitter alkaloids.

Leave potatoes to dry before you store them in a large paper bag. Remove any damaged potatoes before storing.

Shelves, nets, and ropes

Slatted wooden shelves in a cool, dry shed or basement will allow a good flow of air around vegetables, which helps prevent rotting. Place mature vegetables, such as pumpkins and winter squashes, onions, and fall cabbages on the shelves, but be aware that they sometimes start to rot underneath where they press against the wood. Hanging them up in nets or using old nylon stockings avoids this problem.

Onions and garlic are traditionally braided into ropes, using the dried foliage of the bulbs, and hung in an airy place.

Freezing

Freezing is one of the most successful and popular methods for storing vegetable crops. Remember that it's worth taking a little time to prepare the produce before freezing—it can make all the difference to the quality of the end product.

IS FREEZING FOR YOU?

PRO

- Freezing is one of the best methods for home preservation.

CONS

- There may not be enough space in a standard freezer for everything you want to keep in it.
- There is the initial expense of buying a separate freezer and its running costs to take into account—and a power outage can be inconvenient.
- Freezing inevitably damages vegetable texture to some extent, so it is not suitable for produce that will be eaten raw.

The microorganisms that cause decay and deterioration are rendered almost completely inactive by the cold temperatures used in freezing. Frozen vegetables retain virtually all their nutritional value, and their flavor and appearance are also usually well preserved.

Don't waste space in your freezer on vegetables that will keep well enough by other simpler methods, such as those already discussed on pages 116–17. Save this technique for young and tender vegetables that cannot be preserved as successfully by these other methods. As always, use fresh, undamaged produce.

Blanching

Before freezing vegetables for long-term storage, it is important to blanch them first to destroy microorganisms and enzymes, which are responsible for the deterioration of their texture, color, and flavor. You may be tempted to skip the blanching process, but it

Freezing vegetables

Prepare the vegetables for cooking, then blanch them in boiling water and cool them. Most vegetables need two to three minutes' blanching time; root crops and corn cobs need four to seven minutes, depending on their size. Package the vegetables in plastic freezer bags or containers. To save space and prevent deterioration, remove as much air as you can by depressing the lid on a container or squeezing out air from a bag before sealing them.

1 Prepare the vegetables as you would for a recipe; for example, trim the ends of green beans or cut into pieces. Place them into a wire basket (no more than 9 oz/250 g at a time).

To freeze a leafy herb, rinse and finely chop it with a sharp kitchen knife. Place a tablespoonful (15 ml) of herb into each compartment of an ice-cube tray, cover with water, then freeze. Once frozen, remove the ice cubes from the tray and store in a plastic bag in the freezer. Simply add the cubes of frozen herbs when needed to stews or soups.

does improve the quality of frozen vegetables. However, if you plan to eat the frozen produce within two or three weeks, it is not essential to blanch.

Leafy herbs

Among the leafy herbs suitable for freezing—in ice cubes—are basil, mint, chervil, parsley, tarragon, and chives. These can lose their taste and aroma shortly after being picked, but freezing helps retain them (but the leaf texture and color will be altered).

Quick Tip

Power outage

Don't open the freezer door to check the contents during a power outage. Most older freezers allow food to stay frozen for at least 11 hours without power and modern ones for up to 29 hours—but only if the door remains closed.

VEGETABLES FOR FREEZING

You can freeze vegetables such as cabbage, Brussels sprouts, and root crops instead of keeping them in the ground or in clamps (see pages 116–17). Vegetables with a high water content, such as zucchini and tomatoes, tend to collapse when thawed and are usually best cooked in a ratatouille or similar dish before freezing.

Other vegetables suitable for freezing are:

Asparagus

Beans: broad, French, and string

Broccoli

Carrots (young)

Cauliflower

Peas and snow peas

Spinach and Swiss chard

Squashes (young)

Sweet corn

2 Plunge the basket into a pot of rapidly boiling water. Bring the water back to a boil as quickly as possible; then start timing from the moment it boils again.

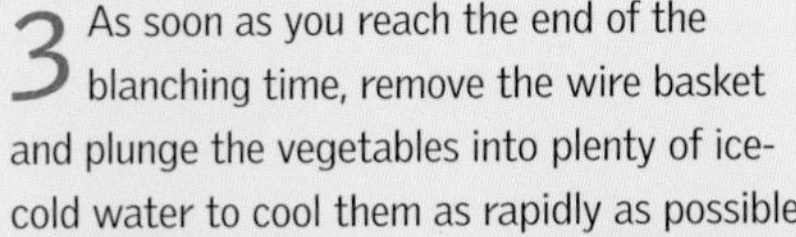

3 As soon as you reach the end of the blanching time, remove the wire basket and plunge the vegetables into plenty of ice-cold water to cool them as rapidly as possible.

4 Drain the vegetables and pack them in suitable portions in plastic freezer bags or containers; extract any air. Label the packages with the contents and the date and freeze them.

Drying vegetables and herbs

Drying, one of the most ancient forms of food preservation, has enjoyed a renaissance in recent years. Think of sun-dried tomatoes! If you don't live in a climate where sunshine can be relied on for drying, don't despair—there are other ways of achieving tasty results.

By removing moisture from your vegetables, you deny microorganisms a vital component. Without a supply of moisture, they can no longer grow—or spoil food.

Getting ready for drying

Prepare vegetables in the usual way for eating or cooking. Cut large or dense vegetables into pieces thin enough to allow thorough drying.

Blanching improves the storage life and quality for some vegetables. Blanch as if for freezing (see pages 118–19), but line the basket with muslin for chopped vegetables. Once blanched, dip the vegetables in ice-cold water briefly to stop them from cooking. Drain well and blot with a paper towel, then put them onto racks for drying. (Use racks, not solid trays, so air can circulate.)

Quick Tip

Making a rack

Stretch muslin or cheesecloth across a wooden frame to make a drying rack. You can use metal racks (such as cake-cooling racks), but line them with muslin to prevent produce from falling through or being marked by the grid.

Oven-dried tomatoes

Heat the oven to 200°F (95°C), and leave the door propped open slightly. The amount of time required for drying tomatoes depends on the variety you use. The higher the moisture content, the longer they'll need in the oven.

1 Put a single layer of sliced tomatoes on a baking tray lined with baking parchment, then put it in the oven.

2 The tomatoes take about 24 hours to dry; you may need to experiment. Check them often. When done, they should be leathery and exude no juice if squeezed.

3 Store dried tomatoes in olive oil in an airtight jar with a tightly fitted lid. Refrigerate and use within three weeks.

Microwaving herbs

A microwave is excellent for drying herbs. Because they contain little moisture in the first place, they are able to dry out without cooking. (However, microwave drying is not suitable for vegetables.) Adjust the timing to suit your microwave oven and use a high setting. If the leaves are not dry and brittle when removed, heat for another 30 seconds.

1 Lay the herbs on a piece of paper towel, then place a second piece on top. Heat in the microwave for two to three minutes.

2 Crumble the herbs and pack them into an airtight container with a tightly fitting lid. Keep in a cool, dark place for up to a year.

STORING AND USING DRIED VEGETABLES

Let dried produce cool down completely before storing it in airtight containers—glass jars with screw lids are ideal. Keep them in a cool, dark place; sunlight fades their color and destroys vitamins. Dried produce can keep for up to a year at 50°F (10°C); warmer conditions reduce their storage life.

Use dried vegetables by adding them to soups, stews, or other liquid-based dishes, simmering until they are rehydrated. Or soak them in water or stock for one to two hours and drain.

Drying methods

Gentle warmth is all that is needed for drying vegetables—enough to remove their moisture, not cook them. There are several ways of providing the warm, dry conditions necessary.

Sun. A reliably hot, dry climate with a minimum air temperature of 85°F (30°C) and humidity below 60 percent for several days is ideal. Bring produce indoors overnight to protect it.

Warm indoor space. A warm, dry place around the house, such as a shelf near the furnace, can be used.

Domestic oven. An oven is fine as long as you keep the temperature low.

Dehydrator. Proprietary dehydrators provide ideal drying conditions.

Drying times vary from six hours in a dehydrator to three to four days outside, depending on the temperature, humidity, and airflow. Check every four to five hours; stir the produce for an even result.

Whatever the method, when ready, peas, beans, or diced vegetables will be crisp. Tomatoes will be dry and leathery.

PREPARING VEGETABLES

Cut vegetables into slices, or dice, before blanching.

PRODUCE	PREPARATION	BLANCHING
Beans, French	Leave whole if small and slender; otherwise, slice like string beans.	2 minutes
Beans, string	Slice as if cooking.	2 minutes
Carrots	Slice ⅛-inch (3-mm) thick or dice.	3 minutes
Celery	Trim and slice across stalks ¼-inch (6-mm) thick.	2 minutes
Eggplant	Slice ¼-inch (6-mm) thick or dice.	3 minutes
Okra	Slice across ¼-inch (6-mm) thick.	Not needed
Onions and garlic	Peel and slice onions ⅛–¼-inch (3–6-mm) thick. Chop garlic finely.	Not needed
Peas	Shell.	1–2 minutes
Peppers	Remove seeds, white parts; slice into ¼-inch (6-mm)-thick strips.	Not needed
Tomatoes	Halve or quarter if small, or slice ¼–½-inch (6–12-mm) thick.	Not needed

Pickles, preserves, and condiments

There is something very satisfying about filling pantry shelves with jars of homemade pickles, preserves, and condiments. You don't need to be a first-class cook—just follow a few simple rules for guaranteed success.

Several preservation techniques come under the heading of "pickles and preserves," but the aim is the same—to prevent food-spoilage organisms (bacteria and fungi) from developing. There are two methods to stop microorganisms in their tracks: heat and chemicals. (The chemicals used are natural ones: sugar, vinegar, and salt.) However, not all methods are suitable for all vegetables.

This is a quick overview of the most common methods. Consult a cookbook for detailed instructions.

HERB-FLAVORED OILS

Bay, chives, oregano, sage, rosemary, tarragon, and thyme are all herbs ideal for adding flavor to a good-quality olive oil. Place sprigs of your chosen herb (or combination of herbs) into a sterilized bottle and fill with the oil. Seal the bottle and store it in the refrigerator for two weeks to allow the flavors to transfer to the oil. You can also add chilies or peeled garlic cloves. Strain the oil; refrigerate and use within three weeks. Herb-flavored oils are ideal for salads, breads, and sauces.

Canning

In the canning process, produce is packed into special jars, covered in syrup or water, and heated to sterilize it. The jar is then vacuum-sealed to prevent further contamination.

Canning is fine for fruit because their acidity prevents the growth of heat-resistant bacteria. However, most vegetables do not have enough acid, so botulism-causing bacteria can escape heat sterilization—and if eaten, the results can be fatal. Tomatoes are the exception because they have enough acid. It is essential to use proper jars fitted with rubber rings and spring clips or screw bands that enable a vacuum to form in the jar after heat processing.

Pickles, chutneys, sauces

Vegetables can be preserved by the acidity of vinegar. Pickles are made from vegetables that remain crisp, and

A simple no-cook mixed pickle

Pearl onions, green beans, peppers, and cauliflower are just a few of the vegetables that can be pickled. Soak them in a salt-water solution before adding them to vinegar—this firms them up and allows the vinegar to penetrate. Use a vinegar of at least 5 percent acidity (check the bottle label).

1 **Prepare the vegetables** as you would normally for a recipe, peeling them and trimming off the ends, if needed, then cutting them into florets, strips, or wedges.

2 **Soak the vegetables** for one to two days in a mixture of 1 pound (450 g) of salt and 5 quarts (4.5 liters) of water. Drain the vegetables, rinse them, and dry them thoroughly.

3 **Pack the vegetables** in an airtight container, leaving a 1-inch (2.5-cm) gap at the top; cover completely with a spiced vinegar (see box, above right) mixed with sugar. The quantity of sugar depends on the volume of vinegar and your taste. Place a layer of waxed paper or plastic wrap on top; then tightly secure the lid. You can store in the refrigerator for up to three months.

ADDING FLAVOR TO VINEGAR

Spiced vinegar adds flavor to pickles and chutneys. Add whole spices, such as cinnamon, cloves, mace, chilies, and peppercorns to a sterilized bottle filled with vinegar; infuse for two months and strain. Refrigerate it and use within three months.

Herb vinegars can be made by adding a handful of bruised sage, tarragon, rosemary, thyme, or mixed herbs to a sterilized bottle filled with white-wine or cider vinegar; infuse for six weeks and strain it. Refrigerate it and use within three months.

they are used raw or are cooked briefly. For the USDA guidelines on both pickling and canning, visit this website: www.foodsaving.com/canning–guide/.

Chutneys are made from a mixture of vegetables and fruit chopped small and cooked slowly until soft and the right consistency. Sugar is always used along with the vinegar so that chutney has a sweeter flavor than pickles. Beets, squash, pumpkin, peppers, and corn are suitable for making a chutney.

Sauces have a pouring consistency. They are cooked with spices and are sieved before sugar and vinegar are added. Tomato and red pepper sauces are two of the most popular types.

Jams and jellies

Fruit is the main component for jams and jellies, but you can also try carrots, pumpkins, or tomatoes. You can add herbs such as mint and rosemary to jellies, too. Jams and jellies use the preservative power of heat and sugar. Cook the produce in an open pan until soft; add sugar and boil the mixture until it reaches the setting point.

Part 2

THE VEGETABLES

6 Lettuce and greens

A simple salad will never be boring when your garden includes a bed of lettuce and greens. The variety of lettuce alone will inspire creative salad-making. However, you can supplement lettuce with a range of spicy and bitter greens, as well as vitamin-rich spinach and Swiss chard.

For delightful salad mixes, grow premixed mesclun blends or experiment with mixing your own for unique salads crafted to your taste. Easy-to-grow arugula, chicories, radicchio, and endive add a tantalizing flavor and colorful accent to salads—and they can be delicious heated, too.

Swiss chard comes in a rainbow of colors and is just one among a huge variety of lettuces and greens.

Lettuce

Great salads start with freshly picked lettuce. Plant a mixture of butterhead, crisphead, looseleaf, and romaine lettuce. With a little luck and experience, in most regions you can enjoy crispy, sweet lettuce for at least six months of the year.

PLANTING GUIDE

What to plant Seeds or transplants.

Starting indoors Sow seeds early to extend the season.

Site preparation Add organic matter to improve moisture-holding capacity.

When Frequent small sowings while weather is cool or in fall.

Spacing *Butterhead* and *romaine* Sow 6–10 inches (15–25 cm) apart, 18–24 inches (45–60 cm) between rows. *Crisphead* Sow 10–12 inches (25–30 cm) apart in rows 18–24 inches (45–60 cm) apart. *Looseleaf* Sow 1–2 inches (2.5–5 cm) apart; set transplants or thin seedlings to 4–6 inches (10–15 cm) apart.

How much For each person, two to four plants every two weeks.

Temperature alert
Lettuce grows best in cool conditions. For a summer crop in most areas, choose heat-tolerant varieties and plant in semi-shaded areas.

Planting

Soil Lettuce will grow best in rich, loose soil with a pH between 6.0 and 7.0. Spread a 2-inch (5-cm) layer of organic matter over the soil and work it in. Before sowing seeds, rake the bed to remove any clumps. When planting lettuce as a succession crop, you should add compost or a balanced organic fertilizer to renew soil fertility between plantings.

Planting Lettuce doesn't keep long after being picked, so make small, frequent sowings. Sow 10 seeds every two weeks (or weekly). You can sow seeds in garden beds, but it is usually better to sow seeds in pots or flats. The germination of delicate lettuce seeds can be disappointing. Seeds will germinate well in soil temperatures of 40–70°F (4–21°C), but poorly in warmer temperatures. Potted seedlings grow quickly and will be ready to transplant within three weeks.

Growing spring crops In cold-winter regions, cover planting areas with plastic to warm the soil a few weeks before planting. Sow seeds and plant transplants four to five weeks before the last expected spring frost.

Planting summer lettuce Lettuce may bolt to seed or develop a bitter taste in high temperatures and during long days. To counteract this, you can choose heat-tolerant and bolt-resistant varieties, plant lettuce in partial shade, or use shade cloth or shading devices. Add extra compost or leaf mold as you dig planting holes for transplants so the soil will retain more moisture. Mulch the soil surface. Water often, which may mean once or twice a day.

Interplant lettuce among tall crops, such as tomatoes, corn, and trellised melons or pole beans. In the humid South, even these measures probably

BEST OF THE BUNCH

'Buttercrunch' Dependable, heat-tolerant butterhead lettuce with buttery texture. 65 to 75 days from seeds.
'Summertime' Heat-tolerant crisphead variety that resists tipburn; medium-size heads. 70 to 75 days from seeds.
'Merlot' Batavian variety with savoyed, ruby-colored leaves; superb taste; heat tolerant. 50 to 65 days from seeds.
'Red Sails' Good looseleaf variety for hot conditions; frilly, reddish maroon outer leaves. 45 to 55 days from seeds.
'Rouge d'Hiver' Rounded leaves with reddish bronze blush; good harvested for baby leaves; buttery texture; tolerates heat and cold. 60 to 65 days from seeds.
'Salad Bowl' Frilly, deeply notched green leaves; resists bolting; sweet flavor. 45 to 50 days from seeds.
'Winter Density' Compact romaine; loose heads of dark green leaves; good for overwintering. 54 days from seeds.

When harvesting a full head of lettuce, use a sharp knife to cut cleanly at soil level. Discard damaged and dirty wrapper leaves after cutting.

won't be enough to produce high-quality lettuce once temperatures soar in May or June. Take a lettuce break and start planting again in September.

Planting for fall Plant lettuce in late summer for a fall harvest. Start with transplants if the soil is still hot. Time plantings so they will reach maturity at the time of the first expected frost date—from the frost date, count back the number of days to maturity; then add an extra week to compensate for slower growth in fall.

Succession planting doesn't work in the fall, so plant a large crop to provide a harvest that will last several weeks. After the first frost, lettuce will keep well in the garden. Cover plants with a row cover when temperatures below 25°F (-4°C) are predicted. These plants will survive temperatures close to 10°F (-12°C). Plastic tunnels provide even greater cold protection.

Overwintering lettuce Young lettuce planted at the time of the first fall frost will survive over winter with protection as far north as Zone 5. Plant in raised beds, which drain better and warm up faster in the spring. Cover the plants with row covers (even if your area has snow cover). Begin checking the plants when warmer conditions arrive in early spring. Harvest overwintered lettuce plants on the small side—they will bolt quickly in response to spring warmth and longer days.

Care

Watering Don't allow lettuce plants to dry out, especially in hot weather. Water whenever the top 2 inches (5 cm) of soil become dry. Don't water in the fall unless there is prolonged dry weather.

Fertilizing When you transplant lettuce, side-dress the plants with blood meal, sprinkling it in a strip 1 inch (2.5 cm) wide. For long-growing crispheads, you can spray with a liquid organic fertilizer once a month until the fall.

Harvesting

Begin harvesting baby lettuce leaves two weeks after setting out transplants. Pick leaves from the outside edges of plants. The plants will continue producing new leaves from the center.

In the fall, harvest entire heads—there won't be much new growth. Harvest head lettuce when the heads are firm. If they are elongated, they will taste bitter. If a long heat wave is predicted, harvest small heads to avoid bolting.

Storing Lettuce is best eaten just after you pick it. To store lettuce, refrigerate it unwashed (unless you need to rinse the leaves immediately after picking to cool them in hot weather, but then dry them) in plastic bags. Looseleaf lettuce will last only a few days; iceberg head lettuce will keep for up to three weeks.

PROBLEM SOLVER

Curled, distorted areas on leaves. Dislodge aphids with a jet of water. Spray persistent infestations with insecticidal soap. Protect new plantings with row covers sealed at edges with soil.

Twisted and stunted or mottled leaves. Destroy plants infected by viral diseases. (Aphids can spread them; see above.)

Holes in leaves. Look for caterpillars, slugs, or snails. For small caterpillars, spray BTK. Cover new plantings with row covers. For slugs and snails, use slug traps or spread a band of sharp sand or diatomaceous earth around plants.

Edges of internal leaves turn brown. A calcium deficiency causes tipburn of head lettuce; it is worst in hot weather. Choose resistant varieties. Undamaged areas of leaves are usable.

Silvery streaks on leaves. Spray plants with insecticidal soap, especially leaf undersides, to get rid of thrips.

Cottony growth on lower leaves. Plants infected by sclerotinia rot, a fungal disease, may collapse. Destroy them; try new plantings in raised beds.

Rusty lesions on leaves; slimy or wet rot at base of plants. Destroy plants infected by bottom rot, a fungal disease. Adding biofungicide to the soil may help prevent the disease in new plantings. Plant new crops in raised beds.

Quick Tip

Cool lettuce

For a supply of lettuce during hot summers (except in the humid South), plant some lettuce in containers on your patio so that you can move the containers into the shade on hot afternoons.

Types of lettuce

Try planting attractive ruffled leaf lettuce and deep red lettuce in beds with annual flowers. Add crisphead, romaine, looseleaf, and butterhead lettuce to your vegetable garden, and there will be a steady supply of ever-changing salad fixings.

▶ Crisphead lettuce

'Burpee's Iceberg' is the variety that brought crisphead lettuce to fame. Iceberg types have dense heads with nearly white leaves at the center.

Make sure you choose crisphead varieties intended for home gardening—varieties that have been developed for commercial production aren't suitable. Crisphead lettuce can be challenging to grow, especially in the humid South. For the best results, plant when at least two months of moderate temperatures will follow.

▼ Batavian lettuce

Batavian lettuce is a loosely headed type of crisphead lettuce that tends to be more flavorful than iceberg types. Many Batavian varieties have purplish or rosy outer leaves.

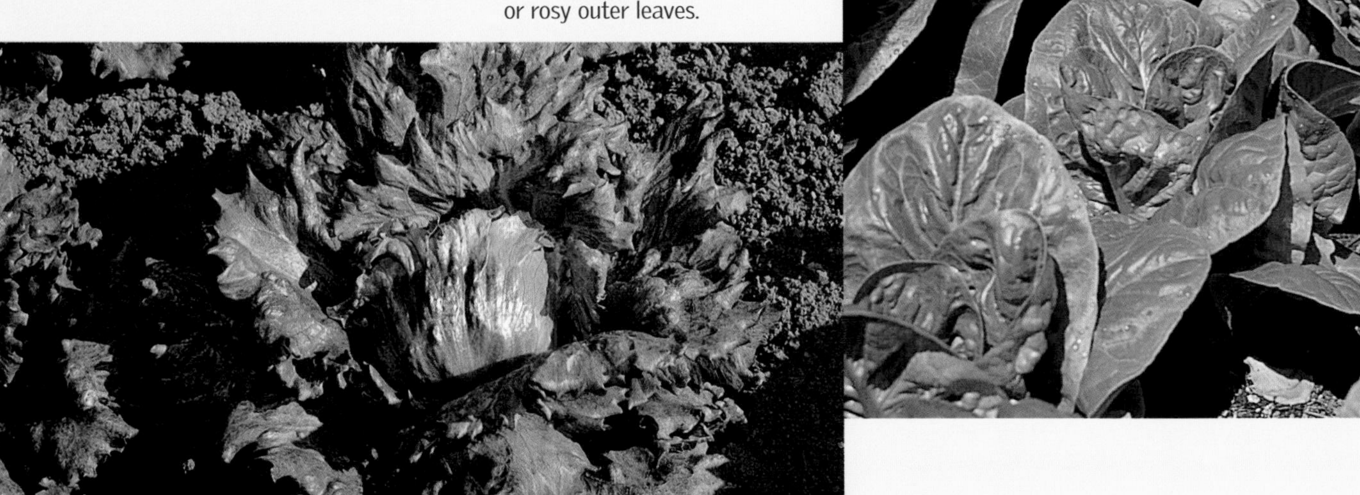

◄ **Looseleaf lettuce**

Looseleaf lettuce (leaf lettuce) is a catchall term for lettuce that doesn't form a head even when mature. The lettuce is easy to grow and the plants are beautiful, with a wide range of leaf colors and forms. Leaves may be smooth or crinkled, ruffled, notched, or curled. They range from green and yellowish green to reddish and bronze. Some varieties are ready to harvest 40 days or less after planting.

◄ **Romaine lettuce**

Also known as cos lettuce, romaine varieties will form upright heads of sturdy leaves that have thick midribs. The heads range from 8 inches (20 cm) to over 12 inches (30 cm) tall when ready for harvest. The leaves may be smooth or ruffled, and some varieties have red-tinged or red-speckled leaves. At its best, romaine lettuce is the sweetest of all lettuce.

▲ **Butterhead lettuce**

Buttery is the perfect way to describe the color and texture of the inner leaves of butterhead lettuce, which is also known as Bibb lettuce. This type of lettuce forms heads of loosely folded, soft leaves. Butterhead lettuce doesn't store or ship well, and it's often expensive to buy at the grocery store or farmer's market. However, butterhead lettuce isn't hard to grow, so it's a good choice for the home gardener. Heat-tolerant varieties are available.

Arugula

Young arugula, or rocket, leaves have a nutty or tangy flavor that becomes peppery and more piquant as the plants grow or the temperature rises. Use its soft, lobed leaves fresh from the garden in salads or pesto, or sauté it lightly.

PLANTING GUIDE

What to plant Seeds.

Site preparation Add organic matter to improve moisture-holding capacity.

When Early to mid-spring and again in fall in the South.

Spacing Sow seeds about 1 inch (2.5 cm) apart in rows 6 inches (15 cm) apart. Don't thin for baby leaves; thin to 6 inches (15 cm) for standard-size plants.

Intensive spacing Sow seeds lightly in a band 2–4 inches (5–10 cm) wide.

How much Per sowing, 1–2 feet (30–60 cm) of row per person.

Planting

Soil Loosen the top few inches of soil, and spread a 1-inch (2.5-cm) layer of compost over it and work it in. Rake smooth to remove clumps.

When to plant Sow arugula every one to three weeks from early to mid-spring (depending on how often you want to harvest). Arugula won't grow well in the summer except in Zones 4 and colder areas. If you want to try late-spring sowings, sow in the shade of tall crops.

Begin sowing again in August. In Zones 5 and 6, make succession sowings in a cold frame for a winter harvest. In Zone 7 and warmer areas, sow directly in the garden. In Florida and some other mild-winter areas, sow through April for a continuous harvest.

Care

Water regularly to prevent the flavor from turning too strong or hot. In arid climates, use a sprinkler when you water to prevent the tender leaves from drying up in the dry heat.

Allow a few plants to go to flower. The flowers are edible, and the seeds will self-sow. Let seedlings spring up in the garden where you want them to grow, or try carefully transplanting them from one spot to another.

Harvesting

Baby leaves will be ready to harvest within a few weeks of sowing. When the leaves grow to about 3 inches (7.5 cm) long, use a pair of sharp scissors to snip off the leaves 1 inch (2.5 cm) above the soil level. The plants will resprout.

If you allow leaves to grow large, sample them often to make sure their flavor is not too hot. Once the flavor turns, pull out the plants and move on to new plantings.

Wash arugula leaves by swishing them in a bowl or sink full of cool water. The leaves may require three or more washings to remove all traces of soil.

Storing For best results, use arugula immediately after picking. If you must store it, wash and dry the leaves thoroughly; then place them in a plastic bag in the refrigerator. They will keep for up to two days.

PROBLEM SOLVER

Small holes in leaves. Flea beetles may be attracted to arugula, especially during hot weather. Cover plantings with a row cover after sowing.

Temperature alert
Arugula grows best in cool conditions. Hot weather can change the flavor of arugula leaves from savory to "skunky."

Endive

Lend a new flavor to salads with endive. Curly endive has narrow, frilly leaves and a tender, tightly packed heart. Broad-leaved endive (or escarole or Batavian endive) forms an open rosette of broader, wavy leaves with a blanched heart.

PLANTING GUIDE

What to plant Seeds or transplants.

Starting indoors Sow seeds four weeks before the desired outdoor planting date.

Site preparation Add organic matter to improve moisture-holding capacity.

When Late summer in mild areas; in the North sow in the spring and again in summer.

Spacing Sow the seeds lightly; thin seedlings or set transplants 8–12 inches (20–30 cm) apart in rows 1–2 feet (30–60 cm) apart.

Intensive spacing Broadcast in wide rows; thin to 6 inches (15 cm) apart on centers for curly endive, 12 inches (30 cm) apart for escarole.

How much Per planting, two plants per person.

BEST OF THE BUNCH

'Batavian Full Heart' Widely adapted escarole. 80 to 90 days from seeds.
'Salad King' Curly endive with dark green leaves. 95 days from seeds.

Planting

Soil Spread a 2-inch (5-cm) layer of organic matter over the soil and work it in. Before sowing seeds, rake the bed well to remove all clumps.

When to plant In the South and other mild-winter areas, plant endive about three months before the first fall frost. Make succession plantings every two weeks until six weeks before the first fall frost.

In the North, sow seeds in spring two to four weeks before the last expected spring frost. You can sow seeds again about three months before the first expected fall frost.

Care

Blanching endive will help prevent bitterness. About one week before harvesting, gather the leaves into a clump and tie twine or slip a rubber band around them. Alternatively, you can cover the plant with an upended pot, with the drainage holes sealed to prevent light from reaching the plant. During cool fall conditions, blanching may not be necessary.

Endive can survive temperatures as low as 10°F (-12°C) with protection. Although broad-leaved types may suffer some damage, the undamaged parts will still be edible.

Extending the season In cold-winter areas, try a succession planting of endive from mid- to late summer. As temperatures fall below 32°F (0°C), protect the plants under plastic tunnels or cold frames. They should continue to grow slowly for harvest through fall and into winter. In wet conditions in fall and winter, endive is prone to rot.

Alternatively, dig up the plants and plant them in pots or buckets of moist sand. Set the pots in a cool root cellar and harvest as needed. They may last for two to three months.

Harvesting

Pick leaves, or cut heads 1 inch (2.5 cm) above ground level. Plants may resprout. Flavor will be sweeter after a frost, and blanched endive hearts are sweeter than outer leaves.

Storing You can store endive leaves in plastic bags in the refrigerator for up to 10 days.

Quick Tip

Inner beauty

The secret to enjoying endive is to pull away the outer leaves, which can be bitter, to reveal the light green, mild-flavored inner leaves.

Chicory

In North America, chicory is an exotic addition to the garden. European gardeners, however, have long appreciated the beautiful leaf forms and flavor of cultivated chicories, including sugarloaf, grumolo, Italian dandelion, and Belgian endive (or Witloof chiory).

PLANTING GUIDE

What to plant Seeds.

Site preparation Add organic matter.

When In early spring and three months or eight weeks before first frost, depending on type.

Spacing *Sugarloaf chicory* and *Italian dandelion* Sow seeds 2 inches (5 cm) apart in rows 18–24 inches (45–60 cm) apart; thin to 10–12 inches (25–30 cm) apart. *Grumolo chicory* and *Belgian endive* Sow seeds about 1 inch (2.5 cm) apart, 18 inches (45 cm) between rows; thin to 6–8 inches (15–20 cm) apart.

How much Per planting, two plants per person.

BEST OF THE BUNCH

'Sugarloaf' Forms a large tight, upright head. 90 days from seeds.
'Grumolo Chicory' Medium-size rosettes; dark leaves. 40 to 55 days from seeds.
'Italian Dandelion' Leaves resemble common dandelion leaves with white midribs. 40 to 55 days from seeds.

Planting

Soil Chicory grows best in rich, loose soil. Work in a 2-inch (5-cm) layer of organic matter. Rake the bed well to remove clumps before sowing.

When to plant Grow fast-growing chicories in the spring for an early harvest. If the weather turns hot before the crop is mature, the leaves may be bitter. Plant Belgian endive in spring, or in fall to winter in mild-winter areas.

For a fall harvest, sow sugarloaf chicory three months before the first fall frost; Italian dandelion and grumolo, six to eight weeks before the frost. Later sowings will overwinter (use protection in the North) for a spring harvest.

Care

Maintain even soil moisture at all times. Blanching improves the flavor. Sugarloaf chicory blanches itself naturally. For Belgian endive, lift four-month-old roots and cut the leaves back to 1 inch (2.5 cm). Plant the roots vertically in a box of moist potting mix and cover the tops with 10 inches (25 cm) of the mix or an upturned pot to keep out the light. Keep in a warm, dark place until the chicons form a month later. For other types, cover with a flower pot (with the drainage holes plugged) when leaves are 10 inches (25 cm) long. Leave it in place for a week. Don't cover wet plants or they may rot.

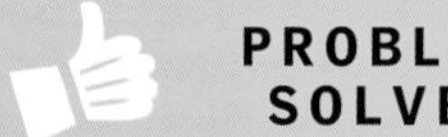

PROBLEM SOLVER

Ragged holes in leaves. Combat slugs and snails by handpicking, setting out slug traps, and spreading a band of diatomaceous earth around the plants.

Harvesting

Use the cut-and-come-again method to snip leaves, or cut whole heads. After a frost the outer leaves of sugarloaf chicory may be mushy, but you can use the heart. If you cut sugarloaf heads in late fall, leave ½ inch (12.5 mm) of the base intact; it may resprout in spring.

Storing Keep sugarloaf heads in the root cellar or refrigerator for a month. Keep leaves of other types in a plastic bag in the refrigerator for 10 days.

Chicory is a perennial, although it is often grown as an annual.

Radicchio

Red heads with white accents make raddichio an eye-catching crop. Chioggia types form rounded heads. Treviso raddichio looks like romaine lettuce, but it has pink-to-red leaves and a distinctive radicchio flavor—a bitter taste that mellows in cool conditions.

PLANTING GUIDE

What to plant Seeds or transplants.

Starting indoors For a spring crop, start seeds six to eight weeks before last expected frost.

Site preparation Add organic matter.

When Two to four weeks before last frost, or six weeks before first frost in hot-summer regions.

Spacing Sow the seeds 1 inch (2.5 cm) apart in rows 18 inches (45 cm) apart; set transplants or thin seedlings to 8 inches (20 cm) apart.

How much Up to five plants per person per planting.

BEST OF THE BUNCH

'Fiero' Elongated, uniform heads; plant in spring or fall. 66 days from seeds.
'Indigo' Fast-growing; tolerates heat; sow in spring or fall. 60 to 72 days from seeds.
'Leonardo' Large red heads; best for fall and winter harvest. 81 days from seeds.
'Red Verona' Heirloom variety; white stems and red leaves. 85 days from seeds.

Planting

Soil Radicchio grows well in most soils. Dig a 2-inch (5-cm) layer of compost into the soil before you begin planting.

When to plant Spring plantings are best in areas with long moderate spring weather or cool summers. Set out transplants two to four weeks before the last-expected spring frost; plant heirloom varieties afterward.

In hot-summer areas, plant six weeks before the first-expected fall frost. If winter temperatures don't drop below 10 °F (-12°C), you can plant seeds in the fall for a spring harvest. In cold-winter areas, cover plants with cold frames in fall.

Care

You should never allow the soil to dry out, because moisture stress leads to bitter flavor. Mulch to control weeds and keep the soil moist. Fertilize every three to four weeks with compost tea or a balanced fertilizer (but fertilize less or not at all in fall).

Heirloom varieties may produce a lot of green leafy growth with no sign of a cabbagelike head. To force them to produce a head, cut back the tops to 2 inches (5 cm) above soil level. The plants will resprout and form heads.

PROBLEM SOLVER

Brown tips on outer leaves. Tipburn is due to heat; change planting time of crops. Undamaged parts are edible.

Elongated core of head. The start of bolting, triggered by heat or long days. Adjust the planting time of future crops.

Heads slimy or rotten at base. Bottom rot occurs in wet conditions. Destroy infected plants. Replant in another spot with good drainage; water less often.

Harvesting

Heads may be ready six weeks after transplanting. Squeeze the heads at the base; they are ready to cut when firm. Remove the outer green leaves to reveal red heads. With protection, radicchio keeps in the garden for a long time; harvest as needed.

Storing Store radicchio heads in the refrigerator in a perforated plastic bag for up to three weeks.

Temperature alert
Grow radicchio when temperatures won't rise above 80°F (26.5°C). Too much heat can make it unpleasantly bitter.

Mesclun

Create simple, unique salads by growing mesclun, a mixture of mild, spicy, and bitter greens. Looseleaf lettuce is a common ingredient, but it's only the starting point. Mesclun is easy to grow in the garden, in containers, or in a cold frame.

PLANTING GUIDE

What to plant Seeds.

Site preparation Add organic matter; prepare a fine seedbed.

When Varies by region; plant mesclun at the same time as lettuce (see pages 128–29).

Spacing Sow seeds lightly in rows 3–6 inches (7.5–15 cm) apart, or broadcast them lightly over a wide row.

How much Plant an area that is 1–2 square feet (30–60 sq cm) per person.

Temperature alert
Most mesclun mixes grow best in cool weather. In summer heat, some bolt; others develop an unbearably hot or bitter flavor.

Planting

Soil Spread 2 inches (5 cm) of compost over the planting area and work it into the top several inches of soil. Rake the planting area to remove all clumps.

Planting prepared mixes The easiest way to grow mesclun is to buy packets of premixed seeds—many different blends are available. You should shake the packet well before sowing to make sure the seeds are evenly blended. You can sow mesclun mixes in rows, but broadcasting the seeds lightly over a wide bed will make harvesting easier.

Planting for custom harvesting
You can concoct your own custom blend by buying a packet of each of your favorite lettuce and greens. Mix a small amount of seeds from each packet in a container; then sow the mix in rows or broadcast. Bear in mind that some fast-growing greens may be more prevalent than others in your mix.

Another way to create custom blends is by planting each component in its own short row. Then you can harvest individual leaves in whatever combinations and proportions you like, depending on whether you want a milder or spicier mix.

Extending the season A mesclun mix will grow well in a cold frame. Sow seeds a week or two before the first expected fall frost. The mix will grow slowly and keep fresh for weeks. If your cold-frame space is limited, regard your planting as a treat for a fresh salad once a week. Sow seeds in furrows 1 inch (2.5 cm) apart. Make sure you vent the cold frame if temperatures inside rise to 65°F (18°C) or above.

Care

Monitor the soil moisture and water as needed to keep the top several inches of the soil moist. Fast-growing mesclun doesn't need fertilizing.

Harvesting

Mesclun will be ready for harvesting four to eight weeks after sowing. You should cut the plants 1 inch (2.5 cm) above soil level. In good weather conditions, the plants will resprout for an additional harvest, although the subsequent cuttings may be more uneven than the first. If the stand seems too crowded, pull out some plants entirely at the time of the first harvest to leave more space for regrowth. Harvest mesclun in cold frames on the small side—when leaves are 3–4 inches (7.5–10 cm) tall.

You should carefully wash the leaves to remove all dirt and grit. Handle the mix gently as you work because the leaves are fragile. Spread the leaves on a clean towel to dry after washing.

Storing Because some components of mesclun will keep better than others, it's best to harvest only as much as needed. You can store mesclun in plastic bags in the refrigerator for up to two days.

PROBLEM SOLVER

Ragged holes in leaves. Look for slugs and snails. Handpick and destroy them, set out slug traps, or spread a band of diatomaceous earth around your patch.

Plants slimy or rotten at base. Various diseases cause rot, especially in cold, wet weather. Destroy infected plants. Replant in raised beds to improve drainage.

To wash the leaves, swish them in a bowl of cool water and repeat as often as needed.

WHAT'S IN THE MIX?

Mesclun mixes can include everything from dandelion greens to fresh herbs and edible flowers.

Bitter greens Curly endive (see page 133), some leafy chicories (see page 134), and radicchio (see page 135) are excellent bitter greens for mesclun.

Cultivated dandelion greens are another bitter green worth trying (these seeds are often labeled as "French dandelions"). The leaves are broader and smoother than those of typical weedy dandelions.

Pick young dandelion leaves for best flavor. If your cultivated dandelions go to flower, pick off the flowerheads before they set seed, or they may become a weed problem in your garden.

Spicy greens Arugula (see page 132), mustard greens, and cress add a hot, peppery flair to mesclun. Mustard greens and cress are generally hardy and disease resistant. Sow and grow them as you would other greens.

Mild greens Looseleaf lettuces (see page 131) and spinach (see page 138) are common mild greens for mesclun. You can also add Asian greens, such as mizuna and tatsoi (see pages 182–83).

Corn salad Also known as lamb's lettuce or mache, this is an iron-rich green that makes a nice addition to mesclun. It forms low rosettes of spoon-shaped dark green leaves. Unlike other greens, corn salad leaves don't turn bitter even after the plants form seed stalks.

Corn salad germinates slowly, so sow it separately and add it to your mesclun at harvest. Soak seeds before planting to speed germination, and keep the seedbed moist. Thin plants to 3 inches (7.5 cm) apart.

Other greens You can clip young beet greens (see pages 194–95), Swiss chard (see pages 140–41), and kale (see page 178) leaves to add rich color and texture to a mesclun mix.

Herbs and flowers For a mix with more complex flavor, you can add a small amount of fresh basil (see pages 259–61), chervil, or fennel leaves (see page 257). Edible flowers, such as pansies, calendulas, nasturtiums, and 'Scarlet Emperor' runner bean blossoms, add contrast of color and form as well as flavor.

A mixture of greens from a variety of plants will provide a blend of colors, flavors, and shapes that will add spark and intensity to your salads.

Spinach

Tasty spinach is one of the most nutritious greens—and one of the most cold-tolerant. Some gardeners think spinach is hard to grow, but that's probably because they've sown spinach in the spring. For the best results, sow spinach in the late summer.

PLANTING GUIDE

What to plant Seeds.

Site preparation Add plenty of compost for this heavy feeder.

When In spring, sow seeds when soil can be worked and eight to ten weeks before first fall frost; sow four to six weeks before first fall frost for overwintering.

Spacing Sow the seeds 1 inch (2.5 cm) apart in rows 18 inches (45 cm) apart; thin seedlings 4–6 inches (10–15 cm) apart.

Intensive spacing Sow seeds 4 inches (10 cm) apart on centers.

How much Per planting, 2 feet (60 cm) of row, or five plants per person.

Planting

Soil Spread 1–2 inches (2.5–5 cm) of compost over the planting area. For extra nitrogen, you should also sprinkle blood meal (1–3 pounds per 100 square feet/0.45–1.5 kg per 9 m sq). Work the amendments into the top several inches of soil.

Planting in spring As the days gradually become longer in the spring, the plants will receive a signal to stop producing leaves and send up a flower stalk. When a warm spell occurs, the heat will provide even more of an "incentive" for the plants to send a stalk, causing them to bolt rapidly and leaf growth to decline. Because of this phenomenon, fall planting often gives better results than spring planting, even in cold-winter areas.

If you sow spinach in spring, sow as soon as the soil can be worked. In Zones 4 and colder areas, plantings in mid- to late spring may be successful if there are no unseasonal hot spells.

Planting in fall For the main fall harvest, plant spinach 8 to 10 weeks before the first hard frost. You'll need to water the bed every day to keep the soil cool enough for germination (seed germination will be poor if soil temperature exceeds 80°F/26.5°C). Make succession plantings until four to six weeks before the first fall frost. The final sowing will produce small plants that will overwinter well.

In mild-winter areas, you may be able to harvest right through winter. In Zones 6 and 7, cover plants with a row cover to extend the harvest through December.

In harsh-winter areas (Zones 4 and colder areas), wait until the first hard freeze; then mulch the young plants with 6 inches (15 cm) of chopped leaves. Cover the mulched bed with a tarp. Remove the tarp and mulch in early spring. The plants will begin growing immediately and produce a heavy crop.

Care

Mulching will keep the soil cool and prevent it from spattering onto leaves when it rains. If your spinach doesn't

Temperature alert
Temperatures above 75°F (24°C) and longer days in late spring can cause bolting. You can choose more heat- and cold-tolerant savoy types.

Quick Tip

Cool success
Spinach can be hard to start growing in the spring—heat and long days can spoil the crop. Try sowing in late summer for a fall harvest, and learn how to overwinter spinach for a spring harvest.

HEAT-TOLERANT SPINACH SUBSTITUTES

If you yearn for fresh spinach—a cold-tolerant plant—in the summer, try growing a spinach substitute. New Zealand spinach and Malabar spinach are heat-tolerant plants with leaves that have a spinachlike appearance and flavor.

New Zealand spinach is a frost-tender plant with branching, sprawling stems. Its seeds are dried fruit with multiple seeds in each. Soak the seeds in warm water before sowing to speed germination. In short-season areas, start seeds indoors in spring and transplant them outside after danger of frost is past. In long-season areas, sow seeds directly in the garden from mid-spring through early summer. Set plants 12–15 inches (30–38 cm) apart in rows that are about 2 feet (60 cm) apart. Harvest the young tender leaves at the growing tips (cut about 3 inches/7.5 cm of stem and leaves) and use them as you would spinach. Plants will resprout, and the harvest should continue until the first hard frost.

Malabar spinach is a tender vine that produces thick, glossy, succulent leaves and thrives in warm, humid conditions. Malabar spinach is not fussy about soil conditions, but won't withstand moisture stress. In the North, start the seeds indoors eight weeks before the last spring frost. Plant transplants outside when all frost danger is past, setting the plants 3 feet (90 cm) apart along a trellis or at the base of a fence in full sun (light shade is beneficial in hot southern gardens). In the South, direct seeding is also an option. Leaves and shoots will be ready to harvest 70 to 80 days from planting. Cut leaves and young stems as desired to eat and as needed to keep the vigorous vines under control.

seem to be growing vigorously, you can feed the plants weekly with a solution of balanced fertilizer.

Harvesting

For the best flavor, harvest spinach early in the morning. You can pick individual outer leaves, cut whole plants 1 inch (2.5 cm) above the soil surface, or pull up whole plants and trim the roots.

Swirl the leaves in a bowl or sink full of water to remove all soil and grit. Remove the leaves, replace the water, and repeat as often as needed.

Storing Refrigerate unwashed spinach in a plastic bag for up to one week. Spinach freezes well.

Smooth-leaved spinach is the best type to grow if you want spinach for a salad.

Spinach leaves may be savoy (crinkled), semi-savoy, or smooth.

BEST OF THE BUNCH

'Indian Summer' Savoy leaves; slow to bolt; disease resistant. 35 to 40 days from seeds.
'Melody' Big, semi-savoy upright leaves; disease resistant. 42 days from seeds.
'Olympia' Smooth, dark green leaves; slow to bolt; excellent productivity and flavor. 45 days from seeds.
'Space' Smooth leaves that are good for planting in spring and fall; freezes well. 35 to 40 days from seeds.
'Tyee' Semi-savoy leaves; vigorous, good for planting any time of year; mildew resistant. 45 days from seeds.

PROBLEM SOLVER

Small round holes in the leaves. Flea beetles cause this damage. To prevent holes, cover planting areas with a row cover immediately after sowing seeds.

Irregular lines or blotches on leaves. Leafminers (larvae of small flies) tunnel through the leaves. If damage is minor, pick and destroy damaged leaves. Cover future plantings with row cover. Check under the covers occasionally—pupae in the soil can emerge and attack plants.

Yellow patches on leaves. If you find gray or purple mold on leaf undersides, the problem is downy mildew. Pull up and destroy infected plants. Replant in a new location in raised beds to improve drainage; plant mildew-resistant varieties.

White areas on leaves. Leaf scorch is due to heat and moisture stress. Mulch and water more often. Time plantings to avoid hot periods.

Stunted plants with mottled leaves. Mosaic disease is caused by a virus that is spread by aphids. Destroy infected plants. Cover new plantings with a row cover to prevent aphids.

Swiss chard

A relative of beets and spinach, Swiss chard is also called leaf beet and spinach beet. Swiss chard is full of vitamins, and there are many varieties in an exciting range of color combinations, making this crop a great candidate for any garden.

PLANTING GUIDE

What to plant Seeds.

Site preparation Add organic matter to poor soils.

When Two to three weeks before last expected spring frost, again in mid- to late summer. In mild-winter areas, plant in fall, too.

Spacing Sow seeds 2 inches (5 cm) apart in rows 1–2 feet (30–60 cm) apart; thin plants 6–12 inches (15–30 cm) apart.

How much Three to five plants per person.

Planting

Soil Well-worked fertile soil needs no special improvement. However, if your soil is sandy or infertile, you should dig in a 2-inch (5-cm) layer of compost before planting.

Extending the season In short-season areas, you can sow some Swiss chard seeds as soon as the soil can be worked. In some years, seedlings won't survive through sudden temperature dips, but when they do, you'll get an early start on the harvest.

Succession sowing may work best in the South—plants can become tough during hot conditions. Sow late-spring sowings in partial shade. New plantings will produce more young tender leaves than older plants.

Care

Thinning Like beet seeds, Swiss chard seeds are dried fruit, each containing several seeds. Seedlings will emerge in clusters; when plants are a few inches tall, thin each cluster to one plant.

Watering Maintaining soil moisture is critical for Swiss chard. Moisture stress is the factor most likely to cause bolting. Check soil moisture regularly, and water whenever the top several inches of the soil becomes dry. In hot-summer areas, mulch in early summer to conserve soil moisture.

This striking variety of Swiss chard has vibrant red veins running through the bright green leaves.

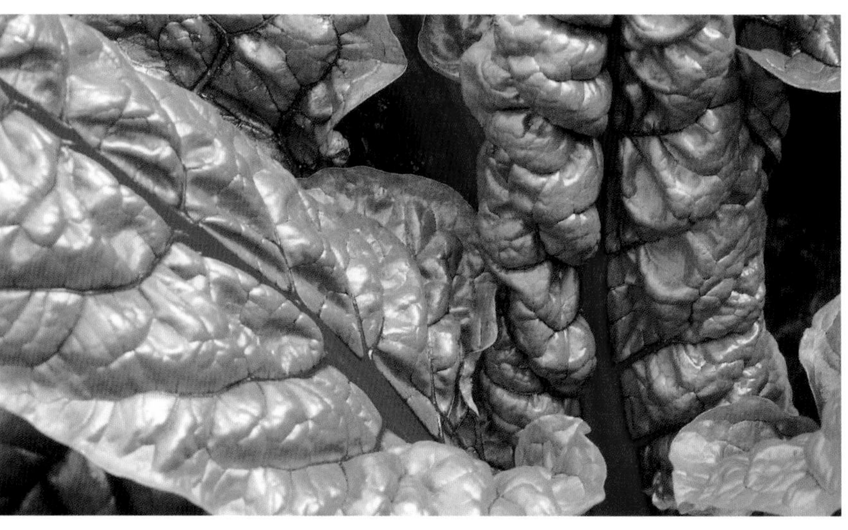

BEST OF THE BUNCH

'Bright Lights' Yellow, orange, pink, violet, and white stalks; mild flavor. 60 days from seeds.

'Golden' Yellow stems turn to a rich golden shade as plants mature; yellow-green leaves; excellent mild flavor. 55 to 60 days from seeds.

'Rhubarb Supreme' Large red stems, with dark green leaves with red veins. 50 to 60 days from seeds.

Fertilizing If you plan to harvest from the same sowing through the season, fertilize once a month with a balanced fertilizer or side-dress with soybean or alfalfa meal (1 pound per 10 feet/0.45 kg per 3 m of row).

Unique foliage and eye-catching colors will make Swiss chard an ideal addition to an ornamental garden.

Harvesting

You can cut all the stems on a plant at once, but leave 2 inches (5 cm) of the plant at the base intact. The plant should resprout, producing a fresh crop of young leaves. You can also harvest individual Swiss chard stems; pick them from the outer edges of the plant. Baby Swiss chard leaves are excellent for adding to a mesclun mix. In general, don't let leaves grow too large—leaves longer than 10 inches (25 cm) may have poor flavor.

If the outer leaves turn yellow or the stalks seem tough, remove them from the plant and compost them—they won't have good eating quality. Remove any flower stalks that appear.

Storing Refrigerate Swiss chard stems and leaves unwashed, but use them as soon as possible. If you harvest a large quantity at one time, you can freeze it (see pages 118–19).

Harvest the leaves using a sharp knife. Use the leaves as you would spinach; you can steam or stir-fry the stems.

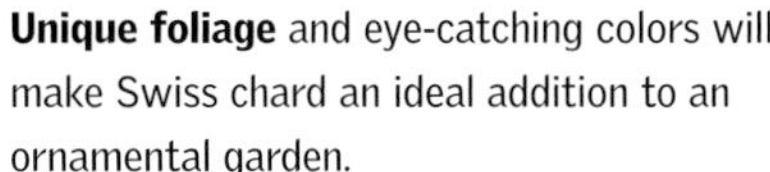

PROBLEM SOLVER

Ragged holes in leaves. Look for slugs and snails. Handpick the pests, set out traps, and surround the plants with a band of diatomaceous earth.

Irregular lines or blotches on leaves. Leafminer larvae tunnel through the leaves. Cover plants early in the season to prevent adults from laying eggs on them. Pick and destroy damaged leaves.

White areas on leaves. Leaf scorch is due to heat and moisture stress. Mulch the soil and water more frequently during hot periods.

Yellow leaves and stunted plants. Root-knot nematodes may attack Swiss chard, especially in the South. Replant in a different location. If nematodes are a problem throughout the garden, solarize the soil to kill the nematodes.

Quick Tip

A winning green

Swiss chard handles heat better than most salad greens. Many gardeners find that a spring planting of this crop will last through summer and into fall without bolting or losing quality.

7 Peas and beans

Prolific and easy to grow, peas and beans belong in every garden. These nitrogen-fixing legumes need less fertilizing than other crops and can even help to improve the garden soil. Plant a sampling of shelling-pea varieties, snap peas, and snow peas in the spring. Once the weather warms, it's bean-planting time, and the choices are almost unlimited. Enjoy a bounty of green beans, wax beans, limas, favas, shelling beans, and more. Some gardeners like fast-producing bush varieties, while others prefer long-season pole varieties—you may want to try both.

Peas start the season in spring and are ready to harvest as early as two months after sowing.

Peas

Plump pea pods sweeten the dreams of gardeners in the spring. Once you've tasted the incomparable sweetness of homegrown peas, you'll find yourself checking your pea vines daily for more of these sugary treasures.

PLANTING GUIDE

What to plant Seeds.

Site preparation Work in organic matter; prepare in fall for early spring planting.

When As soon as the ground can be worked in spring; again in late summer to fall.

Spacing Sow seeds in 6-inch (15-cm)-wide furrows, 1 inch (2.5 cm) deep; thin seedlings to 2–4 inches (5–10 cm) apart.

Double rows Sow seeds 1 inch (2.5 cm) apart in two rows 6 inches (15 cm) apart; allow 2½–3 feet (75–90 cm) between double rows; thin seedlings 2–4 inches (5–10 cm) apart.

How much *Shelling peas* Allow 20 feet (6 m) of row per person (for freezing and fresh eating). *Snow peas and snap peas* Plan 1–2 feet (30–60 cm) of row per person for fresh eating.

Temperature alert
When temperatures soar, check your pea plants daily. Harvest pods extra young, because quality may decline quickly in the heat.

Planting

Soil Because peas are legumes, they don't need supplemental nitrogen and will grow well in average garden soil. Try to prepare your pea bed in fall. Work about a ½-inch (12.5-mm) layer of organic matter into the soil. Shape the soil into a raised bed so that it will drain better and warm up faster in the spring.

When to sow Peas will grow best in 50–70°F (10–21°C), although healthy vines can grow and produce pea pods at higher temperatures. Peas are a spring and fall or winter crop in most parts of the United States and Canada. However, gardeners in the mild-summer areas of the West and North can harvest peas right through the summer.

The spring harvest Succession sowing doesn't work well to spread out the pea harvest. In the cool conditions of early spring, the first sowing will grow slowly. Later sowings will catch up to the early one, and all the plants will mature at once. Instead, sow several varieties—a selection of early, midseason, and late—all on the same day.

This strategy can spread the harvest over a period of six weeks or more. However, in the South, because the weather turns hot quickly, the spring harvest may last as little as two weeks.

The multi-variety sowing strategy will require a fair amount of space, but when you pull out the vines after harvest, you will open up space for warm-season crops, such as cucumbers, peppers, and squash.

Wide rows and double rows For better yields and a more uniform planting, try sowing peas in a wide row or double row. For wide-row planting, open a 6-inch (15-cm)-wide furrow about 1 inch (2.5 cm) deep down the bed, and broadcast the seeds lightly in the furrow. Set up a trellis along the center of the wide row. Peas will grow up both sides of the trellis. Thin as needed.

For double rows, open two narrow 1-inch (2.5-cm)-deep furrows about 6 inches (15 cm) apart. Sow the seeds 1 inch (2.5 cm) apart and cover. Set up a trellis to run between the two furrows. Thin as needed.

Care

Watering Avoid overwatering the young plants. Cold, wet soil will slow root development and may lead to disease problems. When the plants start flowering, water once weekly. Apply as much water as necessary to moisten the soil 9–12 inches

(23–30 cm) deep. You should make sure you deliver the water at soil level, close to the base of plants, and avoid wetting the foliage.

Trellising Nearly all pea crops will benefit from trellising, even varieties that grow only 3 feet (90 cm) tall. Trellising is essential for tall varieties. Create trellises by using twine strung from sturdy stakes or chicken-wire fencing using lengths of metal pipe as stakes. You can insert pea brush—twiggy prunings from trees and shrubs—among the vines as a traditional way to support peas.

Harvesting

Because the sugars in pea seeds start turning to starch immediately on picking, homegrown peas will be at their sweetest just after picking. The critical factors for all types of peas are to harvest before the pods become too mature and to harvest often to encourage continued production.

Shelling peas will be ready for harvest when they are bright green and full, almost rounded. The same is true for petit pois; however, the pods will be only about half the size of regular shelling peas. Snap peas are at their best and ready to harvest when 2–3 inches (5–7.5 cm) long, with small seeds. Snow peas should be flat, bright green, and crisp.

For all types of peas, make sure to harvest before pods begin to lose their sheen. As harvest draws near, visit the pea patch daily to sample a few pods of each variety. Harvest thoroughly when the peas are at the right stage, and then check again a few days later to see how the crop is progressing.

Storing You can store unwashed fresh peas in the refrigerator for two to three days. Keep in mind that they continuously lose sweetness, so you should eat them as soon as possible.

To prepare batches of snow peas for freezing, blanch pods for one minute in boiling water; snap peas, for two minutes. Then chill the peas rapidly in cold water and freeze. You can blanch shelled peas in boiling water for two minutes, chill, and freeze.

PROBLEM SOLVER

White, powdery coating on leaves. Some varieties are highly susceptible to powdery mildew, a fungal disease that likes high humidity with warm days and cool nights. Pull out and destroy infected vines. Replant resistant varieties. Grow peas early in the season to avoid the disease. Weekly sprays of sulfur or baking soda may prevent the disease.

Mottled, distorted leaves and pods. Viral diseases, including pea enation virus, bean yellow mosaic, and pea streak virus, cause these symptoms. Pull up and destroy infected plants. Replant using resistant cultivars. Don't touch wet plants. Cover plants with row covers as long as feasible to prevent aphids from reaching plants; they spread diseases.

Plants turn yellow and die. Root rot or Fusarium wilt are often the cause. Grow future crops in well-drained soil, practice crop rotation, and plant resistant varieties.

Distorted growth and sticky sap. Look for clusters of aphids (small, round green insects), especially at growing tips. Wash plants with a strong stream of water or spray with insecticidal soap.

BEST OF THE BUNCH

'Green Arrow' Small dark green peas on semi-bush plants. 70 days from seeds.
'Maestro' Shelling pea with 9 to 11 peas per pod; 30-inch (75-cm)-tall plants; tolerates powdery mildew. 60 days from seeds.
'Oregon Giant' 5-inch (12.5-cm) snow pea pods remain sweet even when the seeds are visible; disease resistant; 3-foot (90-cm)-tall vines. 70 days from seeds.
'Oregon Trail' Multiple disease resistant; shelling peas on bush-type plants. Up to 70 days from seeds.
'Super Sugar Snap' Thick-walled snap peas on 5-foot (1.5-m)-tall vines; resistant to powdery mildew and pea enation virus. Good for winter crops in mild areas. 64 days from seeds.

Regardless of the type of pea, harvest the pods before they become overly mature, while they can still provide the best flavor.

Types of peas

All peas—shelling peas, snap peas, snow peas, and petit pois—need the same conditions and care. When prime for picking, the tiny seeds of flat snow peas will barely bulge in the pods, while the meaty snap pea pods will have a smooth, rounded profile.

▼ **Shelling peas**

This is the classic garden pea. There are early, mid-season, and late varieties, as well as bush and tall types. Harvest pods when they are full of round seeds but before the pods lose their sheen and bright color. Some varieties produce petit pois, small peas in pods that are only 2–3 inches (5–7.5 cm) long.

▲ **Snow peas**

Crispy, sweet snow pea pods are superb served raw in salads or lightly stir-fried. At their prime, snow pea pods will be 2–3 inches (5–7.5 cm) long, and the tiny seeds will be barely bulging in the pod. Snow pea pods may have fibrous strings, similar to string beans, which are best removed before eating raw or cooked. Snap off one end of the pod and pull the string to remove it. Snow peas are available in both bush and tall varieties.

▲ **Snap peas**

Snap peas offer you the choice of eating the pods when they are young, like snow peas, or allowing the pea seeds inside to enlarge partially before harvesting and eating them, pod and all. The pods are meatier than snow pea pods. It's best not to let the seeds grow as large as peas for conventional shelling, or their sweetness may be lost. Eat snap peas raw or lightly steamed. Most snap pea varieties grow 3 feet (90 cm) high or taller.

ASPARAGUS PEAS

The plant is a member of the legume family, but it belongs to a different genus from either peas *(Tetragonolobus purpurea)* or beans (*Lotus tetragonolobus).* This plant is beautiful, with a low, bushy form, and with its gray-green leaves and brick-red flowers. The asparagus pea makes a great addition to either a flower garden or ornamental kitchen garden.

In mild climates, plant the seeds directly in the garden during the first part of June. After about two months of growth, the plants will begin to produce pods that have four raised ridges, or wings, with frilly edges.

Northern gardeners should begin seeds indoors in the spring and transplant the seedlings to containers. Set the containers outside when the weather is consistently warm. To extend the harvest when fall comes, you can bring the containers inside a greenhouse or a sunny room of your house.

The entire pod is edible when picked young (about 1 inch/2.5 cm long). Older pods will be stringy. The flavor of the pods is similar to asparagus, and they're best cooked as you would asparagus spears—steam lightly, drain, add a little butter, and enjoy. The plants may bear pods for as long as three months if you keep picking them regularly.

Bush beans

For beginners, bush beans are the easiest beans to grow. Bush beans quickly yield a crop on compact plants. Almost all types of beans—for example, snap beans, yellow beans, lima beans, and soybeans—are available as bush varieties.

PLANTING GUIDE

What to plant Seeds.

Site preparation Ensure site is well drained.

When After danger of frost is past; succession plantings until 60 days before first fall frost.

Spacing Sow seeds 1–2 inches (2.5–5 cm) apart in rows about 1½–2½ feet (46–75 cm) apart; thin to 6 inches (15 cm) apart.

Intensive spacing Sow 6 inches (15 cm) apart on centers.

How much Per planting, 5 feet (1.5 m) of row.

Planting

Soil Beans will grow well in average soil. Plant a cover crop the preceding fall (see pages 36–37), dig it into the soil in spring, and let it break down several weeks before planting.

Sowing tips Always sow fresh bean seeds, because seed quality declines quickly. Presoaking bean seeds can cause the seeds to split. Instead, wet paper towels with water, wring them out, then wrap the towels around your seeds and keep them in a jar for a day before planting.

Check the soil temperature before you sow. The minimum temperature that is necessary for green bean seed germination is 55°F (13°C), but 60°F (15.5°C) is better. Bean seeds can rot in cold, damp soil. However, broad beans are the exception to this rule and need to be sown early, while the soil is cold, as soon as it can be worked. You should sow all varieties 1 inch (2.5 cm) deep.

As legumes, beans will provide some of their own source of nitrogen. You can buy inoculant—a bacteria-containing powder necessary for nitrogen fixation—for beans from a seed supplier. Using inoculant may lead to better growth and production in new gardens. However, it will not be necessary if you plant in an area where beans or peas have grown sometime in the past few years.

Succession planting A crop of beans on bush bean plants tends to mature all at once. To spread the harvest, make succession sowings about every two weeks. For later sowings, when the soil is warm and dry, sow seeds 2 inches (5 cm) deep in a furrow to keep them moist. Stop sowing about 60 days before the first expected fall frost.

Care

Bush beans will usually have few problems, as long as you plant them in healthy soil and care for them properly. However, they are susceptible to the same pests and diseases as pole beans (see pages 150–51).

Thinning When you thin bean plants, don't be concerned about precise spacing. Try to preserve only vigorous plants and thin out all the weak plants. Weak plants are more prone to disease, and once disease gets a foothold, it can spread to healthy plants, too.

Fertilizing You should be cautious about fertilizing beans. Too much nitrogen can cause excess leaf growth at the expense of pods. In addition, succulent foliage is more attractive to pests. Your crop may not need any fertilizer, but if you are concerned about nutrient deficiencies, you can try a foliar spray of kelp extract.

Harvesting

As the time of maturity approaches, sample some beans for readiness. The pods should be crisp enough to snap in two at the center when bent, but pod tips should be flexible and bend without breaking. Seeds inside the pods should be tiny. Don't let the pods become overly mature, because their quality will decline fast and the plants will stop producing pods.

For fast, easy harvesting, pull up an entire plant by the roots, turn it upside down, and pull off all the pods. The total yield will be a little lower, but you'll save time and the strain of stooping to pick the beans from low-growing plants. Compost the plants (or destroy them if they show any signs of diseases or insects).

To harvest selectively, use two hands to pull the pods off the plants without breaking the stems or damaging the foliage. Never harvest when plants are wet, or you may spread disease.

For dried beans, wait until much of the foliage has died; the beans should rattle loosely inside the brown or blackened pods. Shell the beans and separate them from the chaff. (For additional harvesting information on special types of beans, such as soybeans and lima beans, see pages 152–55.)

Storing Most types of fresh beans will last for up to one week in the refrigerator. To freeze bean pods, snap off the ends. Blanch small pieces for two minutes in boiling water; whole beans for three minutes. Chill in ice water; then drain and freeze (see pages 118–19). Frozen beans will keep for almost a full year.

If you want to store dried beans, you can test their moisture content by putting several beans in a closed glass container; check 24 hours later. If you see condensation inside the jar, the beans need additional drying before long-term storage. Keep dry beans in airtight jars in a cool, dry place.

BEST OF THE BUNCH

'Black Jet' Black soybeans are good for eating fresh or dried; a vigorous grower. 85 days from seeds.
'Contender' Green bean; grows well in cool conditions and tolerates heat; good for freezing. 45 to 50 days from seeds.
'Derby' Smooth pods stay tender up to 7 inches (17.5 cm) long; produces over long period. 57 days from seeds.
'Dwarf Bees' Runner bean; up to 2 feet (60 cm) tall. 80 days from seeds.
'Envy' Bright green edamame (soy) bean; early bearing. 75 days from seeds.
'Fordhook No. 242' Productive; resists heat and adaptable. 75 days from seeds.
'Maxibel' Stringless filet beans, 7 inches (17.5 cm) long. 50 days from seeds.
'Nickel' Tender filet bean with straight 4-inch (10-cm) pod; concentrated harvest in a short period. 60 days from seeds.
'Pencil Pod' High-yielding yellow wax bean with black seeds; tolerates heat. 52 to 60 days from seeds.
'Romall' Dark green Italian-type bean with rich flavor. 55 days from seeds.
'Royal Burgundy' Purple snap bean; good in cool conditions. 60 days from seeds.
'Windsor' Classic broad bean variety for spring or fall crop. 75 days from seeds.

Bush beans don't require trellising as pole beans do—and they suffer fewer pest and disease problems, making them easier to grow.

Pole beans

Great taste and texture—plus harvesting over a long season from a single planting—motivate many gardeners to choose pole beans instead of bush beans. Pole beans are also space-saving and easy to pick because they grow vertically.

PLANTING GUIDE

What to plant Seeds.

Site preparation Choose a well-drained site; average fertility is fine.

When After danger of frost is past in spring; in mild-winter areas, plant again in late summer for fall harvest.

Spacing *Fence or trellis support* Sow 3–4 inches (7.5–10 cm) apart; thin the seedlings to 6–9 inches (15–23 cm) apart. *Pole support* Sow six seeds at the base of each pole; thin to two to three plants per pole.

How much Per person, 10 plants.

BEST OF THE BUNCH

'Fortex' Green beans up to 11 inches (28 cm) long; filet-bean quality; pick young or as a shelling bean. 60 days from seeds.
'Kentucky Blue' Straight green pods with excellent flavor, uniform vines. 60 to 65 days from seeds.
'Kentucky Wonder Wax' Butter-colored pods, brown seeds; grows well in cool climates; harvest as snap beans and shelling beans. 60 to 65 days from seeds.
'Romano' Flat pods with nutty flavor and crunchy texture. 60 days from seeds.
'Scarlet Emperor' Runner bean with sweet, rich flavor; up to 10 feet (3 m) tall; scarlet-orange flowers. 75 days from seeds.

Planting

Soil Good drainage is important, but average fertility is fine, because—as with bush beans—beans produce some of their own nitrogen. However, for best results, grow a cover crop the preceding fall. Work it into the soil in spring and allow it to break down before planting the beans.

Or you can work in a shovelful of compost at each planting hill where you plan to provide some type of pole support. Allow several weeks for the compost to finish breaking down—unless it is already fully mature.

Supporting the vines Pole beans can stretch as high as 15 feet (4.5 m) if you provide a tall support. You can set up poles or a trellis of stakes and heavy twine before you plant. Many gardeners use tepees for pole beans; however, it can be difficult to harvest bean pods from the upper areas of a tepee. You should set individual poles 6–12 inches (15–30 cm) apart.

Pole beans grow well on a chain-link or wood fence if you run twine from the top of the fence down to the ground for the vines to wind around. Or use cylinders of wire fencing, such as tomato cages, to support the vines.

Sowing seeds All of the sowing information for bush beans supplied on page 148 also applies to pole beans. However, to ensure that your pole beans get off to a strong start, wait until the soil temperature is 65–70°F (18–24°C), if possible.

Care

Watering Keep the top 2 inches (5 cm) of soil moist, but don't let the soil get soggy. Moisture is especially important for germination and, once flowers appear, for seed formation in pods. Once the plants are established, apply a 2–3-inch (5–7.5-cm) layer of grass clippings or straw to conserve soil moisture, especially if you live in a hot-summer area. In a mild-summer area, a 1-inch (2.5-cm) layer should be sufficient.

Fertilizing Because pole beans produce a crop over a prolonged period, they'll benefit from some

Quick Tip

Seed sense

When choosing varieties, think about your climate. If you have long, hot summers, disease and heat tolerance are important. However, if your growing season is short, look for varieties that produce well in cool conditions.

Harvest the beans while they are still young so that the plant continues to produce more flowers and pods.

Many types of beans, including snap, filet, and lima beans, are available as tall, vining cultivars.

supplemental fertilizing, but avoid supplying too much nitrogen. Use a foliar spray of kelp, or side-dress with compost every three weeks.

Ending the season When pole bean plants start to decline, don't try to revive them. Harvest any last pods you can find, and pull out the plants. Don't compost the vines unless you're certain they are free of pests and diseases. (If you live in a mild-winter area, you can start a new planting in late summer or early fall for a fall harvest.) Dismantle your trellis or tepees. Discard the twine and store the poles for next year.

Harvesting

With pole beans, it's important to pick pods on the young side (except for dried beans), because when pods mature on the plant, it signals the vine to stop producing more flowers and pods. Follow the harvesting guidelines for various types of beans described on page 149 and pages 152–55.

PROBLEM SOLVER

Skeletonized leaves. Mexican bean beetle larvae are the problem. Cover young plants with row covers to exclude beetles. Plant early to avoid the heaviest beetle populations. Handpick beetles and larvae. For a large plot, release predatory wasps or spined solider bugs. Destroy plants after harvest, and plant resistant cultivars. Interplant cilantro to attract natural predators. Every seven to ten days, spray neem on undersides of leaves.

Holes in leaves and pods. Bean leaf beetles and larvae feed on plants in midsummer and later. Plant crops early; cover later crops with a row cover. In the future, apply beneficial nematodes at planting time to control larvae.

Pale speckles on leaves. Spider mites are usually worst in hot, dry conditions. Spray plants with insecticidal soap.

Leaves turn yellow and die from bottom to top of vine. This is typical of fungus-related Fusarium root rot. In the future, practice crop rotation. In areas with consistent summer sun and heat, kill the fungus by solarizing the soil in summer for six weeks.

Brown and black blotches on pods. Bacterial blight is the cause, especially during warm, wet weather. Pull up and destroy infected plants. For future crops, use copper sprays to prevent the disease.

Stunted plants with yellowed leaves. Look for aphids or root-knot nematodes. Aphids (small, round insects) will form clusters on plants, especially at leaf tips. Spray with insecticidal soap or insecticidal oil. If aphids are not present, check for galls on roots, a sign of nematodes. Pull up diseased plants and dispose of them. Practice crop rotation. Drench the soil with beneficial nematodes.

Types of beans

There's no end to the possibilities when growing beans. Choose beans based on whether you want to grow bush-type plants or vining pole beans, and whether you want to harvest immature pods, enlarged bean seeds (shell beans), or dry beans.

▼ Shelling and dry beans

The terms "shelling beans" and "dry beans" refer to the stage at which beans are picked, not a specific type of bean. You should pick beans for shelling when the seeds have enlarged but are still soft. The pods will be green but no longer edible. When bean seeds are mature, the pods will turn brown or black and the dry beans will rattle inside. After picking, separate the seeds from the pods and chaff.

▲ Snap bean

Snap beans, green beans, and string beans are different names for the same crop. The name string bean arises from the tendency of pods to develop a "string" along the ridge of the pod, which won't soften even after cooking. However, if you pick pods when they're still young, most won't have a noticeable string. The beans that you pick from these plants are actually immature pods. Many bush-type and pole varieties are available. Some varieties produce purple bean pods, but they turn green when cooked.

◀ French bean

French beans are a gourmet snap bean. Also called filet beans, these varieties are bred to produce thin, long bean pods that have a sweet flavor and delicate texture. It's important to harvest French beans when they are less thick than a pencil. These beans are best eaten fresh; they may not freeze well.

▼ Italian bean

These beans are the same species as regular string beans, but the wide, flat pods are meatier and have a distinctive flavor. Pole and bush varieties are available.

▶ Wax bean

Wax beans is a misnomer, because there's nothing waxy about these yellow snap beans, and, in fact, they are actually crisp. Wax beans are available as both bush and pole varieties. Be sure to harvest them young—once the pods become lumpy, their texture is rubbery and unpleasant. When these beans are at their prime, the pods are covered with tiny hairs. Certain varieties are good as shell beans or as dry beans.

Types of beans (continued)

▼ Runner bean

The perennial runner bean *(Phaseolus coccineus)* is grown as an annual in the United States and Canada. Most varieties are pole beans, but some short varieties are available. Runner beans are also called fire beans (because of their bright red or orange-red flowers) and white Dutch runner beans. The vines grow 12–15 feet (3.7–4.6 m) tall. The seeds are shaped like lima beans, and they can be black or black mottled with dark red. Pick the pods young to eat whole, or use the seeds like lima beans in cooking.

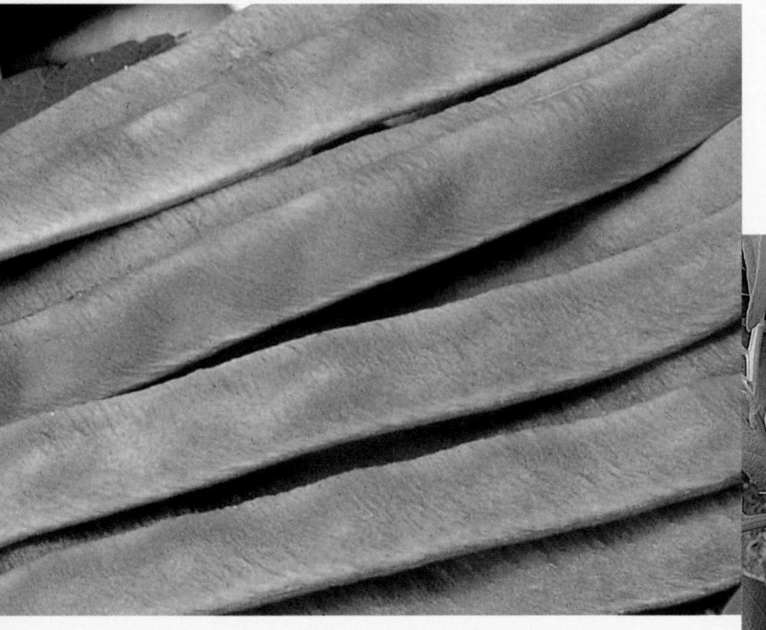

► Fava bean

Fava beans *(Vicia faba)*, or broad beans, grow better in cool conditions and can withstand frost. Plants grow 3–4 feet (90–120 cm) tall, with pods 12 inches (30 cm) long. Pods at the bottom of the plant ripen first. Plant fava beans early in spring for a harvest before the weather turns hot. In Zones 9 and 10, plant in fall for a winter harvest. The beans may have a tough seed coat; if so, slip it off before or after cooking. If you are of Mediterranean, African, or Southeast Asian descent, you may develop a serious reaction to eating fava beans called favism. Consult a doctor to test your susceptibility.

▼ Asparagus bean

Asparagus beans ***(Vigna unguiculata sesquipedalis)*** are also called yard-long beans or dow ghok. Although they grow much longer, for the best quality, harvest the pods when they are 12–18 inches (30–45 cm) long.

Pods bear 10 to 20 seeds each and have a sweet, beany flavor. The vines sport pale blue flowers; the vines are heavy and vigorous, so supply a sturdy trellis. Or you can try interplanting them with a tall corn variety and let the vines twine up the cornstalks. These beans are real heat lovers and will not grow well north of Zone 6. Wait until two weeks after the last expected frost before planting them.

▲ Soybean

Here's a mild and nutty-flavored bean that you can use in any dish that calls for dry beans. High in protein, soybean ***(Glycine max)*** is the only legume that provides all nine essential amino acids. In general, grow soybeans as you would bush beans. Soybeans produce a taproot, so they are drought tolerant. Also, soybeans tend to be free of pest and disease problems. Harvest and store soybeans as you would other dry beans. Edamame is another term for green soybeans.

8 The onion family

Many a memorable recipe begins with onions and garlic sautéed in olive oil. When those dishes are prepared with homegrown onions and garlic, the results are even more delectable. It's easy to tuck onions, garlic, and scallions into your garden.

Leeks, an onion cousin, take a little more space and effort, but the superb flavor of their white fleshy stems is an excellent reward. Delicate chives are equally at home in a vegetable garden bed, herb garden, or flower border.

Onions are sweet, mild, or pungent; white, yellow, or red; and globe- or torpedo-shaped or flattened.

Onions

Full sun, fertile soil, and a specific period of daylight are necessary for onions to form sizable bulbs, depending on the type of bulb. It's possible to stretch these planting guidelines, but your harvest may be less than ideal.

PLANTING GUIDE

What to plant Seeds, sets, or transplants.

Starting indoors Sow 8 to 12 weeks before planting outdoors.

Site preparation Add compost.

When Spring, fall, or late winter.

Spacing *Seeds* Sow ½ inch (12.5 mm) apart in rows that are 12–18 inches (30–45 cm) apart; thin to 4–6 inches (10–15 cm) apart. *Sets or transplants* Plant 4–6 inches (10–15 cm) in rows 12–18 inches (30–45 cm) apart.

Intensive spacing 4–5 inches (10–12.5 cm) apart on centers.

How much *Sweet slicing onions* 3–5 feet (90–150 cm) per person. *Long-keeping storage onions* 10–15 feet (3–4.5 m) per person.

Quick Tip

Seeds and sets

Buy fresh seeds each year; they don't last in storage. Buy sets from a reliable garden center or mail-order catalog. Sets that haven't been stored properly may bolt early, producing poor yields.

Planting

Soil You can tuck onions among other plantings, but they may not do well in heavy soil or dry, sandy soil. To provide good drainage, make a raised bed 4 inches (10 cm) high (see pages 22–23). To prepare a bed for onions, spread an 1½-inch (3.75-cm) layer of compost over the soil and dig it in.

When to plant In the North, plant long-day onions in early spring, so plants will produce plenty of leaves before bulb formation.

Gardeners in mild-winter areas can plant short-day onions in the fall or winter. Fall-planted onions may go dormant during winter, then grow again in early spring, producing bulbs in late spring and early summer.

Gardeners in areas where winter temperatures stay above 0°F (-18°C) can plant intermediate-day onions in fall. In areas with lower winter temperatures, plant in late winter.

Sowing seeds outdoors For spring plantings, sow seeds as soon as the soil is workable. In late summer and fall, time plantings so that the seedlings become established before a dormant period. However, they should not grow larger than pencil thickness—or they may bolt in spring if exposed to prolonged cold temperatures.

Keep the soil moist at all times as the seedlings emerge. They can't break through even a thin soil crust.

Seedlings and transplants Move germinated seedlings to a cold frame, preferrably at 40–50°F (4.5–10°C). Feed them with plant-starter fertilizer every two to three weeks. To prevent foliage from flopping, trim the tops to 2 inches (5 cm) when the seedlings are 4–5 inches (10–12.5 cm) tall.

Plant transplants from a supplier as soon as they arrive. If you raised your own transplants, plant them out in the garden as soon as soil temperatures reach 40°F (4.5°C) in spring. Set the transplants 1–1½ inches (2.5–3.75 cm) deep. Water them in with plant-starter fertilizer or compost tea.

ONION DAYS

Short-day onions require days that are 11 to 12 hours long before the plants stop producing new foliage and start forming bulbs. Intermediate-day onions don't start to form bulbs until days are 12 to 14 hours long. Long-day onions won't form bulbs until the day is at least 14 hours long. A few varieties of onions are day-neutral and will grow well in all regions.

Open a furrow and space the sets evenly along the length, 4–6 inches (10–15 cm) apart, with the pointed end up.

Carefully fill the furrow so that the tips of the sets are barely visible or just below the soil surface.

Planting multiplier onions

Multiplier onions—Egyptian onions, shallots, and potato onions—have a different growth cycle. Plant bulbs or sets in fall; the technique is similar to planting garlic (see pages 166–67). Space bulbs 5–6 inches (12.5–15 cm) apart. In cold-winter areas, plant them 2–4 inches (5–10 cm) deep and cover with several inches of mulch. In milder areas, plant them just below the soil surface and apply a light mulch.

Care

Watering and weeding Water often but lightly at soil level. Avoid wetting the foliage, which can lead to disease. Cultivate gently to remove weeds without damaging the roots. When the soil is warm, apply a mulch of chopped leaves or grass clippings to suppress weeds and conserve moisture. Pull back the mulch when bulbing begins to allow them to mature.

Fertilizing Water the plants with liquid kelp or a balanced fertilizer every three to four weeks from three weeks after planting. Stop fertilizing six to seven weeks before harvesting.

Harvesting

Begin pulling onions as soon as the bulbs are large enough for your needs. As the crop matures, the foliage will turn yellow and flop over. When most of it has flopped, dig out the crop.

In dry conditions, cure the plants in the garden; it takes about one week. Lay the plants in overlapping rows, so the foliage of one row shades the bulbs of the row beneath. If the sun is hot, or if rain is threatening, move the plants to an airy shed, garage, or attic. For multiplier onions, harvest and cure the crop when half the tops die back.

Storing Clip the roots and tops, but leave ½–1 inch (1.25–2.5 cm) of the dry neck (don't cut the tops if you want to braid the onions). Onions with thick necks won't store well, so use them right away.

Store onions at 32–40°F (0–4.5°C) and low humidity. Put them in mesh bags, knotting the bag between each onion, or braid the tops. Hang the braids or bags. Inspect the onions periodically; remove any rotting bulbs. You can also store loose onions (not in bags) in the refrigerator.

PROBLEM SOLVER

Yellowed and wilting leaves. Onion bulbflies lay eggs at the base of plants; the onion root maggots tunnel into the bulbs. Roots will rot. To avoid problems, use row covers from planting until late July. Hard-skinned cultivars are less prone to damage. Remove and destroy all plant refuse at the end of the season.

Rusty stripes on leaves. Thrips feed on the leaves, especially during hot, dry weather. Spray the plants with either insecticidal soap or neem.

Mold on plants; rotting plants. Many fungal and bacterial diseases can affect onions in the humid South. To reduce problems, plant onions in raised beds and sow disease-free seeds in the garden, or start your own transplants.

Young plants bolt. Premature bolting can occur if sets are stored at 40–50°F (4.5–10°C) before planting; large onion transplants are exposed to prolonged temperatures below 45°F (7°C); root damage occurs during cultivation; or there is moisture or nutrient stress. Although the bulbs will be edible, they will not last in storage.

Doubled bulbs. Two half-bulbs may form at the base of one plant if it has suffered from moisture stress.

BEST OF THE BUNCH

'Ailsa Craig' Large sweet onion; long-day variety, but may do well in the South; stores well. 105 days from seeds.
'Prince' Long-day onion with yellow skin; stores well. 106 days from seeds.
'Red Creole' Short-day, red-fleshed onion; keeps well. 95 to 190 days from seeds.
'Super Star' Day-neutral variety; good in all regions; good salad and slicing onion; does not store well. 109 days from seeds.
'Walla Walla' Sweet, white intermediate-day onion. 115 to 300 days from seeds.
'Yellow Granex' Classic short-day sweet onion. 182 days from seeds.

Types of onions

Common garden onions *(Allium cepa)* are available in a wide assortment of varieties. Choose varieties by day-length requirement, color, size, and sweetness. It's also fun and easy to grow multiplier onions, such as shallots or the intriguing Egyptian, or walking, onions.

◀ Red onion

Red-skinned onions may have white, red, or bicolored flesh. Sweet red Bermuda-type onions are excellent slicing onions that can be served raw in salads, sandwiches, and on hamburgers. Some long-keeping red varieties are available, but it can be difficult to get red onions to develop large bulbs.

▶ White onion

Large, sweet white onions are delicious slicing onions for fresh use. Other varieties of white onions produce small bulbs that are an excellent choice for boiling, creaming, and pickling.

▲ Yellow onion

Yellow storage onions are good all-purpose onions and are especially well suited for cooking in soups and stews. Many yellow varieties are easier to grow than other types of onions because they have a tougher skin that is more resistant to attack by insects or disease organisms.

▼ Shallot

Shallots are a special type of multiplier onion, and they are often prized by cooks. Shallot bulbs have a coppery skin and a tapered shape. There are some varieties available from seeds. Each shallot bulb you plant will produce a cluster of up to a dozen baby bulbs. Usually, each bulb consists of two cloves. The flavor of shallots is described as a mixture of sweet onion and garlic.

◄ Egyptian onion

Egyptian onions have several other names, including tree onions, walking onions, and top-setting multiplying onions. The plants form small purplish red bulblets at the top of tall stems. These bulblets aren't seeds—they are tiny bulbs, up to 1 inch (2.5 cm) long. The bulbs are good for pickling or in soups, and they keep well in storage.

If you leave Egyptian onion plants to their own devices, the heavy head of bulblets eventually bends over to the ground, where the bulbs will root and a new cluster of shoots will appear. Let the plants spread, or pick individual bulblets and plant them where you want new plants to grow. 'Catawissa' is a variety that sends out shoots from the cluster of bulblets, sometimes producing two tiers of bulblets. Buy Egyptian onion plants from specialty nurseries or mail-order suppliers.

Chives

Bushy clumps of bright green chives *(Allium schoenoprasum)* are a welcome addition to both kitchen and flower gardens. A sprinkling of chopped chives will lend a light touch of onion flavoring to salads, soups, and cooked vegetables.

PLANTING GUIDE

What to plant Seedlings, divisions, or potted plants.

Starting indoors Sow clusters of seeds in individual pots.

Site preparation Add compost to planting holes.

When Spring, late summer, fall.

Spacing Set seedling clumps, divisions, or potted plants about 8–12 inches (20–30 cm) apart.

How much One plant per person for culinary purposes.

GARLIC CHIVES

For a taste of mild garlic in the form of chives, try garlic chives *(Allium tuberosum)*. They are as easy to grow as chives. Older leaves are coarse, so trim them even if you don't need them. New, tender leaves will resprout quickly. You can grow garlic chives for their white flowering ornamental quality; in this case, don't trim the foliage. Cut off flowerheads before they go to seed to prevent weedy seedlings.

Planting

Soil Dig individual holes for each plant about twice the width of the root ball. Mix the removed soil with a handful of compost.

Starting seedlings Always use fresh seeds; sow several seeds per pot. Keep them in dark conditions at 60–70°F (15.5–21°C) until the seeds eventually germinate. Move the seedlings under lights or to a cold frame. The clumps of seedlings will be ready for planting outside in four weeks. They may grow slowly, but they should be ready for regular harvesting by the second year.

Planting outdoors Chives are hardy up to Zone 3, and they are evergreen in mild-winter areas. When you plant seedling clumps, divisions, and potted plants, make sure they are set at the same depth as they grew previously. Water well after planting.

Care

Chives need little care once they're established. Mulch them with grass clippings to suppress weeds and give a little nitrogen boost. Chives often die back during hot summer weather. However, if you keep them watered, they will send out new growth when temperatures cool down.

Dealing with flowers Cut flowers in late spring before they set seed to avoid a weed problem. (You can add the flowers to salads.)

Dividing In the fall, cut back the tops and dig up the plants for dividing. Pull each plant apart into small sections and replant. You should divide the plants every three years to keep them growing vigorously.

In cold-winter areas, extend the harvest by potting up divisions in 8-inch (20-cm) pots. Leave the pots outdoors until after the first hard freeze; then move them to a cool basement or garage. After three months, bring the pots indoors to a sunny windowsill to stimulate new growth. Snip the leaves as needed until you can replant the chives outdoors.

Harvesting

Use sharp scissors to clip chive leaves, leaving about 2 inches (5 cm) of basal growth when you cut. Harvest as needed when plants are growing vigorously. In hot-summer areas, stop harvesting in June; resume harvesting in September.

Storing Rinse chive leaves and use them right away. Try storing chopped chives in the freezer in ice-cube trays (see pages 118–19).

Scallions

Any young garden onion *(Allium cepa)* can be harvested as a scallion, salad onion, or green onion. However, bunching onions *(Allium fistulosum)* produce scallions with beautiful color and form, plus a richer, less biting flavor than garden onions.

PLANTING GUIDE

What to plant Seeds, transplants, or divisions.

Starting indoors Sow seeds 10–12 weeks before the last expected spring frost.

Site preparation Add compost.

When Spring, summer, or fall.

Spacing Sow the seeds thinly. Thin seedlings, divisions, and transplants to 6 inches (15 cm) apart (non-clumping types, about 2 inches/5 cm apart).

How much *Clumping types* One clump per person. *Non-clumping types* For each person, 20 or more plants.

BEST OF THE BUNCH

'Evergreen Long White' Hardy; plant in spring or fall. 60 to 120 days from seeds.
'Ishikura Improved' Can grow 2½ feet (75 cm) tall; sow in trenches and hill stems to keep white. 50 days from seeds.
'Red Baron' Bright red stem bases, green leaves; best for spring. 65 days from seeds.
'Tokyo Long White' Non-clumping type; long stalks. 65 to 95 days from seeds.

Planting

Soil Loosen the soil several inches deep and enrich individual planting holes with compost. Or you can work compost into the top several inches of soil and shape a low raised bed.

Starting seeds indoors You can grow scallions from seeds like onions (see pages 158–59), but it's often easy to sow seeds outdoors.

Planting In cold-winter areas, sow seeds or set transplants out in spring for a summer harvest. Sow seeds or set transplants out in late summer and fall for a fall and winter harvest in Zone 6 and warmer areas. If you sow seeds outside in summer, plant the scallions in the shade of a taller crop so the soil isn't too hot.

Treat non-clumping scallions as an annual crop. However, after your initial harvest from clumping types, you should replant portions of clumps to perpetuate your crop. In subsequent years, the clumps may send up flower stalks and go dormant. After a rainy period and when temperatures turn cooler, these plants will resprout and produce new stems.

In mild-summer areas, scallions will grow slowly in midsummer, but they will generally come back strongly in late summer and fall.

Care

Mulch the plants with grass clippings to conserve moisture and provide nitrogen. If plants need a growth boost, you can water them with a plant-starter fertilizer.

In Zone 5 and colder areas, mulch plants with straw to protect them from cold. Or pot up divisions and bring them indoors to a cool, bright spot; replant outdoors in early spring.

Harvesting

You can begin harvesting scallions when they are about pencil thickness. Keep harvesting them as needed for fresh eating. You will need to uproot the plants with a trowel rather than pulling them, because the stems break very easily.

With clumping varieties, remove as many stems as you need from a cluster and replant the clump. If you want to increase the number of clumps, separate single shoots and plant them individually. To prevent disease problems, change the location of clumps when you replant, bearing in mind a rotation plan with other members of the onion family.

Storing Scallions will not keep well for longer than about one week in the refrigerator.

Leeks

It takes a little special care to establish leeks in a bed, but their beautiful white stalks add a unique mellow flavor to a wide variety of dishes, including soups, stews, and salads. Leeks have long been a favorite of European gardeners—for good reason.

PLANTING GUIDE

What to plant Transplants.

Starting indoors Sow seeds 10–12 weeks before outdoor planting date.

Site preparation Prepare a bed with deep, loose fertile soil.

When In mild-summer or cold-winter areas, plant in spring. In the South and other mild-winter areas, you should plant in late summer and fall.

Spacing Set the transplants 4–6 inches (10–15 cm) apart, with 12–18 inches (30–45 cm) between rows.

How much For each person, grow 10 plants; more if a prolonged harvest is planned.

Planting

Soil Leeks don't require much special preparation. Spread a 2-inch (5-cm) layer of compost over the planting area and work it into the soil.

Starting seeds indoors Sow seeds in containers that are at least 3 inches (7.5 cm) deep. Keep the containers at 55–75°F (13–24°C)—the temperature in which the seeds will germinate best. You can feed the developing seedlings a solution of plant-starter fertilizer every two weeks.

You should begin hardening off the plants for a spring planting about one week before transplanting. For summer and fall crops, move the seedlings to a protected spot shortly after they germinate.

When to plant In the North, plant leeks in spring for a late summer and fall harvest, setting transplants out in the garden about four weeks before the last expected frost.

In the South and West (Zone 8 and warmer areas), you can plant leeks in late summer or early fall. Gardeners in temperate areas along the Pacific Coast can plant leeks almost any time of the year.

Planting methods One easy way to plant leeks is by using a dibble to open a deep individual planting hole for each seedling. Or you can open a trench approximately 6 inches (15 cm) deep. Set the transplants in the trench, covering the roots and the stem base with soil. As the leeks grow, gradually fill the trench with soil, straw, or chopped leaves.

Care

Watering Leeks require frequent watering. If you hill up soil around the plants (see below), don't water the hills directly, or you will wash away the soil. Instead, let the water pool between the rows and soak into the soil. To avoid disease, try not to water the foliage or stems directly.

Blanching If you plant leeks in a trench, once it is filled, hill up soil around the stems as they grow to blanch them. This keeps the stems white and tender. Be careful not to push soil up to where the leaves branch out from the stalk—otherwise the leeks will be difficult to clean after harvesting.

Even if you plant leeks in deep holes, you can still hill up additional soil around the stems as they elongate. As an alternative to hilling, you can slip a 6-inch (15-cm) length of plastic pipe around each leek to shade the stem.

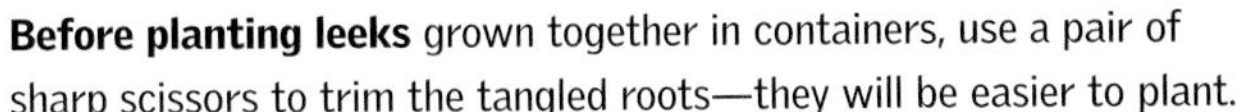

Before planting leeks grown together in containers, use a pair of sharp scissors to trim the tangled roots—they will be easier to plant.

Plant the leeks in individual holes made by a dibble; alternatively, plant the leeks in a trench (you won't need to trim their roots).

Fertilizing You can apply a balanced fertilizer or compost tea about once a month.

Harvesting

Use a garden fork to loosen and unearth leeks when they reach the size you desire. If you have a large planting, you can harvest some early, slender baby leeks. Many varieties will eventually produce stems up to 2 inches (5 cm) in diameter.

You may discover that some of the leeks you harvest have produced small corms or buds at the base. You can separate these "buttons" from the main roots and plant them for an additional harvest.

Storing In most areas of the country, leeks will keep well in the garden into winter. Cover them with a deep straw mulch to protect them from frost.

After digging leeks, you should trim the roots and cut back the green tops. Leeks will keep for several weeks in the crisper drawer of a refrigerator or in moist sand in a root cellar (see pages 116–17).

Before storing leeks, make sure you trim the roots and cut back the green tops to about 3 inches (7.5 cm).

Succulent leek stems and leaves require a lot of moisture. Make sure you water leeks well as they grow.

BEST OF THE BUNCH

'Bleu Solaise' Blue-gray leaves; stems up to 2 inches (5 cm) across; extra hardy. 105 days from transplanting.

'King Richard' Fast-growing; long stalks; good for harvest of baby leeks or full-size leeks. 75 days from transplanting.

'Lincoln' Good as baby leeks or full-size leeks. 50 to 100 days from transplanting.

Garlic

Fall planting sets the stage for a successful garlic harvest. Plants sit dormant or grow slowly through the winter. Once the weather warms up in spring, the plants produce plenty of straplike green leaves that will feed the developing bulbs.

PLANTING GUIDE

What to plant Single cloves.

Site preparation Plant a cover-crop in spring or enrich soil with organic matter before planting.

When In fall, four to six weeks before first expected fall frost.

Spacing *Softneck* Set cloves 6–8 inches (15–20 cm) apart in rows 12 inches (30 cm) apart. *Hardneck* Set cloves 4–6 inches (10–15 cm) apart, with 12 inches (30 cm) between rows.

Intensive spacing Set cloves at standard in-row spacing in rows 6–8 inches (15–20 cm) apart.

How much Per person, about 10 feet (3 m) of row.

Planting

Soil Pick an area in the garden with excellent winter drainage, because cloves can rot in cold, wet soil. To improve drainage, you can hill up soil into a raised bed. Garlic is shallow-rooted, so you will need only a 4-inch (10-cm)-high bed (see pages 22–23).

Planting a green manure crop in spring and digging it into the soil in late summer are good preparation for garlic. If you plan to plant in a spot where another vegetable crop grew during the summer, spread a 2-inch (5-cm) layer of compost over the planting area and work it into the soil.

Planting cloves Separate the cloves from the bulbs just before planting. Discard any damaged, diseased, or puny cloves. (Big cloves produce big bulbs.) Open a planting furrow or, if your soil is loose, just push the cloves into the soil to the proper depth.

In mild climates, set the top of the clove 1–2 inches (2.5–5 cm) below the soil surface; in cold-winter areas, you should plant them 2–4 inches (5–10 cm) below the soil. Water them thoroughly and mulch with straw or chopped leaves. Mulch lightly in areas where cloves will sprout in the fall. However, you should mulch more heavily in areas where soil normally freezes during the winter.

Spring planting Garlic is hardy to Zone 3, but in areas with very harsh winters, even mulched beds of garlic may freeze. Try planting in spring instead, as soon as you can work the soil. Harvest will take place in early fall. Yields will be lower than for fall-planted garlic, but some harvest is better than none.

Care

Watering After the first watering in fall, you may not need to water garlic

GARLIC TYPES

Garlic is available in hardneck (or topsetting) and softneck varieties. Softneck garlic, the type used for garlic braids, is adaptable to many conditions. The bulbs form multiple layers of cloves, and they will last well in storage.

Hardneck garlic grows well in cold-winter areas. The bulbs produce one layer of cloves, which are larger than those of softneck and easier to peel. The cloves have a stronger flavor than softneck. Plants develop a false flower stalk in late spring or early summer. (Cut it off just above the level of the surrounding foliage for best yield.) Hardneck garlic does not keep long in storage.

Quick Tip

Buying cloves

Local farmers might sell garlic at farmer's markets in the fall, or check for a mail-order supplier in your region. For a range of flavors and a longer-lasting supply in storage, try growing both softneck and hardneck garlic.

plants again until spring, depending on the weather. In mild-winter areas, check soil moisture twice a week once the tops sprout; you should water when the top 2 inches (5 cm) of the soil have dried out.

In the spring, you should keep the plants well watered, but not soggy. During the last month of growth, cut back on watering so the bulbs can mature. The roots will still need some moisture, but it's best if the soil stays dry to the depth of the bulbs. Stop watering altogether about two to three weeks before the plants should be ready to harvest.

Weeding Because garlic has upright foliage that doesn't shade out weeds, maintain a weed-suppressing mulch around them. Apply the mulch when planting, and keep it in place until the last few weeks before harvest (but pull back the mulch if it seems to be holding moisture around the bulbs). Cultivate as needed to keep the stand clear of all weeds.

Fertilizing If your soil isn't rich enough to support strong foliage growth, begin fertilizing the plants in spring when growth starts. Spray plants with a complete fertilizer and kelp, or side-dress with blood meal or alfalfa meal once every two weeks. Stop fertilizing by late spring, or you may ruin the flavor and quality of the developing bulbs.

Harvesting

You can start harvesting garlic in the South around mid-May; in the North, mid-July. Yellowed, dry lower leaves are a sign that the garlic bulbs are approaching maturity. In general, plants have only four to six green leaves left at harvesttime; however, some early varieties are ready for harvest when the foliage has barely started to die back.

When about one-quarter of the foliage has dried up, unearth a couple of bulbs and unwrap them. Bulbs ready to harvest have tight wrapper leaves. Inside the leaves, the cloves are fully separated. Don't delay harvest too long, or the outer wrapper leaves will deteriorate.

Either pull out the bulbs by hand or use a garden fork to unearth them. Gardeners in areas with dry summers can cure garlic in the garden. First lay a row of about five plants on the soil; then lay another group of plants on top of this row, with the foliage covering the bulbs of the plants below. Continue piling on the layers until all the garlic is harvested.

Gardeners in areas with humid or rainy summers can spread the plants in a single layer on screens in an airy shed, garage, or greenhouse, or on a covered patio. If conditions are very humid, set a fan on low speed to blow across the plants. Curing will take one to four weeks.

Storing When the garlic is fully dry, clip the tops to ½ inch (12.5 mm) long. If there is any sign of moisture when you cut the tops, the plants haven't finished curing. Cut the roots back to ½ inch (12.5 mm), too. Use a toothbrush or fingernail scrub brush to gently brush soil off the bulbs.

Store bulbs in baskets, burlap bags, or net bags in a dark place at room temperature and low humidity. Or store them at 32–40°F (0–4.5°C) and low humidity. Avoid temperatures between 42–52°F (5.5–11°C), which may prompt the bulbs to sprout.

PROBLEM SOLVER

Silvery streaks and blotches on leaves. Feeding onion thrips reduce plant vigor and can also spread disease. Thrips are worst in hot, dry conditions. Spray plants with a strong stream of water. If the problem persists, spray with insecticidal soap. Destroy crop remains after harvest.

Yellow leaf tips; white mold appears on plants; bulbs rot. Fungal infection causes rot and white mold. It occurs most often in cold, poorly drained soil. Try replanting in a different spot in the garden, and build up a raised bed about 4 inches (10 cm) high for planting.

Clusters of black dots on plants. The dots are black aphids; their feeding will weaken plants. Wash them off with a strong spray of water or spray with insecticidal soap.

Stored cloves develop pits or shrivel. These symptoms are caused by blue mold rot; they result on garlic harvested prematurely or stored in poor conditions.

When garlic plants are cured, the wrapper skins of the bulbs will be completely dry, so that the necks of the plants form a tight barrier to protect the cloves inside.

9 The cabbage family

Nearly every vegetable garden is home to at least one member of the cabbage family. Even if you're not a cabbage lover, chances are you do like some of its relatives, which include broccoli, cauliflower, Brussels sprouts, and kale.

These crops are collectively called brassicas or crucifers because they belong to the botanical family known as Brassicaceae or Cruciferae. This chapter also includes growing advice for some Asian relatives of the cabbage, including Chinese cabbage, pak choi, and tatsoi.

Cabbages and other brassicas are at their best when freshly picked from the garden.

Cabbage

What kind of cabbage should you grow? The answer depends on whether you like to eat cabbage fresh in salads, cooked, or prepared as slaw or sauerkraut. Depending on your region, you may want varieties resistant to clubroot and Fusarium wilt.

PLANTING GUIDE

What to plant Transplants; direct seeding is possible.

Starting indoors Sow two to four weeks apart to spread the harvest; or sow a few varieties with different maturity dates.

Site preparation Plant a cover crop the preceding fall or add compost before planting.

When Depends on climate.

Spacing *Large heads* 18 inches (45 cm) or more apart. *Small heads* 12 inches (30 cm) apart.

How much Per person, 5 to 10 cabbages. (You should consider how much you want to eat—a single cabbage can weigh up to 8 pounds/3.5 kg.)

BEST OF THE BUNCH

'Early Jersey Wakefield' Good early cabbage. Pointed head, excellent flavor. Fusarium resistant (F). 65 days from transplants.

'Ruby Perfection' Stores well. 85 days from transplants.

'Savoy King' Crinkled, dark green leaves. Suitable for planting in any season. 80 days from transplants.

Planting

Soil Cabbage plants need rich, fertile soil. You can boost soil fertility by growing a cover crop and turning it under. Alternatively, spread a 2-inch (5-cm) layer of compost and work it into the soil.

Check the soil pH where you plan to plant cabbages. It should be at least 6.0, but ideally 6.5 to 7.0, to reduce the risk of clubroot.

When to plant Cabbage matures best in cool conditions. If you live in an area where summer temperatures rarely exceed 90°F (32°C), plant cabbage in spring for summer and fall harvest. In warmer areas (Zones 6 and 7), plant in early spring to harvest before summer temperatures top 90°F (32°C). Plant again in late summer for a fall harvest.

In Zones 8 and warmer areas, plant in late winter for a spring harvest and in late summer for a fall harvest. In some mild-weather areas, fall-planted cabbage will overwinter for an early spring harvest.

Extra protection Seedlings can tolerate 40–50°F (4.5–10°C) without problems, but young transplants (with a stem diameter at least as thick as a pencil) exposed to low temperatures may send up a seed stalk prematurely, without forming a head. To protect cabbage transplants from sudden cold temperatures, you can cover the plants with row covers.

Planting an early-season crop in a shallow trench (2–3 inches/5–7.5 cm deep) may help to protect the plants from wind. Fill the trench once the plants are established.

Direct-seeding cabbage Cabbage seeds germinate even in warm soil (up to 90°F/32°C), so you can start seeds for the fall crop directly in the garden. Pamper the seedbed and seedlings to prevent heat stress. Water daily, if needed, and shade the seedbed in hot or dry weather.

Care

Watering Cabbage needs even moisture, especially when the weather is hot (more than 80°F/26.5°C) and when the plants are forming heads. If the soil dries out and heavy rain falls, the sudden rush of water into the plants can cause the heads to split.

Despite your best efforts, you may find that the soil around your cabbages has become too dry. Don't flood the area with water because that will make the heads split, too. Instead, apply a small amount of water daily—2 or 3 cups (475–700 ml) per plant—to gradually restore soil moisture.

To conserve soil moisture, spread a 2-inch (5-cm)-thick layer of organic mulching material around cabbage plants. However, do not allow the mulch to touch the heads, or it may encourage rot.

Weeding Competition with weeds will slow cabbage growth, so cultivate as needed to prevent weeds. Because cabbages are heavy feeders, you should spread a shovelful of compost around each plant before you weed. As you cultivate, you'll work the compost into the soil, providing a nutrient boost for your cabbages.

Fertilizing For a month after transplanting, water weekly with dilute fish emulsion.

Harvesting

You will know when cabbages are ready to harvest because the heads will be firm. Use a sharp knife to cut through the stem below the heads. It is best to cut the heads in the morning—sugars will be at their highest, which yields the best flavor.

If several heads mature at the same time, spread the harvest by breaking a portion of the roots on some of the plants. This reduces water uptake and lessens the risk of split heads during the harvest period. Use both hands to twist a cabbage head about one-quarter turn, or plunge a shovel into the soil at one side of the head.

If a head does split, harvest it right away. Cut away any deteriorating portions and cook the healthy cabbage pieces immediately.

Leave stumps of cut plants in place so they can produce small side heads. Removing all but one side shoot will promote a bigger size of the remaining head. Cut the side heads when 2–4 inches (5–10 cm) across.

Remove cut stumps from the garden after the harvest is complete. Otherwise, diseases and pests may persist in the stump and roots.

Storing Cut off any soiled wrapper leaves, but don't wash cabbages. Store in the refrigerator in plastic bags for two weeks (longer for late varieties). Late-season cabbages store well in the coolest part of a root cellar.

Cabbage heads may be red or green, round, pointed, or flat, with smooth or crinkly leaves.

PROBLEM SOLVER

Plants wilt. Tunnels in roots are from cabbage maggots. Swollen, misshapen roots indicate clubroot. Destroy plants.

To protect new transplants from maggots, slip tar paper or foam rubber below each plant, resting flat on the soil. For clubroot, replant in a different area. Follow a crop-rotation plan; keep soil pH above 6.0, ideally between 6.5 and 7.0.

Leaf wilt may be from harlequin bugs, which are black insects with red and yellow marks. Remove insects by hand daily. Weed out old cabbage-family plants, radishes, and wild mustard, which attract the bugs.

Chewed leaves. Diamondback moth caterpillar, imported cabbageworm, and cabbage looper feed on leaves. Spray BTK as soon as you see small green caterpillars. Handpick caterpillars, too.

Small holes in leaves. Protect young plants from tiny flea beetles with a row cover; older plants aren't harmed.

Lower leaves turn brown. Fusarium wilt is the cause. The plants may yield a harvest, but destroy plants that decline. Choose Fusarium-resistant cultivars.

Deformed or distorted leaves. Look for harlequin bugs or clusters of tiny gray-green aphids at the growing tips. Spray plants with a jet of water to dislodge aphids or spray with insecticidal soap.

Moldy heads. May be caused by fungal white rot or downy mildew; destroy plants. Replant resistant cultivars in another site; space plants farther apart.

Temperature alert
You should plan to plant cabbages so heads will mature in cool conditions.

Brussels sprouts

Eating homegrown Brussels sprouts for the first time is a revelation. Freshly harvested sprouts have a tender texture and nutty sweetness that are completely different from those bought in a supermarket.

PLANTING GUIDE

What to plant Transplants only.

Starting indoors Sow seeds indoors. Move seedlings to a shaded site outdoors; bring back indoors if outside temperatures exceed 80°F (26.5°C).

Site preparation Enrich the soil before planting.

When Early to midsummer in the North and middle states; in the South, when peak summer temperatures have passed.

Spacing *Short varieties* 18 inches (45 cm) apart on centers. *Tall varieties* 24 inches (60 cm) apart on centers.

How much Two to three plants per person.

Temperature alert
Brussels sprouts become sweeter after a frost, so time their planting so they mature in cool conditions.

Planting

Soil Brussels sprouts will need rich, moist, cool soil for the best results, so spread a 2-inch (5-cm) layer of compost over the soil and work it in. You can plant the transplants when they are six weeks old.

Care

Watering Consistent moisture is important for Brussel sprouts. If possible, set out a drip hose and leave it in place throughout the long growing period.

Mulch You can protect Brussels sprouts by applying a mulch, such as loose straw, around the plants. It will help to block the heat.

Fertilizing At planting time, apply a plant-starter fertilizer. You can side-dress with compost or a balanced organic fertilizer when the plants are 12 inches (30 cm) tall.

Harvesting

Sprouts form once temperatures drop to 60°F (15.5°C) at night, starting at the stem base and progressing upward. Begin harvesting when basal sprouts

Easy-to-grow Brussels sprouts can be kept in the garden well into winter. Don't remove the top leaves until you have harvested all the sprouts growing beneath.

are 1–1½ inches (2.5–3.75 cm) in diameter. Snap off the sprouts or cut them free with a sharp knife. To reach them easily, remove basal leaves as you harvest. Pick the sprouts every week or two as needed.

To force the sprouts to mature at the same time, cut off the top 6 inches (15 cm) of the plant five to six weeks before your first average frost date. The sprouts will mature six to eight weeks after the plant top is removed.

The loose, leafy plant top is edible, too. Cook the small leaves as you would collards or kale. Larger leaves aren't as tender and tasty.

Storing Harvest sprouts as you need them. Sprout quality improves with freezes as long as temperatures don't dip below 20°F (-6.5°F). Sprouts on snow-covered plants maintain good eating quality. Dig down into the snow to harvest the sprouts.

Store Brussels sprouts in the refrigerator for a day or two at the most. Don't wash the sprouts before refrigerating them.

BEST OF THE BUNCH

'Bubbles' Tolerates heat; drought resistant. 92 days from transplants.
'Jade Cross Hybrid' Tolerates heat. Blue-green sprouts with mild flavor. 82 days from transplants.
'Oliver' Firm sprouts; vigorous and early bearing. 90 to 100 days from transplants.

PROBLEM SOLVER

The sprouts are loose and tufty. The temperatures were too warm when the sprouts were forming. Alternatively, the soil was not firmed enough at planting time.

Tiny gray or black insects in sprouts. Aphids suck juices from tender sprouts. In the growing period, dislodge aphid clusters by spraying them with a hard stream of water.

Broccoli

Home gardeners can enjoy broccoli over a long season by harvesting not only the large central flower heads but also a bounty of smaller secondary heads.

PLANTING GUIDE

What to plant Transplants.

Starting indoors Fairly easy; seedlings grow fast.

Site preparation Enrich the soil well before planting.

When Soil should be at least 60°F (15.5°C).

Spacing 18 inches (45 cm) apart; 2 feet (60 cm) between rows.

Intensive spacing 15 inches (38 cm) on centers.

How much About three plants per person.

BEST OF THE BUNCH

'Green Comet' Disease and heat tolerant. Easy to grow; doesn't produce side shoots. 40 days from transplants.
'Packman' Large central head; produces plentiful secondary shoots. Tolerates heat. 55 days from transplants.
'Waltham' Drought tolerant; produces side shoots. Good for freezing. 74 days from transplants.

Planting

Soil Soil pH should be at least 6.0 but ideally 6.5 to 7.0. Enrich the soil by planting a cover crop and turning it under or working a 2-inch (5-cm) layer of compost into the soil.

When to plant Set out transplants two weeks before the average last frost date in the North; plant a fall crop 10 to 12 weeks before the first average fall frost. In the South, start seeds in January through March (depending on your hardiness zone). Start seeds again in late July through September for a fall crop. Plant them, and all brassicas, firmly to ensure they crop well.

Protecting young plants Water transplants with plant-starter fertilizer to encourage vigorous growth. Many pests, especially cutworms and flea beetles, attack seedlings, so cover plants with a row cover after planting and use tinfoil collars at soil level.

Care

Watering Keep plants moist, especially in hot conditions (above 80°F/26.5°C). Wet the soil 6 inches (15 cm) deep, but don't keep beds soaking wet. Moisture or heat stress stunts growth. If a plant suffers, pull it out and replant.

PROBLEM SOLVER

Plants form heads too soon. Known as buttoning, this can be caused by overhardening of transplants, too little water, or cold temperatures.

Hollow stems. Too much nitrogen or boron deficiency. Feed plants mature compost or a balanced organic fertilizer. Heads with hollow stems are edible.

See page 171 for additional solutions.

Mulch Use straw or dried grass clippings to keep down weeds and help conserve moisture in the soil.

Harvesting

Make a cut 4–6 inches (10–15 cm) below the heads while buds are firm and tightly closed; tender, delicious side shoots will develop afterward. In warm weather, monitor plants daily—heads quickly overmature. If a head has yellow petals, cut it off and wait for side shoots.

Storing Broccoli lasts about one week in the refrigerator, stored loosely in a plastic bag. For the best quality, cook broccoli as soon as possible after harvesting or freeze it (see pages 118–19).

Broccoli rabe

Broccoli rabe, also called broccoli raab or rapini, is a popular vegetable in China. The tender shoots are delicious when stir-fried with garlic. The flavor is sharper than that of broccoli—in fact, broccoli rabe is related to turnips.

PLANTING GUIDE

What to plant Seeds.

Site preparation Enrich the soil before planting.

When Depends on region.

Spacing Sow seeds 1 inch (2.5 cm) apart, with 18 inches (45 cm) between rows; thin to 6 inches (15 cm) apart.

Intensive spacing Broadcast seeds in wide rows; thin to 3 inches (7.5 cm) apart.

How much Two to four plants per person.

Planting

Soil Enrich the soil by working in 2 inches (5 cm) of compost. Or dig a trench 6 inches (15 cm) deep and 3–4 inches (7.5–10 cm) wide, and fill it with compost to 1 inch (2.5 cm) below the soil level. Add about ½ inch (1.25 cm) of soil and sow the seeds; cover with soil to ground level.

When to plant Begin seeding in the spring when soil temperatures are at least 45°F (7°C). Stop sowing when crops would mature in hot weather (when average daytime temperatures reach above 85°F/29°C). Sow again for a fall harvest, beginning six to eight weeks before the first fall frost and continuing until three weeks before; a light frost improves flavor.

In mild-winter areas, plant from late summer through late fall for a fall and winter harvest.

Planting for overwintering Even in cold-winter areas, you can try planting seeds late, two to three weeks before the first fall frost. When the seedlings germinate, cover them well with a straw mulch. The plants will survive the winter, leading to an extra-early crop the following spring. This works best in well-drained soil.

Care

Improving yields Broccoli rabe is generally easy to grow. Keep the soil moist and side-dress with plant-starter fertilizer or another nitrogen-rich organic fertilizer for a better yield.

See page 171 for solutions to pest and disease problems.

Harvesting

Cut the stems 6 inches (15 cm) long before the flower buds open; plants will send out side shoots for a second cutting and perhaps even a third.

You can blanch or boil the shoots before stir-frying if you want to make the flavor more mellow.

Storing Place unwashed shoots in a plastic bag; they will keep fresh in a refrigerator for up to three days.

BEST OF THE BUNCH

Note: Many seed companies offer only one choice, often not a named variety.
'Spring Raab' Plant for spring and summer harvest. 42 days from seeds.
'Sessantina Grossa' Thick but tender shoots; good for a fall crop or to overwinter. 35 days from seeds.

Temperature alert
Broccoli rabe grows best in cool conditions and will do well in partial shade.

Cauliflower

Cauliflower is broccoli's temperamental cousin. Conditions that are too hot, too cold, or too dry can result in disappointing head development. However, with some perseverance and luck, you can grow snowy white, delicious cauliflower.

PLANTING GUIDE

What to plant Transplants.

Starting indoors Germination is fastest at 80°F (26.5°C). Start to harden off after about four to five weeks.

Site preparation Provide rich soil conditions.

When Depends on your climate.

Spacing Set plants 15–24 inches (38–60 cm) apart; 24–36 inches (60–90 cm) between rows.

Intensive spacing 18 inches (45 cm) on centers.

How much About five plants per person.

Quick Tip

For the best crop

Plant several varieties with different dates to maturity at various times. You'll discover which combination of variety and planting time yields the best results.

Planting

Soil The soil pH should be at least 6.0 but ideally 6.5 to 7.0. Provide fertile conditions by planting a cover crop and digging it into the soil. Or work a 2-inch (5-cm) layer of compost into the soil before planting (see pages 36–37).

When to plant Cauliflower is finicky when it comes to exposure to hot and cold temperatures. The ideal temperature range for growing the plant is 65–80°F (18–26.5°C).

In the North, plant cauliflower for a fall harvest, setting out transplants about 60 to 90 days before the first expected fall frost.

In Zones 7 and 8, you can plant in early spring and again in late summer, but don't set out the transplants more than three weeks before the last average spring frost date.

Cauliflower will grow well as a winter crop in Zones 8b through 10. You should choose varieties that are specially developed for this climate.

Starting transplants Make sure the plants are firmly set in the soil. You can protect spring transplants from cold temperatures by covering plants with row covers or cloches. Water transplants in with a plant-starter fertilizer.

Care

Feeding After the first month, water plants with fish emulsion every two to three weeks (or side-dress with compost or kelp meal). The exception is cauliflower grown in the winter—because it needs to develop more slowly than spring- or fall-grown plantings, it does not require any additional feeding.

Pest protection If pests attack your cauliflower, the resulting stress can ruin the harvest. The best protection is to use a row cover. Make sure it is draped over the plants with all the edges buried well in the soil.

Where conditions are warm, you should choose the lightest type of row

PROBLEM SOLVER

Curds separate and heads are leafy. Temperatures were too high. Plant for fall harvest next time (or an overwinter crop in the South). For spring plantings, try a variety with shorter maturity time.

Curds turn brown. This can result from sunburn; protect future crops from sun. In humid climates, this may also be due to a downy mildew, a fungal disease.

See page 171 for additional solutions.

BEST OF THE BUNCH

'Snow Crown' Fast and easy to grow. White heads up to 8 inches (20 cm) wide. 50 days from transplants.
'Fremont' Self-blanching; good in a variety of soil and weather conditions. 62 days from transplants.
'Violet Queen' Purple head turns green when cooked. 70 days from transplants.
'Maystar' Overwintering type; white heads. 270 days from transplants.

Prevent sun scorch by bending the large leaves over the head and securing them in place.

Purple-head varieties do not require blanching to protect their heads from sunburn.

cover you can find. A thick row cover can cause heat to build up, which can also lead to stress.

Blanching

Flowerheads require protection from the sun to retain their whiteness. You can use twine, tape, or rubber bands to fasten the leaves around the head as soon as you notice any sun scorch. Even self-blanching cauliflower types may require blanching.

Harvesting

Cauliflower is ready to harvest one to two weeks after the head first appears. Cut the stem below the head when the head is 6–8 inches (15–20 cm) in diameter. The heads won't withstand temperatures lower than 25°F (-4°C), so harvest them when they are small rather than waiting until they are larger and risking exposure to such low temperatures.

Storing

Cauliflower heads will keep fresh in the refrigerator for up to four weeks if they are covered in plastic wrap or stored in plastic bags.

Temperature alert
Too much heat or cold can lead to poor production of cauliflower heads.

Kale and collards

A hardy member of the cabbage family, kale is a taste treat that's more nutritious than broccoli. Collards are related to kale and have similar growing requirements, but collards tolerate heat better than kale.

PLANTING GUIDE

What to plant Seeds or transplants.

Starting indoors Start seeds in midsummer for a fall crop.

Site preparation Cover crop previous season or add compost.

When Varies by region.

Spacing *Kale* Sow 3 inches (7.5 cm) apart, 18 inches (45 cm) between rows; thin plants to 12–18 inches (30–45 cm) apart. *Collards* Sow 6 inches (15 cm) apart, 2 feet (60 cm) between rows; thin to 2 feet (60 cm) apart.

Intensive spacing *Kale* Sow 8 inches (20 cm) apart on centers. *Collards* Sow 15 inches (38 cm) apart on center.s

How much Above five plants per person.

Temperature alert
Collards can tolerate summer heat; kale, cold conditions. Both taste best harvested after a frost.

Planting

Soil Kale and collards thrive in rich, evenly moist soil. Turn under a cover crop a few weeks before planting, or spread 3 inches (7.5 cm) of compost over the area and work it into the soil.

When to plant In mild-summer areas, plant as soon as the soil can be worked in spring. Plant again in midsummer for a fall harvest.

In the South or other hot-summer areas, plant kale in late summer only. The plants may produce through the winter. Southern gardeners who want a challenge can sow collard seeds outdoors in fall for an early spring harvest. The plants may grow into fall. Harvest throughout, but their flavor will be less appealing in summer heat.

Care

Feed kale monthly with a plant-starter fertilizer or a side-dressing of compost. Collards grow well without fertilizer, but may yield better when fed. See page 171 for pest and disease solutions.

Cold-weather care To protect fall crops from the cold, mulch around the plants with chopped leaves.

Blanching collards To improve collard flavor, blanch the inner leaves by slipping a rubber band over the plant or tying string around the outer leaves; leave these in place until they are ready to be harvested.

Harvesting

Pick leaves as needed, avoiding tough or yellowed leaves. For cooking, use leaves 6 inches (15 cm) or larger. You can try a cut-and-come-again technique with salad-type kales, cutting plants above the central growing point—you'll have another harvest a few weeks later. Harvest whole plants by cutting the stem just above ground level.

Storing To store the heads, remove excess stem and soiled or yellowed outer leaves. Wrap moist paper towels around the heads and slip them into plastic bags. You can store them in a refrigerator for up to five days.

BEST OF THE BUNCH

Collard 'Vates' Overwinters well. Good steamed or fresh. 55 days from seeds.
Kale 'Laciniato' Tall plants with large leaves; good flavor. 60 days from seeds.
Kale 'Red Russian' Bicolor leaves; young leaves good for salads. 50 to 60 days from seeds.
Kale 'Winterbor' Productive and hardy plant, with ruffled leaves; overwinters well. 55 to 65 days from seeds.

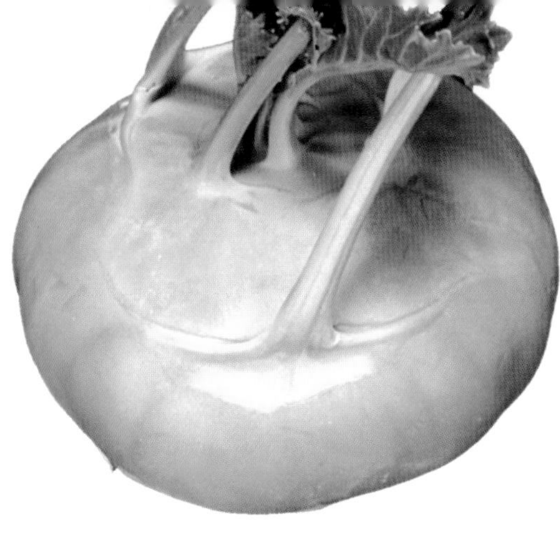

Kohlrabi

The swollen aboveground stems of kohlrabi are delicious whether eaten raw or cooked, and they have a mild, sweet flavor that is comparable to cabbage, turnips, celery, and even cucumbers.

PLANTING GUIDE

What to plant Seeds or transplants.

Starting indoors Easy to start seeds indoors or in a cold frame.

Site preparation Enrich soil as for cabbage (see pages 170–71).

When Spring and late summer in cool- and moderate-summer areas; fall and winter in hot-summer areas.

Spacing 6 inches (15 cm) apart; rows 1–3 feet (30–90 cm) apart.

Intensive spacing 4–6 inches (10–15 cm) apart in a staggered double row.

How much *Seeds* Sow 1–2 feet (30–60 cm) of double row per person; 3–5 feet (90–150 cm) of standard row. *Plants* About 6 to 10 plants per person.

BEST OF THE BUNCH

'Early White Vienna' Compact plants; light green skin and white flesh globes; slow to bolt. 50 to 55 days from seeds.
'Grand Duke' Green skin, resists black rot; 4-inch (10-cm) globes. 48 days from seeds.
'Kolibri' Purple globes with white flesh; tolerates heat. 50 days from seeds.

Planting

Soil Plant a cover crop and turn it into the soil a few weeks before planting. Alternatively, you can work a 2-inch (5-cm) layer of compost into the soil before you begin planting (see pages 36–37).

When to plant You can sow seeds or set out transplants about four weeks before the last expected spring frost and again about four weeks before the first expected fall frost. Be sure to keep late plantings well watered during hot weather.

Gardeners in Zones 9 and 10 can grow kohlrabi through winter. You can sow seeds as long as temperatures are above 40°F (4.5°C).

Care

Feeding Kohlrabi is less prone to pests and diseases than other members of the cabbage family. However, you can feed kohlrabi once a month with a plant-starter fertilizer or by side-dressing it with compost or a balanced organic fertilizer.

Cold-weather care If you are growing kohlrabi for a late fall or winter harvest, cover the plants if nighttime temperatures below 25°F (-4°C) are predicted.

Harvesting

You should harvest spring-grown kohlrabi before the globes swell beyond 3 inches (7.5 cm) in diameter or they may become woody. Cut the plants about 1 inch (2.5 cm) below the globe. Kohlrabi leaves are also good to eat; you can cook them as you would other greens.

If you discover that a globe has turned tough, peel away the outer layers. The center may still be tender and have good flavor.

Storing You can store kohlrabi globes for up to three weeks in the refrigerator if they are wrapped in plastic; or store them in a root cellar for up to three months. In mild-winter areas, leave it in the ground over the winter and harvest as needed.

Kohlrabi globes won't mature well in hot weather, so time your plantings accordingly.

Asian greens

Gardeners in China, Japan, Korea, and other Asian countries grow a variety of cabbage-family cousins that also thrive in our gardens. Chinese cabbages, tatsoi, mizuna, and Chinese broccoli are a few of the most popular varieties.

PLANTING GUIDE

What to plant Direct seeding for most types. Transplants or seeds for Chinese cabbage.

Starting indoors Sow Chinese cabbage seeds indoors for a summer planting.

Site preparation Add plenty of compost just before planting.

When Depends on the type and the climate.

Spacing Depends on the type.

How much to plant Per person, 5 to 10 cabbage plants.

Planting

Soil These crops like rich soil and don't do well in acidic soil. Add a 2-inch (5-cm) layer of compost to provide nutrients and keep the soil moist—Asian greens will tolerate heat better when they grow in consistently moist soil. If you make succession plantings, add another 2-inch (5-cm) layer of compost before sowing or planting each new crop. Prepare a raised bed (see pages 22–23) for choy sum plants.

When to plant Asian greens grow best in cool weather. Northern gardeners can grow spring and fall crops; southern gardeners should plant in late summer for fall and winter harvest.

You can direct-seed spring crops of Chinese cabbage, but start seeds for summer plantings indoors—seeds won't germinate well above 80°F (26.5°C). Space seedlings of heading types 1 foot (30 cm) apart and loose types 6–10 inches (15–25 cm) apart. Thin direct-seeded plantings to these spacings, too—you can use the tasty thinnings in salads.

If temperatures are unusually hot, spring crops of heading cabbages may bolt before the heads form. Sow fall crops three months before the first average fall frost day.

Sowing seeds For Chinese broccoli, sow seeds 2–4 inches (5–10 cm) apart in rows about 1 foot (30 cm) apart; thin to 6–8 inches (15–20 cm) apart. In areas with moderate summers, such as parts of the Pacific Northwest, you can plant succession crops of Chinese broccoli.

For tatsoi, sow seeds a few inches apart and thin them to 6–15 inches (15–38 cm) apart, depending on whether you plan to harvest young leaves or mature plants. Tatsoi is best grown for a fall harvest. You should sow seeds eight weeks before the first expected fall frost if you want a harvest of full heads. You can sow seeds again about three to four weeks before the fall frost.

To grow mizuna, sow seeds 2 inches (5 cm) apart in rows 18 inches (45 cm) apart. Thin the plants 10–12 inches (25–30 cm) apart. You can also plant mizuna intensively by spacing them 6 inches (15 cm) on centers.

Grow choy sum with 4 inches (10 cm) between the plants.

Care

Feeding and mulch Fertilize plants monthly with fish emulsion or with a side-dressing of compost. If the plants are mulched well, tatsoi may survive through winter.

Quick Tip

The name game

Asian greens have many different names, both in English and Asian languages. If you're not sure which seeds to order in garden centers or catalogs, ask a salesperson for advice or call the company's customer service line.

If mizuna is planted intensively, you can harvest the leaves using a cut-and-come-again technique.

Although these plants don't suffer from pest problems as much as regular cabbage and broccoli do, they are prone to slug damage. (For solutions to problems that do occur, see page 171.)

Harvesting

When the stems of Chinese broccoli reach about ½ inch (125 mm) in diameter, cut the stems 3 inches (7.5 cm) above ground level.

For tatsoi, harvest individual leaves from these plants for as long as they survive in the ground.

You can harvest the young leaves of mizuna as soon as three weeks after the seedlings first appear. Use the cut-and-come-again technique if you want just a few leaves.

After the flower buds open on choy sum, use a sharp knife to cut the plant at the base.

Storing Harvested heading cabbages will last approximately two to three months in humid, cool storage. If temperatures drop below 50°F (10°C), the heads will also keep well in place in the garden.

Chinese broccoli doesn't store well, so prepare it right after harvesting. The stems will still taste good even if the flower buds open before harvest.

Choy sum usually has green leaves and stems, but some have attractive red-purple stems.

AN ASIAN CONTAINER GARDEN

If you've never tried eating Asian greens, you may want to experiment with these crops on a small scale. One way to do that is to plant just a few specimens of each in pots or a planter on a sunny terrace or patio. Asian-theme pottery would be an appropriate choice, but use whatever you have available. A 12-inch (30-cm) pot is the right size for a Chinese cabbage or Chinese broccoli plant. Make sure that all containers have adequate drainage holes.

Prepare the potting mix as you would for any other container vegetables (see pages 44–45). Transplant crops or sow seeds into the containers at the same time you would plant them in the garden.

If you have a planter, you can interplant Chinese cabbage, Chinese broccoli, mizuna, and tatsoi, placing the taller crops at the back. Their contrasting leaf colors and unusual shapes will be an attention-getter, and you can educate both yourself and your friends about these unusual crops. For an extra-special touch, insert a trellis at the back of the planter and sow snow peas at the base. Your Asian container garden will supply the fixings for wonderful stir-fries.

Temperature alert
Plant Asian crops early or late; crop quality will be poor if plants mature during peak summer temperatures.

Types of Asian greens

Among the types of Asian greens are Chinese cabbage, choy sum, pak choi, Chinese broccoli, tatsoi, and mizuna. Chinese cabbage can be divided into two categories: Heading cabbage form tight, upright heads; loose Chinese cabbage form loose clusters of long white stalks topped by deep green leaves.

◀ **Loose Chinese cabbage**

Loose Chinese cabbage is also known as Chinese mustard cabbage and pak choi (or bok choy). The plants are usually ready to harvest between 50 and 60 days from transplanting. The leaves are succulent and are especially suited for stir-fries.

▲ **Heading cabbage**

Heading cabbages are also called celery cabbage, michihli, napa, and pe tsai. The heads mature 50 to 60 days after transplanting (90 days from seeds). Use them as you would regular cabbage in stir-fries, salads, or for cole slaw.

▶ **Mizuna**

This attractive plant produces feathery green leaves with white midribs. It's so pretty you may want to include it in a flower garden for its looks alone. The leaves have a mild flavor and are a good addition to a mesclun mix. In cooking, mizuna pairs well with root vegetables, or try it stir-fried with ginger and soy sauce.

Choy sum

This cool-season crop is also known as choi sum and Chinese flowering cabbage. Harvest 30 to 50 days after sowing, when first flower buds begin to open. Use the flower shoots and young leaves in salads or stir-fries.

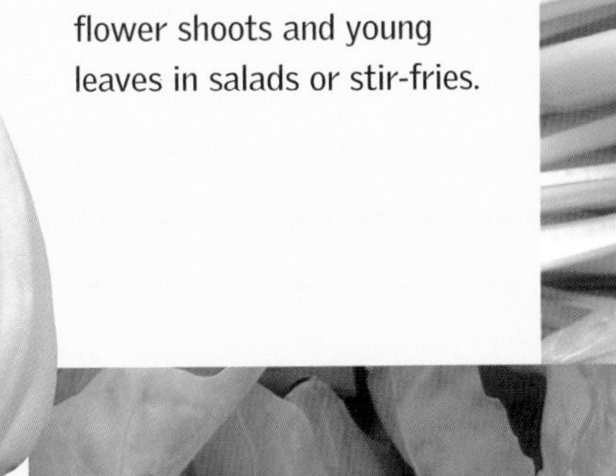

Chinese broccoli

Chinese broccoli, also known as Chinese kale, gai lohn, and gaai lohn, doesn't form large heads. The tender young stems, along with flower buds and leaves, are a tasty addition to stir-fries. Plants mature 60 to 70 days from seeds (faster-maturing varieties are available).

Tatsoi

Tatsoi is also called flat cabbage or rosette pak choi. As these names suggest, it resembles a flattened pak choi plant, with small round dark green leaves at the end of slender stems. Tatsoi is easy to grow and withstands cold temperatures well (hardy to 15°F/-9.5°C).

10 Root and stem crops

Root crops hail from a range of plant families, but they all share the need for the sheltering environment of the soil as they produce succulent storage roots and tubers. Some of our favorite vegetable crops are root crops, including carrots, radishes, and potatoes. A few of these crops, including turnips and beets, also offer a bonus of tender leaves that are delicious when cooked. Some other crops, such as celery and Florence fennel, are grown primarily for their bounty of fleshy, crisp stems.

Freshly dug potatoes are full of goodness extracted from the soil.

Potatoes

You can grow your own potatoes from small tubers or pieces of tubers known as seed potatoes. From these, you can enjoy an astounding selection of delicious potatoes that are not normally found at the grocery store.

Planting

Soil If you add compost regularly to your garden, you don't need to add any extra amendments to your soil before planting potatoes. Check the soil pH and adjust it if needed (see pages 32–33). The proper pH range for potatoes is 5.0 to 6.5; 5.5 is ideal if scab is a problem in your area.

Preparing seed potatoes Potato tubers are swollen stems, not roots. The potato "eyes" are buds, which sprout and produce stems and leaves when the tubers are planted. After acquiring seed potatoes, you can store them in the refrigerator for up to one month before planting.

You can plant seed potatoes whole, or cut them to about the size of a medium egg, with two or three buds apiece. After cutting, you should let the pieces cure for one to two days at 75°F (24°C). Even if you don't cut the seed potatoes, curing them

Red potatoes are just one of the more interesting types of potato to grow.

PLANTING GUIDE

What to plant Seed potatoes.

Starting indoors Pre-sprouting seed pieces is helpful.

Site preparation Check soil pH.

When Three to four weeks before last spring frost; in Zone 7 and warmer, plant a second crop in late summer or fall.

Spacing *Early varieties* 8–14 inches (20–35 cm) apart, 12–18 inches (30–45 cm) between rows. *Late varieties* 30–36 inches (75–90 cm) between rows.

Intensive spacing 18 inches (45 cm) apart on centers.

How much Per person, 15 feet (4.5 m) of row or a 4 x 8-foot (1.2 x 2.4-m) bed.

Quick Tip

Smart shopping

Grocery-store potatoes may have been treated with chemicals that inhibit sprouting and may not be certified disease-free. Buy seed potatoes only at garden centers when in season or from mail-order suppliers.

in a warm place for two days before planting will lead to better growth.

Planting You should make a trench approximately 3–4 inches (7.5–10 cm) deep and wide, set the seed pieces in it, and fill the trench with soil. If you prefer not to dig, or if your soil is heavy and wet, you can lay the tubers on the soil surface and cover them with 4–6 inches (10–15 cm) of straw or composted leaves.

Care

Hilling potatoes Light can cause tubers to develop a green color, which is slightly toxic. To block the light—and to keep the tubers cool and maintain even moisture conditions—hill the plants when the shoots are about 4–5 inches (10–12.5 cm) tall by using a hoe to pull up soil around the plants. Hill the plants again two or three weeks later.

For surface-planted potatoes, use additional mulch piled deeply around the plant instead of hilling with soil. The mulch can be a haven for slugs, so make sure you provide plenty of slug control (see pages 96–99).

Air-dry unwashed tubers for a few hours after you harvest them, then brush off any soil.

Harvesting

Harvest new (small) potatoes when plants are blooming strongly. Harvest whole plants, or reach into the mulch and gently break off tubers, removing a maximum of two tubers per plant.

Watch the vines as the plants mature. Leave tubers in the ground for a few weeks after the tops die back—the skin toughens as they sit, so they'll last better in storage. Frost may kill the vines naturally, but if frost isn't imminent and the vines aren't dying, knock them flat or cut them with a knife to kill them.

Early potatoes take about 60 days to reach maturity; mid-season potatoes need about 80 days; and late-season potatoes need 90 days or longer.

Storing Put unwashed, air-dried potatoes in a dark place at 50–65°F (10–18°C) for five days. For longer storage, move them to a cooler spot (50°F/10°C). Store potatoes for no more than six months.

PROBLEM SOLVER

Brown spots and white mold on foliage. The late blight fungus attacks potatoes in humid conditions, with hot days and cool nights. Brown flecks first appear on leaves and stems, enlarge, and then a white velvety coating appears. Plants will blacken and die. Remove and destroy infected plants. Plant certified disease-free seed potatoes and resistant cultivars. As a preventive measure, use copper-based or compost-tea sprays.

Holes in leaves. Handpick and destroy Colorado potato beetles and their eggs and larvae. Spray *Bacillus thuringiensis* var. *san diego* (BTSD) on larvae. Trap adult beetles by surrounding the plants with a plastic-lined trench; cover plants with a floating row cover until mid-season. Grow early maturing types, and harvest before the beetles appear.

Stunted plants with puckered or yellow leaves. Small bumps on the tubers and hard galls on the roots are from root-knot nematodes; otherwise, suspect a virus. In both cases, destroy infected plants. At future plantings, cover plants with a row cover to keep virus-spreading aphids off. To prevent nematode problems, plant a cover crop of marigolds; apply beneficial nematodes to the soil.

Corky patches on tubers. Caused by scab. Potatoes are still edible; cut away the corky areas. For future crops, adjust soil pH to 5.5; choose resistant cultivars.

BEST OF THE BUNCH

'All Blue' Medium-size potato with blue skin and blue-purple flesh; good for baking and boiling. 80 to 90 days from planting.
'Cow Horn' Purple skin and off-white flesh; long, tubers good for baking and storage. 90 days or longer from planting.
'Cranberry Red' Red skin and pink, smooth flesh. 60 to 80 days from planting.
'Yellow Finn' European yellow-fleshed variety; good for mashing and baking. 80 days from planting.

Types of potatoes

Instead of the typical white potatoes available year-round at the supermarket, why not plant red-fleshed or all blue potatoes? Try 'Butterfinger' or another fingerling variety, and sample unusual heirloom varieties such as 'Cow Horn'.

◀ **Russet potatoes**

The distinctive russeting, or reddish brown color, on their skin distinguishes russet potatoes from other types, as well as the light, fluffy texture of the flesh when it's baked. Most russets have white flesh and an oblong shape. The best-known variety is 'Russet Burbank', but newer varieties are better adapted to various regions of the country. Ask for a russet that will grow well in your area. Russets are also good for mashing and roasting.

▲ **Fingerlings**

Named for their shape, fingerling potatoes usually have yellow flesh, although red- and purple-fleshed varieties are available. Fingerlings tend to have firm flesh, and they are the favorite of many gourmet chefs for steaming, sautéing, and roasting. Some types are excellent for puréeing. Fingerlings are long-season potatoes; however, a few varieties are available that mature in only two months from planting.

▶ **Yellow potatoes**

'Yukon Gold' is the variety that brought fame to yellow potatoes, but there are many other varieties as well, including 'Bintje' and 'Red Gold'. These smooth-skinned potatoes are excellent for baking, boiling, mashing, frying, steaming, and in potato salad.

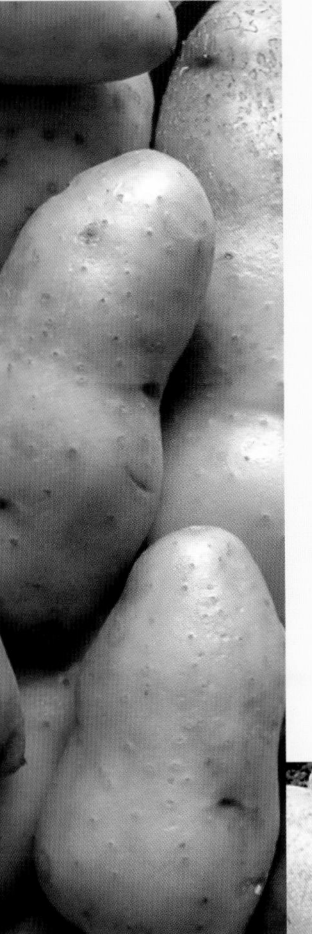

▶ New potatoes

Any potato can be a new potato if you harvest it early. Wait for your plants to start blooming. Once blooming is well under way, try reaching into the soil with your hand to fish out some small tubers, which may be less than 1 inch (2.5 cm) in diameter and up to 2 inches (5 cm) across. Take only a few from each of your plants and allow the rest to mature. New potatoes have delicate skin, so don't scrub them. Wash and cook them gently.

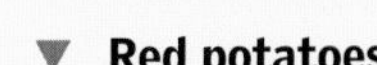

▼ Red potatoes

Red potatoes usually have thin skin and firm flesh. White-fleshed types, such as 'Red Norland', are well known, but there are also varieties with pink flesh and red flesh. The thin skin is often easier to peel than that of other types of potatoes. Try red-fleshed types for an eye-catching potato salad or casserole.

▲ White potatoes

Don't take white potatoes for granted. Round white potatoes are a good choice for making potato chips, and some of the best-known varieties of all-purpose potatoes, including 'Katahdin' and 'Kennebec', are white potatoes.

Sweet potatoes

Here's one root crop that loves warm soil and hot weather—but even if you don't have hot summers, you can grow sweet potatoes. As long as your growing season offers at least 90 days frost-free, you should reap a respectable harvest.

PLANTING GUIDE

What to plant Certified disease-free slips.

Starting indoors Start your own slips indoors.

Site preparation Raised beds are best in the North.

When Two weeks after last expected spring frost; when soil is at least 65°F (18°C).

Spacing Plant 12–18 inches (30–45 cm) apart in rows 3 feet (90 cm) apart; or grow 3 slips per hill, 3 feet (90 cm) apart.

How much Two to four plants per person.

Planting

Soil Here's a crop that doesn't do well with too much nitrogen, so be conservative when preparing the soil. If it is low in organic matter, spread a 1-inch (2.5-cm) layer of compost and work it into the soil before planting. However, be careful—too much compost can cause brown areas to appear on tubers if they are kept in storage. Make sure you remove any rocks and debris as you work the soil.

Warming the soil Sweet potatoes won't grow well in cold soil. To warm soil in the North, you can make a raised bed about 8 inches (20 cm) high and 1 foot (30 cm) wide (see pages 22–23). Cover the raised bed tightly with a layer of IRT (infrared transmitting) or standard black plastic. Then cut Xs through the plastic at the desired spacing down the center of the bed.

Planting slips Slips—sprouts cut from tubers—ordered via mail order may look wilted or dead when they arrive, but they should recover quickly after planting. Open a planting hole several inches deep (at an X if the bed is layered with plastic) and insert the slips deeply enough so that only a few leaves show above the soil level.

Care

Avoiding the cold In short-season areas, cover the beds with row covers after planting to protect the slips from cold winds and possible late frosts. Any exposure to frost will kill the foliage. Alternatively, you can cover each young slip with a cloche.

At the end of the growing season, if early frosts are predicted, spread a row cover over all of the sprawling foliage—this will extend the season a little longer.

Watering and feeding After the first few weeks of growth, sweet potatoes generally don't need watering or fertilizing. In fact, pampering the plants can cause excessive vine growth rather than

BEST OF THE BUNCH

'Centennial' Classic high-yielding variety; good for short-season areas. 90 days from planting.
'Georgia Jet' Large roots; good in cool climates. 85 to 90 days from planting.
'Regal' Reddish purple skin and orange flesh; productive. Disease resistant. 110 days from planting.
'Sumor' Creamy white skin, white flesh. Disease resistant. 115 days from planting.
'Vardaman' Bush type ideal for small gardens. Golden skin and orange flesh. 95 days from planting.

Temperature alert
In short-season areas, use plastic mulch to warm the soil and row covers to protect plants from chilly conditions.

root growth. Cut back on water in late summer or the developing roots may crack.

Harvesting

If possible, time your harvest to dig the roots just before frost kills the vines. However, if frost strikes before you harvest the plants, dig up the roots immediately because decay can spread rapidly from frost-killed foliage to the roots.

Storing Don't plan on storing your sweet potatoes for more than a few weeks unless you do the following: Bring harvested roots into a warm area (80–95°F/26.5–35°C) to cure for about 10 days. Move them to a cool area (60°F/15.5°C), and wrap them individually in newspaper or spread them out on racks. They will keep for several months like this, but will last only a week or so at higher temperatures. Exposure to cold (below 50°F/10°C) can cause chilling injury.

PROBLEM SOLVER

Stunted plants. Root-knot nematodes stunt growth. Plant a dense cover crop of marigolds where you want to grow sweet potatoes. After they are dug under and break down, plant the slips. Choose nematode-resistant varieties.

Chewed leaves. Sweet potato flea beetles are probably the culprits. In warm-season areas, plant late to avoid this pest, or cover early plantings with a floating row cover.

Tunnels in roots. In southern gardens, larvae of the sweet potato weevil feed inside roots. Also watch for reddish black weevils on the leaves. Destroy all infested foliage and roots. Buy certified weevil-free slips for new crops. Don't grow morning glories—they harbor weevils.

Heat-loving sweet potatoes, a member of the bindweed family (and a cousin of the morning glory), will thrive where summers are long and hot.

Sweet potatoes have a sweet, tender flesh. Choose traditional orange-fleshed types or firmer white-fleshed sweet potatoes.

Quick Tip

Disease alert

Look for multiple disease-resistant varieties, such as 'Carolina Bunch' and 'Excel'. To prevent the spread of diseases, out-of-state producers cannot ship slips to gardeners in California and some other states.

Carrots

With well-worked soil, proper thinning, and regular watering, you can enjoy crunchy carrots with flavors that are far more sweet and satisfying than any carrot you can purchase at the grocery store.

PLANTING GUIDE

What to plant Seeds.

Site preparation Prepare soil the season before planting.

When Sow seeds until average daily temperature exceeds 85°F (29°C); sow again six weeks before first fall frost. In areas with cooler summers, you can continue sowing until six weeks before the first fall frost.

Spacing Allow 6–12 inches (15–30 cm) between rows; for a winter harvest, space rows 4–5 inches (10–12.5 cm) apart.

How much Per person, 20 to 40 carrots (6–12 feet/1.8–3.6 m of row per person) per seeding for fresh eating.

Temperature alert
Hot spells can cause split roots and bitterness. You can grow carrots when temperatures are below 85°F (29°C), but 60–65°F (15.5–18°C) is ideal.

Planting

Soil Loose, even soil without clods or rocks is essential for long, straight carrot roots. Be realistic about your soil when you choose varieties. If the best you can provide is 2 inches (5 cm) of loose, stone-free soil, select round varieties such as 'Thumbelina'. If you have heavy soil, you can create a miniature raised bed to grow your carrots (see pages 22–23).

To prepare the soil, dig in 2 pounds (0.9 kg) of compost per square foot (30 cm sq) as deeply as you can.

Sowing seeds Make sure you water the area thoroughly before you sow seeds. It can be difficult to sow tiny carrot seeds individually, but with practice and patience, you can sow seeds about ½ inch (1.25 cm) apart. Sow the seeds over shallow furrows, spreading them lightly by hand if necessary. Or use a sowing aid, which is available from mail-order catalogs.

Carrot seeds germinate slowly and wash away easily. Sow seeds ¼ inch (6 mm) deep and cover them with compost or vermiculite to avoid crusting. You can sow radish or lettuce seeds along with the carrot seeds; the fast-germinating radish and lettuce seedlings will mark the rows.

Plant a crop for winter harvest in a block with rows spaced closer together; it's easier to insulate a block than a long row (see *Storing*, opposite).

Thinning The seeds will germinate in one to two weeks. Thin the rows of seedlings once or twice as needed. When the seedlings reach 2 inches (5 cm) high, thin them to 1–2 inches apart. If you seeded heavily, you may pull more seedlings than you leave in

Roll about a dozen seeds between your thumb and finger to sow one seed at a time.

When seedlings reach 2 inches (5 cm) tall, use nail scissors to clip extra seedlings.

place, but don't be faint-hearted—crowded carrot plants will never produce good roots.

For blocky varieties, thin a few weeks later, leaving plants 3–4 inches (7.5–10 cm) apart. You can use the pencil-thin thinnings in salads.

If your plants come up poorly and leave gaps, make sure you reseed the gaps. Otherwise, you'll be inviting weed problems.

Care

Watering If there is no rain, water seeded rows daily. Apply the water gently, or open a trench in the space between two rows and add water slowly to the trench. To prevent weeds from sprouting in the trench, fill it with shredded leaves.

After carrots are established, reduce watering, but don't let the soil dry out completely. If it does, restore soil moisture gradually—with moderate watering for several days rather than one drenching—or the roots will split and their flavor may be ruined.

Mulching Make sure you weed carrot rows frequently when the seedlings are small. After the last thinning, mulch the area completely with hay or shredded leaves, pulling mulch close to block the sunlight. This will prevent the carrots from developing green shoulders.

Quick Tip

Interplanting

Plant parsnips with your carrots so you can harvest some of both crops each time you raid your in-ground winter supply. To prevent the larger parsnips from casting shadows on the carrots, make sure you leave plenty of space between the two.

Carrots are available in many shapes, including round golf-ball-size carrots and finger-size types known as fingerlings.

Harvesting

At the expected time of maturity, check the size of the carrot roots every few days by poking your finger into the soil around them. Pull out individual carrots by hand as desired when they reach the right size. To harvest several roots at once, insert a garden fork beside the row to loosen the soil.

Storing In general, store carrots at 32°F (0°C) and high humidity. Carrots will rot in cold, wet soil, but you can store a fall crop in a well-drained garden bed into winter by applying a thick insulating mulch. When air temperatures drop to 20°F (-6.5°C), cover the carrot bed with 1 foot (30 cm) of straw or leaves.

As you work, poke tall stakes into the ground at the end of the rows to serve as markers. Spread a plastic sheet over the mulch and weight it with rocks (mulch loses its insulating quality if it gets wet). Leave bare ground on all sides of the mulched area to prevent mice from invading the bed.

To harvest, pull back one section of plastic, brush away the mulch, and dig out the roots. Then replace the mulch and plastic.

PROBLEM SOLVER

Roots split. Heat, dry soil, rapid soil moisture changes, or too much nitrogen fertilizer can cause splitting.

Tunnels in roots. Rust-fly maggots or wireworms may cause tunnels. To deter the maggots, drench the soil with beneficial nematodes before planting. Cover seeded areas with row covers from planting to harvest.

Forked, distorted roots. Root-knot nematodes are probably the culprit. Plant nematode-resistant varieties and rotate crops. Applying beneficial nematodes to the soil before planting may provide a few months of control.

Yellow or small dark brown spots on leaves. These are signs of leaf blight, one of two types of fungi that appear late in the season. Remove and destroy infected leaves. Plant disease-restistant cultivars; practice crop rotation.

Bitter flavor. Usually caused by hot conditions, avoid planting when roots would mature in hot weather. Too much nitrogen fertilizer can also ruin flavor.

BEST OF THE BUNCH

'Caroline' An improved Chantenay type, will grow well in clay soil; 7–8 inches (17.5–20 cm); 65–80 days from seeds.
'Nantes Half Long' Great for eating raw or cooking; slim, 7 inches (17.5 cm) long. 70 days from seeds.
'Parmex' Round baby carrot; smooth skin does not need peeling; 1–2 inches (2.5–5 cm) long. 60–70 days from seeds.
'Touchon' Good for fresh eating and in-ground storage; 6–8 inches (15–20 cm) long. 65 days from seeds.

Beets

If you hanker for pickled beets, roasted beets, or borscht, you'll be pleased to learn that beets are easy to grow in almost any soil. The sweet, colorful roots are a tasty treat any time of year, and beet greens are one of the best greens for cooking.

PLANTING GUIDE

What to plant Seeds or transplants.

Starting indoors Sow seeds six to eight weeks before last spring frost; harden off and transplant outside four weeks later.

Site preparation Dig the soil deeply; remove rocks and clumps.

When Sow several plantings from early to late spring. Sow again in midsummer.

Spacing Eight to 10 seeds per foot (30 cm); rows, 18 inches (45 cm) apart; thin seedlings to 4–6 inches (10–15 cm) apart.

Intensive spacing Broadcast seeds lightly over a 15–18-inch (38–45-cm)-wide bed.

How much Per person, a row 5–10 feet (1.5–3 m) long or a 3 x 5-foot (1 x 1.5-m) bed.

Temperature alert
Beets thrive in moderate temperatures, from 50–65°F (10–18°C).

Planting

Soil When planting beets for the first time, test the soil before planting. The ideal pH is 6.5. If you have chalky or recently limed soil, it might be deficient in boron. Carefully sprinkle 1–1½ tablespoons (6–9 g) of household borax along 100 feet (30 m) of row and work it into the soil. Use borax sparingly—it can be toxic.

Work the soil well and remove rocks or chunks of soil that could interfere with root growth. To boost yields, dig in a 5-gallon (19-liter) bucketful of compost or 3 cups (700 ml) of dried seaweed per 100 square feet (9 sq m).

When to plant Sow seeds in spring two to four weeks before your last spring frost. Make sure you check the soil temperature before planting. The soil should be at least 50°F (10°C) if you've had previous problems with damping-off.

You should keep spring plantings small and make new plantings every three weeks. In hot-summer areas, stop sowing about 60 days before the full summer heat begins.

Sow seeds again six to eight weeks before your first expected fall frost. This will be your fall storage crop, so sow only once, planting as much as you think you'll need to last through the winter. Depending on the variety, you'll harvest about 15 pounds (7 kg) of beets per 10 feet (3 m) of row.

In mild-winter areas, sow seeds in fall to harvest throughout winter.

Sowing and thinning Each knobbly beet "seed" is not really a seed, but is, in fact, a dried fruit that contains several tiny true seeds. Presoak these seeds for 12 hours before sowing to help speed germination. Seedlings will sprout in clumps. Use small scissors to snip off unwanted seedlings at ground level.

Because beet seeds won't germinate well in heavy clay soil, transplants are a better choice. If you buy transplants, another benefit is that you won't need to thin seedlings. Set each plant at the desired final spacing.

If you're starting your own seeds indoors, sow one seed per peat pot, and thin seedlings to one plant per pot when the first true leaves emerge.

Care

In the North, spring crops will grow faster when covered with a row cover, which will provide protection from chilling winds. If a heavy freeze is a threat, also cover with a row cover.

When direct-sowing during the summer, keep the soil constantly moist or germination will be poor.

Preventing weeds To prevent weed competition and to conserve moisture, you should water your stand of beet seedlings well and then put down a layer of mulch between the rows at least 4 inches (10 cm) deep. If slugs are a problem in your garden, wait until the plants are a few inches tall before mulching.

If weeds spring up around your beets, pull them carefully by hand rather than using tools. Tools may nick the developing beet roots and leave them open to disease organisms.

Harvesting

Cut young beet greens for salads beginning about one month after planting. Rinse the greens repeatedly in a sink full of cold water before use to remove any grit.

For baby beets, try lifting some roots about 40 days after planting. Full-size beets should be ready to pick two to three weeks later. Roots that are Ping-Pong to golf-ball size have optimal flavor. Storage varieties, such as 'Lutz Greenleaf', will taste good even when as large as a softball. Golden beets maintain quality up to hardball size.

Storing Store beet greens in plastic bags up to 10 days in the refrigerator. Freshly harvested beets will last refrigerated in plastic bags up to three weeks. For long-term root storage, you can pack the beets in containers of moist sand or peat and keep them in an unheated basement or garage (40–50°F/4.5–10°C is ideal). Sort the beets by size before packing—small beets won't last as long as large roots.

You can also store beets in a clamp (see pages 116–17) in mild-winter areas. In cold-winter areas, dig an outdoor pit and line it with dry leaves or straw. Layer the beets on top, then cover with a heavy layer of mulch.

Quick Tip

Salad treat

Use the first thinnings for salads. A continued gradual harvest will allow the remaining roots to enlarge.

A versatile vegetable, both the root and the leaves of beets are edible.

PROBLEM SOLVER

Black spots or brown hearts on roots. Caused by lack of boron. Cut away the discolored parts; the rest is edible. If soil is chalky or has recently been limed, add boron by raking in 1½ teaspoons per square yard (7.5 ml per sq m) of borax or feeding plants with calcified seaweed.

Holes in leaves. Ragged holes may be caused by slugs, beet armyworms, or garden webworms. Handpick caterpillars or spray them with BTK when small; use your preferred method to control slugs.

Tunnels in leaves. Spinach leafminer larvae leave tunnels. Destroy infested leaves. Cover newly planted areas with row covers to prevent damage.

Brown spots on leaves, which then deteriorate. Cercospora leaf spot can cause these symptoms. Pick and destroy diseased leaves. Developed roots are edible; look for resistant varieties.

Young plants go to seed. Due to exposure to temperatures below 50°F (10°C) or lack of moisture. Adjust planting times to avoid cold exposure; use mulch and/or an irrigation system for consistent soil moisture.

BEST OF THE BUNCH

'Burpee's Golden' Sweet, nonstaining golden flesh; large and tasty greens for salads or cooking. 55 days from seeds.
'Chioggia' Roots reveal rings of red and white when sliced; sweet; use greens in place of spinach. 54 days from seeds.
'Cylindra' Long, dark red roots good for making pickled beets. 60 days from seeds.
'Lutz Green Leaf' Dark beet, tasty greens; good for storage. 70–80 days from seeds.
'Red Ace' Fast-growing, dependable, and somewhat resistant to leaf spot. Tasty greens; sweet roots. 50 days from seeds.

Radishes

Most vegetables grow slowly and steadily, but radishes (a member of the cabbage family) race to the finish line—they are ready to pick as soon as three weeks from planting day. Radishes have zesty color and flavor that add appeal to any meal.

PLANTING GUIDE

What to plant Seeds.

Site preparation No special preparation needed.

When As soon as soil can be worked in spring; succession plantings throughout the season.

Spacing 1 inch (2.5 cm) apart, 6 inches (15 cm) between rows; thin 2–4 inches (5–10 cm) apart.

Intensive spacing 2 inches (5 cm) apart on centers.

How much Per person, 2–3 feet (60–90 cm) of row per planting.

WINTER RADISHES

Deeply worked, slightly acid, cool soil is best for winter radishes (or daikons). Sow spring varieties early in spring; or sow in midsummer for a fall harvest. In mild-winter areas, sow in fall to early winter. Sow seeds 2–3 inches (5–7.5 cm) apart with 10 inches (25 cm) between rows. Thin 4–8 inches (10–20 cm) apart; keep the soil moist. Harvest roots when they are 2 inches (5 cm) across.

Planting

Begin sowing in early spring and sow a new planting every 10 days. You can try sowing straight through summer into fall, but in hot-summer areas, summer radishes are disappointing—heat and drought toughen the roots and intensify their "heat." Take a break during summer, but enjoy radishes through fall and winter.

Care

In loose, moist soil, radish seeds germinate almost overnight. Mulch thinly with grass clippings after seeding to conserve soil moisture. Sow small patches of radishes in nooks and crannies among other crops, such as between cabbage-family transplants. Harvest the radishes before the other crops grow enough to shade them.

Harvesting

Pick radishes when they are up to 1 inch (2.5 cm) across (except winter radishes, see box, left). Don't let the roots grow larger, or they'll become woody, have a sharp taste, and may crack. Pick the roots all at once while their quality is prime.

Storing Cut off the plant tops and refrigerate the roots.

PROBLEM SOLVER

Gray, rotted roots. Caused by fungal root rot. Plant resistant types. Follow a crop-rotation plan for cabbage-family crops.

Worms in deformed roots. Keep larvae of cabbage maggot off plants, particularly in spring and fall, by using row covers.

Large, deformed roots. Clubroot makes foliage turn yellow and wilt. Destroy the plants. Replant in a different site with well-drained soil.

BEST OF THE BUNCH

'Cherry Belle' Round, scarlet red. 24 days from seeds.
'French Breakfast' Elongated radishes; crisp, mild flavor. 23 days from seeds.
'Fuego' Barrel-shaped radish; disease resistant. 25 days from seeds.

Whether elongated or round, radishes are enjoyable in salads and other dishes.

Parsnips

The sweet nutty flavor of these roots improves after frost, making parsnips a star of the fall and winter garden. Parsnips have a reputation for being hard to grow, but that's only to get the plants established—otherwise, they are usually trouble free.

PLANTING GUIDE

What to plant Seeds.

Site preparation Work the soil deeply and enrich with compost.

When In spring, from two weeks before to two weeks after last frost date. In mild-winter areas, in late fall for spring harvest.

Spacing Sow seeds thickly in rows 18–24 inches (45–60 cm) apart; thin plants 4–6 inches (10–15 cm) apart.

Intensive spacing 6 inches (15 cm) on centers.

How much Up to 30 plants per person.

BEST OF THE BUNCH

'Harris Model' Long, slim roots with few side roots. 120 days from seeds.
'Andover' Canker-resistant, sweet-tasting. 120 days from seeds.

Temperature alert
Roots have poor eating quality if they mature above 75°F (24°C), so avoid a spring planting in areas with hot summers.

Planting

Soil To prepare the planting area, dig the soil about 18 inches (45 cm) deep, removing all stones and clods. Spread a 3–5-inch (7.5–12.5-cm) layer of well-rotted compost, and thoroughly mix it into the soil. Or to save labor, dig a trench or individual planting holes. For a trench, loosen the soil, then dig an 18-inch (45-cm)-deep trench. Fill it with well-rotted compost mixed with soil, open a furrow, and sow the seeds.

To make planting holes 6 inches (15 cm) apart, use a digging bar to open holes a few inches across and 18 inches (45 cm) deep. Fill each hole with compost mixed with soil. Open a small hole in the compost with a dibble. Sow several seeds at each spot.

Establishing seedlings Make sure you always use fresh parsnip seeds. Instead of using soil, you should cover the seeds with sand or vermiculite to prevent crusting.

Care

Side-dress with compost or a balanced organic fertilizer once during the growing season. Once seedlings are a few inches tall, apply a mulch of chopped leaves to conserve moisture and suppress weeds.

PROBLEM SOLVER

Cankers on roots. The fungus that causes cankers thrives in wet conditions. Replant in a raised bed that drains well. Check soil pH and raise it to 7.0 if needed. Practice a crop-rotation plan.

Small swellings on roots. Root-knot nematode can cause the main root and side roots to swell. To prevent future problems, you can plant a cover crop of marigolds. Practice crop rotation.

Harvesting

Young roots are more tender than large roots, but flavor is usually best after a frost. Use a garden fork to loosen the soil around the roots before pulling out the plants.

Storing Parsnips store well in the garden. Apply mulch 6–12 inches (15–30 cm) thick over the bed to insulate them; dig roots as needed throughout fall and winter. Or let the roots freeze in place and harvest them in the spring.

If winters in your area are mild or wet, dig all the roots in late fall. They will last for several weeks stored in the refrigerator. For longer storage, pack them in damp sand (see pages 116–17).

Turnips and rutabagas

White turnip roots and succulent greens are a treat that you can enjoy in both spring and fall, while the substantial roots of a rutabaga (also called swede turnips) grow best in cool fall conditions, or even throughout the winter in mild areas.

PLANTING GUIDE

What to plant Seeds.

Site preparation Work soil well.

When Sow turnips in spring and midsummer to fall; rutabaga, in early to midsummer.

Spacing Sow 2 inches (5 cm) apart, in rows 18 inches (45 cm) apart. Final spacing if growing turnips for roots is 4–6 inches (10–15 cm); final spacing for rutabaga, 8 inches (20 cm).

How much *Turnips* 5 feet (1.5 m) of row per person for storage; less for fresh eating. *Rutabaga* 8 feet (2.4 m) of row per person for storage.

Temperature alert
Cool conditions and frost bring out the best in turnips. Roots that mature in the heat will have an unpleasantly strong flavor.

Planting

Soil Loosen the soil well to 6 inches (15 cm) deep. Remove any rocks and clods and dig in a 2-inch (5-cm) layer of compost. Test your soil and make sure the pH is not lower than 6.5 (see pages 32–33).

Spring turnip crops Turnip seeds are readily available from garden centers and mail-order suppliers. Choose fast-maturing varieties to plant in spring.

Begin sowing the seeds about one month before the last-expected spring frost. You can sow seeds every three weeks until one month before you expect high temperatures to average 80°F (26.5°C).

If you live in an area with mild summers, continue sowing every three weeks or once a month throughout the summer.

Fall and winter turnips For a fall harvest, begin sowing turnip seeds about eight weeks before the first-expected hard frost; choose varieties that are good for storage. Make sure you keep the seedbed moist; the seeds should germinate quickly and do well in hot soil.

Gardeners in areas with mild winters can plant turnip seeds in September and October.

Rutabaga crops For specific rutabaga varieties, you may have to try specialty seed companies or seed exchanges.

In most regions, you should plant rutabaga seeds in early to midsummer for a fall harvest (about 90 days before the shift to cool weather patterns in your area). In mild-winter areas, you can also try sowing rutabaga seeds in early fall.

Care

Rich soil with plenty of moisture will produce crispy, tender turnips. Dry conditions, especially during hot weather, will produce harsh-tasting

BEST OF THE BUNCH

Rutabaga 'American Purple Top' Purple-red skin aboveground, yellow skin below. Yellow flesh turns orange when cooked. 90 days from seeds.
Turnip 'Hakurei' Sweet roots and delicious greens. 38 days from seeds.
Turnip 'Purple Top White Globe' Heirloom variety with sweet roots up to 6 inches (15 cm) across. Pink or purple shading on root shoulders. Greens are good for cooking. 55 days from seeds.
Turnip 'Seven Top' Grown only for its productive greens. 45 days from seeds.
Turnip 'Tokyo Cross' Spring turnip. Tasty greens; harvest roots 2–6 inches (5–15 cm) across. 35 days from seeds.

roots. However, avoid overwatering—too much rain or water can cause enlarging roots to crack.

After seedlings are established, mulch with clean straw, shredded leaves, or grass clippings for weed control and to keep the soil cool.

Harvesting

Baby turnips are ready for harvest as soon as one month after planting. Rutabagas are slower to mature, needing from 90 to 120 days to reach a harvestable size.

For spring plantings, you can pick individual turnip leaves as desired. If you are growing a patch of turnips for only the greens, shear the tops about an inch (2.5 cm) or so above the base of the stems.

Baby turnips about 1 inch (2.5 cm) in diameter may be ready for harvest in only 25 days from planting. You should monitor the weather and finish the harvest of spring-planted turnips before the weather turns steadily hot.

In the fall, wait to harvest the roots until after a frost, which will improve the flavor. If possible, dig the turnips when they are about 2–3 inches (5–7.5 cm) across for the best flavor and tenderness. Some varieties are reputed to stay tender up to 6 inches (15 cm) across. You can cut the leaves as you need them, but do so before they reach 12 inches (30 cm) long.

Harvest rutabagas when they are about 6 inches (15 cm) across, as you need them.

Storing Turnip roots will last in the refrigerator for two to three weeks in plastic bags. You can refrigerate greens, too, but they're best cooked as soon as possible after harvest. You can also store turnips in damp sand (see pages 116–17). Leave turnips in the ground only until the time of hard freezes, which will crack the roots.

Rutabaga can withstand hard freezes if well mulched. Or dig and store them for up to six months in a humid root cellar at 32°F (0°C).

PROBLEM SOLVER

Tunnels in roots. Due to cabbage root maggots; damage is worst early in the season. Cover spring crops tightly with row covers. Plant only in late spring or midsummer (for fall harvest).

Swollen, distorted roots; wilting leaves. Clubroot is the cause. Practice a crop-rotation plan. Add lime to raise soil pH. Remove and destroy infected plant materials.

Small holes in leaves. Caused by flea beetles; prevent problems by covering crops with row covers.

Turnips are cabbage-family crops and are susceptible to some of the same problems. See page 171 for additional problems and solutions.

Harvest rutabagas in the fall for use throughout the winter.

Quick Tip

Getting your greens

For more turnip greens from thinnings, sow the seeds closer than the standard 2 inches (5 cm). For only greens, allow 1–4 inches (2.5–10 cm) for final spacing between plants.

Celery

Garden-grown celery has a delightful crispness and full flavor you'll never get from store-bought celery. It's wise to choose at least two varieties the first time you grow celery, because some types of this temperamental plant may not do well in your area.

PLANTING GUIDE

What to plant Transplants.

Starting indoors After soaking seeds in compost tea for six hours, sow seeds eight weeks before last frost in soil at 65–70°F (18–21°C); keep moist. Harden plants, then transplant.

Site preparation Enrich soil; add composted manure if needed.

When Set out transplants after danger of frost has passed.

Spacing Set transplants about 9–12 inches (23–30 cm) apart in rows 24 inches (60 cm) apart.

Intensive spacing 12 inches (30 cm) apart on centers.

How much Six plants per person.

Temperature alert
Celery needs three to four months of 65–80°F (18–26.5°C) outdoors. When above 80°F (26.5°C), stems may become stringy.

Planting

Soil Dig in a 1½-inch (3.75-cm) layer of compost 4 inches (10 cm) deep. To add moisture retention and nutrients, you can dig a 12-inch (30-cm)-deep trench; fill it with compost mixed with composted manure and add 2–3 inches (5–7.5 cm) of soil.

When to plant If summer heat is intense in the Midwest and Mid-Atlantic, set out transplants in late summer. In Zones 9 and 10, plant in November; harvest in spring.

Care

If temperatures dip below 45°F (7°C), cover plants with cloches (remove on warm days to avoid overheating plants).

To blanch nonblanching varieties, mound soil around the stalks when they are 12 inches (30 cm) tall, or wrap the stems of a plant in brown paper and tie it in place. Alternatively, plant celery in trenches in the same manner as leeks (see pages 164–65).

Watering and feeding Ideally, use a drip irrigation system. Or for only a few plants, sink watering reservoirs (such as soda bottles) between them. Water weekly with fish emulsion or side-dress with ½ pound (20 g) blood meal per 10 plants; then mulch.

PROBLEM SOLVER

Holes in stalks. Handpick and kill slugs. Spread diatomaceous earth or crushed eggshells around plants. Set out traps.

Rotted stalks. Destroy plants infected by fungi or bacteria. Use a crop-rotation plan. Water soil, not stems; allow air circulation.

Misshapen leaves with sticky coating. Wash aphids off plants with jet of water. Spray plants with insecticidal soap.

Young plants form seed stalks. Bolting results from temperatures below 50°F (10°C). Protect plants by using cloches.

Harvesting

Cut plants at the base before frost. In fall, heap straw or leaves around plants to protect from frost, or use cloches.

Storing Store celery in plastic bags in the refrigerator for several weeks. Or put plants with roots attached in boxes with moist sphagnum moss or soil around the roots for up to four months.

BEST OF THE BUNCH

'Utah 52-70' Resists bolting. 100 days from transplants.
'Ventura' Strong seedlings; bright green stalks. 85 days from transplants.

Celeriac

Sow some celeriac this year and enjoy its mild celery flavor with nutty overtones in your cooking without the hassle of growing celery. Celeriac and celery are closely related, but celeriac produces skimpier tops and a fat, fleshy root.

PLANTING GUIDE

What to plant Seeds or transplants.

Starting indoors Sow seeds 8 to 10 weeks before last expected spring frost. In cool-summer, short-season areas, sow in early spring.

Site preparation Add compost.

When Set plants out in spring when daytime temperatures consistently exceed 55°F (13°C).

Spacing Set transplants or thin seedlings 8–10 inches (20–25 cm) apart in rows 2 feet (60 cm) apart.

Intensive spacing 12 inches (30 cm) apart on centers.

How much Up to 10 plants per person if storing.

Temperature alert
In hot-summer areas, plant outdoors in late spring to early summer, so the roots will mature during cool weather.

Planting

Work in 2 inches (5 cm) of compost over the area to be planted—it will help the soil to retain moisture. Test the soil (see pages 32–33); the best pH range is 6.0 to 6.5.

For summer sowings, shade the seedbeds on hot, sunny days until the plants are established. You can water in transplants with a plant-starter fertilizer.

Care

Celeriac doesn't tolerate heat well. You should provide a lot of water and mulch to keep the soil cool.

During summer, you can pull back some soil from the crowns of the roots; then with your thumb, rub off the side shoots. This will make the roots smoother and easier to peel after harvesting.

Harvesting

Smaller roots will have better texture and quality than large roots. Try harvesting celeriac when the roots are 3–5 inches (7.5–12.5 cm) across. Cut off the leaves and compost them, or add the leafstalks and leaves to soup stock in place of celery stalks and leaves. Scrub the roots well. Tender roots may be enjoyable for eating raw. Peel away the tough outer parts before cooking celeriac.

Storing In mild-winter areas, you can overwinter celeriac roots right in the garden. In cold-winter regions, you should dig the roots in fall and store them in boxes packed in damp sand in a cool basement or garage (see pages 116–17).

You should avoid storing celeriac near vegetables with strong flavors, such as onions, because the roots may pick up their flavors.

PROBLEM SOLVER

Tunnels in leaves. Celery leafminers feed internally in leaves. Snip off leaves that show tunnels and destroy them. If leafminers are a serious problem in your area, cover the crop with row covers to prevent adults from laying eggs.

BEST OF THE BUNCH

'Large Smooth Prague' Uniform roots about 4 inches (10 cm) in diameter. 110 days from transplants.
'Diamant' Vigorous grower; resists pithiness. 110 days from transplants.

Salsify and scorzonera

Expand your root-crop repertoire with two crops that have a reputation for having an unusual taste. Salsify and scorzonera (or black salsify) resemble slim carrots—however, their flavor is reminiscent of oysters.

PLANTING GUIDE

What to plant Seeds.

Site preparation Work the soil deeply and remove rocks.

When As early as possible in the spring. In Zones 7 and 8, sow also in late sumer; in Zones 9 and 10, plant in fall.

Spacing Sow thickly in rows 15–18 inches (38–45 cm) apart; thin seedlings to 4–6 inches (10–15 cm) apart.

Intensive spacing 6 inches (15 cm) on centers.

How much Up to 10 feet (3 m) of row per person.

Scorzonera roots have black skin. Salsify roots (above) are whitish with side roots.

Planting

Soil Salsify and scorzonera roots are long and slender. For best results dig the soil well at least 1 foot (30 cm) deep and remove any rocks. Avoid adding fresh nitrogen sources, such as manure, which may cause forked roots. Work a 1-inch (2.5-cm) layer of finished compost into the soil.

Establishing seedlings Use fresh seeds and sow thickly. The seeds may take up to three weeks to germinate—never let the seedbed dry out during this period.

Once the seedlings appear, water the bed well and gently pull out excess seedlings or cut them off at ground level, leaving seedlings at least 4 inches (10 cm) apart.

The plants will grow best when temperatures are below 75°F (24°C). In mid-latitude areas, spring weather may turn too hot too fast; but in fall, frosts may stop growth before the roots mature. Experiment to see which season works best for you.

Care

These crops don't need much special care and almost never suffer from pest problems. When they are young, remove any weeds but be careful not to mistake the grasslike foliage of the crops for weeds. Water as needed to keep the soil moist.

Harvesting

Try clipping some scorzonera foliage to add to green salads, leaving enough at the base to allow regrowth.

The roots will grow up to 1 inch (2.5 cm) in diameter and 8–12 inches (20–30 cm) in length. While you can harvest them as soon as they reach full size, keep in mind that their flavor will improve after exposure to frost.

You should cook the roots before peeling them or you'll lose their delicate flavor. After peeling, serve the cooked roots with melted butter and lemon or add them to soups or stews.

Storing The roots will store well in the ground. Mulch them thoroughly with a deep layer of chopped leaves or straw in cold-winter regions.

If you dig a full crop, store the roots in damp sand (see pages 116–17). The roots will last only about a week in the refrigerator in plastic bags.

BEST OF THE BUNCH

Salsify 'Mammoth Sandwich Island' Variety with roots to 1½ inches (3.75 cm) in diameter. 120 days from seeds.

Scorzonera 'Belstar Super' Variety with long roots. 80 days from seeds.

Florence fennel

With its feathery, licorice-scented foliage and attractive form, Florence fennel is a great addition to a flower garden. The harvest of crunchy "bulbs" (swollen stem bases) is delicious raw in salads or appetizers and irresistible braised or grilled.

PLANTING GUIDE

What to plant Seeds or transplants.

Starting indoors Six to eight weeks before last spring frost.

Site preparation No special preparation needed.

When Varies by region.

Spacing Set transplants about 10–12 inches (25–30 cm) apart on centers; thin direct-seeded rows to same spacing.

How much Up to five plants per person per planting.

Planting

Florence fennel will grow well in most average flower or vegetable gardens and doesn't require any particular soil preparation.

Alternatively, you can grow this unusual crop in a sunny patio planting; it will do well in a pot.

When to plant In mild-summer areas, sow seeds after danger of frost has past. Seeds and seedlings are small and delicate, so keep the soil fully moist for two weeks after sowing.

In areas with hot summers, a spring planting may not grow well. Instead, sow in midsummer for a fall harvest. In Florida, you can sow seeds in September or October.

If you buy transplants or start your own, you can plant them outdoors two weeks before the last spring frost, but plan to protect them if temperatures will drop below 25°F (-4°C).

Care

For the best yields, you should water the plants regularly and feed them by watering with fish emulsion every three weeks.

When the bulbs are about the size of an egg, push the soil up around them to blanch them; this will make the bulbs more tender.

PROBLEM SOLVER

Plants bolt without forming swollen stems. Disturbing the roots can cause bolting, so apply mulch to control weeds instead of cultivating around the plants. Sow seeds instead of transplanting.

Harvesting

Florence fennel bulbs can grow to a large size, but smaller bulbs are better for eating. You can harvest the bulbs as soon as 65 days after planting, but some varieties require up to 100 days to mature. Ideally, harvest bulbs when 3–5 inches (7.5–12.5 cm) across.

Storing You can wrap Florence fennel bulbs in plastic and store them in the refrigerator for two to three days after cutting.

To harvest Florence fennel, cut off the bulbs at soil level using a sharp knife.

Quick Tip

Worthy plant

You may have to search to find these seeds in catalogs (try looking under finocchio, another name for this traditional Italian favorite). The choice of varieties will be small; however, it's worth your while to find and plant Florence fennel.

11 Tomatoes and other heat lovers

Tomatoes and peppers rate as favorite vegetables for most home gardeners. These colorful, flavorful fruit are excellent for fresh eating, cooking, and preserving. Eggplant was once an unpopular cousin, but more gardeners are discovering how delicious it tastes grilled or combined with other ingredients for creative appetizers and sauces. Tomatillo, a prolific tomato relative, deserves a place in every salsa-lover's garden. Okra rounds out this group of heat-loving crops. You can grow this traditional southern favorite in most regions by choosing early yielding varieties.

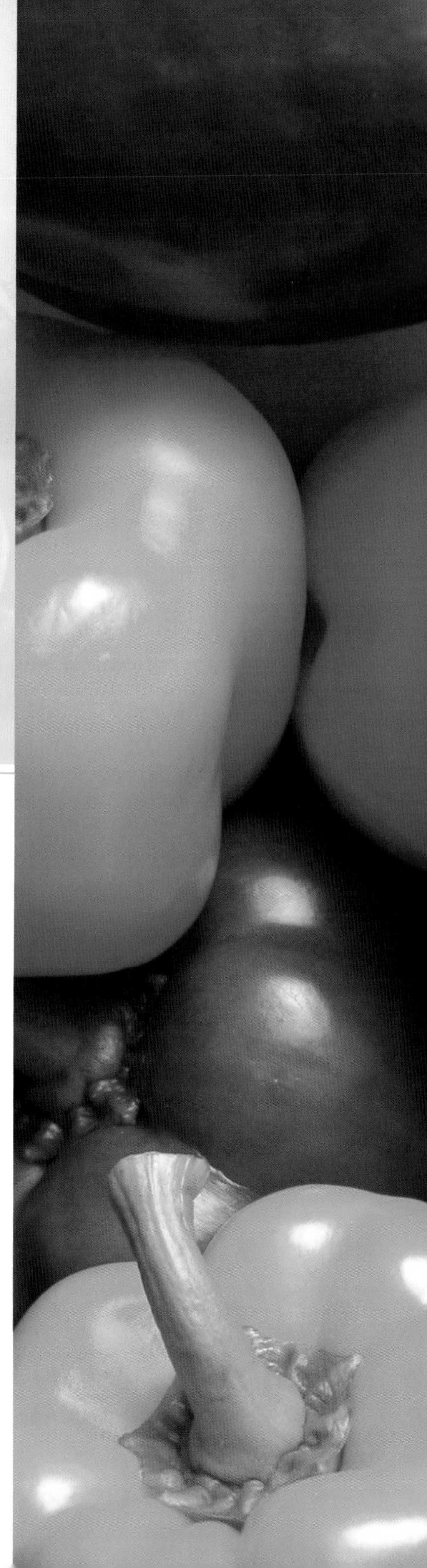

Sweet bell peppers are versatile staples of Mexican and Italian cuisine.

Tomatoes

The temptation of tomatoes has lured many a gardener to plant just a few too many plants. It's difficult to rein in your enthusiasm for garden-fresh tomatoes, especially when such a wide range of types is available.

PLANTING GUIDE

What to plant Transplants or rooted cuttings.

Starting indoors Sow seeds six to eight weeks before your last frost date.

Site preparation Loosen the soil and add organic matter.

When After danger of spring frost is past; 12 to 14 weeks before first fall frost.

Spacing Set plants 2–4 feet (60–120 cm) apart, depending on the type of tomato.

How much Two to four plants per person; one or two cherry tomato plants per household.

Planting

Soil Loosen the soil about 10 inches (25 cm) deep; then work a 2–3 inch (5–7.5 cm) layer of compost into the top several inches of soil. To warm up the soil faster, shape the soil into a raised bed 6 inches (15 cm) high.

When you dig planting holes, add compost to the removed soil. Create a mixture that's half soil and half compost for refilling the holes.

Choosing what to grow Consider what you want from the plants: an early harvest, large fruit, best flavor, disease resistance, or an extended harvest period—no single variety provides all of these qualities. If you have space, grow several varieties with different characteristics.

Determinate, indeterminate, and semideterminate are terms used to describe how a tomato plant develops. Determinate plants are bushy, reaching 3 feet (90 cm) tall. Their side branches are short, and each side branch produces a flower cluster at the branch tip at about the same time. The fruit form and ripen in two to three weeks.

Indeterminate plants produce a lot of suckers from the main stem; each sucker expands into a rambling branch. The branches flower and set fruit as long as conditions are good.

Semideterminate plants have characteristics of both types. They produce suckers, but not as many as indeterminate tomatoes. These plants will stop growing when they reach 3–5 feet (90–150 cm) tall.

Tomato varieties are also classified as early season, mid-season, or late-season producers. Early season types produce fruit as early as 60 days after transplanting. Mid-season varieties take from 65 to 75 days from transplanting to first harvest. Late-season varieties require more than 75 days to set fruit.

Encouraging early plantings Every gardener anticipates the first tomato of the season. There are several tips that will lead to early production. However, the first tomatoes of the season will be small and may not have the rich flavor you expect from a homegrown tomato. The plants will have less foliage and thus can't produce as many sugars, which are the fuel for excellent flavor.

One strategy for getting better flavor from an early crop is to grow varieties that produce fruit in the shortest possible time. You won't have to plant these varieties as early, so they won't have to get established during cold, short days. These plants grow faster overall, producing more foliage, more sugars, and better fruit.

Temperature alert
Tomatoes may not set fruit in temperatures above 90°F (32°C) or below 55°F (13°C). Fruit set should resume when the weather changes.

For an early harvest, start seeds three to six weeks earlier than the recommended transplanting time. Start to harden off the transplants by reducing water and fertilizer if conditions are too cold to harden them off outdoors.

You can cover the soil with black plastic or IRT (infrared transmitting) mulch—ideally the preceding fall. The mulch will warm the soil and keep it dry, which is important for early planting. Leave the mulch in place until the end of the season.

Once you set plants outside, cover them with cloches. Alternatively, set up tomato cages right after planting and wrap them with clear plastic to create a mini-greenhouse. Or, if you are growing more than three early plants, set up a tunnel over the plants using wire hoops covered by clear plastic or row covers.

Remove the protective coverings once the weather reaches the right range for tomato growth. Otherwise the plants will overheat, and that can damage plants and developing fruit.

Starting plants from cuttings

In the South and some parts of the Southwest, gardeners can harvest tomatoes well into fall. However, the tomato plants set out in spring may succumb to stress, pests, or disease before fall comes around. For a reliable fall crop, start a new set of plants in midsummer, either from seeds or by taking cuttings from the plants set out in spring.

Choose suckers that are about 4–5 inches (10–12.5 cm) long, and use scissors or pruners to cut them off. Remove the bottom set of leaves and place the cuttings in a container of water or moist sand. The cuttings should root easily.

Plant the rooted cuttings in pots or into a garden bed. Water them thoroughly for the first few days while they adjust to their new setting. If the cuttings are free of disease and insect pests, these plants will develop quickly and fruit well.

Transplanting to the garden

Whether you raise your own transplants or buy them at a garden center, be sure to properly harden them off before transplanting. The day before transplanting, water them with fish emulsion or compost tea. If the transplants are tall and rangy, remove the first couple of true leaves and lay the bare stretch of stem on an angle in a shallow trench.

1 Gently slide the plant out of its pot, supporting the stem of the plant between your thumb and index finger.

2 Set the plant deeply, so that the first true leaf is just above soil level.

3 Refill the planting hole. Shape a small berm around the plant to capture and hold water, and water the plant well.

Staking and training Using stakes, trellises, or cages to train tomato plants will provide several benefits. The plants will have fewer disease problems because the fruit won't rest on the ground and air can circulate better through the foliage. The fruit will also be easier to reach for harvesting. You'll need to maintain the plants more often to train them, so you'll be more likely to spot potential pest and disease problems early, when you can still take effective steps to control them.

Make sure you install the method of support at the same time you set transplants in the garden. Otherwise, you may damage the plant roots, or the plants may grow large enough to flop over before you get around to setting up the supports.

You can train plants on single vertical stakes or on a tepee made of four long bamboo poles—one plant per pole. Stakes will work for determinate or indeterminate plants, but prune indeterminate plants so they don't overgrow the support.

Determinate plants also do well when supported by a horizontal wire framework. Set out hoops as you would for a protective plastic tunnel, but make the tunnels out of wire mesh fence or concrete reinforcing wire. The plants will grow up through the wire grid, which will support them.

Another method is to surround each plant with a sturdy cage. The funnel-shaped cages sold at garden centers will support determinate and semideterminate plants, but they aren't strong enough for large indeterminate plants. Instead, make cages out of wire-mesh fencing and sturdy wooden stakes. Use fencing with mesh squares at least 5 inches (12.5 cm) square.

Trellis systems will also work well for indeterminate plants. If you use twine as the vertical part of the trellis, choose plastic twine instead of sisal twine. Sisal will stretch under the weight of the heavy vines.

Pound a 6-foot (1.8-m) stake into the ground at least 6 inches (15 cm) from a newly planted transplant.

Care

Pruning side shoots You'll need to prune indeterminate tomatoes to train them to a stake or trellis. Pruning results in fewer but slightly larger fruit. Unpruned plants may develop dense foliage that blocks air circulation and leads to disease. They may also eventally become so large and heavy that they'll topple a trellis (caged tomatoes generally don't need pruning). As a general rule, allow the first few suckers to develop into fruiting branches. After that, you should prune out all other side shoots.

Fasten the stems to the stake using soft cloth strips or plant ties. As the plant grows, add strips or ties every 12 inches (30 cm).

Semideterminate plants will benefit from light pruning. Wait until the plants form a first flower cluster, then remove all but one or two suckers below that flower cluster. Do not prune the sucker immediately below the cluster.

You should prune indeterminate and semideterminate plants more lightly in Zone 6 and warmer. They need more foliage to shield fruit from the summer sun.

Don't prune determinate plants. You'll have a smaller harvest, and the plants may produce too little foliage to shade the fruit, which can lead to sunscald.

Watering In general, a tomato plant needs 3–5 gallons (11–19 liters) of water per week. However, soil type, relative humidity, rainfall, and mulch affect the rate at which soil dries out. Check soil moisture regularly, and when you do water, moisten the soil 8 inches (20 cm) deep. Early in the season, watering with heated water (80°F/26.5°C) will help to warm the soil.

After the soil is thoroughly warm, apply a mulch of straw, plastic, or paper. Mulching helps conserve soil moisture and prevents disease spores from splashing up onto plants from the soil.

Fertilizing Don't overfertilize the plants, especially with nitrogen, or they may produce excessive leaves

Remove suckers when they're 3–4 inches (7.5–10 cm) long. Bend them to the side with your fingers to break them off the plant.

Use your fingers to pinch out the growing points of tomato vines when they reach the top of a trellis.

and no fruit. If you're concerned about soil fertility, side-dress plants with a balanced organic fertilizer when the first fruit form. Continue to side-dress every three to four weeks while plants are growing.

Harvesting

Gardeners in the Deep South who plant for an early harvest may start harvesting ripe tomatoes in May. Tomatoes ripen from the inside out. Once the skin color changes from green to the mature color, the fruit are fully ripe. Ripe fruit can drop from the plants, so inspect the ground around your plants when you harvest. Many heirloom varieties are prone to cracking. To prevent this, harvest them two days before they are ripe and let them finish ripening indoors.

Extending the harvest If frost is predicted, cover the plants with a tarp, sheet, burlap bag, row cover material, or large cardboard box in the late afternoon; remove the cover the next morning once temperatures rise above freezing. This can extend the harvest by two or three weeks.

At the time of the first frost, root-prune the plants. Use a spade to slice down into the soil in a circle around the plant, 1 foot (30 cm) away from the base of the plant. This cuts roots, which triggers the plant to ripen fruit more quickly.

When frosts occur more often, cut an entire plant at the base, take it indoors to a garage or basement, and hang it upside down. The fruit will ripen slowly. Alternatively, pick all fruit when the season ends. Use green fruit for pickling or cooking. Fruit that are at least three-quarters of their mature size and have started to change color will ripen if stored in the right conditions.

Storing Ripe tomatoes won't last long, and refrigeration will ruin their flavor. Use them quickly or store them by canning. To ripen underripe tomatoes off the vine, place them in a paper bag or a dark cupboard at 65–70°F (18–21°C). Leave them in a single layer—don't stack them.

If you have a large quantity of underripe tomatoes, spread them out on a shelf in a cool pantry, garage, or basement. Cover them with layers of newspaper. Check them frequently, and remove any fruit that are ready to use, as well as any that are starting to rot.

PROBLEM SOLVER

Brown or black spots on leaves. Suspect early blight fungus, Septoria leaf spot, or another fungus. Destroy infected leaves. Prune foliage to improve air circulation. Spray with a copper-based fungicide every 7 to 10 days. Destroy severely infected plants. Practice crop rotation.

Greenish black, water-soaked spots on leaves; gray-green spots on fruit. Signs of late blight, a fungal disease; it is worst in warm, wet weather. If conditions do not change, destroy infected plants.

Distorted growth, wilting plants. Spray plants infested by aphids or whiteflies with insecticidal soap.

Mottled, crinkled leaves. Mosaic virus is spread by aphids. Destroy the infected plants. Use a row cover at planting time. Keep tobacco away from the plants.

Plants wilt in the afternoon. Lower leaves yellow and die. This is Fusarium or Verticillium wilt. Destroy the plants. Plant in raised beds to improve drainage.

Stunted plants. Swellings on roots are a sign of root-knot nematodes. Destroy the infected plants. Replant resistant varieties in a new area. Plant a cover crop of marigolds in infested areas.

Brown or black area on bottom of fruit. Blossom-end rot occurs if there is not enough calcium in developing fruit, which occurs when the soil dries out. Unaffected parts of fruit may still be edible. Check soil moisture regularly and mulch to maintain even soil moisture.

Large holes in fruit. Slugs and snails eat tomatoes close to ground level. Keep fruit up off the ground. Remove the pests.

After harvest, fruit have sunken spots that rot. Anthracnose, a fungal disease, is worst when fruit rest on soil, especially in wet weather. Keep the fruit off the soil.

Types of tomatoes

From tiny currant tomatoes to oversized beefsteaks, you'll want to grow some of every kind of tomato. However, keep in mind that fresh tomatoes won't keep for long, and a large tomato vine can be amazingly prolific.

▲ Paste tomatoes

Pear-shaped paste tomatoes (or roma tomatoes) have thick walls and small seed cavities. Most varieties are determinate. You can choose 'Roma' or 'San Marzano', an heirloom variety, to make tomato sauce or paste.

▶ Slicing tomatoes

The bread and butter of the tomato world, slicing—or salad—tomatoes are round and juicy with a rich taste. Although most slicers are red, orange and yellow varieties are also available. You can choose between determinate or indeterminate plant varieties. Some slicers are early season plants, but most of them are mid-season types. Two classic slicing tomatoes are 'Better Boy' and 'Celebrity'.

◀ Beefsteak tomatoes

The giants of the tomato world, beefsteaks produce fruit that weigh 2 pounds (0.9 kg) or more each. The fruit are wider than deep, and the flesh is juicy. Classic varieties include 'Beefmaster' and 'Big Beef'. 'Brandywine' is a popular heirloom type.

▲ Cherry tomatoes

A single indeterminate plant produces hundreds of fruit in clusters, and they may be red, orange, golden, or white. The fruit are usually sweet and juicy. Currant tomatoes produce fruit the size of currants. 'Supersweet 100', 'Tiny Tim', and 'Sweet Million' are the best-known varieties.

▼ Heirloom tomatoes

For a feast of unusual colors, shapes, and flavors, try some heirloom tomato varieties. The names often give a clue to their flavor or appearance: 'Cherokee Purple' tomatoes are dark pink and purple when ripe and have a rich flavor, while 'Green Zebra' will bear small yellow green fruit with green stripes when ripe. Heirloom tomato plants may be either indeterminate or semideterminate.

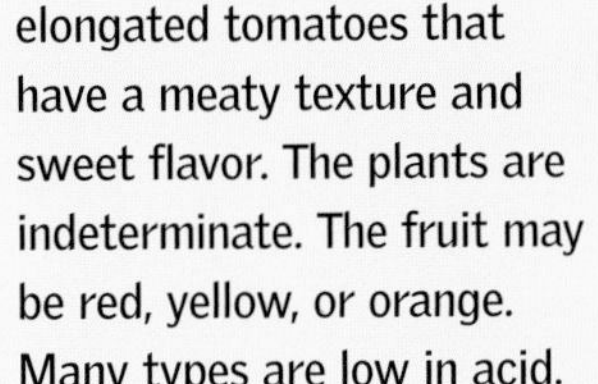

▲ Pear, plum, and grape tomatoes

These plants produce clusters of small pear-shaped or elongated tomatoes that have a meaty texture and sweet flavor. The plants are indeterminate. The fruit may be red, yellow, or orange. Many types are low in acid.

► Patio tomatoes

Ideal for containers, these compact determinate tomato plants bear small slicing-type tomatoes. One patio tomato plant will generally produce 30 to 40 egg-size tomatoes. Some types also grow well in hanging baskets.

Tomatillos

Green tomatoes, the recommended substitute for tomatillos, are no comparison to the delightfully tart flavor of tomatillos (also called husk tomatoes or Mexican green tomatoes). The bushy plant produces small tomato-like fruit with firm flesh.

PLANTING GUIDE

What to plant Seeds or transplants.

Starting indoors In short-season areas, four to six weeks before the last frost.

Site preparation Add organic matter to boost fertility.

When After all danger of frost has past.

Spacing Sow seeds 6 inches (15 cm) apart; thin seedlings or set transplants 2–3 feet (60–90 cm) apart.

How much One plant a person.

BEST OF THE BUNCH

'Purple' Deep purple fruit; good as a garnish. 70 days from transplants.
'Mexican Strain' Large fruit and high yields. 65 days from transplants.
'Gigante' Very large, fleshy, sweet fruit. 86 to 100 days from transplants.
'Toma Verde' Early-maturing; green fruit. 60 to 70 days from transplants.

Planting

Soil Make sure you loosen the soil well. If you are sowing seeds, work a 1-inch (2.5-cm) layer of compost into the soil. If planting transplants, add a shovelful of compost to each planting hole and mix it lightly.

Starting seeds indoors Sow seeds indoors four to six weeks before the last spring frost date. Use 4-inch (10-cm) pots or larger containers so that the seedling roots will have plenty of room to expand.

Planting outdoors Sow seeds or set out transplants when the soil is thoroughly warm (80°F/26.5°C). If planting transplants, pinch off the lower leaves and set the plant on an angle in a shallow trench, with only the top 4 inches (10 cm) of the plant above soil level. The plants will root along the stem.

Protecting plants from cold In cool-summer areas, covering the soil with black plastic two weeks before planting will help warm the soil and promote strong growth. If you are setting up a plastic-covered planting bed for eggplant, squash, or melons, extend the area enough for your tomatillo plants, too. Cover the plants with a row cover to protect them from chilly air temperatures for the first few weeks after planting. (After that, the plants will probably outgrow the covers.)

Care

Although tomatillo plants generally are problem free, they are susceptible to the same pests and diseases as tomatoes. If your tomatillos develop a problem, turn to pages 208–209 to find the solutions.

Watering Don't overwhelm your tomatillos with water. Water them deeply once a week if conditions are dry. Mulch the soil to retain moisture and suppress weeds.

Fertilizing Side-dress tomatillos with a balanced organic fertilizer or feed them with a fish-emulsion solution when the plants start to bloom. Avoid overfertilizing the plants, or they may produce a lot of lush foliage but no fruit.

Staking Tomatillo plants are bushy, but can grow up to 5 feet (150 cm) tall. Without support, the fruiting branches may end up sprawled on the ground, which makes harvesting difficult. To ensure an easy harvest, corral each plant inside a tomato cage or tie plants to a trellis.

Harvesting

To determine when to harvest the fruit, watch for the papery husks to change from green to tan or pale gold. Once the husks change color, pick some of the fruit and taste them. Green fruit will be tarter than those left on the plants until they turn yellow.

It will be easier to remove the husks and the sticky coating on the fruit if you set the fruit in a bowl of warm water for one minute.

Frost will kill tomatillo plants. Be sure to strip off all the fruit at the end of the season, or they will reseed themselves and can become a weed problem the following season.

Storing Tomatillos will keep for one week at room temperature. The ideal storage conditions are 40–50°F (4.5–10°C) and high humidity. However, tomatillos can be stored in the refrigerator, too. Leave the husks intact and put the fruit in paper bags (not plastic); they will keep in the refrigerator for up to one month. Tomatillos freeze well: Remove the husks, wash the fruit, and freeze them whole in plastic bags.

Tomatillo fruit are packaged inside delicate, paper-thin husks, resembling Chinese lanterns.

Peppers

Peppers are a great crop for the gardener who's short on time. They have few problems, don't demand daily harvesting, and when the weather and soil conditions are right, they're very prolific. You can even grow them in a patio container.

PLANTING GUIDE

What to plant Transplants only.

Starting indoors Worth it if you want unusual varieties.

Preparing the site Warm soil; remove soil cover seven days before planting.

When to plant After all danger of frost has passed.

Spacing Plant in blocks, setting plants 18–24 inches (45–60 cm) apart on a grid.

How much to plant *Bell peppers* Three plants per person; more if you plan to freeze some. *Hot peppers* Two plants per household; more if you cook a lot of spicy food.

Planting

Soil Peppers need moderately rich soil. Side-dress plants with compost or fish emulsion every three weeks. Don't use a high-nitrogen fertilizer; otherwise your plants will produce leaves, not fruit.

Coping with a cool climate If your springtime is cool, cover your planting area with black plastic a week before planting. Cut slits in the plastic for planting and leave it in place all season to warm the soil, conserve moisture, and prevent weeds. Providing a row cover at planting time can supply extra warmth and protection from wind.

Planting Set plants about 18 inches (45 cm) apart and plant them in a double- or triple-row block rather than a single row. The exception to this is areas with cool, cloudy summers. Cool-climate gardeners should space plants farther apart for better air circulation and to allow the maximum light to reach each plant.

Care

Watering Pepper plants can suffer from water stress during dry periods. Use a drip-irrigation hose—heavy watering from overhead can wash away pollen and reduce the fruit set.

To stake or not to stake? When staked or supported, the branches can't break under the weight of a prolific crop. Use a sturdy stake or a mid-size tomato cage.

Letting plants sprawl has one big advantage: It's easier to cover the plants with a blanket overnight if

Quick Tip

Frozen food

When you need some frozen, chopped bell pepper for cooking, remove it from the freezer and use a spoon or fork to separate chunks of the fruit from the mass of frozen flesh. Reseal and return the container to the freezer.

Some types of hot peppers need to ripen to their full color before they are ready for picking.

PROBLEM SOLVER

Misshapen, mottled leaves. Viruses are usually the culprit, and there is no cure. Plants may grow out of the problem. To prevent it, choose virus-resistant types.

Poor fruit set. Peppers set fruit at 65–85°F (18–29°C). If your plants aren't forming fruit, it's probably too hot or too cold. Wait a week or two. When the weather changes, the fruit will probably start to set again.

Dark patches on fruit. Lack of calcium causes blackened areas on the bottom, called blossom-end rot. You can't undo this problem; however, you can still eat undamaged parts of the fruit. To prevent it from occurring again, water frequently because a lack of moisture disrupts the calcium supply within the plant.

Dry, whitish areas on fruit. Caused by sunscald—too much exposure to hot sun. If you garden in an area with a lot of hot weather and bright sun, plant your peppers close together in a block—this will enable the leaves to shade the developing fruit.

Red bell peppers achieve their full sweetness when the fruit is a rich red. However, you can harvest them when green.

an early frost might cut the harvest short. Covering staked plants takes more time and care.

Harvesting

With bell peppers, leaving fruit on the plant suppresses further fruit production. So start the harvest early by picking some fruit while it is green, although it won't be as sweet as fully ripe fruit. Continue picking as needed while the fruit change from green to their mature color. However, be sure to let some fruit reach full ripeness because they'll have the sweetest flavor.

Cut peppers off the vine with pruners or a sharp knife. If you try to yank off the fruit by hand, you might break off most of a branch along with the fruit.

Wear gloves and glasses or sunglasses when harvesting hot peppers to protect yourself from the burning effects of capsaicin—the substance that gives hot peppers their heat.

Storing Peppers will keep in the refrigerator for up to two weeks. When frost threatens at the end of the season, pick all the remaining fruit. You can chop it into chunks and package it in freezer containers or plastic bags; then freeze it.

Types of peppers

Variety truly does add spice when it comes to peppers. One basic way of dividing peppers is by flavor: sweet or hot. Beyond that, there's an amazing range of colors, shapes, and hotness. A pepper's degree of hotness is rated in Scoville heat units. Mildly hot peppers have a low score; very hot peppers, a high score.

▼ **Bell peppers**

With a sweet flavor and crisp texture, bell peppers are excellent when eaten fresh in salads, cooked in casseroles and sauces, baked for stuffing, or roasted. These mild peppers rate 0 Scoville heat units. Bell peppers are about 3 inches (7.5 cm) wide and 4 inches (10 cm) long.

Most bell peppers start out green, and you can harvest them at the green stage. However, for full sweetness and flavor, allow some to ripen to their mature color, which may be bright red, orange, yellow, or purple.

▶ **Cayenne peppers**

You can pick long and slim cayenne peppers when green or fully ripe. Their mature color may be red, yellow, or purple, and their heat-unit rating ranges from 30,000 to 60,000. Cayenne peppers are popular for making salsa and for use in Cajun cooking.

▲ **Poblano peppers**

These heart-shaped, thick-walled peppers can be stuffed and are often used to flavor chili. The 4-inch (10-cm)-long fruit are dark green to red when mature. These Mexican favorites are slightly hot, with a rating of 1,000 to 1,500 heat units. When dried, they are called ancho peppers.

▼ **Thai peppers**

These small peppers have an intensely hot flavor, and their Scoville rating is 150,000. They may remain green when mature or turn bright red. They are used often in Asian cuisine. These bushy plants are also attractive as ornamental plants.

▼ **Habanero peppers**

These orange peppers are hot, hot, hot! Their Scoville rating is 200,000 heat units and higher. The peppers ripen from green to gold to orange. Handle these peppers with extreme care—make sure you avoid getting the juice on your skin or in your eyes.

▲ **Banana peppers**

Named for their shape, banana peppers are a good choice for frying. The fruit grow up to 6 inches (15 cm) long and turn yellow, orange, or red when ripe. Banana peppers have a Scoville rating of 100 to 500, and these mild peppers are suitable for eating fresh in salads and sandwiches.

Eggplant

With the right care, your eggplant crop will produce a beautiful harvest of fruit in an array of sizes, shapes, and colors. You'll need to outwit pests, especially in the North—and protect the eggplants from cold soil and cold air.

PLANTING GUIDE

What to plant Transplants.

Starting indoors Provide bottom heat for germinating seeds; optimal temperature is 80°F (26.5°C).

Site preparation Add compost to improve soil fertility; in short-season areas, warm the soil by covering it with black plastic.

When Set out transplants two to six weeks after the last spring frost date; in the South, plant again four months before the first fall frost.

Spacing Allow 18–24 inches (45–60 cm) between transplants.

How much Two to three plants per person.

Temperature alert
Eggplants will sulk in cold soil. Long periods of chilly weather can injure plants, and frost ends their season.

Planting

Soil Eggplants need fertile, well-drained soil. You should spread a 1-inch (2.5-cm) layer of compost over the planting area and work it into the top several inches of soil. Or you can dig planting holes for transplants, adding one or two trowel scoops of compost to the bottom of each hole.

Starting seeds Sow seeds eight weeks before the planting date. Seeds take one to two weeks to germinate and will probably sprout irregularly. After the first true leaves appear, transplant seedlings carefully into 4-inch (10-cm) pots (or larger). The goal is to avoid crowding the roots during the long period before you set out plants in the garden.

Coping with a cool climate
Prewarm the soil by covering it with black or infrared-transmitting (IRT) plastic two weeks before planting. You can also encircle the young plants with rocks or bricks after planting. They will absorb heat during the day and release it at night. Cover the plants with a row cover when temperatures below 60°F (15.5°C) are predicted.

Another option is to grow small-fruited varieties in containers. The soil mix in the container will warm up rapidly, and you can move the containers to a protected spot whenever a cold spell threatens.

Care

Watering Mulching the soil may be helpful in hot, long-season areas, but be sure the soil is fully warm before applying mulch. Water plants at soil level to avoid wetting the foliage, because disease spreads more rapidly when foliage is wet.

Fertilizing You can fuel strong growth by fertilizing the plants regularly, but don't overwhelm them with nitrogen, or the result may be

BEST OF THE BUNCH

'Black Beauty' Heirloom purple variety; holds well after harvest. 73 days from transplants.
'Dusky' Good producer in short-season areas; oval, deep purple fruit are disease resistant. 80 days from transplants.
'Fairy Tale' Purple-and-white-striped fruit with few seeds. Good producer. 60–65 days from transplants.
'Pingtung Long' Asian-type eggplant; long, narrow lavender fruit; compact plants that tolerate humidity and heat well. 75–90 days from transplants.
'Rosa Bianca' Round, rosy pink fruit with white streaks; mild flavor, good for stuffing. 70–85 days from transplants.

lush foliage and no fruit. Apply half-strength fish emulsion every two weeks. Or side-dress with a balanced organic fertilizer once a month in long-season areas. In short-season areas, a single side-dressing after plants have set their first few fruit should be sufficient.

Staking Fruit on plants that flop onto the ground may become misshapen. Staking or caging large-fruited varieties will help to ensure that the fruit remain straight and develop evenly. Also, keeping the plants upright will help prevent sunscald, because the foliage will shade the developing fruit.

Harvesting

To guarantee fine flavor, color, and texture, begin harvesting eggplants while they're small—only about one-third of their mature size. Shiny skin is desirable; eggplants with dull skin may be bitter and woody. The plants often bear sharp spines on the stems, so wear long sleeves and gloves to harvest. Cut the stems with a knife, leaving 1 inch (2.5 cm) of stem attached to the fruit.

Storing Eggplants are not easy to store, and refrigerators are usually colder than the ideal temperature. If possible, store eggplants between 40–50°F (4.5–10°C) and in high humidity. Even in these conditions, eggplants will last 10 days at most.

You can grow dwarf bushy eggplants in a container on the patio—an ideal option in cool-weather areas.

PROBLEM SOLVER

Small holes in leaves. Flea beetles can be a serious pest. Cover new transplants with a row cover and seal the edges using boards or soil. Remove the covers when flowers begin to open. Dust the plants with flour.

Skeletonized leaves. Colorado potato beetles eat the leaves, but not the veins. Cover plants with a floating row cover until mid-season. Alternatively, mulch the plants with deep straw. Handpick and destroy the beetles, eggs, and larvae. You can spray the larvae with *Bacillus thuringiensis* var. *san diego* (BTSD).

Leaves turn yellow and drop off. Look for webbing and tiny red spider mites on leaf undersides. Spray plants with insecticidal soap or horticultural oil.

Brown or water-soaked spots on leaves; spots on fruit. Various fungal and bacterial diseases cause leaf spots. If the symptoms are mild, plants may produce usable fruit. Destroy all infected plants, including roots, at the end of the season. Rotate the crops. Keep future plantings stress free and plant early-maturing varieties. Avoid watering the foliage. Don't handle plants when wet.

Plants wilt. Wilting may be due to moisture stress or waterlogged soil. If soil moisture is adequate, check the roots. Small knots or galls indicate root-knot nematodes. To combat them, add organic matter to the soil. In areas with steady summer sun, solarize the soil to kill nematodes. If no galls are present, and if leaves wilt on only one side, suspect Verticillium wilt. To avoid this disease in the future, practice crop rotation; destroy infected plant material.

Odd-colored fruit. This problem is usually due to heat and moisture stress. Keep plants well watered during hot weather. Otherwise the fruit are too mature—old fruit may look bronzed.

Okra

Okra pods are a good source of vitamins, minerals, and fiber when added to soups and stews—or try them grilled or pickled. In the South and desert Southwest, okra plants are impressively tall, reaching up to 10 feet (3 m) high.

PLANTING GUIDE

What to plant Seeds or transplants.

Starting indoors Only in short-season areas; seedlings can be difficult to transplant.

When Two to four weeks after last spring frost; in long-season areas, succession plant until 16 weeks before first fall frost.

Spacing Sow seeds 4 inches (10 cm) apart in rows 1½–3 feet (45–90 cm) apart. Thin seedlings or set the transplants 1–2 feet (30–60 cm) apart.

How much One to four plants per person (plants are more productive in the South) for fresh eating; more for storing.

Temperature alert
Okra loves hot weather. The plants can't withstand frost and won't grow well until soil temperatures reach 70°F (21°C).

Planting

Soil Okra will grow best in fertile soil that is barely acid, neutral, or slightly alkaline. Because okra prefers somewhat dry soil, don't overdo adding organic matter. Too much soil nitrogen will promote foliage growth at the expense of pod formation. Before planting, you should loosen the soil up to 1 foot (30 cm) deep to promote strong, deep root growth.

In the North, try covering the soil tightly with plastic mulch to speed soil warming. Be sure to check the soil temperature before planting; okra will languish when planted in soil that is cooler than 70°F (21°C).

Planting tips Okra is a summer crop in the North. Gardeners in the South and warm parts of the West can make succession plantings for harvest well into fall.

Okra seeds have a hard outer coat. To crack the outer coat and speed germination, you can place the seeds in a freezer overnight or soak them in water for 24 hours before sowing.

If you start seedlings indoors or sow seeds in a protected outdoor seedbed, make sure you handle the seedlings with great care when transplanting. Seedlings are brittle and the roots don't readjust easily if disturbed.

Spacing depends on where you live and what variety you plant. Small, bushy okra varieties do well at close spacing. In hot-weather areas, large varieties need a lot of room to spread—plant them at the maximum recommended spacing.

Care

Okra is generally trouble-free. As insurance against disease problems in wet-summer areas, sow seeds in raised planting ridges or raised beds to ensure good drainage.

Watering Okra is more drought tolerant than most other vegetable crops. Even in hot weather, watering once every seven to ten days is usually sufficient. In drought areas, mulch with chopped leaves to help keep soil moisture even, but be sure the soil is thoroughly warm and the plants are at least 6 inches (15 cm) tall before mulching.

Fertilizing Okra may not need any supplemental fertilizer, but if you're concerned about soil fertility, you can side-dress plants with fishmeal or a balanced organic fertilizer when they first bloom.

Harvesting

Once the pods start to form, you should check the plants frequently. Pick the pods when they grow 3–4 inches (7.5–10 cm) long—larger pods will be woody and unappealing. Use pruners to cut through the thick stems.

Most varieties bear spines that can cause skin irritation. You should protect your skin by wearing long sleeves, long pants, and gloves when harvesting. Even spineless types may have a few spines.

In late summer, cut plants back by 24 inches (60 cm) to stimulate growth of side branches, which will encourage more pod production. If frost is predicted, pick all the pods.

Storing It is best to eat okra pods when freshly picked, but they will keep in the refrigerator for up to three days. You can store a large harvest by freezing the pods.

You can grow okra in the North. Plants will be smaller, but early-yielding varieties still produce an adequate crop.

PROBLEM SOLVER

Yellowed leaves, stunted growth. Root-knot nematodes are a soil-dwelling pest that is especially problematic in sandy soils in the South. Destroy the infested plant debris. Add plenty of organic matter to the soil to encourage beneficial fungi. Solarize the soil to kill nematodes. Rotate crops.

BEST OF THE BUNCH

'Annie Oakley II' Tender, spineless pods; early yielding; grows well in all regions. 48 days from seeds.

'Cajun Delight' Semi-dwarf plants; good for northern gardens; dark green, spineless pods. 55 to 70 days from seeds.

'Clemson Spineless' High yielding; produces spineless pods on bushy plants. 56 days from seeds.

'Red Burgundy' Red stems and pods on bushy plants; pods turn green when cooked. 53 to 80 days from seeds.

Quick Tip

Floral treat

Okra is related to hibiscus, and its large creamy white or red flowers resemble hibiscus blossoms. These bushy plants with showy blooms will look right at home in your flower garden.

12 Vine crops

From the fleeting pleasure of fresh melons to the reliable keeping quality of winter squash, vine crops offer gardeners plenty of reward. By growing early-maturing varieties, even gardeners in chilly northern zones can grow melons and pumpkins. Cucumbers and summer squash will grow in any garden if they are protected from troublesome insects.

Planting in the proper conditions and keeping plants healthy will avoid disease problems, too. So set aside as much space as you can for vine crops—and remember that if you grow them vertically on a trellis, they are space efficient and easy to harvest.

Vine crops require a considerable amount of garden space, rich soil, and warm, sunny weather.

Cucumbers

When trained on a trellis, cucumbers are a space-efficient crop. There are also bush varieties that grow well in containers. People who can't digest cucumbers easily will appreciate the burpless varieties that are available.

PLANTING GUIDE

What to plant Seeds or transplants.

Starting indoors Sow seeds two weeks before last frost. *Greenhouse types* Sow from mid-fall through early spring.

Site preparation Add organic matter to improve fertility and moisture-holding capacity.

When After danger of frost has past; also in midsummer.

Spacing Sow seeds 3 inches (7.5 cm) apart in a row at the base of a trellis; thin seedlings or set transplants 12 inches (30 cm) apart. Or sow six to eight seeds per hill, with hills 3–4 feet (90–120 cm) apart; thin to three plants per hill.

How much *Slicing variety* One plant per person for fresh eating. *Pickling variety* About 10 plants.

Planting

Soil Spread a 2-inch (5-cm) layer of compost and work it into the top several inches of the soil.

Speeding up the season Vigorous, fast-growing cucumber plants are more likely to withstand the stresses of insect damage and disease. If you take the proper steps, you can plant up to one month earlier than the usual recommended planting time.

Cover the soil with black plastic for two weeks before planting to help warm the soil. After planting, cover the plants with a plastic tunnel or row cover. Monitor temperatures under the cover; remove it when temperatures underneath are close to 90°F (32°C).

Seedlings don't transplant easily, so use 2- to 4-inch (5- to 10-cm) peat pots when starting transplants indoors. Sow three seeds per pot, and when the seedlings emerge, cut off the two weakest seedlings, leaving the strongest one in each pot. Transplants grown in a cold frame will be better acclimated for the shift to a garden bed.

Planting for late harvest You can start a second crop of cucumbers in midsummer by sowing seeds into the garden bed. However, until the seeds germinate, you may need to shade the soil surface to keep it cool.

Greenhouse cucumbers Choose European seedless varieties, which don't require pollination. They need a constant temperature of 70°F (21°C). Sow seeds as you would for starting seedlings indoors; move the seedlings to 20-inch (50-cm) pots.

Care

Watering Proper watering is needed for good fruit development. A drip irrigation system maintains even soil moisture without wetting the foliage, which is important to avoid diseases.

Trellising cucumbers Use posts and heavy netting or wire for a vertical or A-frame trellis. Or use wire-mesh fencing to make a tunnel over the row, and train the vines to grow along the top sides of the tunnel. (For greenhouse cucumbers, see pages 80–81.)

Feeding You can spray plants with kelp spray when they flower to help improve the fruit set.

Quick Tip

Finding a male

When hand pollinating a cucumber (or squash) flower, it doesn't matter if the male flower is from the same plant or another one.

Harvesting

Harvest cucumbers in the morning while the fruit is still relatively cool. It's important that you don't let the fruit become too large, or it may become bitter or pithy.

You can pick pickling cucumbers when they grow to about 3–4 inches (7.5–10 cm) long (2 inches/5 cm for gherkins); 6–8 inches (15–20 cm) is ideal for slicing cucumbers. You can allow most burpless types to grow 10–12 inches (25–30 cm) long.

If you miss harvesting a cucumber and it grows too big, you should remove it from the vine anyway; otherwise it will suppress production of more fruit.

Storing Plunge cucumbers into cold water to chill them; then store them loosely in plastic bags in the refrigerator for up to three days. For the best pickle quality, make pickles with freshly picked fruit.

BEST OF THE BUNCH

'Alibi' Disease-resistant pickling type; also good for fresh eating. 50 days from seeds.
'Bush Pickle' Grows well in containers; medium-green pickling variety. 45 days from seeds.
'Calypso' Medium-green fruit; tolerates diseases. 53 days from seeds.
'Lemon' Heirloom variety; lemon yellow, round fruit with sweet flavor. 65 to 70 days from seeds.
'Marketmore 76' Tolerates powdery mildew, mosaic, and other diseases; slender dark green slicing variety. 58 days from seeds.
'Salad Bush' Good for small spaces and containers. Disease tolerant; smooth-skinned slicing variety. 57 days from seeds.
'Sweet Slice' Burpless, sweet flavor; tolerates mildews, scab, and other diseases. 62 days from seeds.

Outdoor cucumber flowers must be pollinated to set fruit. To hand pollinate, remove a male flower (one without a swelling behind the bloom), strip off the petals, and press its center into the center of the female flowers (see page 227).

PROBLEM SOLVER

Skeletonized leaves. Striped cucumber beetles eat leaves; their larvae feed on roots. Spotted cucumber beetles also feed on the plants. Cover plants with a row cover to block beetles. Plant early or late to avoid peak beetle populations.

Brown patches on leaves. Handpick gray squash bugs and nymphs from the undersides of leaves. Scrape egg clusters off, or use a knife to cut out parts of leaf with eggs attached; destroy them. Spray young bugs with insecticidal soap. Bugs gather in mulch, so don't mulch future planting. Destroy infested debris.

Powdery coating on leaves. Spray plants with baking soda or sulfur spray when powdery mildew appears. Destroy infected plant material. Train future plantings on trellises to improve air circulation. Choose resistant varieties.

Plants wilt suddenly. If wilt starts on one part of the plant, bacterial wilt is the problem; destroy the plants. It is spread by cucumber beetles; in the future, use a row cover until blossom time. Nonbitter varieties are less attractive to the beetles.

Mottled leaves and bitter fruit. Suspect cucumber mosaic virus. Destroy infected plants; plant resistant varieties.

Fruit is oddly shaped. Can be due to poor pollination or inconsistent watering during fruit development. Water regularly and hand pollinate. Pollination can cause oddly shaped fruit on greenhouse types.

Poor yield; tunnels in fruit. In the South, plant early to avoid pickleworms. Spray *Bacillus thuringiensis* or beneficial nematodes in the early evening once a week and after rain, starting in June.

Plants don't set fruit. Male flowers appear before female flowers, so female flowers may not be present yet. If they are, wet weather or lack of bees hindered pollination. Hand pollinate.

Zucchini and summer squash

Summer squash *(Cucurbita pepo)* includes zucchini, yellow squash, Lebanese squash, and scallop squash. These squashes have thin, tender skin and mild white or creamy flesh. The fruit enlarge rapidly, and picking them encourages continued production.

PLANTING GUIDE

What to plant Seeds or transplants.

Starting indoors Sow seeds two weeks before the last frost.

Site preparation Add compost to enrich the soil.

When In spring when soil temperature reaches 60°F (15.5°C); again 60 to 90 days before first fall frost.

Spacing Sow seeds in hills or set transplants about 2–3 feet (60–90 cm) apart.

How much One to three plants per person.

Quick Tip

Quantity control

When deciding how much to plant, keep in mind that yield per plant will be higher in hot-summer areas than in cooler areas. Heat spurs rapid fruit production and growth; a midsummer planting may start to produce fruit within five weeks.

Planting

Soil Mix a 1-inch (2.5-cm) layer of compost into the soil if you want to plant transplants in rows. If planting seeds in hills, add several shovelfuls of compost to each hill.

Sowing seeds Plant seeds in slightly raised planting mounds, or hills. Sow six to eight seeds a few inches apart in a ring. Thin each hill to the two or three strongest plants.

Speeding up the season In both warm-season and cool-season areas, helping summer squash plants adjust to the garden quickly and grow rapidly improves the chance of harvest success. Vigorous, fast-growing crops are more likely to avoid the stresses of insect damage and disease. When you take the proper steps, you can plant up to one month earlier than the standard recommended planting time.

Cover soil tightly with black plastic for two weeks before planting to help warm the soil. In addition, cover the plants with a plastic tunnel or row cover after planting. Monitor the temperatures under the cover, and remove the cover once temperatures underneath climb to 90°F (32°C).

Starting transplants inside gives you a head start toward the harvest, too. Squash seedlings don't transplant easily, so use peat pots if possible. The roots will need space to expand, so choose 3- or 4-inch (7.5- or 10-cm) pots. Sow three seeds per pot, and when the seedlings emerge, cut off the weakest seedlings, leaving only the strongest one in each pot.

Transplants raised in a cold frame will be better acclimated for the shift to a garden bed.

BEST OF THE BUNCH

'Black Beauty' Classic zucchini with dark green fruit; open growth habit. 60 days from seeds.

'Eight Ball' Dark green, round zucchini. 40 to 50 days from seeds.

'Gold Rush' Golden yellow zucchini with creamy flavor; vigorous grower. 45 to 52 days from seeds.

'Peter Pan' Green, bushy scallop squash; good raw or cooked. Best when 4 inches (10 cm) or under. 48 days from seeds.

'Ronde de Nice' Round, milky green zucchini; harvest as baby fruit or at size of a tennis ball. 50 to 60 days from seeds.

'Spineless Beauty' Medium-green zucchini; spineless. 48 days from seeds.

'Sunburst' Bright yellow scallop squash with a blotch of green at each end; early bearing; firm but tender even when fully mature. 50 to 52 days from seeds.

'Sundance' Golden yellow scallop squash; pick small or at 6 inches (15 cm) across for stuffing. 52 days from seeds.

'Yellow Crookneck' Yellow squash with sweet flavor and firm flesh; vigorous grower. 58 to 65 days from seeds.

Care

Mulching Mulching helps conserve soil moisture, which in return will help produce better-quality fruit. It also keeps fruit off the soil surface, reducing disease and rot problems. However, mulch can shelter pests, especially squash bugs. So whether to mulch squash depends on the problems you encounter in your garden (see *Problem Solver,* right).

Fertilizing When fruit appear, side-dress with 1 cup (225 g) of balanced organic fertilizer per plant or spray with a fish-emulsion-and-kelp solution.

Hand pollinating Hand pollinating can improve fruit set. First, identify the male and female flowers. Female flowers have a small swelling at the base below the blossom.

You can use a cotton swab or artist's paintbrush to collect pollen from male flowers and transfer it to the female flowers. Alternatively, pick a male flower, pull off the petals, and rub the pollen, which looks like yellow grain, directly on the stigma—the central structure in the female flower. A single male flower has enough pollen to pollinate several female flowers. For best results, you should pollinate flowers daily.

Harvesting

When the fruit appear, check summer squash (especially zucchini) daily. Fruit quality declines if the fruit become oversized. Small fruit are tender and have excellent flavor. Use scissors or pruners to cut the squash from the plants, leaving about 1 inch (2.5 cm) of stem attached. For yellow squash and zucchini, 3–6 inches (7.5–15 cm) long is ideal. Harvest scallop squash when 3 inches (7.5 cm) across. You can allow scallop squash to mature, with a hard rind, and harvest them like winter squash (see page 229).

Most summer squash plants have hairy or spiny stems and leaves. To avoid skin irritation, wear long sleeves and gloves when harvesting.

Storing Store the squashes unwashed in plastic bags for up to four to five days in the refrigerator.

Smooth, spineless varieties are just one of the many types to choose. Also look for virus-resistant varieties or parthenocarpic types—these can set fruit without pollination.

PROBLEM SOLVER

Plants wilt suddenly in midsummer. Inspect stem bases for holes and debris, signs of squash borer larvae. Slit the stem with a knife; remove and kill the borers. Heap soil over the damaged area to keep it moist until the stem heals. Inject stems with *Bacillus thuringiensis* var. *kurstaki* (BTK) or beneficial nematodes.

Plants wilt suddenly. If wilt starts on part of the plant, the problem is bacterial wilt; destroy the plants. It is spread by cucumber beetles; in the future, use a row cover until blossom time. Nonbitter varieties are less attractive to beetles.

Fruit is oddly shaped. Can be a result of inconsistent watering during fruit development or poor pollination. Water regularly and hand pollinate.

Poor yield; tunnels in fruit. In the South, plant early to avoid pickleworms. Spray *Bacillus thuringiensis* or beneficial nematodes in the early evening once a week and after rain, starting in June.

Plants don't set fruit. Male flowers appear before female flowers, so female flowers may not be present yet. If they are, wet weather or lack of bees hindered pollination. Hand pollinate.

Fruit have pitted skins. The fruit have been exposed to temperatures below 40°F (4.5°C) for several days. At the end of the season, use a row cover, or harvest fruit when a cold spell is predicted.

Small fruit turn moldy. Fruit may rot if plants have been overfertilized with nitrogen. Try hand pollinating and cut back on fertilizing.

Leathery area at blossom end of fruit. Squash suffer from blossom-end rot due to a lack of calcium in the developing fruit when it doesn't get enough water. Mulch the soil to conserve moisture and water regularly.

Pumpkins and winter squash

It would take a mighty big garden to grow just one of each popular type of pumpkin and winter squash. These bountiful and delicious squashes are available in a truly amazing variety of shapes, forms, and colors.

PLANTING GUIDE

What to plant Seeds or transplants.

Starting indoors Sow seeds three weeks before the last spring frost.

Site preparation Add compost and cover with black plastic to speed soil heating.

When Varies by region and plant type.

Spacing Sow hills or plant transplants of bush and compact varieties 2–4 feet (60–120 cm) apart in rows about 5–6 feet (150–180 cm) apart. Sow hills or plant transplants of large varieties 6 feet (180 cm) apart.

How much As many vines as space will allow; most vines produce four to five fruit.

Quick Tip

Native gardener

One space-saving trick is to plant squash and pumpkins next to sweet corn and train the vines to grow beneath and between the corn rows. This planting style was used by Native Americans.

Planting

Soil Winter squash and pumpkins are usually planted in hills, but their vines and roots spread widely. To ensure their fertility and moisture-holding capacity, spread a 2-inch (5-cm) layer of compost over the entire planting area and work it into the soil.

These crops also do well planted directly in a mature compost pile, as long as the vines can sprawl in full sun.

Two weeks before you plant, wet down the planting area thoroughly and cover it tightly with black plastic mulch to speed soil warming. (This may not be necessary in the Deep South or in hot-summer areas in the West.)

When to plant

Winter squash and pumpkins won't grow well until soil temperature is 60°F (15.5°C). A temperature of 70°F (21°C) is ideal. To ensure the warm soil and air conditions that these plants like, hold off planting until two to four weeks after the last spring frost. Gardeners in the North will do best to start with transplants rather than direct-seeding. (See pages 226–227 for raising summer squash transplants.)

In the hot, long-season parts of the South and West, where cold soil is not a concern, calculate the planting time by counting back four to five months before the first expected fall frost.

Hill planting Form hills for sowing seeds or setting transplants. If you've spread black plastic, use a knife to cut a circular hole 1–2 feet (30–60 cm) across for each hill. Mix a half-bushel (17.5 liters) of compost into the soil for each hill, and shape a low raised mound 1–2 feet (30–60 cm) across. Sow five or six seeds per hill or set two transplants per hill. When you thin seedlings, leave the two strongest plants per hill.

You can plant squash and pumpkin hills along one edge of your garden and train the vines out across the surrounding lawn or other surface. The vines will cast shade that may weaken or kill the grass, which can be an advantage if you want to expand your garden next year.

Care

Watering Pumpkins need a lot of water or the fruit won't develop to full size. As a rule of thumb, supply 2–3 gallons (7.5–11 liters) of water per hill each week if it doesn't rain. Or dig a test hole to monitor soil moisture. When you water, soak the soil up to 1 foot (30 cm) deep. Withholding water as the fruit near maturity will hasten ripening.

If you haven't used plastic mulch, you should leave the soil surface bare, because organic mulches can harbor squash pests. Once the vines begin to elongate, the spreading foliage will shade the soil and slow moisture loss.

Feeding Side-dress the plants with compost or balanced organic fertilizer when the first blossoms appear.

Pinching and thinning If the squash and pumpkins are planted closer than standard recommendations, control their growth by pinching the growing tips after the first several fruit have set. Although the fruit may not turn out as sweet as they could—because there won't be as many leaves to supply sugars to them—this is a better choice than facing the chaos of rampant squash vines taking over your garden. Plus, crowded vines are more prone to disease and insect problems.

If a vine sets too many fruit, the fruit will compete for sugars and nutrients, and all of the fruit will be small at maturity. If you want larger fruit, especially for jack-o'-lantern–type pumpkins, remove some of the developing fruit from each vine.

Harvesting

When winter squash and pumpkins are ripe, the rind turns slightly dull. The rind should be tough enough to withstand light pressure from a fingernail. For best keeping quality, harvest winter squash and pumpkins before the first frost, ideally before temperatures drop below 40°F (4.5°C). Cut the fruit off the vines, leaving 2 inches (5 cm) of stem attached to the fruit. Handle them carefully: If the stem breaks off, there will be an entry point for decay organisms.

Storing

Cure squash at 85–90°F (29–32°C) for several days to promote hardening of the rind; then move the fruit to a cool area. Temperatures of 50–60°F (10–15.5°C) and humidity of 50 to 75 percent are ideal. Some types last for four months in these conditions. Before moving squash to storage, wipe the rind with a 10 percent bleach solution to improve its keeping quality.

PROBLEM SOLVER

Brown patches on leaves. Handpick gray squash bugs and nymphs from the undersides of leaves. Scrape egg clusters off, or use a knife to cut out parts of a leaf with eggs attached; destroy them. Spray young bugs with insecticidal soap. The bugs congregate in mulch, so don't mulch future plantings. Destroy infested debris.

Powdery coating on leaves. Spray plants with baking soda or sulfur spray when powdery mildew appears. Destroy infected material; choose resistant types.

Plants wilt suddenly in midsummer. Inspect stem bases for holes and debris, signs of squash borer larvae. Slit the stem with a knife; remove and kill the borers. Heap soil over the damaged area to keep it moist until the stem heals. Inject the stems with *Bacillus thuringiensis* var. *kurstaki* (BTK) or beneficial nematodes. Wrap the first 3 feet (90 cm) of each stem with aluminum foil.

Plants wilt suddenly. If wilt starts on one part of the plant, the problem is bacterial wilt; destroy the plants. It is spread by cucumber beetles. In the future, try using a row cover until blossom time.

Poor yield. In the South and Midwest, plant early to avoid pickleworms. Spray either *Bacillus thuringiensis* or beneficial nematodes in the early evening once a week and after rain, starting in June.

Plants don't set fruit. Male flowers appear before female flowers, so the female flowers may not be present yet. If they are, wet weather or lack of bees hindered pollination. Hand pollinate.

Small vines can bear four to five small fruit. Medium-size pumpkins and large squashes can handle three or four fruit per vine. For large pumpkins, leave two to three fruit per vine.

Types of winter squash

There are three species of winter squash: *Cucurbita pepo, C. moschata,* and *C. maxima.* Pepo squashes don't need curing. Moschata squashes grow well in the South, but they can be grown in Zone 4. Maxima squashes grow best in cool conditions.

▼ **Butternut squash**

This favorite winter squash is a reliable producer and has good keeping quality. Butternut squashes have elongated or hourglass-shaped fruit, which is orange or tan. Because they have a solid stem, these moschata squashes are not vulnerable to squash vine borer. There are many cultivars to choose from, including the classic variety 'Waltham'.

▲ **Acorn squash**

One of the smallest types of winter squash, acorn squash can have green, gold, or white rinds. These ribbed fruit are a pepo type, and their flavor is more nutty and not as sweet as some other types of squashes. 'Table Ace' is early-bearing and has dark skin, while 'Cream of the Crop' has a creamy white rind.

◀ **Delicata squash**

Green stripes on white skin make this oblong fruit a beauty. This winter pepo squash is good for baking and stuffing. It's also called sweet potato squash and has dry flesh. A bush variety, 'Bush Delicata', is available.

▲ **Kabocha squash**

These large maxima squashes can be dark green or bright orange. Orange varieties, such as 'Sunshine', resemble squat pumpkins with very thick stems. The flesh is sweet and delicate.

◀ **Hubbard squash**

Perhaps the least attractive winter squash, hubbards are large, lumpy, blue-gray squashes with pointed ends. However, these maxima squashes offer thick, dry, sweet flesh and impressive yields, easily more than 10 pounds (4.5 kg) apiece. 'Blue Ballet' is a more compact plant that bears fruit about half the size of regular Hubbard squash.

▶ **Spaghetti squash**

Named for its stringy flesh, this winter pepo squash has oblong yellow fruit. When cooked, the flesh separates into strands. Many people use spaghetti squashes, such as 'Vegetable Spaghetti', as a pasta substitute. Its delicate flavor comes forward when you prepare it with cinnamon or a light curry seasoning.

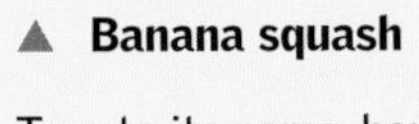

▲ **Banana squash**

True to its name, banana squash is very long, but unlike bananas, it sports a gray-green or pinkish rind. This is a winter maxima squash, and it is good for making pies, baking, and puréeing. Banana squashes can grow more than 2 feet (60 cm) long.

Types of pumpkin

Pumpkins are a type of winter squash, but unlike other winter squashes, they do not develop a fully hard rind. Small-space gardeners can grow mini-pumpkins. Gardeners with room for sprawling vines can grow jack-o'-lanterns—and giant pumpkins.

▶ Giant or jumbo pumpkin

Monstrous maxima pumpkins can grow to an amazing size (1,200 pounds/ 544 kg or larger) if you give them special care and feeding. 'Prizewinner' and 'Atlantic Giant' are famous varieties that have won prizes at fairs and competitions.

◀ Jack-o'-lantern

These classic smooth-skinned, round pumpkins are pepo pumpkins. They range in size from 2 to 25 pounds (0.9 to 11 kg). Many of the small varieties, such as 'Small Sugar', are good for cooking and making pies. Intermediate and large varieties are popular for carving or painting. 'Howden Field' is probably the best-known large variety.

▶ Mini-pumpkin

'Jack Be Little' is one of the most popular of these tiny flattened pumpkins, which are usually about 4 inches (10 cm) across. The vines are short, and each vine produces up to a dozen single-serving pumpkins. These small pepo pumpkins are fun to decorate or eat.

▶ White pumpkin

These unusual pumpkins have become popular as seasonal decorations and for painting. 'Lumina' and other varieties are maxima pumpkins; 'Baby Boo' is a white-skinned pepo pumpkin. The vines need excellent care because the skin color dulls when the plants are stressed.

Melons and watermelons

Most melons grow on sprawling vines and need a lot of space, and all melons need warm weather to grow and ripen fruit. However, with the advent of early-ripening varieties and bush-type plants, even gardeners in Zone 4 can grow melons.

PLANTING GUIDE

What to plant Seeds or transplants.

Starting indoors Sow seeds indoors three to four weeks before last spring frost.

Site preparation Add organic matter to increase moisture-holding capacity.

When After all danger of frost is past; wait until soil is 70°F (21°C). In long-season areas, sow early-maturing varieties again three to five weeks later.

Spacing *For muskmelons and cantaloupe* Sow seeds or set transplants 4–6 feet (1.2–1.8 m) apart. *For watermelons* Sow seeds or set transplants 5–7 feet (1.5–2.1 m) apart.

How much As many vines as space allows. Most produce three to five fruits per vine.

Temperature alert
Melons won't develop a nice flavor unless they ripen in warm conditions. Northern gardeners need to choose fast-growing varieties and start the crop early.

Planting

Soil Spread a 2-inch (5-cm) layer of compost over a planting area that receives full sun and work it into the soil. For spring planting in northern areas (or if you want to start an early crop), moisten the soil and cover it tightly with black plastic mulch.

Starting seeds in containers Soak watermelon seeds overnight before planting them. Use 4-inch (10-cm) peat pots or plastic pots. Plant two seeds per pot and cut off the weaker one after the first true leaf appears. Handle the seedlings carefully when transplanting them to avoid damaging the lanky stems or prolific roots.

Planting outdoors Cut 2-foot (60-cm)-diameter holes through the plastic mulch and create slightly raised hills for sowing seeds or setting transplants. After planting, cover the plants with a medium-weight row cover. Keep the row covers on as long as possible. You can leave the row covers in place after flowers appear if you hand pollinate often.

Care

Watering Melons have a high water content, so it is important that you don't let the plants suffer moisture stress. Drip irrigation is ideal for melons. However, you should hold off watering in the final week before the expected harvest. This will help concentrate the sugars in the fruit to produce sweeter, more flavorful melons. Also, excess watering can cause melons to split.

After you harvest your first round of melons, water the plants again; then monitor watering as the next round of melons ripens.

BEST OF THE BUNCH

'Ambrosia' Muskmelons with peach- or salmon-colored flesh with excellent flavor and aroma; tolerates powdery mildew. 86 to 100 days from seeds.
'Earlidew' Honeydew melon that grows well in cool conditions; yellow-green flesh. 80 to 85 days from seeds.
'Fastbreak' Early-bearing muskmelons with 5 pound (2.25 kg), netted fruit with very sweet golden flesh. 85 days from seeds.
'Honey-I-Dew' A white-fleshed melon that has good disease tolerance. 80 to 85 days from seeds.
'Passport' Hybrid honeydew melon with sweet flesh that ripens quickly. Good disease resistance. 73 days from seeds.
'Sugar Baby' Watermelon with 10-pound (4.5-kg) fruit; thin dark green rinds and sweet flesh. 95 days from seeds.
'Yellow Doll' Watermelon with bright yellow, sweet flesh in small 3–5 pound (1.5–2.5 kg) fruit. 80 days from seeds.

Supporting fruit There are several advantages to trellising muskmelons and watermelons with small fruit. It lifts the fruit up off the ground, away from slugs, snails, and mice. It keeps the fruit from soil contact, which can lead to disease. And it allows more sun to reach the fruit and speed ripening. If you grow melons up a welded wire trellis or fence, support the fruit in slings made from old panty hose or mesh onion bags tied to the trellis.

For vines that are growing at ground level, keep the fruit off the soil by placing each fruit on a board, brick, flat rock, or coffee can.

Fertilizing Try using a kelp spray at flowering to promote better fruit set.

Harvesting

As the expected harvest date nears, check the fruit regularly for signs of ripeness. The tendril by the stem where a fruit is attached to the vine dries up at about the time of ripening, although this may happen up to a week before the melon is ripe.

For watermelons, carefully roll the melon so that you can see the ground spot—the area that rests on the soil. This will be greenish white while the melon is developing, but will change to yellowish when it is ripe. The surface of the melon will become a little rough. Try the thump test—ripe watermelons (on the vine) will have a dull sound rather than a sharp sound. When ripe, use scissors or pruners to cut the fruit from the vine.

For muskmelons, try the slip test. Gently lift and pull the fruit. Ripe fruit should detach from the vine with almost no pressure. Also, try sniffing the blossom end of the fruit. Ripe fruit will usually give off a pleasant, sweet aroma.

Storing Melons and watermelons are best used as soon as possible. Underripe fruit may continue to ripen a little off the vine if left at room temperature. Uncut watermelons will last for one to two weeks at a cool room temperature. Refrigerated cut pieces of watermelon or muskmelon will keep for a few days.

PROBLEM SOLVER

Skeletonized leaves, especially young plants. Striped cucumber beetles eat melon leaves and lay eggs at the base of the plants. The larvae feed on the roots. Spotted cucumber beetles feed on many plants. The larvae are also called corn rootworms. Cover plants with a floating row cover to block beetles.

Powdery coating on leaves. Spray plants with baking-soda spray when powdery mildew symptoms first appear. Improve air circulation. Remove and destroy infected plant material. For future crops, choose resistant varieties.

Plants wilt suddenly. Fusarium wilt, a soilborne disease, is probably the problem. The strain that attacks melons is different from the one that attacks cucumbers and tomatoes. Rotate crops and use disease-tolerant varieties. Plant your next melon crop in a new area, and be careful not to contaminate it with soil from other garden beds.

For the best melons, allow plenty of room for vines to sprawl, and make sure your patch is in a sunny spot in the garden.

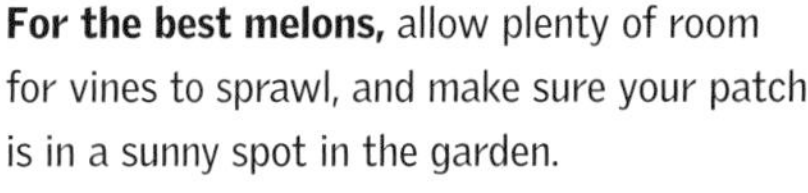

Quick Tip

Regional choices

In cold-weather areas, you should grow early-ripening varieties of muskmelons and watermelons. If you have a long, warm growing season, you can also grow crenshaw, casaba, and honeydew melons. You should ask local experts for recommendations of melons that do well in your area.

Types of melons

Gardeners who love melons have a satisfying array of sweet choices to grow. Botanically speaking, melons are *Cucumis melo,* while watermelons are *Citrullus lanatus.* Within those two species, there's a wide range of varieties.

▶ Muskmelon

We often call these melons "cantaloupes," but true cantaloupes are more often grown in Europe than North America. Most varieties identified as cantaloupes in American seed catalogs are really muskmelons.

Muskmelons are a good choice for gardeners in any part of the country. Some varieties ripen in as little as 75 days from seeds. Muskmelons usually give off a musky aroma, and they have netted skins and orange flesh (although there are green- and white-fleshed muskmelons, too). True cantaloupes often have prominent ribs (like some pumpkins), and they don't slip off the vine when ripe.

◀ Crenshaw melon

Crenshaws are also winter melons. These large oval melons can weigh as much as 10 pounds (4.5 kg). They have smooth, dark green skin that lightens to yellowish green as it ripens. The flesh is salmon or pinkish orange and has a rich, sweet flavor.

▼ **Honeydew melon**

Honeydew melons have smooth skin and green or white flesh. (Varieties with orange flesh are available, too.) While honeydews don't have a strong fragrance even when ripe, their flesh is wonderfully sweet and refreshing. Many hybrid varieties are well suited to cool-summer areas.

▲ **Watermelon**

There's a watermelon for any garden. Bush types produce small, sweet melons that may weigh 5 pounds (2.25 kg). Icebox-type melons produce sizable melons on manageable vines. If you want to grow classic watermelons weighing 20 pounds (9 kg) or more, you can do that, too, if you can provide space for the sprawling vines. Take your pick of varieties with white, peach, yellow, orange, pink, or classic bright red flesh. Seedless varieties are available too, but you must grow at least one vine of a pollinator type as well. (Seeds of the pollinator variety are often included in the packet.)

13 Corn

"Boil the water before you pick" is a saying from sweet-corn growers who enjoy the experience of eating sweet corn as soon as possible after it has been harvested. They know that the sugars in the corn start to turn to starch as soon as the cobs are removed from the plant, reducing its flavor.

Every vegetable gardener should try growing sweet corn at least once. Although your crop may not produce 100 percent perfect ears, the experience of eating freshly grown sweet corn is not to be missed. Just for fun, you may want to consider trying a patch of popcorn, too.

Yellow kernels of sweet corn are at their sweetest at the moment the cob is picked. Homegrown sweet corn will always be sweeter than store-bought corn.

Sweet corn

The joy of eating fresh corn repays the effort it takes to grow this crop well. Sweet corn has many requirements, but with proper preparation and well-chosen varieties, a successful harvest can be yours—even if you live in a short-season area.

PLANTING GUIDE

What to plant Seeds or transplants.

Starting indoors Sow seeds one week before the last spring frost.

Site preparation Add compost and nitrogen supplement; make raised beds, if possible.

When After danger of frost is past. In the South and other long-season areas, do succession plantings every two weeks until three months before fall frost.

Spacing Sow seeds 3–4 inches (7.5–10 cm) apart in rows 3 feet (90 cm) apart. Thin seedlings or set transplants about 10 inches (25 cm) apart, but up to 2 feet (60 cm) apart for tall varieties.

Intensive spacing Sow seeds 3–4 inches (7.5–10 cm) apart in double rows 1 foot (30 cm) apart; allow 3 feet (90 cm) between double rows; thin seedlings or set transplants 1 foot (30 cm) apart. Do not choose tall varieties.

How much For fresh eating and freezing, 30 plants per person.

Planting

Soil The ideal preparation for corn is to plant a nitrogen-fixing green manure, such as alfalfa or clover, the preceding fall (see pages 36–37). Leave the crop in place through winter, and dig it into the soil two weeks before you plan to plant.

If you are concerned about soil fertility or if you're planning to plant intensively, spread 2 inches (5 cm) of compost over the planting area. Add a nitrogen-rich supplement, such as fish meal, blood meal, or cottonseed meal, sprinkling a light coating over the compost. Work the compost and supplement into the top several inches of soil. If possible, shape the planting area into a raised bed to speed soil warming and ensure good drainage.

Choosing what to grow Sweet corn is available in early-, mid-, and late-season varieties. Generally, early-season varieties are shorter, and they are the best choice in short-season areas and for small plantings.

You can grow corn with yellow kernels, white kernels, or bicolor kernels. These are available with "regular" sweetness (called sugary varieties), sugar-enhanced, or super-sweet. Super-sweet varieties are two to four times sweeter than standard varieties. They keep their sweetness and crispness better when frozen than other types do. However, super-sweet seedlings tend to be less vigorous and more cold sensitive than standard varieties. Also, you must isolate super-sweet varieties from other corn plantings that tassel at the same time, because if super-sweet ears are pollinated by non-super-sweet varieties, the ears will not develop properly. To isolate a super-sweet planting, make sure you plant it at least 400 feet (120 m) away from field corn or standard or sugar-enhanced sweet corn.

Sowing seeds The usual sowing depth is 1 inch (2.5 cm), but sow the seeds a little more shallowly (and more thickly) in cool soil. Sow a bit deeper in hot conditions. To protect emerging seedlings from being uprooted by birds (seeking to eat the seed kernels), sow the seeds in a shallow trench and cover them with a row cover.

If the soil is dry at planting time, water the seed furrows thoroughly before putting the seeds in place. Then cover the seeds, firm them in place, and water lightly.

As an alternative to the usual sowing and thinning method, sow seeds in pairs at your planned final spacing (such as 10 inches/25 cm apart). If both seeds germinate, nip off the weaker seedling. For sweet corn,

The spiky male flowers, or tassels, stand above the female flowers with silks—both on the same plant.

the ideal germination temperature range is 70–85°F (21–29°C). Open a furrow and drench it with water if the soil is dry at planting time.

No matter which sowing method you use, always set up small corn plantings as a block consisting of at least four rows. The rows may be as short as 4–5 feet (120–150 cm). Block planting helps ensure a good transfer of pollen from the tassels (the male flowers) to the silks (female flowers).

Starting seeds indoors Gardeners in short-season areas can get an earlier start by sowing seeds in peat pots or individual plastic pots. Two weeks after the seeds germinate, you should move the containers to a cold frame or protected outdoor area to harden off for one week. Transplant the seedlings gently to avoid disturbing the corn's delicate roots.

If you use plastic containers, soak them thoroughly so the root ball will slip easily out of the container. With peat pots, peel away the top rim of the pot so that it can't be left exposed and wick moisture away from the roots.

In longer-season areas, sowing sweet corn seeds directly in the garden is generally the best choice.

Care

Watering If plants are water-stressed, plant growth will come to a standstill, even if the plants appear vigorous. Using drip irrigation is best because it's an easy way to deliver water evenly throughout the stand, even when the stalks are tall. Check the soil moisture and water when the top 2 inches (5 cm) have dried out. When you water, make sure you soak the soil at least 6 inches (15 cm) deep. Mulching the soil with organic mulch will help conserve moisture.

If you don't have a drip irrigation system, make furrows between your rows of corn as shallow "irrigation ditches." When you need to water, direct the water into these ditches and let it soak into the surrounding soil; you won't have to direct the water at the foliage or directly at the base of the plants (which could destabilize them).

BEST OF THE BUNCH

'Ambrosia' Bicolor, sugar-enhanced variety; grows 6½ feet (2 m) tall. 75 days from seeds.

'Gourmet Gold' Popping corn variety. 105 days from seeds.

'How Sweet It Is' White super-sweet hybrid; holds sweetness well after harvest. 87 days from seeds.

'Indian Summer' Bicolor super-sweet hybrid; grows 7 feet (2.1 m) tall. 80 days from seeds.

'Northern Xtra-Sweet' Yellow super-sweet hybrid; grows 5 feet (1.5 m) tall. 67 days from seeds.

'Silver Princess' White sugar-enhanced variety; up to 7 feet (2.1 m) tall. 75 days from seeds.

'Silver Queen' Longtime favorite standard variety; grows 8 feet (2.4 m) tall. 92 days from seeds.

Temperature alert
Corn seeds tend to rot in cold soil, so wait until the soil is warm before planting them; the soil should be at least 65°F (18°C).

POPCORN

Homegrown popcorn is a healthy snack, and a fun project to try with children. Plant popcorn as you would regular sweet corn. Because you don't need to harvest before the weather turns cold, you can plant popcorn in a garden bed after you harvest early broccoli or lettuce. As few as six ears of corn can produce 5 quarts (5.5 liters) of popcorn, but remember that you need to plant a small block to ensure good pollination.

You should care for your popcorn plants as you would sweet corn. The difference comes at harvest-time. Instead of picking the ears when the silks dry up, leave them on the plants until all the stalks have turned dry and brown; then snap off the ears, pull down the husks, and put the ears in a warm, dry place to cure. Putting the ears in mesh onion bags and hanging them to cure works well. Curing generally takes four to five weeks.

The goal is to get the moisture level in the ears in the right range for successful popping. To tell when your popcorn is dry enough, select an ear, use your thumbs to remove the kernels from the husk, and try popping them. If the kernels won't pop, allow the ears to continue to cure for another week; then try the popping test again. Once you've had success with a test popping, remove the rest of the kernels and put in sealed jars; store them in a cool, dry spot. The kernels should retain good popping quality for several years.

Grow popcorn to provide a tasty—and healthy—snack. Try popping short-cob varieties in a suitable container in a microwave oven.

Unfurling, bright green leaves above the female silks soak up the sun, producing plenty of sugar to pump into succulent ears of tender kernels of corn.

Stalk management When the plants reach about 12 inches (30 cm) tall, you should use a hoe to hill up extra soil around their stalks. This will make the plants better able to withstand any strong gusts of wind.

Do not remove any suckers (the small side stalks). They will not harm the plants or reduce yields; however, removing them could injure the stalks and leave them open to invasion by disease organisms.

When the stalks are 12–18 inches (30–45 cm) tall, feed them with a complete fertilizer, and repeat the feeding when the tassels appear.

Ensuring pollination To help good pollination on a windless day, shake the cornstalks when the tassels are shedding pollen. This will help to distribute the pollen to the silks.

Alternatively, shake the tassels over an opened envelope to collect the pollen. Carefully sprinkle the pollen onto the silks.

Quick Tip

Corny border

You can prepare a bed for corn along a sunny boundary line of your property. It will provide a summertime privacy screen and a delicious harvest to boot. Alternate sweet corn with sunflowers from year to year as a mini crop-rotation plan.

Harvesting

Ears of corn will be ready to pick when the silks turn brown and dry up. To test for ripeness, you can pierce the kernels of an ear—if it's ripe, a milky liquid should leak out. (However, for super-sweet types, the liquid stays clear even when the ears are ripe.) Generally, ears will ripen at the same time in a single planting, so check your corn patch daily once the silks start to turn brown.

Remove the ears by twisting them down, away from the stalks. After the harvest is complete, remove any crop debris from the garden so pests cannot use it to overwinter.

Storing It's best to eat sweet corn as soon as possible after picking, or quickly blanch and freeze it. You can freeze the kernels on the cob or stripped off. Super-sweet varieties hold their sweetness better than other types when frozen.

PROBLEM SOLVER

Skeletonized leaves. Look for metallic blue-green beetles on the leaves. These are Japanese beetles; they are at their worst in midsummer. Handpick and destroy the beetles. Japanese beetle larvae feed on the roots of crops, especially lawn grasses. Apply milky spore *(Bacillus popillae)* powder to your lawn to kill larvae and reduce future beetle populations.

Leaves have purplish coloring. This is probably due to a lack of phosphorus and is worst when the soil is cool. Spray plants weekly with compost tea or liquid seaweed spray until soil is fully warmed.

Stunted plants. Uproot a plant and look for white larvae among the roots—these are corn rootworms. If only a few are present, your crop may survive and produce a harvest. Drench the soil with parasitic nematodes to fight the rootworms. At the end of the season, remove and destroy all corn residue and cultivate the soil well. Practicing crop rotation should solve the problem.

Tunnels in tips of corn ears. Corn earworms tunnel into the tips of ears, leaving debris around the entrance holes. Cut off damaged tips—the rest of the ears are fine to eat. To prevent problems in the future, use an eyedropper to apply several drops of vegetable oil to the silks at the tip of each ear from four to six days after the silks first appear. Choose tight-husked varieties in the future.

Small worms eating tassels and corn stalks. These are European corn borers, which tunnel into corn ears. When they appear, spray with *Bacillus thuringiensis* var. *kurstaki* (BTK). Respray a few days later if worms are still present.

Corn is king in the vegetable garden for many people. Sturdy stalks can eventually tower to an impressive 8 feet (2.5 m) tall.

14 Perennial and annual herbs

Every garden needs herbs, but if you don't have room for a separate herb garden, don't fret! Perennial herbs, such as sage, thyme, marjoram, oregano, and rosemary, have lovely form, foliage, and flowers that will make delightful edgings or accents in a flower garden. You can tuck annual herbs, such as summer savory, dill, and basil, in and around your vegetables.

Herbs are generally undemanding and rarely suffer pest and disease problems. Many may even repel pests, and several produce flowers that attract beneficial insects to your garden.

Feathery fronds of fennel take center stage alongside sage and mint in this herb garden.

Mint

Peppermint *(Mentha piperita)* and spearmint *(M. spicata)* are popular types of mint, a highly fragrant perennial herb. However, you can also choose from a wide variety of flavored mints, including orange mint, apple mint, and pineapple mint.

PLANTING GUIDE

What to plant Rooted cuttings, divisions, or potted plants.

Site preparation Sink a root barrier into the soil before planting.

When Divisions in fall; rooted cuttings or potted plants when they are available.

Spacing About 12–18 inches (30–45 cm) between plants.

How much One plant of each type you want to grow.

Planting

Soil Mints like moist, well-drained soil. To prepare for planting, dig a hole at least 12 inches (30 cm) in diameter and 12 inches (30 cm) deep.

This perennial herb can quickly spread and engulf a garden bed, so you will need to control it by sinking a root barrier into the soil before planting. You can use a clay drainage tile or a plastic bucket with the bottom cut out. Position the barrier into your planting hole, but leave 2–3 inches (5–7.5 cm) sticking up above soil level. Fill the container with the removed soil, and plant the mint inside the barrier.

You can start your mint planting with divisions or rooted cuttings from another plant. Alternatively, purchase mint from your local garden center. Even if it is a small plant, mint establishes quickly and provides plenty of tender leaves for harvesting.

Care

Pruning Mints are hardy and fast-growing plants, and they respond well to frequent cutting. Always pay particular attention to shoots at the edge of the clump. If these are allowed to grow unchecked, they may spill over the side of the root barrier and root into the soil outside.

Dividing You should dig your mint clumps every few years and divide them, replanting small sections and leaving them room to spread. Be careful how you dispose of excess plant material. Discarded mint can easily take root in a compost pile.

Mints occasionally suffer from problems such as spider mites, aphids, flea beetles, and diseases. However, the problems usually aren't serious.

Growing indoors You can grow a pot of mint indoors in winter. Root cuttings to start your mint plant. Potted mints don't need as much sun as some other indoor herbs, but good air circulation is crucial.

The plants will try to spread and may become pot-bound. To prevent this, unpot them regularly, divide, and repot. Pinch the stems frequently so they don't become rangy.

Harvesting

Cut sprigs frequently, beginning shortly after new growth emerges in spring. Shear plants after flowering so they produce new growth by fall.

Storing Tie bunches of mint stems loosely and hang them to dry in a warm, airy spot. Store whole leaves in airtight containers. You can freeze leaves in well-sealed plastic bags.

Quick Tip

Aromatic choice

Visit an herb garden or garden center specializing in herbs to see and smell a variety of mints so you can choose your favorites for your own garden. Foliage color, shape, and fragrance vary among the species.

Oregano

The intense aroma and unmistakable flavor of true oregano are invaluable for seasoning tomato-based dishes, roasted meat, and vegetables. Try Greek oregano *(Origanum vulgare* subsp. *hirtum,* or *O. heracleoticum)* or Italian oregano *(O. majoricum).*

PLANTING GUIDE

What to plant Potted plants; rooted cuttings, divisions.

Site preparation No special preparation needed.

When Potted plants in spring; divisions in fall.

Spacing Set plants 12 inches (30 cm) apart.

How much One or two plants per person.

Planting

Soil Oregano needs both excellent drainage and good air circulation to thrive; moderate fertility is sufficient. Choose a site in full sun; however, in hot-summer areas, select one where there is some afternoon shade.

Greek oregano is a hardy plant as far north as Zone 4; Italian oregano is hardy to Zone 6.

Care

Watering If soil conditions are too wet, oregano will be subject to rot and fungal diseases. Let the top inch of the soil dry out between waterings.

Pruning Snip stems frequently to encourage branching and delay flowering. If desired, you can cut all stems to within 2 inches (5 cm) of ground level in August to encourage fresh growth.

Dividing Over time, the plants will spread moderately by sending out runners. If you want to increase your planting of oregano, dig up and divide the plants in the fall, or take stem cuttings in spring or fall.

Winter care Oregano may survive the winter in pots placed on a sunny windowsill with good air circulation.

PROBLEM SOLVER

Yellow specks on leaves. Look for webbing and tiny spider mites on plants. Spray plants with water or insecticidal soap. Mites are usually at their worst during hot, dry conditions.

You can use rooted stem cuttings to start oregano at a windowsill.

Harvesting

Begin harvesting lightly as soon as the plants are about 6 inches (15 cm) tall. The plants will flower in early summer. The best time to harvest leaves for drying is when the flower buds have set but are not yet open.

Storing Oregano is best used fresh. If you harvest it in the morning for use later that day, wash and refrigerate the stems or store the stems in a jar of water on your kitchen counter.

To dry oregano, hang bunches of stems in a warm, dry place. Don't strip the leaves from the stems. They will last longer if you store whole stems in glass containers in a dark place. Remove the leaves from the stems just before using.

Quick Tip

Telltale scent

"Oregano" is applied to a range of plants, but some have nearly no aroma or flavor. At the nursery, rub the leaves of any plant labeled oregano and inhale to check for scent. Greek oregano is the classic culinary oregano; Italian oregano is milder.

Thyme

English thyme *(Thymus vulgaris),* also called French thyme and common thyme, forms a low bushy mound with pink to purple flowers in midsummer. Thyme's sharp woodsy flavor and peppery aroma make it a favorite for meat and poultry dishes.

PLANTING GUIDE

What to plant Potted plants, rooted cuttings, or seeds.

Site preparation No special preparation needed.

When Spring or summer.

Spacing Set plants 8–12 inches (20–30 cm) apart.

How much One or two plants for culinary use; as desired in ornamental plantings.

Planting

Soil A garden bed needs no special preparation before planting thyme, which grows fine in average soil. However, thyme must have good drainage, so plant it in a raised bed, if possible. Thyme does best in full sun, but it will tolerate partial shade.

It's possible to grow thyme indoors on a sunny windowsill during the winter. The best choice for this is lemon thyme *(T. x citriodorus).* Plant it in a pot or hanging basket or as a filler in a window-box planting. Feed potted thyme plants with diluted fish emulsion twice a month.

Care

Although it's a member of the mint family, thyme is not an aggressive grower. It is usually trouble-free, thriving even in dry conditions once it is established.

Replanting Over time, thyme plants become woody and scraggly. It's best to dig out plants every three years or so and replant new ones. Buy potted plants from a garden center, or start your own by rooting cuttings from the original plants. Take cuttings in spring or early summer before plants bloom. Stick the cuttings in moist sand to root. Or dig and divide established plants in spring. Replant the most vigorous divisions and add the rest to your compost pile.

Winter care English thyme is hardy to Zone 4. Use an airy mulch, such as pine branches, to overwinter in the northern part of its range.

Harvesting

Cut leafy stems as needed during the growing season. In early summer, just before the plant blooms, make a full harvest by shearing the plant 2 inches (5 cm) above ground level. The plant will resprout and can be cut again in the same manner in late summer.

Storing When you make a full harvest, gather stems in a bunch and put them in a paper bag, tip end down. Hang them to dry in a warm, airy place. Strip dried leaves from the stems. Store the leaves in an airtight container.

Quick Tip

Other thymes

You can grow citrus thymes *(T. x citriodorus* and *T. pulegioides)* for culinary use, but their flavors are not as consistent as English thyme. Other species of thymes are used as low ground covers along pathways and in ornamental beds.

PROBLEM SOLVER

Yellow specks on leaves. Look for signs of tiny spider mites on plants such as their webs. Spray plants with water or insecticidal soap. Mites are usually more prevalent during hot, dry conditions.

Sage

While not as showy as ornamental sages, culinary sage *(Salvia officinalis)* has beautiful gray-green, purplish, or variegated foliage. Cooks treasure sage's pungent flavor as a seasoning for stuffing, soup, meatloaf, egg dishes, and sausage.

PLANTING GUIDE

What to plant Seeds, potted plants, or rooted cuttings. Some varieties may not come true to type from seeds.

Site preparation No special soil preparation needed.

When Seedlings and potted plants in spring; rooted cuttings in summer.

Spacing Plant 18–24 inches (45–60 cm) apart.

How much Start with two plants; increase your supply as needed by rooting cuttings.

Planting

Soil Sage will need full sun except in areas with hot summers, where it may do better in partial shade. It thrives in light, well-drained soil. Avoid heavy soil, or plants may become diseased.

To start sage from seeds, sow them in containers indoors in early spring. When 3 inches (7.5 cm) high, harden them off, then transplant outdoors.

Varieties with gray-green leaves are the hardiest (Zones 4 to 5). Variegated sages may be hardy only to Zone 7. Due to lack of winter chill, culinary sage may not renew growth from year to year in Zones 9 and 10.

Care

Watering Water plants regularly only until they become established. Afterward, sage prefers dry conditions and needs water only during drought.

Pruning After the first year, cut sage plants back by one-half to two-thirds after new growth begins to appear in the spring—this will encourage tender growth. Fertilize at the same time, too.

Sage becomes straggly after three or four years. Take some cuttings each year in late spring and root them to renew your supply. You can also take cuttings in fall to root for growing indoors during the winter.

Winter care In areas that are too cold for sage to overwinter, grow it in a container. When the season ends, move the container to a cool, protected spot and allow the plant to go dormant. Take it back outdoors the following spring.

Try growing a pot of sage on a sunny windowsill indoors for a supply of fresh leaves in the winter. Compact varieties are best for indoor growing. If flowers form, clip them off right away; if seeds form, the plant may die.

Harvesting

Potted plants will be ready for harvest in the first year. If you have started plants from seeds, pinch the stem tips periodically to encourage branching; begin harvesting in the second year.

Cut stems in early summer just before they bloom, taking 6–8 inches (15–20 cm) of growth. Harvest only once in the first year. In subsequent years, harvest two or three times as regrowth allows.

Storing To dry sage, tie stems in bunches and hang them in a warm place with good air circulation. Sage can become moldy in the drying process. As you remove dried leaves from the stems, inspect them; discard any that are moldy. You can also freeze fresh sage (see pages 118–19).

BEST OF THE BUNCH

Note: These are attractive cultivars, but they are not as flavorful as culinary sage.
'Berggarten' Compact growth; reaches 12 inches (30 cm) tall; blue-gray leaves.
'Tricolor' Broad leaves with green centers edged in purple or white.

Rosemary

A beautiful evergreen shrub, rosemary *(Rosemarinus officinalis)* has narrow, leathery leaves that are useful for seasoning meats, bean dishes, roasted potatoes, and in baking. Some varieties grow up to 6 feet (180 cm) tall in areas where they are hardy.

Planting

Soil Light, well-drained soil with full sun is best for rosemary. Most varieties are hardy only in Zones 8 to 10.

Care

Watering Once established in the garden, water rosemary only during droughts. In most cases, rosemary won't need any supplemental feeding. If plants are not thriving, try side-dressing with compost. If that helps, side-dress once every other year.

Cuttings Propagate rosemary by taking cuttings or by layering. Take 6-inch (15-cm) cuttings from stem tips in late spring. After cuttings root, plant them directly in the garden.

Gardeners in the North can take cuttings in late summer, root them, and pot them for overwintering inside.

Growing rosemary indoors To succeed indoors, rosemary needs at least 4 hours of direct sun or 12 hours of artificial light daily. Plants do best with cool nights (about 55°F/13°C).

Rosemary doesn't like constantly moist soil conditions; however, if it dries out to the point of wilting, it probably won't recover. You should monitor the soil moisture of potted rosemary often. When the soil is moderately dry, water it thoroughly. If the leaves turn brown, it is a sign that the plant has been overwatered.

Harvesting

Snip leaves as needed for fresh use. To harvest rosemary for drying, cut stems back to a few inches above the point when growth has become woody. Don't cut more than one-quarter of the plant's growth at a time.

Storing Hang cut branches to dry in an airy spot, or spread stems to dry on racks. Strip dried leaves from stems and store them in airtight containers.

PLANTING GUIDE

What to plant Potted plants; rooted cuttings.

Site preparation No special preparation needed.

When Any time of year in Zones 8 to 10; otherwise, when nighttime temperatures exceed 55°F (13°C).

Spacing As periennials, 4 feet (120 cm) apart; as annuals, set 1–2 feet (30–60 cm) apart.

How much One or more plants, depending on the growth rate.

BEST OF THE BUNCH

'Arp' Overwinters to Zone 6 with protection.

Temperature alert
Rosemary is a tender perennial. Most varieties won't survive outdoors where winter temperatures drop below 5°F (-15°C).

SWEET BAY

A tender perennial, sweet bay *(Laurus nobilis)* won't survive winter north of Zone 8. Plant young potted bays outdoors in moderately rich soil in full sun or partial shade. Once established, they need little watering. Indoors, treat bay the same as rosemary.

You should harvest the leaves as you need them or for drying. To dry bay leaves, put them between two flat boards with weights on top for two weeks, so that they dry flat. Store them in airtight containers.

French tarragon

The anise-flavored leaves of the shrubby perennial French tarragon *(Artemisia dracunculus)* help create memorable sauces, dressings, and flavored vinegars. Use this strongly flavored herb sparingly, and add it to a dish toward the end of cooking.

PLANTING GUIDE

What to plant Potted plants or rooted cuttings.

Site preparation No special preparation needed.

When Spring or fall.

Spacing Set 18–24 inches (45–60 cm) apart.

How much One plant; increase your supply from cuttings or by division as needed.

Planting

Soil French tarragon will grow well in average soil in full sun or partial shade. However, excellent drainage is essential or the plant may rot. It may take two years for a plant to become fully established, so harvest lightly during the first year of growth.

French tarragon is winter hardy to Zone 4. In hot-summer areas, it may go dormant in the summer, but it will put out a flush of new growth in fall; try planting the herb in partial shade in these areas.

In Zones 9 and 10, French tarragon may not come back after the winter season because of insufficient cold to meet its dormancy requirement.

Care

Propagating This herb needs little special care. However, tarragon roots tangle and intertwine as they grow, eventually choking themselves off. To keep your tarragon vigorous, dig and divide plants every two or three years.

You can also propagate tarragon from stem cuttings taken in late spring or summer. Snip 6-inch (15-cm) lengths from the ends of stems, strip the lower leaves, and stick the cuttings in a container of moist sand. Cuttings should root within four to six weeks and can be planted in the garden.

Cut the plants back in the fall; remaining foliage will die in the winter. You should mulch the roots in cold-winter areas.

Harvesting

You can harvest small quantities of tarragon as needed. For established plants, cut all the stems when they reach about 10 inches (25 cm) tall. Leave 2 inches (5 cm) of growth intact at the base of the plants. The plants will resprout. You can make a second large harvest late in the season if you want.

Storing You can use tarragon fresh or freeze it (see pages 118–19). You can also dry tarragon, but it will probably lose some flavor during the drying process. Another way to preserve its flavor is by making tarragon vinegar (see page 123).

Quick Tip

Leaf alert

Be sure you buy the genuine French tarragon. Don't confuse it with Russian tarragon, which can be grown from seeds—you'll be let down by Russian tarragon's inferior flavor.

PROBLEM SOLVER

Powdery white coating on leaves. Powdery mildew is a fungal disease that is worse during cool, wet weather. Wait until plants are dry; then thin stems to improve air circulation. If symptoms are not severe, a baking soda spray may help.

Marjoram

A type of oregano, the leaves of marjoram *(Origanum majorana)* have a similar, but sweeter flavor. Marjoram is attractive as an edging plant in a flower garden or a hanging basket. The leaves are good for seasoning fish, meat, poultry, and vegetable dishes.

PLANTING GUIDE

What to plant Transplants, rooted cuttings, or potted plants.

Starting indoors Difficult because of low germination and slow growth.

Site preparation No special preparation needed.

When After last spring frost.

Spacing Allow 6–8 inches (15–20 cm) between seedling clumps or plants.

How much One or two plants; several clumps of seedlings.

Quick Tip

Indoor success

Marjoram overwinters nicely as a potted plant on a sunny windowsill. Therefore, no matter what zone you garden in, you can buy sweet marjoram once, and, with proper management, enjoy it year after year.

Planting

Soil Marjoram grows well in soil with low-to-moderate fertility, but it needs excellent drainage. Plant it in full sun and don't crowd the plants.

This plant is a tender perennial, hardy only to Zone 6.

Raising transplants Raising your own marjoram transplants can be challenging. Few of the seeds will germinate, and the tiny seedlings will grow slowly. You should sow seeds about 8 to 12 weeks before the last expected spring frost date.

If you'd prefer an easier way to get started with marjoram, ask a friend for rooted cuttings, or buy a potted plant from a nursery.

Care

Weeding and watering If you plant small transplants, weed diligently until they become established. Weeds can easily choke the transplants.

Marjoram does not like constantly moist soil. Always allow the top inch of soil to dry out between waterings. However, if the plants start to wilt, water them well.

Winter care After the first fall frost, shear the plants to 1 inch (2.5 cm) tall. Dig them out of the garden and pot them to bring indoors. If you live in an area where marjoram is hardy or marginally hardy, you can try leaving it in place with a covering of mulch to overwinter.

An alternative to digging plants from the garden is to take cuttings in midsummer. The cuttings should root in about three weeks; plant the rooted cuttings in pots. Bring the pots indoors to overwinter. You can plant these new plants outdoors the following spring.

Harvesting

You can begin harvesting small sprigs of marjoram as required about six weeks after planting. You should trim the plants regularly to keep them from getting straggly.

Just before the flower buds form, shear the plant back to a few inches tall. In some areas, plants may sprout enough new growth to provide a second harvest. Marjoram flowers are also edible.

Storing Dried marjoram retains its flavor well. Hang stems to dry in a warm, dark place. You can store it in airtight containers with the leaves still attached to stems. Strip the leaves from the stems as needed for use. You can also freeze marjoram leaves (see pages 118–19).

Chamomile

Delightful chamomile offers the choice of growing a perennial, an annual, or both. Roman chamomile *(Chamaemelum nobile)* is a low-growing, spreading perennial; German chamomile *(Matricaria recutita)* grows as an upright annual.

PLANTING GUIDE

What to plant *Roman chamomile* Potted plants or divisions. *German chamomile* Seeds.

Site preparation Prepare a fine seedbed for German chamomile.

When *Roman chamomile* In the spring. *German chamomile* In spring or fall.

Spacing *Roman chamomile* Set plants 12–18 inches (30–45 cm) apart. *German chamomile* Thin the seedlings to about 6 inches (15 cm) apart.

How much *Roman chamomile* Start with a few plants; increase by dividing. *German chamomile* Sow a 2 x 2-foot (60 x 60-cm) area with seeds.

Planting

Soil Roman chamomile, which is hardy to Zone 4, does best in moist, humus-rich soil in full sun or light shade. Spread a ½-inch (12-mm) layer of compost over the soil and work it in before planting.

Sow German chamomile seeds in light, well-drained soil, in full sun. You should wait until soil temperatures are at least 55°F (13°C).

Care

Watering Water the plants to keep the soil moist; Roman chamomile will generally prefer slightly wetter conditions than German chamomile. Mulch the plants to suppress weeds.

Roman chamomile will spread to form a low-growing ground cover. Both plants are easy to grow and generally are pest-free.

Propagating To propagate Roman chamomile, you should divide the plants in spring and replant them 12–18 inches (30–45 cm) apart.

German chamomile will self-sow if you leave a few flowers on the plant to dry and drop their seeds. However, don't leave too many flowers on the plants, or you may have so many seedlings that they will soon become a weed problem.

Harvesting

Cut chamomile flowers carefully when they are fully open. Pinch individual flowers off Roman chamomile; cut whole stems of German chamomile. Fresh flowers are edible and can be added to salad.

Storing You can spread the flowers on screens or sheets of paper to dry in a cool, airy place. Store dried flowers in sealed glass containers.

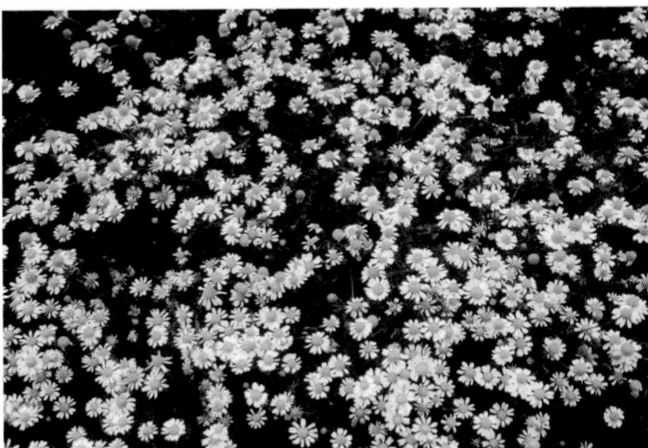

German chamomile (above) has a sweeter flavor than Roman chamomile (top left). The fragrant flowers are used as a tea.

Quick Tip

In the family

Chamomile belongs in the same family as ragweed. People who are allergic to ragweed and other members of the sunflower family should use caution, especially when consuming chamomile.

Parsley

Curly parsley *(Petroselinum crispum* var. *crispum)* is used as a garnish. Italian, or flat-leaved, parsley *(P. crispum* var. *neapolitanum)* has a tangy, sweet flavor. Parsley is a biennial, and it will grow well in a pot on a sunny window indoors, too.

PLANTING GUIDE

What to plant Seeds or transplants.

Starting indoors Keep seeds warm (with soil temperature at 75°F/24°C) and moist.

Site preparation Loosen the soil to accommodate the taproot.

When Sow seeds outdoors when soil temperature is 50°F (10°C); sow indoors six to eight weeks before last spring frost.

Spacing Thin the seedlings to 3 inches (7.5 cm) apart, then thin a second time to 8–10 inches (20–25 cm) apart; allow about 8–10 inches (20–25 cm) between transplants.

How much Three to six plants per person.

Planting

Soil Rich, moist soil is best for parsley, in full sun or light shade. Loosen the soil; work 1 inch (2.5 cm) of compost into the top several inches of soil.

Starting seeds To direct-sow seeds in the garden, try fluid seeding (see page 56). Or, before sowing seeds, soak them overnight in water or rinse them for a few hours in running water (put the seeds in a fine-mesh bag).

If starting seeds indoors, keep the seed flats warm and cover with damp newspaper or plastic wrap. If the seeds don't germinate after two weeks, slip the flat into a plastic bag, seal it, and put it in the freezer for two days. Transplant the seedlings when they are four to six weeks old; avoid damaging the taproot.

Sow seeds indoors in early summer for a fall crop in the North. Mulch with straw or protect with a row cover to overwinter for a spring harvest.

Care

Feed monthly with fish emulsion. Keep soil moist. In the South, if the plants decline, make a new sowing or plant new transplants in fall for a more reliable fall and winter harvest.

Parsley flowers after two years. The flowers will attract a range of beneficial insects to the garden.

PROBLEM SOLVER

Stunted plants. If roots are forked and distorted, suspect root-knot nematodes. Apply beneficial nematodes to the soil before planting to provide a few months of control. In hot-summer areas, solarize the soil and replant.

Harvesting

Harvest the leaves when the plants are 6 inches (15 cm) tall. Cut stems about 1 inch (2.5 cm) above the crown so the plants can produce more leaves.

Storing For short-term storage, wash the leaves, blot dry, and put them in a plastic bag in the refrigerator. To freeze leaves, spread them on a baking sheet and put it in the freezer; place frozen leaves into freezer containers.

Curly parsley has frilly, but bitter, leaves that look pretty in a flower garden.

BEST OF THE BUNCH

'Forest Green' Curled type with ruffled leaves; flavor is not bitter; upright stems keep leaves clean; holds color well.

'Italian Dark Green' A classic flat-leaf variety; tall stems, aromatic leaves.

Cilantro and coriander

The young leaves of *Coriandrum sativum* are called cilantro, and the seeds are coriander. Both plant parts are desirable. Cilantro, with its cool, refreshing flavor, is a popular herb worldwide. Coriander seeds have a citruslike flavor.

PLANTING GUIDE

What to plant Seeds.

Site preparation Add organic matter to improve moisture-holding capacity.

When Sow seeds in spring and fall; in cool-garden areas, sow in summertime, too.

Spacing Sow seeds 2 inches (5 cm) apart; thin seedlings 6–8 inches (15–20 cm) apart.

How much Up to 3 feet (90 cm) of row per planting.

Planting

Soil Cilantro grows well in average garden soil. Add some compost to increase moisture-holding capacity, but be sure the soil is well drained.

Sowing Cilantro will prefer cool conditions. Sow seeds in spring 1 inch (2.5 cm) deep (presoak them if you want). Make succession plantings as desired every two weeks until the weather turns hot, at which time the plants will go to seed prematurely and offer a poor harvest of leaves and seeds.

If you stop sowing during summer heat, sow again in late summer for a fall harvest. In areas that have hot summers, skip the spring planting, but succession plant from fall through winter. Stop sowing in early spring, before the weather heats up.

Care

In cool-winter areas, shield cilantro plants over winter in a plastic tunnel. They may survive to produce an early spring harvest. Or try planting cilantro in a pot to grow indoors on a sunny windowsill or under lights.

Heat and long days will prompt the plants to form flower stalks. The flowers attract beneficial insects. If you leave some seed heads unharvested, plants may self-sow.

Harvesting

You can begin clipping leaves when the plants are about 6 inches (15 cm) tall. You should stop harvesting the leaves when newly sprouted leaves are feathery looking and the plants start to grow taller.

As the flowerheads set seeds, the fresh seeds will smell and taste bad. However, when the seeds begin to dry out, the flavor and aroma are transformed. By the time seed heads are ready to harvest, the unpleasant smell should disappear. Cut coriander seed heads after they turn brown.

Storing Fresh cilantro leaves are the most desirable. For short-term storage, wash the leaves, pat them dry, and store them in plastic bags for up to five days in the refrigerator.

To dry leaves, put them loosely in a paper bag and place in a frost-free refrigerator for one month. The leaves will dry inside the bag, but remain fairly green and aromatic. You can also freeze the leaves (see pages 118–19).

You can dry the seed heads in a warm, airy place. Hang them upside down over a sheet, or hang them enclosed in paper bags to catch the seeds as they drop. If the seeds don't drop on their own, rub the seed heads gently between your palms. Store the seeds in airtight jars.

Dill

An annual herb, dill *(Anethum graveolens)* produces a stem clothed with lovely feathery leaves, and compact varieties are available, too. Use dill leaves in salads and fish and potato dishes. Dill seeds are a crucial ingredient in pickling spices.

PLANTING GUIDE

What to plant Seeds.

Site preparation Boost organic-matter content of poor soil.

When Spring to midsummer; again in fall.

Spacing Sow seeds lightly in rows 10 inches (25 cm) apart, or sow randomly in a patch of desired size; thin seedlings to 10 inches (25 cm) apart. Space rows 2 feet (60 cm) apart if growing to harvest seed heads.

How much Up to 10 seeds per sowing in the garden; two to three seeds per pot.

Planting

Soil Dill prefers rich, well-drained soil. Choose a site in full sun but sheltered from wind; in the South, there should be light afternoon shade. Work in a 1-inch (2.5-cm) layer of compost if planting in a new garden that is sandy or low in fertility. Avoid clay soil; the roots may rot.

Sowing Begin sowing seeds in early spring when the soil is dry enough to work. Sow small quantities and make repeat sowings at two- to three-week intervals to extend the foliage harvest (dill plants can go to seed quickly).

If you plant dill in pots, sow two pots and stagger planting dates by about two weeks. You can harvest leaves from one pot, then harvest from the other while the first one regrows.

After the first year, dill usually self-sows as far north as Zone 3. Seedlings are not easy to transplant, so to ensure an early crop in the location of your choice, sow some seeds there in fall.

Care

Dill likes moist conditions, so check the soil moisture regularly. If you have mulched around the plants, they will need less watering. If not mulched, dill may need watering twice a week in dry weather. Water at soil level to avoid wetting the foliage. Stake tall plants that seem at risk of falling or blowing over.

In containers, pull out dill plants as soon as they begin to look fatigued. Afterward, you can sow fresh seeds.

Harvesting

Dill is usually ready to harvest two months after sowing, but you can snip individual leaves earlier. Take your main harvest before the plants flower.

To harvest dill seeds, cut off the seed heads as soon as seeds turn light brown or start falling. Handle them gently to avoid knocking seeds loose. You should leave one seed head uncut so the plants will self-sow.

Storing Dill leaves remain fresh for a few days in the refrigerator. Stick the stems in a jar of water and cover the leafy tops with a plastic bag.

Hang leafy stems to dry in a cool shaded spot. Strip dry leaves from the stems and store in airtight containers.

Leaves wrapped in aluminum foil or resealable plastic bags will keep well in the freezer up to a month, or freeze in ice cubes (see pages 118–19).

Hang seed heads upside down in paper bags, or with a sheet spread below the heads to catch the seeds. Seeds separate easily from heads when dry; store them in airtight containers.

BEST OF THE BUNCH

'Fernleaf' Compact; good for containers and in flower gardens.
'Dukat' Produces plentiful foliage before setting seeds; excellent foliage flavor; 10-inch (25-cm) seed heads.
'Mammoth' Vigorous and matures to seed quickly.

Fennel

The threadlike leaves of fennel *(Foeniculum vulgare)* have a licorice flavor that enhances fish, cheese, eggs, beans, rice, and other dishes. Gardeners also harvest the small, licorice-flavored seeds to use in cakes, cookies, and Asian cooking.

PLANTING GUIDE

What to plant Seeds.

Site preparation Add organic matter, if needed.

When Late spring or early summer; in Zone 6 and South, late summer.

Spacing Sow the seeds lightly; thin the seedlings 10–12 inches (25–30 cm) apart.

How much One to two plants for culinary use; as desired in ornamental gardens.

Planting

Soil Fennel prefers full sun, good drainage, and soil with moderate to high humus. If your site is low in organic matter, spread 1–2 inches (2.5–5 cm) of compost and work it into the soil before planting.

Fennel is a perennial that is hardy as far north as Zone 6, but it can be grown as an annual in colder zones. Sow individual seeds lightly in the area where you want plants to grow. Keep the seedbed moist, and thin the seedlings as needed.

Care

Fennel likes moist conditions, but don't keep the soil too wet or the plants may rot. Stake plants when they reach about 18 inches (45 cm) tall to protect them from flopping over when in flower.

Harvesting

You can start snipping leaf tips for fresh use when the plants grow to about 6 inches (15 cm) tall. Cut the leafy stems for freezing before the plants bloom.

If you plan to harvest the seeds, watch the seed heads carefully; you should harvest them as soon as the seed color changes from green to brown. Make sure you handle the seed heads carefully—fennel will self-sow, and self-sown seedlings can become a weed problem. To avoid accidental sowing of seeds at harvesttime, hold a paper bag open below a seed head and snip it so that the head drops directly into the bag.

Storing Store leafy stems in the refrigerator for up to a week with the stems in water and a plastic bag over the leaves.

Fennel foliage is not easy to dry; freezing in ice-cube trays is a better choice (see pages 118–19). Or you can store leaves wrapped in aluminum foil or in small resealable plastic bags for about one month in the freezer.

For seed heads, place them in paper bags in a warm, dry place so that the seeds can dry completely. Store the seeds in airtight containers.

Florence fennel (see page 203) has an aniseed-flavoured foliage that can be used as a herb.

Quick Tip

Ornamental style

With its grand size, soft foliage, and umbrella-shaped clusters of flowers, fennel is a wonderful choice for a background plant in an ornamental border. Bronze fennel, which has a coppery tinge to the foliage, is especially attractive.

Summer savory

The leaves of summer savory *(Satureja hortensis)* have a peppery taste akin to thyme. Summer savory is a great addition to egg dishes and soups, and it is also an excellent choice for flavoring stir-fries of mild vegetables, such as summer squash.

PLANTING GUIDE

What to plant Seeds.

Site preparation Prepare a fine seedbed.

When Begin sowing one week before last spring frost; continue sowing to midsummer, if desired.

Spacing Sow the seeds lightly; thin the seedlings to 8–12 inches (20–30 cm) apart.

How much Two or three plants for fresh use; more for drying or companion planting.

Planting

Soil Summer savory will thrive in average, well-drained soil. However, it requires full sun.

Sowing Always sow fresh seeds, because the seeds lose their potency quickly. Scatter the seeds on top of the soil or in a shallow furrow. Lightly cover them with fine soil or potting mix. If kept moist, the seeds should germinate in less than a week.

Care

Summer savory is generally trouble-free, but keep the young plants moist until they are established. Be sure to thin seedlings to the recommended spacing, because crowded plants may develop disease.

Clearing up Summer savory is an annual and will die back at the end of the season. Uproot any remaining stems after they are killed by frost. If you allow the flowers to go to seed, summer savory may self-sow.

Harvesting

Cut sprigs from the plants, as needed, beginning about six weeks after the seedlings emerge. Before summer savory flowers, make sure you harvest some of the leaves. You can make a large cutting before the plants bloom in midsummer. If you cut them about 3–4 inches (7.5–10 cm) above the soil level, the stems will resprout.

Cutting the stems may delay flowering. However, once the plants bloom, they serve as a wonderfully fragrant filler for flower arrangements.

Storing You can hang bundles of stems to dry in an airy place. Strip the dry leaves from the stems and store them in airtight containers.

Cut sprigs of summer savory when the plants are at least 6 inches (15 cm) long. They are often used to flavor bean dishes.

Quick Tip

Natural repellent

Summer savory is reputed to repel Mexican bean beetles, so consider a row of savory on either side of your bean patch. An extra advantage is that it will grace your garden with white or lavender-pink flowers in late summer.

Basil

Fresh basil *(Ocimum basilicum)* is a favorite herb for many. It is appreciated for its flavor and aroma, as a companion plant in the vegetable garden, and for its lovely foliage colors and forms in ornamental plantings.

PLANTING GUIDE

What to plant Seeds; transplants.

Starting indoors Sow seeds four to six weeks before the last expected spring frost.

Site preparation Add compost to poor or sandy soils.

When After all danger of frost is past.

Spacing Set plants or thin seedlings to 12 inches (30 cm) apart, dwarf types 6–8 inches (15–20 cm) apart.

How much Up to six plants per person—but dwarf types produce less than large-leaved types.

Planting

Soil Basil needs rich, moist, well-drained soil. If the soil is sandy or low in organic matter, work a 1–inch (2.5-cm) layer of compost into the soil.

Plant basil in full sun except in the Deep South, where it likes partial shade. If sowing seeds in the garden, wait until the soil is 60°F (15.5°C).

Transplants Northern gardeners can set out transplants in late spring or early summer. In the South, set out transplants earlier in the spring; sow seeds in the garden again in June and July, and plant transplants again in August to ensure a good harvest.

Care

Watering and feeding Keep the soil moist, not wet. When the soil is warm, apply mulch to conserve moisture. In midsummer, side-dress plants with blood meal. Feed monthly with a fish-emulsion-and-seaweed solution.

If you're growing tall varieties on a windy site, stake plants to prevent them from blowing over.

Planting indoors For best results, use dwarf types, and put them under supplemental light. Don't harvest too heavily, but pinch the stem tips often to prevent flowers from forming.

Harvesting

Begin pinching stem tips when plants are 6 inches (15 cm) tall to promote leaf production. Every two weeks, cut stems just above a leaf node. Don't remove more than one-third of a plant's foliage at one time. If plants go to flower, cut them back by one-third; they may resprout tender leaves.

Storing Store fresh, leafy stems in a jar of water (unrefrigerated) for up to one week; change the water daily.

You can freeze leaves in resealable plastic bags. Freeze them in a flat layer so you can break off pieces as needed.

PROBLEM SOLVER

Large holes in leaves. Put out slug traps. Handpick slugs and snails. Surround plants with a band of diatomaceous earth.

Plants drop leaves or wilt suddenly. Pull and destroy plants infected by Fusarium wilt. Replant resistant cultivars in a different spot. Be sure plants have good soil drainage and free air circulation.

Dark spots on leaves and stems. Pick off leaves and stems infected by fungal diseases. Destroy severely infected plants. In the future, provide good air circulation; plant in well-drained soil.

Temperature alert
Basil can't withstand frost, and even a spell of cool temperatures well above freezing can slow growth and stunt the plants.

Types of basil

Basil may have smooth, crinkled, or ruffled leaves, and the foliage may be green or purple. Try mixing and matching the wide range of variations available to create a new twist for your favorite recipes.

▶ **Thai basil**

Thai basil has a delicate clove flavor and scent. It tends to be more compact than other basils, with thinner, smaller leaves. 'Siam Queen' is a popular variety.

▲ **Italian basil**

Classic varieties, such as 'Genovese', 'Italian Large Leaf', and 'Nufar' (Fusarium resistant), are widely grown for use in pesto and tomato-based sauces. Some varieties have smooth, green leaves; others have crinkly foliage. The flowers, which most gardeners discourage, are white. All basil flowers attract bees.

▶ **Purple basil**

'Purple Ruffles', 'Red Rubin', and other purple varieties have gorgeous purple leaves, and their flowers are usually pink or lavender. Purple basils are attractive additions to flower gardens, and they add a beautiful accent to salads. In general, purple basils are not quite as vigorous as the green-leaved basils. Some have purple stems as well as purple foliage.

◀ **Dwarf basil**

These compact varieties can grow up to 12 inches (30 cm) tall and have small leaves. The plants form a tight globe of foliage. Varieties such as 'Spicy Globe' and 'Fine Green' (also called 'Fino Verde') are good for tucking into small spaces, containers, and window boxes. You can try dwarf basil as an edging plant for a flower bed.

▶ **Scented basils**

Scented basils include plants with cinnamon, lemon, lime, licorice, and other flavors infused with the taste and aroma of basil. Holy basil *(Ocimum sanctum)* has a strong camphor scent. Lemon basil *(O.* x *citriodorum)* has small leaves and grows to about 15 inches (38 cm) tall.

15 Permanent plantings

Reserve a section of your garden for crops that need a permanent home. Asparagus and rhubarb are perennials that will resprout each spring, producing delicious stems for harvests that may span two decades or more. Although Jerusalem artichoke and horseradish are underground crops that can be planted each year in a new spot, most gardeners choose to give these crops a permanent home because it makes for easy replanting and keeps their potentially invasive nature under control.

Artichokes are beautiful perennials that are hardy to Zone 7. In colder zones, gardeners can grow artichokes as annuals.

Asparagus

Succulent asparagus spears await gardeners who invest time and space in an asparagus patch. This long-lived perennial produces fernlike fronds after the harvest, providing an attractive backdrop when grown at the back of a bed.

Planting

The preceding fall, test the soil pH; it should be between 6.5 and 7.5. Loosen the soil 12 inches (30 cm) deep, and dig a 1–2-inch (2.5–5-cm) layer of weed-free compost into the top several inches of soil.

Choose a spot with well-drained soil where up to 6-feet (1.8-m)-tall asparagus fronds won't shade your other vegetables. The site should be protected from wind to help prevent the tall fronds from blowing over.

Seeds or crowns Asparagus plants started from seeds produce more than those planted as crowns. However, germination is difficult, and slow-growing seedlings are easily taken over by weeds. You'll have better success with crowns from mail-order suppliers or garden centers.

Planting crowns Shallow planting produces equal or better results than crowns planted 12 inches (30 cm) deep. Soak the crowns in water or compost tea for 20 minutes before planting. Dig a trench, form mounds of soil (or mixed soil and compost) in it, then drape the crowns over the mound. Cover the crowns with a few inches of soil. As stalks poke up through the soil, add more soil, leaving the tips of the stalks exposed.

Spacing considerations You can fit a larger number of crowns in a wide trench by staggering two rows of

PLANTING GUIDE

What to plant One-year-old crowns (look for plump roots).

Site preparation Loosen the soil the preceding fall; if the soil is poorly drained, prepare a raised bed for planting.

When About four weeks before last-expected spring frost.

Spacing Allow 18–24 inches (45–60 cm) between crowns and 3–4 feet (90–120 cm) between rows.

Intensive spacing Stagger two rows of crowns in a 2-foot (60-cm)-wide trench; allow 2 feet (60 cm) between crowns in the row.

How much Five crowns per person for fresh eating; double that if also freezing.

Temperature alert
Asparagus requires a cold-winter dormant period, so gardeners in some areas in Florida won't be able to grow asparagus.

To plant asparagus crowns, dig a shallow trench 4–8 inches (10–20 cm) deep and at least 12 inches (30 cm) wide.

Shape a small mound of soil, position the crowns, then spread their roots so that they radiate out in all directions; top with soil.

crowns in it. However, this is not recommended in humid-summer areas, because close spacing can lead to disease problems. In areas with humid summers, you should space the crowns 2 feet (60 cm) apart with at least 5 feet (1.5 m) between the rows for better air circulation.

Care

Watering Drip irrigation is the best watering method for the first two years after planting the crowns. Make sure the bed receives 1 inch (2.5 cm) of water a week during the summer. After that, an established stand is self-sufficient.

Mulch A permanent mulch helps suppress weeds and retain moisture. Apply a 2-inch (5-cm) layer of chopped leaves or finely shredded bark. Make sure that you renew the mulch every fall.

Weeding You should weed often while the stand becomes established. Hand weeding is preferable because cultivating tools can damage the asparagus roots. If you plant a variety that is not all male, some plants will produce seeds. Seedlings that sprout won't develop into worthwhile plants, so pull them out.

Feeding Fertilize the stand in late spring or early summer, after harvest ends, to stimulate fern growth. Side-dress with compost or an organic fertilizer (analysis 4-5-4 or similar) at 2 pounds per 100 square feet (0.9 kg per 10 sq m).

Motherstalk method With this approach, allow one of the first spears from each crown to produce ferny foliage. The frond will feed the crown throughout harvest,

Cut or snap off the stems at or below ground level, but avoid damaging the emerging spears.

which can lengthen the harvest period. Do not allow the plants to suffer moisture stress during harvest.

Fall and winter care In the South, leave the fronds in place in winter to reduce soil erosion. If the soil freezes in winter and the foliage yellows, cut it back to 12 inches (30 cm). Pull out rotting stems in spring.

Harvesting

In the South and Far West, you can harvest spears one year after planting. In the first year, harvest for about two weeks; the following year, four weeks; and the year afterward, six to eight weeks. Gardeners in the North should wait until two years after planting.

Harvest before bracts on the spear tips start to open, when the spears are 6–10 inches (15–25) tall. Cut spears with a sharp knife, or snap them off with your fingers. Harvest every other day; daily above 85°F (29°C). End the harvest when three-quarters of spears are pencil thickness or less.

Storing After cutting the spears, cool them quickly. Asparagus is best the day of harvest, but you can refrigerate it for five days (see pages 114–15).

PROBLEM SOLVER

Chewed areas on spears, brown insect eggs on spears. Asparagus beetles chew on spears and foliage. Handpick and destroy them. To prevent beetles from overwintering under mulch, delay mulching until late fall. You can plant nectar-producing flowers near your asparagus to attract beneficial insects, such as tachinid flies and lady beetles, which prey on the beetles. Destroy fern fronds in late winter, before new growth starts. Cover the asparagus bed with a floating row cover to prevent beetles from reaching the spears early in spring.

Needles turn yellow and drop. Asparagus rust or needle blight can cause this problem. If you've planted a rust-resistant variety, needle blight is the problem. It is worst during warm, wet conditions. Cut and destroy affected foliage. Plant your stand at a wide spacing to help prevent diseases.

New growth stunted and bushy. Asparagus aphids suck sap, causing foliage to take on a "witches broom" look. Natural predators keep these aphids in check. In severe cases, spray the fronds with insecticidal soap.

BEST OF THE BUNCH

'Jersey King' Green spears with purple tips; predominantly male plants; adapts well to a wide range of conditions; disease resistant.
'Jersey Knight' All-male cultivar; green spears with purple spear tips; vigorous growth; resists Fusarium wilt, crown rot, and rust; does well in heavy soil.
'Purple Passion' Not an all-male variety; large purple spears; sweet flavor; spears turn green when cooked.
'UC 157' Grows well in California and other hot regions; bracts on spears stay tight even in hot weather; spears have low fiber content; rust tolerant.

Globe artichoke

Sculptured foliage, unusual flower stalks, and attractive flowers make globe artichokes a fine candidate for an ornamental flower garden as well as the vegetable garden. However, the unopened flower buds are appreciated by food lovers.

PLANTING GUIDE

What to plant Seeds, root divisions, or container plants.

Starting indoors Start seeds in February or late summer.

Site preparation Work the soil 12 inches (30 cm) deep; add plenty of organic matter.

When Varies by region.

Spacing *Rootstocks and container plants* Set 3–4 feet (90–120 cm) apart. *Seedlings* (for annual production) Set 2–3 feet (60–90 cm) apart.

How much Two to four plants per person.

Planting

Loosen the soil 12 inches (30 cm) deep. For perennial plantings, remove all perennial weeds (including roots). Spread a 6-inch (15-cm) layer of compost and work it into the soil.

Artichokes are perennial, but they are not hardy north of Zone 7. However, gardeners in colder zones can grow artichokes as annuals if they start seedlings indoors early and can provide plants with at least 90 frost-free growing days in the garden.

Artichokes grow best in cool, foggy conditions, so they won't grow well in areas with hot, dry summers. For gardeners with hot summers and mild winters, grow artichokes as annuals. Start the seeds in late summer and grow the plants through the winter.

Planting divisions and container plants An early fall planting is best, but you can plant whenever root divisions or container plants are available at your local nurseries. Set the root divisions with the crown just at soil level.

Starting seedlings Consult your local Cooperative Extension Service for advice on the correct time to sow seed indoors in your area. Seeds germinate best between 70–80°F (21–26.5°C). As seedlings develop, cull out stunted or albino plants (artichoke seeds are not always uniform). After the first true leaves emerge, move the seedlings into individual 4-inch (10-cm) pots.

There are two methods in which you can trick seedlings into reacting as if they've lived through a winter, which helps them to produce flower buds in one season. One way is to refrigerate seeds for two weeks before sowing. An even more effective method is to place potted seedlings outdoors in a cold frame or other sheltered spot as soon as possible, when temperatures are still below 50°F (10°C) for part of each day. Make sure to protect the seedlings or bring them back indoors if frost threatens. Transplant into the garden after all danger of frost is past.

Care

Watering Artichoke plants wilt dramatically when they're moisture-stressed. However, the foliage will recover after watering. Water well if dry spells occur during the active growth periods.

Feeding You should feed both annual and perennial plantings monthly during active growth with fish emulsion or a side-dressing of compost or cottonseed meal.

Temperature alert
In cold-winter regions and hot-summer areas, grow sensitive globe artichokes as annuals instead of as a permanent planting.

Maintaining perennial plantings

After the harvest in spring, clear away any dead leaves and use a pair of loppers to cut off the bases of the flower stalks. Cut the plants down close to ground level in late spring. You should cease watering for several weeks to allow the plants to rest, then resume watering. The plants will resprout.

Divide the plants if they become crowded and overgrown. Cut the crowns into portions, each with at least two buds, and replant right away. If winter temperatures drop below 20°F (-6.5°C), you should cover the crowns with 8 inches (20 cm) of straw or other loose mulch.

Harvesting

The time of harvest will depend on where you live and whether you're growing the plants as annuals or perennials. Perennial plantings bear a heavy crop in spring, sometimes a smaller crop in fall. Spring-planted annuals produce flower buds in fall. Fall-planted annuals produce flower buds the following spring.

Cut flower buds when the scales are still tight and waxy, just as the tips of the scales at the base of the bud begin to lift. Use a sharp knife to cut through the stem 1–2 inches (2.5–5 cm) below the bud. (The stems are edible, too.) Mature plants growing as perennials will produce up to 12 flower stalks a season, with several flower buds on each stalk.

If you allow buds to go to flower, you will inhibit production of more buds. However, if you like artichoke flowers for flower arrangements, for attracting bees and butterflies, or simply for their beauty, you can grow one plant as your supply for flowers.

Storing Globe artichokes are best eaten right after picking, but you can store them in the refrigerator for up to two weeks.

PROBLEM SOLVER

Black or green insects on plants. These aphids can spread viral diseases that will ruin your crop. Spray plants with a strong stream of water to wash them off. Spray seriously infested plants with insecticidal soap.

Dark brown trails in buds and holes in stalks. Larvae of artichoke plume moths tunnel in the stalks and flower buds. Spray plants with *Bacillus thuringiensis* or a solution of parasitic nematodes when small caterpillars are visible. Cut plants to ground level once a year; discard or destroy the plant material.

Stunted, misshapen plants. Curly dwarf virus and other viruses cause these symptoms; there is no treatment. Remove and destroy the infected plants. You should replant in a new area using disease-free root divisions.

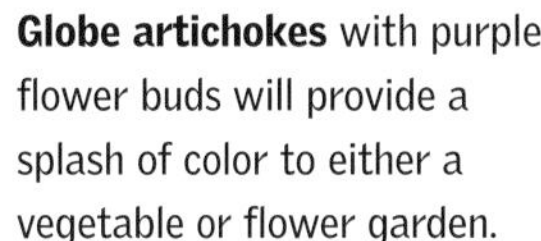

Globe artichokes with purple flower buds will provide a splash of color to either a vegetable or flower garden.

BEST OF THE BUNCH

'Green Globe Improved' Heavy producer, best for perennial plantings. 180 days from seeds.

'Imperial Star' Best variety for starting from seeds; buds are sweet and slow to open. 95 days from transplants.

'Violetta' Rich purple buds; spineless plants; good for annual or perennial plantings. 85 days from transplants.

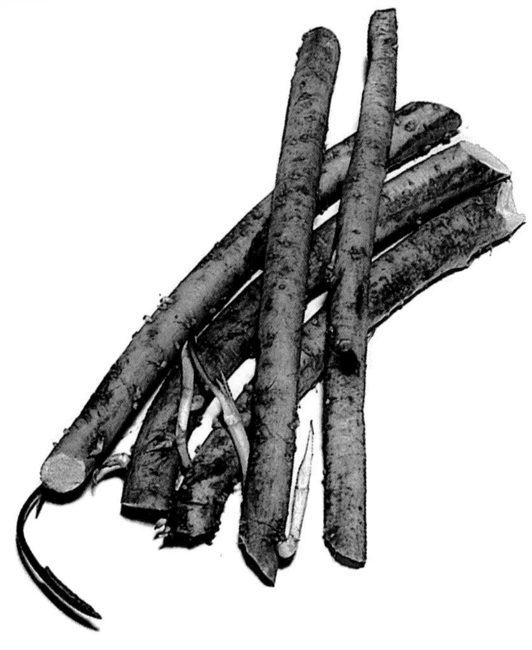

Horseradish

One horseradish root is all that's needed in most gardens to provide a satisfactory supply of this pungent ingredient for condiments and sauces. Choose a site for horseradish carefully. If it wanders uncontrolled, you'll have a weed problem.

PLANTING GUIDE

What to plant Root cuttings.

Site preparation Work the soil at least 12 inches (30 cm) deep and add organic matter.

When Early spring.

Spacing Set roots at least 12 inches (30 cm) apart.

How much A single root may be all you need; don't overplant.

Temperature alert
This hardy perennial grows well in most areas in North America, except in parts of Florida, where winters are too mild to meet the plant's dormancy needs.

Planting

The preceding fall dig an 18-inch (45-cm)-deep hole for one plant. Add a few gallons (several liters) of compost or rotted manure to the bottom of the hole, then return the soil. Mark the prepared spot so you can find it in the spring.

Getting started You can order a root from a commercial source or buy it at a local garden center. Or you can accept a root from a friend who already has horseradish. Choose a slender straight root about 8 inches (20 cm) long.

Open the planting hole and set the root in place either vertically or on a 45-degree angle, narrow end down, with the root 2–3 inches (5–7.5 cm) below soil level. Fill in the hole and water the planting well.

Care

Water early on if the soil is dry. Don't fertilize unless growth seems sluggish; avoid a high-nitrogen fertilizer. You should watch the adjacent beds to make sure stray plants do not emerge. Pest and disease problems are rare.

Keeping your stand going The easy way to perpetuate a horseradish stand is to allow a few side roots to remain in the soil when you harvest the main roots in late fall. Or dig out all the roots and cut side roots from main roots. Replant the side roots immediately or store them in sand in a root cellar or in a plastic bag in the refrigerator. Replant the stored roots in early spring.

Replant horseradish in the same spot each year to reduce the chance of stray roots left in the soil sprouting around the garden. Alternatively, you can plant the root in a bottomless container sunk into the soil.

Harvesting

After a few fall frosts, dig up the main roots, which may be 2 inches (5 cm) wide. Cut off the side roots. Keep or replant the side roots as needed; discard the rest (but not in a compost pile, where they can root). To extend harvest into winter, leave some main roots in place and mulch them well.

You can leave horseradish in the garden through winter and harvest in early spring. Avoid harvesting horseradish roots after shoot growth starts, because flavor will be poor when the plants are actively growing.

Storing Let the harvested roots dry for a few days. Store them in either the refrigerator or a root cellar; grate or grind roots as needed.

Jerusalem artichoke

Italian gardeners gave this North American member of the sunflower family the name *girasole* (sunflower), which led to the name Jerusalem artichoke. This crop produces tubers with a nutty flavor and crisp texture similar to water chestnuts.

PLANTING GUIDE

What to plant Tubers.

Site preparation Dig the soil several inches deep and add organic matter.

When Fall or early spring in the North; in the South, until early summer.

Spacing Set tubers about 2 feet (60 cm) apart in rows 3–4 feet (90–120 cm) apart.

How much One plant can yield 2–10 pounds (0.9–4.5 kg) of tubers, depending on the soil fertility, weather conditions, and variety.

Planting

Jerusalem artichokes will grow best in rich sandy loam, but they can thrive in clay or sandy soils with sufficient organic matter. You should spread a 2–6 inch (5–15 cm) layer of compost and work it into the soil.

Jerusalem artichoke is an annual, but the tubers survive in the soil and overwinter as far north as Zone 3. Production is more reliable in cold-winter areas than in the Deep South, but southern gardeners can enjoy a good harvest, too.

Choose tubers grown in your region; they will be best adapted to your climate conditions. It's easiest to plant whole tubers. If you cut tubers into pieces, be sure each piece has at least one eye, and plant the pieces immediately after cutting. Set the tubers 3–4 inches (7.5–10 cm) deep.

The plants are vigorous, so plant this crop in the same spot each year. It will be easier to see any "escaped" sprouts and uproot them. Alternatively, you can dig a 6–12-inch (15–30-cm)-deep trench around the planting and line it with a vertical root barrier made of metal or heavy plastic.

Care

Water the young plants until they're established, and mulch to conserve soil moisture. Once the plants are growing strongly, they will shade out weeds and be self-sufficient. In general, don't fertilize the plants, or their growth may be too rampant. Pest and disease problems are rare.

Harvesting

Wait until after frost to harvest. Dig through the patch, starting 3 feet (90 cm) away from the base of the plants to ensure you don't miss far-flung tubers. Tubers have tender skin, so handle them gently.

In the South, where frosts may not arrive until January, you can speed the harvest by cutting down the stalks in November. Wait two to three weeks, then dig up the tubers. As long as the tubers haven't resprouted, the flavor and texture should be desirable.

Jerusalem artichokes are tasty baked, boiled, pickled, or sliced raw in salads. You can put cut slices in a mild vinegar or lemon juice solution to prevent them from browning.

Storing Put the tubers into cold, moist storage right away, either in a root cellar or in plastic bags in the refrigerator. If you prefer, you can leave the tubers in the soil and dig them as needed through the winter. In cold-winter areas, mulch to prevent the bed from freezing solid.

Quick Tip

Diabetic treat

The tubers contain inulin instead of starch. Inulin is a carbohydrate that breaks down into fructose during digestion, and fructose is a type of sugar that diabetics can metabolize.

Rhubarb

The tart stems of rhubarb must be cooked—however, they are delicious when added to sweetened sauces and desserts. The arching stems and large fanlike leaves add drama equally well to vegetable gardens or perennial flower beds.

PLANTING GUIDE

What to plant Divisions or seeds.

Starting indoors Start seeds indoors in late summer for plants to be grown as annuals.

Site preparation Loosen the soil and add organic matter; choose a well-drained site.

When Plant divisions as soon as soil can be worked in spring.

Spacing Set divisions 3–4 feet (90–120 cm) apart.

How much One plant per person.

Planting

Loosen the soil in the planting area about 10 inches (25 cm) deep. Spread 3–4 inches (7.5–10 cm) of compost or rotted manure over the area and work it into the soil. Alternatively, dig individual planting holes 12 inches (30 cm) deep. Mix the removed soil from each hole with about 3 gallons (11 liters) of compost or well-rotted manure. Refill the hole with the mix.

Planting divisions You should set the divisions so that the buds are no more than 2 inches (5 cm) below the soil surface. If you're concerned about wet soil conditions, create planting mounds raised about 6 inches (15 cm) above the surrounding soil. Set the divisions in the mounds so that the buds are just below the soil surface.

Growing as an annual Sow the seeds indoors in late summer in soil mix in 4-inch (10-cm) pots. After about 8 to 10 weeks, when the seedlings have three to five leaves, transplant them into the garden. Shade them if the weather is hot. Fertilize the plants once a month through the winter. Protect the plants from hard freezes. Begin harvesting stalks in March or early April. The plants will die or decline by June. Dig them out and compost them.

Care

After the stems emerge, lay 3–4 inches (7.5–10 cm) of clean straw, compost, or chopped leaves around the plants. When temperatures are over 80°F (26.5°C), keep rhubarb well watered, but not soggy.

Fertilizing Feed plants in spring with compost and midsummer with fish emulsion. You can harvest in fall instead of spring, but wait until late fall to avoid creating a rush of new growth just before frost.

Fall and winter care Clear away all stalks and leaves in fall to prevent disease organisms from overwintering. After the soil freezes, cover the crowns with 2–3 inches (5–7.5 cm) of straw mulch. Remove half the mulch in spring before new growth emerges.

Dividing Crowns may be ready to divide three years after planting. If plants aren't divided, they may decline and die within 10 years after planting. Divide in spring before growth starts or in fall after growth stops. Thrust a shovel into the soil next to the base of the plant and lever out the entire crown. Use your hands or a hatchet to break the crown up into fist-size pieces. Each piece should have at least one bud and one large root piece.

Temperature alert
Rhubarb suffers during hot, humid summers in the Deep South; in mild-winter areas, temperatures may not drop low enough. In these areas, grow rhubarb from seeds as an annual.

Replant them as soon as possible. You can use extras to expand your patch if desired or give them away.

Harvesting

Don't harvest any stalks during the first year of growth. The following year, harvest a few stalks from each plant. Beginning the third year, you can harvest for two months, but don't remove more than one-half of the stalks at any one time.

Grasp a stem with your hand and gently twist it; then snap it free at the base. Cut off the leaves and compost them (never eat rhubarb leaves—they contain oxalic acid, a toxin). When most of the emerging stalks are thin, it's time to stop picking for the year.

In the spring, rhubarb plants may send up flower stalks. Cut these off or allow them to bloom, especially if the rhubarb is in a flower bed. Remove the stalks before the seeds dry and fall. Allowing the plants to flower may leave an open spot at the center of the crown. This allows the remaining buds more space to develop and reduces the need to divide the plants as often.

Storing Rinse the stems with water or wipe them clean with a moist cloth. Store stalks in perforated plastic bags in the refrigerator, where they will last for two weeks. You can also cut rhubarb stems into pieces for freezing.

Quick Tip

Forcing rhubarb

To force rhubarb indoors, dig clumps in fall and let them freeze outside. Pot them up and move to a 45–60°F (7–15.5°C) basement or garage. Put them inside trash bags to exclude light. Check the pots every few weeks; harvest stems as they appear.

PROBLEM SOLVER

Sap on stems; stems decay. Rhubarb curculios do not usually cause serious damage, but if plants are heavily infested, destroy them. Pull any dock plants nearby, because the larvae feed on dock and then pupate in the soil, producing the next generation of adults.

Plants don't leaf out, or they leaf out but then die back. This is a sign of crown rot, which is caused by a fungus. Dig out the plants and destroy them. Replant in a well-drained spot. Be sure to plant disease-free divisions.

BEST OF THE BUNCH

'Canada Red' Thick, dark sweet stalks.
'Valentine' Vigorous grower for cold conditions; sweet red stalks.
'Victoria' Green stalks with rosy sheen at base; not stringy; less variable than other varieties when started from seeds.

In mild-winter areas, force dormant rhubarb in the garden by covering it with a large bucket. Uncover it a month before the rhubarb is due to sprout.

Rhubarb grows vigorously and you will need to divide it periodically to avoid overcrowding.

Glossary

acidic
With a pH value below 7.0.

alkaline
With a pH value above 7.0.

All-America Selections (AAS)
New varieties of vegetables that have been tested and rated by this organization before they are released for sale to the public. AAS judges present awards to superior varieties.

annual
A plant that germinates, flowers, sets seeds, and dies within one season.

bacillus thuringiensis (BT)
A bacterium that infects and kills the larvae of various leaf-eating insects. The variety *kurstaki* infects caterpillars, such as cabbage worms. The variety San Diego kills larvae of Colorado potato beetlea and other beetles.

balanced fertilizer
A fertilizer that contains equal amounts of nitrogen, phosphorus, and potassium—the three main plant nutrients.

bare root
A transplant that has been lifted from the open ground instead of grown in a container.

beneficial insects
Insects that pollinate garden crops or prey on or parasitize garden pests.

beneficial nematodes
i) Nematodes that prey on certain garden pests.
ii) Nematodes that help break down organic matter in the soil or compost piles.

blanching
i) Growing a crop such as chicory in darkness to avoid bitterness and grow pale, tender shoots.
ii) Heat treatment of vegetables before freezing, to halt the action of the enzymes that cause deterioration.

bolting
Premature flowering of vegetables, such as lettuce, usually making them unfit for eating.

brassica
A member of the cabbage family, botanically known as Brassicaceae or Cruciferae.

broadcast
Scattering over the soil in a random fashion; the term applies to seeds and fertilizers.

canker
A dead spot on a plant stem caused by a fungus or bacterium; a disease that is typified by formation of cankers.

cap
A hard crust that forms on the soil surface, usually after rain or watering.

catch crop
A fast-growing crop that can be grown in between two longer-term crops.

check
An interruption in the steady development of a plant, caused by adverse conditions such as cold weather.

clamp
A storage method for vegetables, often roots, which involves covering them with an insulating layer of straw and soil.

cloche
A small, movable row or plant cover used to warm soil or protect plants from cold or wind.

cold frame
An area enclosed by walls and a transparent glass or plastic cover for plant protection; similar to a cloche but in a fixed position.

compost
The decomposed remains of plants and garden waste, used as a soil conditioner.

compound fertilizer
A fertilizer with more than one plant nutrient.

corm
A swollen, solid underground stem that resembles a bulb.

cotyledon
A seed leaf of an embryo plant; the first leaf or pair of leaves that develops. Cotyledons are usually a different shape and size to the "true leaves" that follow.

cover crop
A crop sown to prevent soil erosion, suppress weeds, and conserve soil moisture; sometimes synonymous with green manure crop.

crown
The junction of the roots and stems in some perennial plants. Asparagus and rhubarb are two vegetables that sprout from crowns.

curing
Placing harvested crops in specific temperature and humidity conditions for a length of time to prepare them for storage.

cut-and-come-again
A method of harvesting by cutting off plant parts just above the central growing point so that plants will resprout and produce additional harvestable leaves or stems. This harvest technique is most commonly used with lettuce.

cuttings
Sections of plant stems, leaves, or roots that are removed from a plant and induced to sprout roots and grow into a new plant.

damping off
A fungal disease that infects germinating seeds and seedlings, causing them to rot at soil level, topple over, and die; it prefers cool, moist conditions. Damping off can rot seeds before they sprout.

diatomaceous earth
A crystalline mineral product that can be scattered on the soil as a barrier against soft-bodied pests, such as slugs and snails. It can also be sprinkled on plants so that the sharp edges of the particles pierce the insect's protective outer coverings, leading to dehydration and death.

dibble
A tool for making planting holes in the soil or planting mix.

divisions
Sections of perennials formed by pulling or cutting one plant apart into several pieces. Many perennial herbs can be separated into divisions, which can be replanted, eventually increasing the supply of the herb.

drip hose
A garden hose or a part of a drip irrigation system that has small holes or openings. When attached to a water source, drip hoses emit water slowly, providing even watering.

dormant
Alive but not actively growing or developing; in a state of suspended animation until the appropriate conditions for growth are present.

draw hoe
A hoe for making furrows in the soil for sowing seeds, or for drawing up soil around plants.

F1 hybrid
The first generation of plants resulting from a cross between two known parents.

fluid seeding
Sowing seeds suspended in a gel or similar fluid medium. This helps prevent the seeds and newly germinated seedlings from drying out and also helps space the seeds in the row.

forcing
Placing plants in a dark, sometimes warm position so that the resulting growth is pale and tender, without bitterness. Used for plants such as chicory and rhubarb.

friable
Soil that is crumbly and worked to a fine, even texture, suitable for seeds or planting.

fungicide
A substance used to kill fungus diseases or prevent disease spores from germinating.

furrow
A long, shallow depression in the soil in which seeds are sown.

green manure
Plants that are grown to be dug into the soil to improve its fertility and structure. Leguminous plants are often used because of their ability to convert atmospheric nitrogen into a form that can be used by plants.

grow bags
Commercial sacks of growing mix in which vegetables can be grown from seed to maturity. They are commonly used for vegetables such as tomatoes, sweet peppers, and eggplants. A bag of potting mix can be made into a grow bag by punching drainage holes in the side that will be facedown, then cutting slits in the top face to insert plants. Careful attention must be paid to watering, because the small amount of growing mix in the bag is prone to drying out.

growing mix
Commerical sowing, potting, and all-purpose soil prepared for raising and growing plants in containers.

handpicking
Removing garden pests from plants by hand or using implements such as tweezers or chopsticks. You can kill the pests by physical methods such as crushing them or dumping them into a bucket of soapy water.

harden off
To gradually accustom plants raised under cover (in a greenhouse, cold frame, or indoors) to colder conditions in the open, thus preventing the change in conditions causing a check to growth.

heirloom variety
An open-pollinated, cultivated form of a plant that has been in cultivation for a long period of time (generally before 1940).

herbicide
A substance used to kill plant growth.

hilling
Method involving pulling soil up around plants. This may be to stabilize the root system in the soil so that the plant is less likely to be blown over or to protect the edible parts of the plant from light to improve their eating quality.

hose-end dilutor
A hose attachment filled with a concentrated solution of fertilizer or other chemical. The solution is diluted to the correct application rate by the water flowing through the hose.

humus
Decomposed organic matter, which is a valuable addition to soil, improving its structure and capacity to hold water.

inoculant
A powder containing bacteria that interact with the roots of a leguminous plant (such as bean and pea) to enable nitrogen fixation to occur. Commercial inoculants are crop-specific.

insecticidal soap
A commercial formulation of fatty acids that can be diluted with water and sprayed on plants to kill some types of insect pests.

insecticide
A substance used to kill insects.

intensive planting
Setting crops more closely than the standard spacing recommendation for that crop in order to make the best use of available space; it requires careful crop management and soil enriched with high levels of organic matter for a successful harvest.

IRT
Abbreviation for infrared transmitting plastic, a specialized type of plastic mulch that contains a pigment (usually green or brown) to maximize transmission of near infrared radiation (which warms the soil), but block visible light (which would stimulate weed growth under the plastic).

larva(e)
Immature stage of an insect—for example, caterpillars are the larvae of moths and butterflies; grubs are the larvae of beetles.

leaf mold
Decomposed leaves from decidious trees, which should be composted separately from other garden waste because they take longer to rot down.

legumes
Plants, such as peas and beans, belonging to the family Fabaceae. These plants have specialized roots that, in association with specific soil-dwelling bacteria, can convert atmospheric nitrogen into nitrate (a form of nitrogen that can be absorbed by plant roots). Also, the fruit or seeds of plants in this family.

loam
Fertile soil consisting of a mixture of sand, clay, silt, and organic matter.

main crop
A crop produced through the main part of the growing season, as opposed to particularly early or late crops. Main-crop varieties are those varieties that will produce their crop through this part of the season.

microorganism
A living organism that can be seen only with the aid of a microscope. In gardens, particularly important microorganisms are those that help to break down organic matter in the soil, and those that cause plant diseases—often fungi, bacteria, or viruses.

mulch
A layer of organic or inorganic matter placed over the soil surface to protect it from cold, heat, or wind or to retain soil moisture.

nematode
Microscopic, threadlike soil-dwelling animals. Some types cause diseaselike symptoms in plants, such as stunting and yellowing, by parasitizing plant roots. Others are helpful to gardeners because they break down organic matter or parasitize plant pests.

nitrogen-fixing
The ability to convert atmospheric nitrogen into a useful form for plants. Nitrogen-fixing bacteria live in nodules on the roots of legumes, which have this ability; they need less fertilizing than many other crops.

NPK
An abbreviation for nitrogen, phosphorus, and potassium, the major essential plant nutrients. A fertilizer package that states "N:P:K 7:7:7" means the fertilizer contains 7 percent nitrogen, 7 percent phosphorus, and 7 percent potassium. Usually only the numbers are given, but they are always in the order nitrogen, phosphorus, potassium.

open-pollinated
Plants whose flowers have been fertilized by those of the same variety in the field, not by hybrids that are a deliberate cross between two different varieties. The plants produced from open-pollinated varieties will be the same as their parents; hybrids produce a new variety, which will not breed true.

organic
i) Deriving from anything that has once been alive; usually applying to manures and composts that consist of decomposed plant or animal remains.
ii) A method or substance thought to do minimal ecological damage, such as organic gardening, in which plants are grown without the use of chemical pesticides or fertilizers and the presence of beneficial insects and organisms are promoted, while soil fertility is maintained; an "organic pesticide" is a pesticide of natural origin as opposed to a manufactured chemical.

organic matter
Soil additives and improvers of organic origin such as compost, leaf mold, farmyard manure, seaweed, and spent hops.

overwinter
To keep tender plants through the winter in a dormant or protected state so that they will last through or survive the winter.

pan
A hard area some distance below the soil surface through which roots will find it difficult to penetrate. It often occurs when soil is cultivated to the same level for a number of years.

perennial
A plant that persists from year to year.

pH
The measure of acidity or alkalinity of soil. A reading of pH 7.0 is neutral: higher than pH 7.0 indicates alkalinity, while a reading lower than pH 7.0 indicates acidity.

photosynthesis
The process in which plants manufacture sugars from sunlight.

plant out
To transplant young plants raised under cover or indoors into a garden bed; also set out. The plants may need to be hardened off.

plug plants
Commercially available seedlings that have been raised in individual soil blocks, ready for planting out.

pot up
To plant rooted cuttings or seedlings in individual pots.

plumule
The tip of the shoot as it emerges from the seed, protected by the cotyledons.

potager
A formal, decorative vegetable garden, usually on a small scale.

pricking out
Transplanting seedlings to a wider spacing shortly after germination in order to give them room to develop.

propagator
Equipment used for raising seeds or cuttings, allowing you to control the conditions to give seedlings a better start. It usually consists of a tray or trays with plastic covers to maintain high humidity, and it may also provide a method for heating the soil.

radicle
The tip of the root as it emerges from a newly growing seed.

respiration
The process in which plants break down sugars for energy, using oxygen from the air and releasing carbon dioxide.

rhizome
An underground stem that often looks like a root. Weeds with rhizomes are difficult to control because any portion of rhizome left in the soil has the ability to grow new shoots and roots to make new plants.

rose
A plastic or metal fitting for a watering-can spout or hose that has small holes to break up the water into droplets. A "fine" rose has the smallest holes and gives the lightest spray, and you should use one for delicate plants such as young seedlings.

rotation
Moving groups of crops to a new position in the vegetable garden each year to avoid the build up of specific pests and diseases and to avoid the depletion of specific soil nutrients.

root cellar
An underground or partially underground insulated area that remains consistently cool, designed for storing food crops.

rosette
A cluster of leaves that sprout from a central point and radiate in all directions.

row cover
A lightweight synthetic fabric that allows a high proportion of sunlight, air, and moisture to penetrate, but that provides some protection from cold air temperature and wind; also called floating row cover. If properly sealed, a row cover also provides an effective physical barrier against insects. Row cover may also refer to a lightweight plastic cover, but plastic row covers trap more heat than floating row covers and must be closely monitored to avoid overheating plants.

self-sow
To grow from seeds that were distributed naturally in the garden from the seed stalks of plants already growing.

set out
See plant out.

side-dress
To apply fertilizer in a band to the soil surface alongside growing crops.

slow-release fertilizer
A fertilizer that releases its nutrients gradually over a long season instead of all at the same time. The fertilizer is often manufactured in the form of pellets coated with varying thicknesses of a material, which is gradually broken down by moisture and warmth. Some fertilizers, such as bonemeal, are naturally slow-release types.

soilless compost
A growing compost that does not contain loam (soil); it is usually based on peat or a peat substitute.

solarize
To cover and seal an area of wet, bare soil with a sheet of heavyweight clear plastic, which will promote soil heating. Its purpose is to kill disease organisms, nematodes, and sometimes weed seeds.

stale seedbed
A technique for reducing weeds among vegetable seedlings. The seedbed is prepared for sowing; then it is left for a short period to allow the germination of weed seeds that have been brought near the soil surface by cultivation. These weed seedlings are then killed with minimum soil disturbance before the crop is sown.

stolon
A creeping underground stem that produces new shoots and roots.

subsoil
The infertile layer of soil below the more fertile layer of topsoil in which plants grow.

successional sowing
To make a series of small sowings of a crop about 7 to 10 days apart. This technique is useful for ensuring a longer harvest period and avoiding a glut.

taproot
A long, deeply penetrating root that tends to regenerate if the top growth is removed, such as on a dandelion.

tender
Describing a plant that is adversely affected by cold weather or frost.

thinning
The process of removing seedlings in a newly germinated row to provide sufficient space for those that remain.

thrips
Tiny, delicate winged insects that feed on plants, causing streaking or browning of leaves and stems, as well as distorted growth.

tilth
The condition of a well-worked soil that has been reduced to a fine, crumbly texture. (*See friable.*)

topsoil
The uppermost fertile layer of soil in which a plant's roots grow. (*See subsoil.*)

trace elements
Plant nutrients that are vital but required in only tiny amounts and include such elements as iron, magnesium, copper, and boron. A deficiency of these nutrients can produce a range of noticeable symptoms, such as yellowing of the leaf between the veins, but it can be corrected by specialized trace-element fertilizers.

transpiration
The process in which water is absorbed by the roots, passes through the plant, and evaporates through the leaves.

transplanting
To move young plants to a fresh position to give them more space to develop.

tuber
An underground plant-storage organ such as a potato.

variety
Horticulturists use this term as a synonym for cultivar (cultivated variety), which is a cultivated form of a plant that results from controlled breeding techniques or selection. In this sense, varieties are named forms of a crop, such as 'Kentucky Wonder' beans. Botanists use the term to denote a group of plants that vary in some significant way from others in the same species, but that are not distinctly different enough to warrant being classified as a separate species.

Resources guide

Listed below you'll find organizations that provide gardening information, which can be a useful supplement to the material in this book, such as a resource for finding the frost zones in your region. All these organizations have Web sites. If you don't have access to a computer at home, you can visit a local library and seek the help of staff.

In the United States

Nonprofit associations

American Horticultural Society
Provides home gardeners with gardening and horticultural education, with the help of a network of experts.
River Farm
17931 East Boulevard Drive
Alexandria, VA 22308
Toll-free: (800) 777-7931
Local tele: (703) 768-5700
(Fax) (703) 768-8700
Publications Fax: (703) 768-7533
Web site: www.ahs.org

American Horticultural Therapy Association
Advances the practice of horticulture as therapy to improve human well-being.
3570 E. 12th Avenue, Suite 206
Denver, CO 80206
Toll Free: (800) 634-1603
Local tele: (303) 322-2482 (AHTA)
Web site: www.ahta.org

Consumer Affairs
Information specific to the selection, preparation, and use of home canning jars.
P.O. Box 2729
Muncie, IN 47307-0729
Tele: (800) 240-3340
Web site: www.homecanning.com

The Herb Society of America
Promotes the use of herbs through educational programs and research.
9019 Kirtland Chardon Road
Kirtland, OH 44094
Tele : (440) 256-0514
Fax: (440) 256-0541
Web site: www.herbsociety.org

Native Seeds/SEARCH
Seeks to preserve the seeds that connect Native American cultures to their lands.
526 N. 4th Avenue
Tucson, AZ 85705-8450
Tele: (520) 622-5561
Fax: (520) 622-5591
Web site: www.nativeseeds.org

Regional advice

United States Department of Agriculture
Government department to assist farmers but also provides a plant database, weather information, and food preservation and canning details.
1400 Independence Avenue
S.W. Washington, D.C. 20250
No telephone number available
Web site: www.usda.gov

The National Gardening Association
Nonprofit leader in plant-based education.
11100 Dorset Street
South Burlington, VT 05403
Tele: (802) 863-5251
Web site: www.garden.org

Cornell University Department of Agriculture
Offers a wide variety of information on gardening, including vegetables, soil, and houseplants.
134A Plant Science Building
Cornell University
Ithaca, NY 14853
Tele: (607) 255-4568/1789
Fax: (607) 255-9998/0599
www.gardening.cornell.edu/

University of Illinois Extension
Provides horticultural hints and tips.
547 Bevier Hall
905 S. Goodwin
Urbana, IL 61801
Tele: (217) 265-6410
Fax: (217) 244-0191
Web site: www.urbanext.uiuc.edu/hortihints

The Massachusetts Department of Agricultural Resources
Offers links to a range of information on growing vegetables in home gardens.
1251 Causeway Street, Suite 500
Boston, MA 02114
Tele: (617) 626-1700
Web site: www.mass.gov/agr/gardening/vegetables/

The Ohio State University
Ohio State's horticulture and crop science department provides information for growing plants in the United States and Canada.
16 Howlett Hall
2001 Fyffe Court
Columbus, Ohio 43210
Tele: (614) 292-3866
FAX: (614) 292-3505
Web site: plantfacts.ohio-state.edu

EXTOXNET
A cooperative effort of University of California-Davis, Oregon State University, Michigan State University, Cornell University, and the University of Idaho to provide information on pesticides.
No address or telephone number available
Web site: ace.orst.edu/info/extoxnet

Resources

Avant-Gardening
Information on frost zones in the United States.
Creative Organic Gardening
P.O. Box 732
Ramah, NM 87321
Tele: (505) 783-4412
Web site: www.avant-gardening.com/zone

BUGS
An organization devoted to reducing our reliance on potentially toxic agricultural chemicals in urban landscape environments.
P.O. Box 76
Citrus Heights, CA 95611
Tele: (916) 726-5377
Web site: www.organiclandscape.com

The GreenWeb Company
Detailed information on vegetables and herbs, including seed tapes.
P.O. Box 1657
Glendale, CA 91209
No telephone number available
Web site: www.boldweb.com/greenweb.htm

Kitchen Gardeners International
An organization devoted to the growing and cooking of homegrown garden produce.
7 Flintlock Drive
Scarborough, ME 04074
Web site: www.kitchengardeners.org

Milberger's Nursery and Landscaping
An information resource, including details on frost dates in the United States.
3920 North Loop 1604 E.
San Antonio, TX 78247
Tele: (210) 497-3760
Web site: www.plantanswers.com

Southern U.S. Cuisine
Provides information on home canning.
No address or telephone number available
Web site: southernfood.about.com/od/canning

Superb Herbs
A general site on growing and using herbs.
2379 Red Barn Road
Marietta, GA 30064
Tele: (877) 493-5987
Web site: www.superbherbs.com

LifeTips
Supplies hints and tips on vegetables, including pickling and preserving information.
One First Avenue, Suite 200
Charlestown, MA 02129
Tele: (617) 886-9001, ext. 201
Tele: (877) 454-3384
Web site: vegetable.lifetips.com

In Canada

Seeds of Diversity Canada
Canada's premier seed exchange for the passionate gardener.
P.O. Box 36, Station Q
Toronto, Ontario M4T 2L7
Tele: (866) 509-SEED
Web site: www.seeds.ca

Books

Bradley, Fern Marshall and Barbara W. Ellis (eds) *Rodale's All-New Encyclopedia of Organic Gardening*
Rodale, Inc., PA

Cebenko, Jill Jesiolowski and Deborah L. Martin (eds) *Insect, Disease & Weed I.D. Guide*
Rodale, Inc., PA

Editors of Reader's Digest *The Reader's Digest New Illustrated Guide to Gardening*
Reader's Digest, NY

Fedor, John *Organic Gardening for the 21st Century*
Readers Digest, NY

McGee, Rose Marie Nichols and Maggie Stuckey *The Bountiful Container*
Workman Publishing, NY

Smith, Shane *Greenhouse Gardener's Companion*
Fulcrum Publishing, CO

Waters, Marjorie *The Victory Garden Kids' Book*
Globe Pequot, CT

Magazines

Mother Earth News
Ogden Publications, Inc.
1503 SW 42nd Street
Topeka, KS 66609-1265
Toll-free: (800) 234-3368
Web site: www.motherearthnews.com

Organic Gardening
33 East Minor Street
Emmaus, PA 18098
Toll-free: (800) 666-2206
Web site: www.organicgardening.com

Suppliers

Listed below are suppliers of seeds and gardening equipment. You can find common seeds and equipment in your local garden center, but a wider range of seeds and specialized equipment is available through mail-order catalogs and the Internet. All of these companies have Web sites. If you don't have a computer at home, you can visit a local library and seek the help of staff.

In the United States

Abundant Life Seed Company
Specializing in seeds of rare and endangered varieties of food crops.
P.O. Box 157
Saginaw, OR 97472
Tele: (541) 767-9606
Fax: (866) 514-7333
Web site: www.abundantlifeseeds.com

Anioleka Seeds USA
Supplier of heirloom and open-pollinated seeds.
1475 SunGlo Drive
Grants Pass, OR 975273
No telephone number available
Web site: www.vegetableseed.net

Charley's Greenhouse
Provides greenhouse kits and garden supplies.
17979 State Route 536
Mt. Vernon, WA 98273
Toll-free: (800) 322-4707
Web site: www.charleysgreenhouse.com

Down to Earth Distributors, Inc.
Distributor of organic fertilizers and soil amendments. No address available.
Toll-free: (800) 234-5932
Customer Service (Local): (541) 485-5932
Web site: www.down-to-earth.com

Earthcare Environmental Ltd.
Provides a range of products for home testing of soil, available in the United States and UK.
Eagle House
14 Queens Road
Coventry, CV1 3EG, UK
Tele: 44 (247) 663-0832
Fax: 44 (247) 663-0846
Web site: www.solvita.co.uk/

Gardener's Supply Company
An extensive range of gardening products including seed-starting equipment, plant supports, watering equipment, composters, and organic pest controls and fertilizers.
128 Intervale Road
Burlington, VT 05401
Toll-free: (888) 833-1412
Web site: www.gardeners.com

Gardens Alive!
Specialists in organic pest control, natural fertilizers, and natural lawn-care products.
5100 Schenley Place
Lawrenceburg, IN 47025
Tele: (513) 354-1483
Web site: www.gardensalive.com

Harris Seeds
A seed supplier that also gives comprehensive information for the home vegetable gardener.
355 Paul Road
P.O. Box 24966
Rochester, NY 14624-0966
Toll-free fax: (877) 892-9197
Web site: www.harrisseeds.com

Heirloom Seeds
A good source for heirloom vegetable, flower, and herb seeds.
P.O. Box 245
West Elizabeth, PA 15088
Tele: (412) 384-0852
Web site: www.heirloomseeds.com

The Herb Quarterly
Subscription magazine about herbs and herbal lore.
No address or telephone number available
Web site: www.herbquarterly.com

Ed Hume Seeds
Specializing in seeds for short season and cool-climate gardens.
P.O. Box 73160
Puyallup, WA 98373
Tele: (253) 435-4414
Web site: www.humeseeds.com

Johnny Selected Seeds
Contains a wide variety of vegetable seeds and gardening tools.
955 Benton Avenue
Winslow, ME 04901
Tele: (207) 861-3900
Web site: www.johnnyseeds.com

J. W. Jung Seed Company
A great on-line catalog of high-quality seeds.
335 S. High St.
Randolph, WI 53957-0001
Toll-free: (800) 247-5864
Web site: www.jungseed.com

Lee Valley Tools
For serious gardeners, a mail-order and retail supplier of gardening tools.
No address available
Toll-free: (800) 871-8158
Web site: www.leevalley.com

A. M. Leonard, Inc.
Suppliers of gardening equipment.
241 Fox Drive
Piqua, OH 45356-0816
Toll-free: (800) 543-8955
Web site: www.amleo.com

Nichols Garden Nursery
Supplier of herbs and rare seeds by mail.
1190 Old Salem Road NE
Albany, OR 97321–4580
Tele: (541) 928–9280
Web site: www.gardennursery.com

Peaceful Valley Farm & Garden Supply
Educational resources and forums and a comprehensive selection of organic-gardening seeds and supplies.
P.O. Box 2209
125 Clydesdale Court
Grass Valley, CA 95945
Tele: (530) 272–4769
Web site: www.groworganic.com

Palintest USA
Supplier of soil testing kits.
21 Kenton Lands Road
Erlanger, KY 41018
Toll-free: (800) 835–9629
Local: (859) 341– 7423
Web site:
www.palintest.com/soil_testing_kits.htm

Park Seed Company
A wide range of seeds, plants, and bulbs, and details on seed tape.
1 Parkton Avenue
Greenwood, SC 29647
Toll-free: (800) 213–0076
Web site: www.parkseed.com

Pinetree Garden Seeds
Wide variety of vegetable seeds.
P.O. Box 300
New Gloucester, ME 04260
Tele: (207) 926–3400
Web site: www.superseeds.com

Renee's Garden Seeds
Seeds for heirloom and cottage garden flowers, aromatic herbs, and gourmet vegetables from around the world.
7389 W. Zayante Road
Felton, CA 95018
Toll-free: (888) 880–7228
Web site: www.reneesgarden.com

Seed Savers Exchange
A good source for heirloom seeds.
3094 North Winn Road
Decorah, IA 52101
Tele: (563) 382–5990
Fax: (563) 382–5872
Web site: www.seedsavers.org

Seeds of Change
Supplier of organic seeds.
No address available
Toll-free: (888) 762–7333
Web site: www.seedsofchange.com

SoilPerfect
A specialist in soil testing to help maintain healthy soil.
1511 East Main Street
Belleville, IL 62222
Tele: (618) 233–0445
Fax: (618) 233–7292
Web site: www.soilperfect.com

Stokes Seeds
Distributor of flower, vegetable, herb, and perennial seeds, selling to both home gardeners and commercial growers.
P.O. Box 548
Buffalo, NY 14240–0548
Tele: (716) 695–6980
Web site: www.stokeseeds.com

The Territorial Seed Company
Supplier of vegetable seeds, including organic seeds.
P.O. Box 158
Cottage Grove, OR 97424–0061
Toll-free: (800) 626–0866
Web site: www.territorial-seed.com

Thompson & Morgan Seedsmen Inc.
Supplier of seeds for vegetables and herbs, including some organic seeds.
P.O. Box 1308
Jackson, NJ 08527-0308
Toll-free: (800) 274–7333
Fax: 888-466-4769
Web site: www.thompson-morgan.com

Union Tools
Supplier of heavy-duty gardening tools.
No address or telephone number available.
Web site: www.uniontools.com

Veseys
Supplier of vegetable seeds and organic seeds in Canada and the United States.
P.O. Box 9000
Charlottetown
Prince Edward Island, Canada, C1A 8K6
Tele: (902) 368–7333
Toll-free: (800) 363–7333
Web site: www.veseys.com

Virtual Seeds
Specializing in unusual home-garden vegetable seeds.
92934 Coyote Drive
Astoria, OR 97103
Tele: (503) 458–0919
Web site: www.virtualseeds.com

In Canada

Halifax Seed Co. Inc.
Supplier of seeds and other gardening products.
5860 Kane Street
P.O. Box 8026, Stn. "A"
Halifax, Nova Scotia B3K 5L8
Tele: (902) 454–7456
Web site: http://shop.itnweb.com/halifaxseed/

Lee Valley Tools
For serious gardeners, a mail-order and retail supplier of gardening tools.
No address available
Toll-free: (800) 267–8767
Web site: www.leevalley.com

Stokes Vegetable Garden Seeds
Supplier of seeds and accessories.
P.O. Box 10
Thorold, Ontario L2V 5E9
Toll-free: (800) 396–9238
Web site: www.stokeseeds.com

Index

Please note that page references for main entries are in **bold** numerals.

D

E

F

G

T

Photo credits and acknowledgments

Photo Credits

Abbreviations: T = Top; M = Middle; B = Bottom; L = Left; R = Right

Back Cover: Garden Picture Library Juliette Wade (T); **Bud Cole** (BL); **Mark S. Courtier** (BR).

Agrohaitai Ltd www.agrohaitai.com**:** 181 (B), 183 (MR). **Anthony Blake Photo Library:** Maximilion Stock Ltd 258 (BR). **Ian Armitage:** 124; 181 (TL); 182 (ML, BR); 274; 275. **T. C. Bird:** 37; 74 (BR); 76 (TL); 103; 162. **David Cavagnaro:** 210 (TR). **Jane Courtier:** 24 (TL); 36 (BR); 77; 96; 101 (BL); 149 (BL); 165 (TL, TR); 271 (T). **Flora Graphics Inc:** 231 (ML). **Garden Picture Library:** Lamontagne 17 (B); Juilette Wade 19 (BL); Eric Crichton 20 (B); Ron Sutherland 22 (T); Friedrich Strauss 26 (TR); Mel Watson 28; Gary Rogers 29 (R); Friedrich Strauss 32 (TL); Linda Burgess 35 (B); Christopher Gallagher 42 (TL); Janet Sorrell 44 (BL, BR); Mayer/Le Scanff 47; David Cavagnaro 127; Jacqui Hurst 173; Stephen Hamilton 209 (TL); Mayer/Le Scanff 215; Philippe Bonduel 230 (ML); David Cavagnaro 231 (MR); Philippe Bonduel 232 (B); Lamontagne 233; Mayer/Le Scanff 234 (TL); David Cavagnaro 240; Bob Challinor 245; A. I. Lord 253 (TL); Laslo Puskas 253 (MR); Jerry Pavia 257 (BR); Mayer/Le Scanff 258 (TL); Jerry Pavia 261 (M); Clive Nichols 263; Leigh Clapp 267; Howard Rice 271 (BR). **Gardens Monthly:** Jacqui Dracup 93. **Gardening Which?:** 183 (B). **GardenWorld Images:** 201; 202 (B). **John Glover:** 5; 12; 18 (R); 21 (BL); 27 (T, B). **Jerry Harpur:** Bob Dash 16; Chaumont 22 (TL); Jane Adams 23 (BR); New York Botanics 25 (ML); Maggie Geiger NYC 26 (TL); Dr. John Rivers 29 (TL); Old Rectory, Sudborough 141 (TR); 185; 251. **Marcus Harpur:** Geoff Whiten 23 (TR); Gelmham House 25 (MR). **Harris Seeds** www.harrisseeds.com: 232 (T). **Neil Hepworth:** 63. **Holt Studios:** 98 (L). **JB Illustrations:** 17 (T); 41 (TR); 58 (BR); 117 (T). **Johnny's Selected Seeds:** www.johnnyseeds.com 231 (TR). **J. W. Jung Seed Co** Phone: (800) 247-5864 www.jungseed.com; **R. H. Shumway's** Phone: (800) 342-9461 www.rhshumway.com; **Totally Tomatoes** Phone: (800) 345-5977 www.totallytomato.com; **Vermont Bean Seed Company** Phone: (800) 349-1071 www.vermontbean.com**:** 9 (TM); 230 (TR); 169; 179 (B); 199; 229; 230 (TR). **Krivit Photography:** Mike Krivit 2. **Mariquita Farm (USA)** Phone: (831) 761-3226 www.mariquita.com**:** 137 (T); 175; 160 (TR, BM); 203 (TL); 212; Jeanne Byrne 235; 260 (ML, BR). **Photolibrary.com:** Kathryn Kleinman 239; Schnare & Stief 242 (TR). **Photos Horticultural:** (TR); 13; 40 (TL); 45; 65; 72–73; 128; 140 (BR); 143; 147 (BR); 155 (BR); 161 (BL, MR); 177 (TL, MR); 188 (TL); 191 (ML, BR); 193; 202 (TL); 213; 221; 225; 261 (BR). **Dr. Barrington Rudine:** 236 (B). **Denis Ryan:** 7 (BR); 34 (TL); 38 (TL); 42 (BR); 48 (TL); 54 (TL); 56 (TL); 71; 74 (TL); 75; 80; 82 (TL); 91; 95 (TL, BR); 97; 99; 109; 110; 112 (TL); 120 (TL); 149 (BR); 187; 214 (BR); 223; 242 (BL). **Le Scanff-Mayer:** Le Jardin Plume 6 (B); St Jean-de-Beauregard 10; Le Jardin Plume 15; 'La Hussonniere' 18 (TL); 'Potager Arc-en-Ciel' Chateau de Bosmelet 20 (TL); Les Jardins du Prieure N. D. d'Orsan Maisonnais 24 (BR); Le Jardin Plume 31; 101 (T); 234. **Seminis** Dan Croker www.seminisgarden.com**:** 44 (TL); 139 (BL); 152 (MR); 211 (B); 236 (T). **Jason Smalley:** 36 (TL); 151 (ML); 157; 243 (BL). **Sygenta Group, ROGERS ®:** Super Sugar Snap 146–47 (M); Cream of the Crop 229; Kentucky Blue 150. **Thompson and Morgan (UK) Ltd** Phone: 01473 688 821www.thompson-morgan.com**:** 19 (MR); 48 (BM); 130; 131 (MR); 133; 134 (B); 136; 138; 139 (BM); 145; 146 (BL, M); 151 (TL); 152 (BL); 153; 154 (ML, BR); 155 (TL); 156 (TL); 163; 164; 165 (BL, MR); 166; 167; 170; 171; 172; 178; 186 (BR); 188 (BM); 189 (M, BR); 195; 196 (BR); 197; 210 (M, B, R); 211 (T); 216 (TR, MR); 217 (BL, M); 219; 222 (TL); 227; 228; 231 (BM); 232 (M); 254 (BR); 261 (TL); 268; 269; front endpaper. **Roy Williams:** 1; 3; 8 (TL, BL, TM, BM, MR); 9 (TL, BL, BM, MR); 30 (TL); 34 (M, BM, BR); 49; 50; 51; 57 (TL); 88; 92 (TL); 100; 116 (TL); 125; 126 (TL); 131 (TL); 132; 134 (TL); 135; 137 (MR); 140 (TL); 142 (TL); 144; 148; 158; 160 (ML); 168 (TL); 174; 176; 179 (TL); 180; 183 (TL, TR); 184 (L); 186 (TL); 188 (TR); 189 (TR); 190; 192; 194; 196 (TL); 198; 200; 203 (BR); 204 (TL); 205; 206; 211 (MR); 214 (TL); 216 (BL); 217 (TR); 218; 220; 222 (L); 224; 226; 230 (BR); 237 (TL, BR); 238 (TL); 244 (TL); 246; 247; 248; 249; 250; 251; 252; 254 (TL); 255; 256; 257 (TL); 259; 262 (TL); 264 (TL); 266; 270; 272; 273; 276; 277; 278; 279. **Mark Winwood:** 6 (TL); 14 (TL); 7 (TM, BL); 32 (TR); 33; 34 (MR); 35; 38 (BM, BR); 39 (BL, BM, BR); 40 (BM, BR); 41 (BL, BR); 43 (TL, M, BL); 46 (TL); 52; 53; 54 (BL, BM); 55; 56 (BM, BR); 57 (BL, BM); 58 (TL); 59; 60; 64; 66; 67; 68; 69; 78; 83; 84 (TL, MR); 86; 87; 90; 92 (BL, BM, BR); 94; 98 (MR); 102; 108 (TL); 111; 112 (BR); 113; 114 (TL, MR); 115; 116 (MR); 117 (BM, BR); 118; 119; 120 (BM, MR, BR); 121; 122; 123; 129; 141 (B); 159; 192 (BM, BR); 207 (BL, BM, BR); 208 (BL, BM); 209 (TM); 264 (BM, BR); 265.

Acknowledgments

Toucan Books would like to thank the following for their assistance in the preparation of this book:

Pat Alburey, Ian Armitage, Nick Armitage, Susan Bosley at ROGERS ® Brand vegetable Seeds, David Cavagnaro, Dan Croker at Seminis, Liz Dobbs, Polly El Mahdi at Sanders Garden World, Christine Faull at Sygenta International AG, Andrew Griffin at Mariquita Farm, Paivi Jamsen at Kotimaiset Kasvikset, Marylin Keen at Thompson and Morgan (UK) Ltd., Shirun Li at AgroHaitai Ltd., Julia Paul at American Takii Inc., Hugh and Eleanor Paget, Gloria and Barry Rudine, Denis Ryan, Dotti Schultz and Maureen Artco at Jung Seed, Jess Walton, Mia Stewart-Wilson, Ashley Warren at Photos Horticultural, Mark Winwood.

Gardening Consultants

Trevor and Brenda Cole graduated from Britain's Royal Botanic Gardens. Trevor is a gardening author and editor and is the main horticultural consultant for Reader's Digest Canada. Brenda had a regular column in the *Ottawa Citizen* for more than 20 years. They live in Kinburn, Ontario.

NT
AB
SK
MB
BC
ON
WA
MT
ND
MN
OR
ID
SD
WI
WY
IA
NE
NV
IL
UT
CA
CO
KS
MO
AZ
OK
AR
NM
MS
TX
LA
AK
HI